W9-BNH-385

DATE DUE			
JAN 6			

69572
Rougemont

St. Procopius College Library
Maple Ave. and College Road
Lisle, Illinois

The Idea of Europe

THE IDEA OF
EUROPE

BY

DENIS DE ROUGEMONT

❖

Translated by NORBERT GUTERMAN

THE MACMILLAN COMPANY · *NEW YORK*
COLLIER-MACMILLAN LTD. · *LONDON*

COPYRIGHT © THE MACMILLAN COMPANY 1966

All rights reserved. No part of this book may be reproduced or utilized in any form or by any means, electronic or mechanical, including photocopying, recording or by any information storage and retrieval system, without permission in writing from the Publisher.

FIRST PRINTING

The Macmillan Company, New York
Collier-Macmillan Canada, Ltd., Toronto, Ontario

Library of Congress catalog card number: 66-15369

PRINTED IN THE UNITED STATES OF AMERICA

THE AUTHOR wishes to thank the following for permission to reprint copyrighted material in this book:

Agenzia Letteraria Internazionale and George Allen & Unwin Ltd. for an extract from Benedetto Croce, *History of Europe in the Nineteenth Century*, translated by Henry Furst.

George Allen & Unwin Ltd. for an extract from Friedrich Nietzsche, *Beyond Good and Evil*, translated by Helen Zimmerman; and for an extract from Luis Diez del Corral, *The Rape of Europe*, translated by H. V. Livermore.

Bobbs-Merrill Company for an extract from Immanuel Kant, *Foundations of the Metaphysics of Morals*, translated and edited by Lewis White Beck. Copyright 1959 by The Liberal Arts Press, division of the Bobbs-Merrill Company.

Bollingen Foundation and Routledge & Kegan Paul Ltd. for an extract from Paul Valery, *History and Politics, Collected Works*, translated by Denise Folliot and Jackson Mathews.

Cambridge University Press for an extract from *The Greek Bucolic Poets*, translated and edited by A. S. F. Gow.

Cornell University Press for an extract from *The New Science of Giambattista Vico*, translated by Thomas Bergin and Max H. Fisch. Copyright 1948 by Cornell University.

J. M. Dent & Sons Ltd. for an extract from Dante Alighieri, *De Vulgari Eloquentia*, in *A Translation of the Latin Works of Dante*, translated by A. J. Ferrers Howell.

Farrar, Straus & Giroux, Inc., and George Weidenfeld & Nicolson Ltd. for an extract from Dante Alighieri, *Monarchy and Three Political Letters*, translated by Donald Nicholl.

Farrar, Straus & Giroux, Inc., and Faber and Faber Ltd. for an extract from T. S. Eliot, *On Poetry and Poets*. Copyright © 1957 by T. S. Eliot.

Fordham University Press for an extract from Hilaire Belloc, *The Crisis of Civilization*, (Fordham University Press, 1937).

Harcourt, Brace & World, Inc., for an extract from Count Hermann Key-

69572

serling, *Europe*, translated by Maurice Samuel. Copyright 1928 by Harcourt, Brace & World, Inc., copyright 1956 by Maurice Samuel.

Harcourt, Brace & World, Inc., and Faber and Faber Ltd. for an extract from T. S. Eliot, *Notes Toward the Definition of a Culture*. Copyright 1949 by T. S. Eliot.

Harper & Row, Inc., and Basil Blackwell & Mott Ltd. for an extract from *Social Organization, The Science of Man and Other Writings*, Henri Saint-Simon, *Selected Writings*, translated and edited by F. M. H. Markham.

Holt, Rinehart and Winston, Inc., and Routledge & Kegan Paul Ltd. for an extract from Karl Jaspers, *Man in the Modern Age*, translated by Eden and Cedar Paul.

Alfred A. Knopf, Inc., and George Allen & Unwin Ltd. for an extract from Oswald Spengler, *The Decline of the West*, translated by Charles F. Atkinson. Copyright 1926, 1928 by Alfred A. Knopf, Inc.

W. W. Norton & Company, Inc., and George Allen & Unwin Ltd. for an extract from Jose Ortega y Gasset, *The Revolt of the Masses*. Copyright 1932 by W. W. Norton & Company, Inc. Copyright © 1960 by Teresa Carey.

Oxford University Press, Inc., for an extract from Arnold J. Toynbee, *The World and the West*. Copyright 1953 by Oxford University Press.

Charles Scribner's Sons for an extract from F. M. Dostoevsky, *The Diary of a Writer*, translated and annotated by Boris Brasol. Copyright 1949 by Charles Scribner's Sons.

Sheed & Ward, Inc., The Society of Authors and Mr. Christopher Dawson for an extract from Christopher Dawson, *The Making of Europe*.

Dr. Jan van Loewen Ltd., International Copyright Agency, for an extract from Ernst Juenger, *The Peace*, translated by Stuart Hood. Copyright 1948 by Ernst Juenger and Stuart Hood.

Yale University Press and The Bodley Head Ltd. for an extract from Paul Hazard, *The European Mind* (1680–1715), translated by J. Lewis May; published by Hollis and Carter 1953. Copyright 1953 by Yale University Press.

CONTENTS

Preface

WHAT YOU ARE about to read is not a history of Europe, but merely a chronicle—illustrated with quotations—of how men from the time of Homer to the present day have come to think of Europe as a cultural entity.

So much has been written on the subject! One recent work on the history of the European idea lists nearly two thousand names in the index of authors, and it excludes all but the best and most important. I have singled out for quotation those of most immediate interest—men who were actually present at the origins of our civilization or at moments when crucial problems were just emerging on the historical scene, and besides these "eyewitnesses to history," some of the writers who first urged plans for a European federation such as is beginning to take shape before our eyes.

In all these successive references to Europe, which run the gamut from the mythological to the factual, which include utopian dreams and practical plans, and which show how one writer has taken up and developed the ideas of his predecessors, a few general themes stand out. I draw them up here, in the hope that they may serve as guideposts to the reader as he works his way through a maze of quotations taken from twenty-eight centuries of literature, history, and philosophy in twelve ancient and modern languages.

1. Europe is much older than the European nations. Their lack of unity and their ever more illusory claims to absolute sovereignty endanger its very existence. If only they could unite, Europe would be saved, and with it all that remains valuable in its richly creative diversity.

2. From the moment of its birth, Europe has fulfilled a function not only universal but in fact universalizing. It has furthered the one-world concept, first by exploring the world, and then by supplying the intellectual, technological, and political means for achieving eventual unity of "the human race." Europe still has

a worldwide mission, but will not be able to discharge it until it has gathered its scattered powers in a federation of Europe.

3. A united Europe is not some latter-day economical or political expedient, but an ideal which the finest, most far-seeing minds have approved for the last thousand years. Long before that, Homer gave Zeus the epithet *europos,* "the far-seeing."

4. As we shall learn from the myth of Cadmus (quoted a little later), Europe is only to be found in the process of creating it. The true way to define Europe is to build Europe. The task is much less one of setting limits in historical time and geographical space than one of ceaselessly rekindling the fires of Europe's particular genius, which happens to be universal.

When I undertook this work, I had little idea of the scope and complexity of the subject. As the reader proceeds from discovery to discovery with me, I hope he will share my pleasure in composing it.

It remains for me to thank those who have advised and guided me. First of all, M. Hjalmar Pehrsson, head of the publishing department of the European Center of Culture, whose idea this anthology was, and to whom I am largely indebted for the labors of research involved.

Among the contemporary historical writings which have inspired me, I should first mention Gonzague de Reynold's monumental eight-volume work, *La Formation de l'Europe.* Next, Carlo Curcio's two exhaustive volumes entitled *Europa, Storia di un'idea;* Heinz Gollwitzer's exemplary study of European ideology in the eighteenth and nineteenth centuries, *Europabild und Europagedanke;* and three basic works on European internationalism by Jacob ter Meulen, Christian L. Lange, and Théodore Ruyssen. How fitting that the authors are, respectively, Swiss, Italian, German, Dutch, Norwegian, and French.

To those who follow in the same path—may they come soon! —I wish to say that this first rash attempt to do justice to a limitless subject can certainly be improved. I am sure that there are other sources unknown to me, but I doubt that there are any that are more reliable.

D. DE ROUGEMONT

PART ONE
THE ORIGINS

From Hesiod to Charlemagne
(from 900 B.C. to A.D. 1000)

1: Protohistory of a Nameless Continent

WHERE DOES THE name Europe come from?

What does it mean

When did people begin to speak of Europe as an entity? Was it in the period of Victor Hugo and Mazzini? Or only since Coudenhove and Briand? Or even as recently as the Congress of The Hague (May, 1948)?

We have tried to answer this question—or rather, these questions—by going back over the course of the centuries.

Paul Valéry, Proudhon and Saint-Simon, Voltaire, Leibniz, Sully, Pius II, Dante . . . Most historians as a rule do not go farther back than Pierre Du Bois, who served as legal adviser to Philip the Fair, and who, early in the fourteenth century, drew up the first project for a union of European States.

We have decided to go much farther back.

Our search has led us to strange frontiers and legendary epochs.

The earliest mention of "Europe" occurs in a work by Hesiod, dating from about 900 B.C.[1] The first to describe Europe and to compare it with Asia was Hippocrates. But it is not until the eighth century, after the battle of Poitiers (A.D. 732), that we find the first mention of Europe as not just a geographical but a human entity, defended by "Europeans." The Carolingian Empire marks a high point in the awareness of a united Europe. It was, however, followed by an era of warfare and prolonged dis-

---

[1] According to Victor Bérard's demonstration in his *Résurrection d'Homère* (published in English as *Did Homer Live?*), chap. viii, Hesiod lived *c.* 900 B.C. and Homer *c.* 800 B.C.

putes over the right of investiture. Our inquiry into the origins of the term, therefore, ends in the eleventh century.

During the fourth glacial epoch nearly half the plains and mountains were covered with a thick crust of ice. When this had melted, the continent was turned into a vast swampland and then into virgin forest. As a result of these upheavals, by about 8000 B.C. the civilization that produced the fascinating cave paintings of Lascaux and Altamira had been destroyed.

In the Middle East an entirely different civilization was being born—a civilization of husbandmen and city-dwellers, not of nomads and hunters. It spread via the Mediterranean coast, along the belt of olive groves which stretched from the shores of Asia Minor to Portugal, and gradually moved inland from the coast to the forests of the interior.

The continent was taking its present form. By 6000 B.C. England had become an island and the Channel was growing wider. At about the same time, the swamps and land bridges between Denmark and Scotland were submerged by the North Sea.

Colonists from Asia Minor and the Aegean sailed up the Vardar and the Danube and cleared the fertile black lands of the Ukraine and the shores of the Baltic and the North seas. They ventured up the Rhine Valley and across present-day Belgium, south and west of the Seine and the Loire. They burned the forests wherever they went, and cultivated the ash-enriched land for a time, only to move on and repeat the process somewhere else. Progress was slow.

Another stream of settlers, coming by sea from the shores of present-day Egypt and the Near East, gradually moved up through Italy and the Rhone Valley, spread southwest to Spain, and via Languedoc and the Cévennes moved northward to the Swiss plateau where they built their lake cities. The same people occupied the Seine Basin and even ventured as far as England.

Toward the end of the third millennium B.C. the techniques of metal-working invented in the Near East (gold, copper, and bronze) had spread throughout the continent. Here we yield the pen to M. André Varagnac, one of our best guides to the proto-history of the continent:

With the beginning of metal-working appears the first great religion, that of the megaliths—the dolmens and the menhirs. The history of religion usually makes no mention of this strange mystical current, whose strength and persistence is still attested by thousands and thousands of monuments all over western Europe. Its precise origin is still shrouded in mystery, but it certainly came from the Near East. Its victorious advance oddly associates the conquest of metals with the conquest of souls—much as three thousand years later in the Spanish conquest of the New World. Whatever mysterious rituals may have been observed, veneration of the dead was deeply rooted in the peasant mind. The cult and its visible stone structures reached the most distant islands of northern Scotland. The people who practiced this faith went east to Jutland, north to Scandinavia, and across northern Germany, taking their copper pots and weapons with them. As early as the first half of the second millennium B.C., a system of maritime trade had been set up, linking the Mediterranean with its northern counterpart, formed of the Baltic, the North Sea, and the Channel.[2]

Around the beginning of the last millennium B.C., a kind of common civilization seems to have spread over the greater portion of the continent. It was marked by the rite of burning the bodies of the dead, remains of which attest to how widespread the practice was.

A few centuries later, Greece and Etruscan Italy were exporting the refined products of their arts and crafts to the west and to the north. The Vix vase illustrates this so-called Hallstatt epoch. It gave way to the Celtic civilization in the fifth century B.C.

The Celts—the Gaels of Ireland, England, and Brittany, the Gauls and the Galates who reached Asia Minor in the third century B.C.—spread over the greater part of the western peninsula, with the exception of Greece and Italy, where they made but swift and brutal inroads (at Rome and Delphi). Their decentralized empire—a loose continental federation of peoples linked

[2] André Varagnac, "Comment est née l'Europe?" In *La Table Ronde*, No. 113.

by the Druidic cult—is a kind of negative prefiguration of the future Europe, fated to be shaped by the thought, the art, and the laws of the very two Mediterranean nations which were so mysteriously inaccessible to the Celts. Caesar's conquest of Gaul marked the beginning of the secular fusion of the continental and Mediterranean worlds. Out of this fusion Europe was born.[3]

As for its prehistory, then, or more accurately its protohistory—of which we have just retraced a few stages—it is that of a nameless continent, populated slowly, civilized and developed by men who came from the shores of the Near East, importing their ideas and techniques.

But who baptized this continent? When? Under what auspices? And what is the meaning of its name?

2 : The Myth of the Rape of Europa

> As for Europe . . . neither is it known whence the name of Europe was derived, nor who gave it name, unless we say that Europe was so called after the Tyrian Europa, and before her time was nameless, like the other divisions. But it is certain that Europa was an Asiatic, and never even set foot on the land which the Greeks now call Europe, only sailing from Phoenicia to Crete, and from Crete to Lycia.
>
> —HERODOTUS (IV, 45)

EUROPA WAS AT FIRST a goddess, one of the three thousand Oceanids, "a holy company of daughters [of Oceanus] who with the lord Apollo and the Rivers have youths in their keeping." We owe to the poet Hesiod, who lived in Boeotia around 900 B.C., this earliest mention of the name "Europa." It occurs in line 357 of his *Theogony*. Among the countless Oceanid sisters—of whom he mentions only about forty—Hesiod names Asia and Metis (or Reason), Zeus's first wife.

Much later the name Europe reappears, no longer a goddess but a legendary woman. Her father was Agenor, King of Tyre in

---

[3] Hegel, and later Ranke, strongly emphasized the importance of the conquest of Gaul; both see it as the event that created historical Europe.

Phoenicia, himself a descendant of Neptune. Her eyes were so beautiful, as her Greek name indicates, and her skin so refulgently white, that Zeus himself fell in love with her. Metamorphosed into a bull, he abducted her from her home on the shores of Asia Minor and carried her off to Crete, where she became a queen and mother of the kings of the Minos dynasty.

This legend doubtless inspired many works by earlier poets which have not survived; it is referred to by Herodotus and Thucydides among others. We possess a late Greek version of it —the famous idyll by Moschus, which dates from the second century B.C., when Alexandrian literature was at its peak. It is probable that Moschus, a learned, precious poet from Syracuse, was inspired by traditional paintings, frescoes, mosaics, mixing bowls, decorated vases, and engraved stones. He provided the vernal scenery which Western poets, sculptors, and painters have used for twenty centuries in their sensual and imaginative reinterpretations of the myth—works ranging from the metope of Selinus to the bas-relief decorating a modern railway station in Geneva, from Ovid to Victor Hugo, and from the creator of the Aquileia mosaics to painters such as Veronese, Titian, Claude Lorrain, and Tiepolo.

To Europa, the Cyprian once sent a sweet dream at the hour when the third watch of night begins and dawn is near, when sleep, resting sweeter than honey on the eyelids, unbinds the limbs but fetters the eyes in his soft bonds, and the tribe of true dreams fares afield. Then Phoenix' daughter Europa, maiden still, slumbering in her chamber beneath the eaves, fancied two continents contended for her, Asia and that which faces it, and they wore the shapes of women. One had a stranger's form, but the other was like to a woman of her own country and clung the closer about her daughter and kept saying how she herself had borne and nurtured her. But the other, laying strong hands upon her, drew her nothing loth away, for by the will of aegis-bearing Zeus, the figure said, Europa was destined to be hers. But the girl with beating heart sprang in terror from her couch and coverlet, for she saw the dream as it were a waking vision, and long she sat silent, and still before her opened eyes she had the pair; but at last the maiden timorously raised her voice. "What power above has sent me such visions? What dreams are these

that fluttered me as I lay on my strown couch slumbering so
sweetly? Who was the stranger that I beheld in my sleep? How
yearning for her seized my heart; and she, how fondly she wel-
comed me, and looked at me as though on her own child! May
the blessed gods but grant the dream have good fulfilment for
me."

Therewith she rose and sought her dear companions, coevals
born in the one year with her, noble maidens and well-loved,
with whom she always played when she arrayed herself for the
dance, or made her body bright with bathing at some torrent's
mouth, or culled fragrant lilies in the fields. And quickly they
came to her, each with a basket for flowers in her hand; and to
the meadows by the sea they went, where their company was
ever wont to gather, delighting in the roses that grew there and
the murmur of the waves. Europa herself carried a golden
basket, a thing for wonder and amaze, a masterwork of Hephaes-
tus, which he gave to Libya when she came to the Earthshaker's
[Poseidon's] bed, and she to the fair Telephaassa, her kins-
woman. And to the maid Europa, her mother Telephaassa gave
that splendid gift, whereon gleamed many a figure of cunning
craftsmanship. Wrought in gold thereon was Inachus' daughter
Io, a heifer still and not in woman's shape; and on wandering
feet she trod the salt-sea paths like to one swimming. And the
sea was fashioned in inlay of blue. High on the brow of either
coast folk stood gathered and watched the heifer faring over the
deep. And thereon too was Zeus the son of Cronos lightly touching with his hands the heifer, child of Inachus, whom by the
seven-mouthed Nile he changed back from a horned cow to a
woman. The streaming Nile was wrought in silver, in bronze the
heifer, and Zeus himself in gold. About the rounded basket
below its rim Hermes was fashioned, and stretched hard by him
Argus dight with unsleeping eyes, from whose crimson blood
there sprang a bird that gloried in the varied hues of its wings,
which it had spread as a swift ship spreads its sails, and with its
pinions covered the lip of the golden basket. Such was the fair
Europa's basket.

Now when the maidens were come to the flowery meadows,
one took delight in this bloom, one in that. One would choose
out scented jonquils, another hyacinths, violets another and
thyme another (in those spring meadows the ground was thickset with blossoms), and others too culled emulously the fragrant
tresses of golden saffron. But the princess, as she gathered in her
hands the splendor of the blushing rose, shone in their midst as
the foam-born goddess shines among the Graces.

Yet not for long was she to gladden her heart with flowers, nor guard her maiden girdle unsullied. For truly no sooner had the son of Cronos marked her than his heart was troubled, tamed by the sudden shafts of the Cyprian who alone can subdue even Zeus himself. Therefore to escape the wrath of jealous Hera and with purpose too to beguile the maiden's simple mind, he hid his godhead, changed his shape, and became a bull—not such a one as feeds in the byres, or cleaves a furrow as he drags the curving plough, or grazes with the herds, nor like to one broken to draw the loaded wain. All his body was gold-hued save for the white circle which gleamed in the center of his brow. His eyes were bright and lightened with desire, and from his head the horns sprang symmetrical like crescents of the horned moon when her rim is halved. Into the meadow he came, nor did his coming scare the maidens, but desire arose in them all to approach and stroke that lovely bull whose heavenly fragrance from afar outdid even the sweet scent of the meadow. Before the feet of peerless Europa he stopped, and licked her neck, and charmed the maid; and she caressed him, and gently with her hands wiped the deep foam from his mouth, and kissed the bull. But he lowed softly—thou wouldst say it was the sweet note of a Phrygian flute playing that thou heardest—and crouched before her feet, and bending his neck towards her looked at her, and showed her his broad back. And she cried to the deep-tressed maidens, "Hither, dear friends and comrades, that we may mount this bull and so enjoy ourselves, for surely he will make seats for all and take us on his back, so gentle he is, and mild to look upon, and kindly, no whit like other bulls. Reason, sound as a man's, informs him; it is only speech he lacks."

So saying, with a smile she seated herself upon his back, but when the rest would have done likewise straight the bull sprang up master of her he wished, and swiftly came to the sea. And Europa turned to her loved companions with cries and outstretched hands, but they could not come to her. And the bull reached the shore, and sped on like a dolphin treading the wide waves with hooves unwetted. Then as he came the sea grew smooth, and all round before the feet of Zeus the sea-beasts frolicked. The dolphin from the depths gamboled for joy over the swell. The sea-nymphs rose from the waters and advanced in rank mounted all on sea-beasts' backs. The thunderous Earth-shaker himself made smooth the waves over the main and led his brother on his briny road, and about him gathered Tritons, those deep-toned trumpeters of the sea, blowing on their tapering shells a bridal strain.

Meanwhile Europa on the bull-back of Zeus with one hand held the long horn of the beast and with the other drew up the purple fold on her breast for fear it should trail and be wetted by the infinite waters of the gray sea; and on her shoulders the deep robe bellied like the sail of a ship and made a light burden of the girl. But when she was far from her native land and neither sea-swept shore nor steep mountain could be seen, but sky above and the boundless deep beneath, she looked about her and thus broke silence. "Whither art thou bearing me, thou bull divine? Who art thou? How dost thou traverse ways so hard for cattle and fear not the sea? Swift ships may roam the sea but bulls dread that briny path. What pleasant draft is there for thee, or fodder, from the main? Art thou then some god? A god at least might act as thou dost. The dolphins of the deep fare not on land nor bulls in the sea, but thou over land and sea speedest undismayed, and thy hooves are as oars to thee. Verily soon thou wilt rise aloft above the gray mists and fly there like the swift birds. Alas all too ill-fated am I that I left my father's halls and with this bull make strange seafaring, a wanderer and alone. But thou, Lord of the gray sea, Earthshaker, encounter me, I pray, with kindness, for I think I see thee smoothing this voyage before me. For not without god's aid do I traverse these watery ways."

So spoke she, and the horned bull thus addressed her. "Take heart, maiden, and fear not the swelling main. I am Zeus himself, although when nearly viewed I seem to be a bull, for I can put on what semblance I will. It was longing for thee that sent me forth to measure so much sea in likeness of a bull. But now Crete, which nurtured me myself, shall receive thee, and there shall be thy bridal. And to me thou shalt bear famous sons and all shall be kings among mortal men."

So he spoke, and as he said it came to pass. Crete came into sight; Zeus took on him again his proper shape, and loosed her girdle, and the Hours arrayed her couch. She that had been a maid forthwith became the bride of Zeus and bore children to the son of Cronos and so anon was made a mother.[4]

The true significance of the myth, for us at least, surely lies in the dream with which the idyll opens—the two lands contending for Europa, "the land of Asia and the land which faces it." One is the already civilized continent and the other the conti-

---

[4] Moschus, *Europa* II, in *The Greek Bucolic Poets,* trans. A. S. F. Gow (Cambridge: Cambridge University Press, 1953), pp. 128-32.

nent that has no name, that lacks a name and a spirit, and will obtain them by violent means, but only with the help of Zeus himself.

The theme of the two contending women appears even earlier in the *Persae*, by Aeschylus, the admirable account of the battle of Salamis, produced in 473 B.C., only seven years afterward. The subject of this tragedy is the rivalry between Europe and Asia, the former represented by indomitable Greece, the latter by docile Persia.

The dream of Atossa, mother of Xerxes:

> Methought two women stood before my eyes
> Gorgeously vested, one in Persian robes
> Adorn'd, the other in the Doric garb.
> With more than mortal majesty they moved,
> Of peerless beauty; sisters too they seem'd,
> Though distant each from each they chanced to dwell,
> In Greece the one, on the barbaric coast
> The other. 'Twixt them soon dissension rose:
> My son then hasted to compose their strife,
> Soothed them to fair accord, beneath his car
> Yokes them, and reins their harness'd necks. The one,
> Exulting in her rich array, with pride
> Arching her stately neck, obey'd the reins;
> The other with indignant fury spurn'd
> The car, and dash'd it piecemeal, rent the reins,
> And tore the yoke asunder; down my son
> Fell from the seat, and instant at his side
> His father stands, Darius, at his fall
> Impress'd with pity: him when Xerxes saw,
> Glowing with grief and shame he rends his robes.
> This was the dreadful vision of the night.
> When I arose, in the sweet-flowing stream
> I bathed my hands, and on the incensed altars
> Presenting my oblations to the gods
> To avert these ills, an eagle I behold
> Fly to the altar of the sun; aghast
> I stood, my friends, and speechless; when a hawk
> With eager speed runs thither, furious cuffs

The eagle with his wings, and with his talons
Unplumes his head; meantime the imperial bird
Cowers to the blows defenseless.[5]

The Greek hawk that swoops down on the Persian eagle prefigures the defeat of Xerxes, who appears at the end of the tragedy, crushed and deserted. In the work of Moschus, a relatively
late product, we find a symbolic expression of events of more
general significance which took place at least a thousand years
before it was written.

According to most recent writers on the subject,[6] Europa was
an Asiatic deity before she became a heroine of legend. In brief,
she was a local and poetic version of the Great Goddess, whose
cult dominated the Near East from the Euphrates to the Bosporus and the Nile.

Another scholar, the poet Robert Graves,[7] translates "Aerope"
(Europa) as "broad face," and presents her as a lunar symbol,
while both Zeus and the bull, according to him, are solar symbols
par excellence.

In actual fact, the background of the Greek myth is Semitic.
It is part of an Assyrian-Hebrew complex to which the Bible
makes frequent and very precise allusions, and at the center of
which are legendary poems, such as the epic of Keret (discovered
at Ras Shamra in 1929). Keret was king of the Sidonian-Tyrians,
that is the Canaanites, whom the Greeks called Phoenicians,
and who were Semites—the Hebrews of the sea. Actually Keret
stands for Crete; the Keretites (Cherethites) mentioned by
the prophet Zephaniah (2:5) are Cretans. On the other hand,
the god El, father of the Yahweh of the Hebrews, was a bull-god
with a predilection for kidnaping girls on the shores of Canaan,
Tyre, and Sidon—in the region the Greeks called Phoenicia. His

[5] Aeschylus, The Persians, vss. 181–208, trans. Robert Potter.
[6] See especially W. Technau, Die Göttin auf dem Stier, quoted in Gonzague de Reynold, La Formation de l'Europe (Fribourg: L.U.F., 1944; and
Paris: Plon, 1937), Vol. I, and in Jürgen Fischer, Oriens, Occidens, Europa-
Begriff und Gedanke "Europa" in der späten Antike und im frühen Mittel-
alter (Wiesbaden: Franz Steiner Verlag, 1957).
[7] Robert Graves, The Greek Myths (London: Penguin Books, 1955).

headquarters was at Kaphtor (Crete). He was also the great god of Edom, which is the same name as Adam, and which stands for "red" or "Phoenix"—whence the Phoenicians. (According to Herodotus the Phoenicians came from the Erythrean Sea, that is, the Red Sea.) We may lastly note that according to Victor Bérard a symbol which turns up frequently in archaic Greek intaglios, that of "a star close to a sun and crescent moon," clearly indicates the design's Phoenician origin.[8] Everything points to the Semitic ancestry of the Greek myth, a finding which will come as no surprise to readers of Bérard's works on the Homeric poems and the Bible, and on the Semitic origins of a great number of Greek gods and place names. According to ancient Greek chronicles, the events in question took place in the sixteenth century B.C. In the nineteenth century no notice was taken of these chronicles, but the most recent archeological investigations have confirmed their documentary value.

Whatever the value of these various hypotheses and arguments, when we go back to the Greek myth we find that Europa was the name of a female power who was abducted from Asia and fertilized by the male god who ruled over the Olympus of the continental Greeks. The great gold mask found in the ruins of Mycenae—a solar Zeus dating from the decline of Crete and the Cretan cult of the Great Mother—casts light on the birth of Hellenic Europe and at the same time is a reflection of it. What the myth expresses is a religious mutation within a civilization that moved from the Near East to an obscure western land mass, to which it eventually gave the name of its abducted heroine.

We shall not quote here the famous versions of the rape of Europa by Ovid and by Diodorus (first century B.C.). They are merely imitations of Moschus, whose idyll we reproduced in its entirety because in a way it sums up the etymology of an artistic tradition handed down over the centuries.

However, apart from the dream at the beginning, Moschus' allegory does not evoke or prefigure any historical or psychlogi-

---

[8] Victor Bérard, *Did Homer Live?* Trans. Brian Rhys (London: J. M. Darbe and Sons, 1931), p. 190.

cal reality. There is nothing in common between the idyll *Europa* and Europe's subsequent history.

Horace made something more of the myth. Although he keeps the traditional trappings, he was the first to give it historical, universal meaning. At the conclusion of his *Ode to Galatea*, Venus addresses these moving and solemn words to Europa:

> . . . bene ferre magnum
> Disce fortunam; tua sectus orbis
> Nomina ducet.

So did Europa, too, entrust her snowy form to the treacherous bull and turn pale before the deep alone with monsters, and at the peril of mid-sea—she who before had been so bold. Erstwhile among the meadows, absorbed in flowers, and wearing a garland due to nymphs, now she beheld naught in the glimmering night except the stars and waves. Soon as she touched Crete, mighty with its hundred cities, "O father," she exclaimed, "O name of daughter, that I forsook, and filial duty, by frenzy overmastered! Whence have I come and whither? A single death is too light for maidens' faults. Am I awake and do I lament a hideous deed, or am I free from sin and does some empty phantom mock me, which brings a dream as through the Ivory Gate it flees? Was it better to travel o'er the long waves, or to pluck fresh flowers? If anyone would now but deliver the infamous bullock to my anger, I would strive to rend it with the steel and break the horns of the monstrous creature just now so fondly loved. Shameless I left my household gods; shameless I keep Orcus waiting. Oh, if any god hear these laments, let me wander naked among lions! Before hideous wasting seizes upon my comely cheeks and the fresh lifeblood departs from the tender victim, while beauteous still, I seek to feed the tigers. 'Worthless Europa,' my father, though far distant, urges, 'why dost thou hesitate to die? On this ash thou canst hang thyself with the girdle that happily has followed thee. Or if the cliffs and rocks sharp for death allure thee, come! give thy body to the hurrying gale, if thou wilt not rather card a mistress' wool, thou of royal blood, and be given o'er, a concubine, to the mercies of some barbarian queen!'"

As she thus complained, Venus with treacherous laugh stood by, and her son with unstrung bow. Soon when the goddess had had sport enough, "Refrain from anger and hot passion," she exclaimed, "when the hated bull shall give thee horns to be mangled! Thou knowest not that thou art the wife of Jove invincible. Cease thy sobs! Learn to bear becomingly thy great destiny! A region of the earth shall take thy name." [9]

Four centuries later, the myth was attacked and denounced—proof that it was still very much alive—by Christian polemicists. Some, like Prudentius, denounced its immorality; others, like Lactantius who was followed by St. Jerome, sought to divest it of its miraculous character: "Europa was abducted by the Cretans in a ship whose emblem was a bull." [10]

However, Isidore of Seville, in the seventh century, confines himself to a two-line summary of the primitive account. Thereby, thanks to the lasting success of his *Etymologies*, it was passed on to the schools of the Middle Ages.

Unlike Lactantius and St. Jerome, who had merely removed the pagan religious content from the myth, the Middle Ages occasionally attempted to endow it with a Christian content. One is reminded of Simone Weil, who, in our own day, reinterpreted other myths, particularly that of Prometheus, in the same spirit. A touching example is that of the fourteenth-century monk Pierre Bersuire, who supposed the Phoenician coast to stand for worldliness, and Crete for the Christian life of contemplation. According to him, the rape of Europa symbolizes the passage of the soul from the temporal to the eternal:

The maiden Europa stands for the soul . . . Jupiter for the Son of God who, to redeem the soul, changed into a bull, that is, took on corporeal form by assuming human flesh. He came and dwelt amongst us here below in this vale of trouble and tears . . . The faithful should follow His example, for He is a true and certain guide.

The geographer Mercator, whose famous *Atlas* appeared in 1595, observed that the bull-god "does aptly represent the

[9] Horace, *The Odes and Epodes,* trans. C. E. Bennett (The Loeb Classical Library [Cambridge, Mass.: Harvard University Press; London: William Heinemann, Ltd.], 1914).

[10] Note that St. Jerome's "rationalistic" interpretation had already been advanced by Herodotus—a euhemerist before Euhemerus—who wrote (Book I): "Certain Greeks . . . landed in Phoenicia, at Tyre, and ravished Europa, the king's daughter; they may have been Cretans."

natural disposition of the European." This author cares less for
the divine origin of the fable than for the ethnographic sense it
may embody:

Some, scorning these fables, say that she [Europa] was ravished and carried off in a ship, bearing the figure of a bull on its
prow. Others recognized the vessel as bearing the effigy of the
tutelary Jupiter and of the bull. Palephatus says that a Candian
named Taurus carried off Europa, capturing the king's daughter
along with other girls from Italy or the Tyrrhenian region. There
are some who say that there existed a legion of warriors who
bore, among other emblems, that of the bull. Some say that the
ravished girl was thus named because of her beauty. Indeed, the
bull, supposed by them to have carried off Europa, does aptly
represent the customs and natural disposition of the European.
He is the possessor of a kind of noble courage; he is insolent,
embellished by his horns, white in color with a broad throat and
a thick neck, the leader and commander of the stud farm. Although he displays great continence, he exhibits extreme ardor
when confronting the opposite sex, then he again becomes chaste
and moderate. Such is virtually the natural disposition of Europeans, especially those who live farthest north.

From the Renaissance onward, in fact, the myth has been no
more than a "noble subject" for painters and poets. Rémy Bel-
leau, Ronsard, André Chénier, and Victor Hugo all treated it as
a kind of exercise in the style of the ancient idyll. For instance,
Hugo writes:

> Un ouvrier d'Egine a sculpté sur la plinthe
> Europe dont un dieu n'écoute pas la plainte.
> Le taureau blanc l'emporte. Europe, sans espoir,
> Crie, et baissant les yeux, s'épouvante de voir
> L'Océan monstrueux qui baise ses pieds roses.

> [A craftsman from Aegina has carved upon the plinth
> The figures of Europa and a god heedless of her plaint.
> The white bull is carrying her off. Hopelessly she
> Shrieks, and, casting down her eyes, is appalled to see
> The monstrous Ocean lapping her rosy feet with his kisses.]

Leconte de Lisle catches something of Horace's tone in the
speech he puts in the mouth of Zeus (not Venus):

Et quand la terre, au loin, se fut toute perdue,
Quand le silencieux espace Ouranien
Rayonna, seul ardent, sur la glauque étendue,
Le divin Taureau dit; —O Vierge ne crains rien.
Viens! Voici l'île sainte aux antres prophétiques
Où tu célébreras ton hymen glorieux,
Et de toi sortiront des Enfants héroiques
Qui régiront la terre et deviendront des Dieux!

[And when the earth, far off, was finally lost from view,
When the vast soundless Uranian space above
Alone spread warmth and light over the sea-green deeps,
Then the divine Bull spoke: "O Virgin, there is naught to fear.
Come! Here is the sacred isle in whose prophetic caves
Thou art to celebrate thy glorious nuptials.
From thee shall stem a line of Heroes
Who shall rule the earth and who shall be as gods!]

These poets express only too well the distance that separates literature from its deep archetypal theme, the gulf between original myth and reality—the drama of historical Europe. Let us get back to the thread of our own theme, to the relation between the religious evolution which the myth symbolizes and Europe still standing in the wings of history. A fine contemporary historian, Gonzague de Reynold, is particularly helpful here: [11]

Europa came to us from Asia, mother of all the great religions, source of all the great myths. Europe, under the guise of Europa, appears in the earliest of the myths that express a crude, pantheistic religion—earth and fertility worship, the religion of the Great Mother, in which everything is simultaneously one and many.

As soon as it reaches the shores of the eastern Mediterranean, the myth encounters busy maritime activity, a life of piracy and trade, conflict and bartering, a life which it reflects to such a point that it has long been accounted for in terms of cultural history. Soon after it reached the Mediterranean, the myth of Europa took root in Crete. There it became the symbol of a whole civilization intermediate between Greece and Asia.

[11] *Op. cit.,* I, 112, 110, 111.

A powerfully organized state with its own laws, its own arts, and its own wealth, a seafaring, colonizing state, Minoan Crete spread the cult of Europa associated with that of Zeus throughout the Aegean world, including continental Greece. Now the Greek genius takes it over, enrolls it in its own polytheistic religion, and humanizes it. As the male principle becomes victorious over the female principle, a hierarchy of values appears which is no longer Asian but European.

What is Europe?

Europe came from Asia.

Europa was abducted from the East by a Northern god.

. . . .

Zeus-Jupiter now became the god par excellence, the root and principle of Greek polytheism. He it was who preserved unity among the multiple divinities, each of whom was worshiped according to differing local traditions. With him a long and obscure development reaches culmination. The elementary energies, progressing from hypostasis to hypostasis, have become ever more concrete, more and more humanized. At the same time, however, Zeus marks the beginning of another evolutionary process, one that will lead from gods to men. In the Cronide Zeus appears the god-man whose mission is to dominate the world and govern it, to make it possible for men to live in it. He will take the Oceanid Metis, or Reason, for his first wife, but he will absorb her into himself, lest he beget by her a son stronger than himself, and Athena-Minerva, who is produced out of his head, stands for the active, inventive, artistic intelligence, the symbol of Hellenic genius. His second wife will be Themis, i.e., Justice. Later he will marry Mnemosyne, Memory, and he will have the Muses by her. His last wife, Juno the jealous, Hera-Juno, will be Morality. Is he not the very symbol of the great civilization which, in time, gave birth to European civilization?

. . . .

The cult of Europa will remain associated with that of Zeus, but, in a secondary capacity, as it were. What becomes of it?

As we shall see, the cult moved northward and spread gradually throughout Hellas. From Crete it extended in three directions: (1) via Corinth, north to Thessaly, eastward across Thrace, and down into northern Asia Minor; (2) via Boeotia, west to Phocis, Locris, and up into the mountains of Epirus (to which Europe gave the name); and (3) by way of the islands and along the coasts, as far as those parts of Syria and Phoenicia where the myth had originated in the first place. Throughout all this, the local traditions get tangled with each other, the legend becomes complicated and blurred. As the goddess recedes into the background, the continent comes to the fore.

3:   The Myth of Japheth

FOR US TODAY, the myth of the rape of Europa conveys no more than a general westward current of civilization from the Semitic Near East to the "nameless continent," as tribes in search of new lands settled here, bringing their own religions and technical inventions with them. Now we turn our attention to another old myth, one that is much less well known today, but to which we owe the fact that from a very early date "Europe" came to signify a distinct geographical entity: one of the three parts of the known world.

We are referring here to a tradition independent of Greece, which goes back to the Bible as interpreted by the Church Fathers in the fourth century. We call it the Myth of Japheth.

According to St. Jerome (A.D. 346–420) in his *Liber hebraicarum questionum in Genesim,* as well as according to St. Ambrose (born in A.D. 340), Noah gave each of his three sons, Shem, Ham, and Japheth, one of the three parts of the world for their inheritance, and these were Asia, Africa, and Europe, respectively.

This mythical threefold division of the earth was to dominate all medieval geography. It is based upon chapters 9 and 10 of Genesis, in which we read that Noah's sons upon leaving the Ark were ordered by their father to fill the earth with their posterity. They were not treated equally, for only Shem and Japheth, who had covered their father's nakedness when he was drunk, were blessed by Noah: "Blessed be the Lord God of Shem; and Canaan [son of Ham] shall be his servant. God shall enlarge Japheth, and he shall dwell in the tents of Shem; and Canaan shall be his servant." (Gen. 9: 26–27.)

In the eyes of St. Ambrose, the sons of Shem were to be accounted good, those of Ham wicked, and those of Japheth "indifferent"—that is, pagan, "attached to the things of this world," but capable of conversion.[12]

Over the centuries that followed, such commentators as Paulus Orosius and Philastre de Brescia picked up St. Ambrose's tripartite division and elaborated upon it. According to St. Augustine, Japheth was the common ancestor of the peoples of the West, comprising Europe and Africa, while Shem was the common ancestor of the peoples of the East. In Genesis (9:27) he read a prophecy, *prophetica benedictio*, which he interprets as follows: The tents of Shem represent the Church; Japheth, through his posterity, will "enlarge" as far as the domain of Shem, that is, the peoples of Europe will be converted to the true God. The word all these exegetes stress is the one we underlined in the verset quoted above: *dilatet* in the Vulgate. Japheth (or Yepheth, from *phatah*, "to enlarge, to spread") denotes latitude, width, expansion. Thus, according to Isidore of Seville, the spread of the Roman Empire over Europe and the rest of the *orbis terrarum* prefigured that of the Christian Church. Thus the geographical term "Europe" takes on religious significance. According to Isidore, the posterity of Japheth includes the Cappadocians, the Cilicians, the Ionians, the Thracians, the Gauls, and the Spanish: "These are the peoples of the lineage of Japheth, who will possess all Europe [*omnem Europam*] from Mount Taurus in Middle Asia to the Britannic Ocean."

Jürgen Fischer cites a dozen authors from the fifth century to the fifteenth who link the various "nations," or families, peopling Europe, each with its distinct language, to Japheth and his twenty-three or twenty-six sons and grandsons. We may note in passing that some of these same authors divide the human race into three classes: free men, the sons of Shem; soldiers, the sons of Japheth; and slaves, the sons of Ham.

It is surely unprovable, but possible, that in the minds of these authors the relation between Japheth and Europe was confirmed by the Greek translation of the [Biblical] allegory. To

[12] We follow here the argument of Jürgen Fischer, *op. cit.*, pp. 10–19, "Die Japhet-Historie."

the Latin *latus* ("wide, extended") corresponds the Greek *eurus*, from which derived the poetic form *europos*—the latter becoming "Europe" by homophony.[13]

Thus there would be a link—problematic, to be sure, and perhaps based on a play on words—between Genesis and Greek mythology. By incorporation within the system of the Incarnation, Europe becomes a concept acceptable to the Fathers of the Church. So interpreted, the myth of Japheth expressed the state of things on the continent in the second half of the first millennium since Christ. The "indifferent" pagan mass bearing the name of Europe was in fact in process of being Christianized.

The Japhetic origin of Europe went virtually uncontested until the nineteenth century. Joseph de Maistre, like Bossuet before him, still regards it as an established dogma. Vico made it the starting point for speculations as to how languages originated. Campanella wondered whether Japheth's "expansion" to the tents of Shem might not signify Europe's domination over the Arab world. . . . Voltaire, however, set out to refute the legend by employing one of his favorite devices, literal interpretation carried *ad absurdum:*

I leave it to men more learned than myself to show how the three children of Noah, who were the only inhabitants of the globe, shared it among themselves in its entirety; how each of them, living some two or three leagues from one another, went out in all directions to found powerful empires; and how Javan, Noah's grandson, peopled Greece on his way to Italy; how they called themselves Ionians because Ion sent colonies to the shores of Asia Minor; and how this Ion was obviously Javan, if we just change the *I* to *J* and *on* to *van.* These tales are being told to children, but the children don't believe a word of them.[14]

Children are not always good judges, however, and in this instance Voltaire's childish argument misses the point. The migration of the "Phoenician" Semites to Ionia, where Homer lived and wrote (some of them passed through Cadmus' Boeotia), is well attested today.[15]

[13] J. Fischer, *ibid.*, p. 15.
[14] *Essai sur les Mœurs et l'Esprit des Nations.*
[15] Cf. V. Bérard, *op. cit.*

Surprisingly enough, although the Japheth legend enjoyed immense popularity among clerics of all ranks for fourteen centuries, only two or three humanists ventured to suggest that it would have been more consistent with Christian tradition to call our continent "Japhetia" than to call it "Europe." Thus Guillaume Postel wrote in the sixteenth century:

Non, est, quod repetatur, eam partem terrae, quam fabulae Europam dixere, Japetiam debere dici, ob primum illum Japetum non tantum illius, sed universi orbis principem institutum.[16]

4: Cadmus, or the Quest for Europe

LEGENDS AND ARCHEOLOGICAL finds together reveal that there was another point of contact (or of contamination) between the Greek myth and the Biblical one. Let us first consider the Greek legends.

Agenor, king of Tyre, had left the delta region of the Nile to settle in the land of Canaan. There he had five sons and one daughter, Europa. When the latter had been carried off and ravished by the divine bull (or by Taurus, king of Crete) Agenor sent his five sons to look for her. Since they did not know where the bull had taken her, each of them set out in a different direction. Phoenix went westward across Libya as far as the site of the future Carthage, where he gave his name to the *Punici* (from *Poeni*). He returned to Canaan, empty-handed, and the country was subsequently renamed Phoenicia in his honor. Cilix went to what was later called Cilicia, Phineus to the region of the Dardanelles, Thasus first to Olympia in Greece and from there to the island of Thasos. Cadmus, who was to be the most famous of the five brothers, went first to Rhodes, then to Thrace, and from there to Delphi. When he asked the oracle where he might find Europa, the Pythoness advised him to abandon his quest. He should instead follow a cow and, at the spot where the cow drops from exhaustion, Cadmus should

[16] Quoted in F. J. Schneider, *Japeta* (Stuttgart, 1927).

build a city. He bought a cow marked with a white full moon on each flank, and drove it without respite eastward across Boeotia, until it sank down exhausted at the place where the city of Thebes now stands.

Thus we see that the Quest for Europe—according to this group of legends, reported by Pausanias, among others—is identical with the historical travels of the Phoenicians. We also see why, from these fabled beginnings, it is so hard "to find Europe!" It was in pursuit of her mythical image that the five brothers discovered her geographical reality, and the most active of them founded a city. Here is a most instructive lesson for us today: *To search for Europe is to build Europe!* In other words, it is the search that creates her.

But we have left in abeyance the matter of how the two myths here come together. According to Robert Graves:[17]

Aegnor is the Phoenician hero Chnas, who appears in Genesis as "Canaan"; many Canaanite customs point to an East African provenience, and the Canaanites may have originally come to Lower Egypt from Uganda. The dispersal of Agenor's sons seems to record the westward flight of Canaanite tribes early in the second millennium B.C., under pressure from Aryan and Semitic invaders.

At all events, this flight corresponds to the great adventure of those early *descubridores,* the Phoenicians. Victor Bérard gives us a striking résumé of the complex of symbols and historical facts which his "Phoenician" thesis makes intelligible for us: [18]

In like fashion the Phoenicians of pre-Homeric times had set out to discover in the Mediterranean a Western continent which in their tongue they must have called the Land of the West, *Ereba*. It was their Egyptian masters who had given them the idea of this "fair Amentit," of this mysterious West which Egypt made the everlasting abode of the blessed dead. Out of this quest for *Ereba* the Hellenes created the legend of the lovely Europe "of the West," who was sought by her brother Kadmos "of the East" at the bidding of their father Agenor, king of Tyre. Passing from Phoenicia over to Crete, on from Boeotia into

[17] *Op. cit.,* I, 196.
[18] *Op. cit.,* pp. 177–78.

Illyria, Kadmos had moved towards this land of the evening which the Greeks called Hesperia.

Amentit, Europe, Hesperia—three names for that Land of the West which the dwellers in Tyre and Sidon doubtless first imagined as a solid tract of earth, a mighty continent, like one of those they might be familiar with nearer home—Asia, Libya.

And how many years must these questers of passages have taken to break this solid tract up into islands, peninsulas, and lesser territories, and finally, after thinking they had found it at last, first in Crete, then in Greece, then in Italy, to bring it down to the size of the Spanish peninsula?

Even so, there were those in ancient times who could never reconcile themselves to this disappointing fact: they wanted to carry the quest of Kadmos yet farther, find a home for this other world yet farther and farther in the West. And when, beyond Kalypso and the Pillars of Hercules, the boundless ocean stretched before their sight, they held that Hesperis, daughter of Atlas—Atlantis—had foundered in these waters, and some modern sailors have still thought to find her, and some geographers and geologists still persist in seeing her there.

However, the full significance of the Cadmus legend is still far from exhausted by this reference to the discovery of the Land of the Setting Sun. For—to follow Victor Bérard again—the ancients almost unanimously attributed the introduction of the alphabet into Greece to Cadmus, and situated the coming of Cadmus early in the fifteenth century. Now, recent archeological finds confirm this date. Via Crete, the alphabet came to us from the Phoenicians; the latter colonized Boeotia and founded families there. From the noble dynasties of "Cadmeans" descend a number of scholars like Bias and Thales of Miletus (two of the Seven Sages), who later founded Greek prose and philosophy in Ionia, where Homer lived. Nor should it be forgotten that Hesiod, who was the first to mention Europe, was born and lived in Boeotia.

Finally, we may note two other points of mythological affinity. If Agenor, father of Europa, was the Canaan of Genesis, then he was the son of Ham "who shall be a servant." The Greco-Phoenician myth would intersect with the legend of Japheth at this point—a circumstance raising new uncertainties and intro-

ducing new complexities. Europa would then be a descendant
of Ham according to the classical legend and the Phoenician
interpretation of it, and yet, according to the Biblical tradition,
the western continent was promised to the descendants of
Japheth.

No less curious is the striking, but disconcerting, similarity
between the Japheth of Genesis, one of Noah's sons, and the
Iapetus of mythology. He was the Titan father of Prometheus
and hence grandfather of Deucalion, the Noah of the Greeks.
Classical times considered Iapetus the ancestor of the human
race. *Audax Iapeti genus*, Horace wrote. The Western tradition
had no trouble assimilating both ancestors. Bossuet wrote: "Japheth who populated the greater part of the west remained
famous there under the celebrated name of Iapetus." [19]

We shall see how this seeming confusion is accounted for.

5: The Etymologies

ETYMOLOGY IS TOO often presented to us as a science by those
who practice it without art. By tracing the filiations of sign and
sound, which can sometimes be done quite straightforwardly,
the etymologist looks for *significations*, regarding the primitive
ones as more authentic than the recent ones, which it derives
from the former. Practiced as a science, it rarely finds real significations; etymology is chiefly a list of errors, mistaken analogies, puns, and boners; practiced as an art, it finds only too many
"significations," and only its choice among these is significant.
In other words, what we learn from it is the preferences of a
"true" root's discoverer, rather than the "true" meaning of a
word.

This is why it is interesting to recall here some of the "origins"
which were beleived in various epochs to account for the name
"Europe"—in spite of Herodotus, who thought no mortal could
ever hope to discover its true meaning.

[19] Jacques Bénigne Bossuet, *Discours sur l'Historie Universelle* (1681).

a) To begin with, there is the picturesque interpretation advanced by Johannes Goropius, a sixteenth-century physician of Brabant. It is based on the traditional beliefs that the name "Europe" is of Hebrew origin and that our continent was Japheth's inheritance. The purpose, then, as we have seen above is to supply a Biblical root for the term, which otherwise might awkwardly recall the immoral love of the king of the pagan gods for a daughter of Tyre, a city repeatedly cursed by the Prophets. According to Mercator, Goropius wrote:

We see that Japheth is promised enlargement, or as others interpret it, joy, which he was to obtain when Christ had redeemed us by his death. Thus *E* means a legitimate marriage; *Ur*, excellent; *Hop*, hope: hence *Europ* stands for excellent hope of a legitimate marriage; this was natural in this part of the earth, which Noah had given Japheth for his dwelling place. For, even though the descendants of Shem were for many centuries allied with God as the race of Abraham, they nevertheless repudiated it. But the marriage by which Christ joined himself to Europe—His Church—will never be dissolved: therefore Japheth's inheritance is rightfully called Europe.

b) But this was not the only whimsical etymological explanation: there is a Celtic one. In their *Atlas de géographie ancienne et moderne,* published in 1829, the Lapies, father and son, traced "Europe" back to the Celtic *wrab,* which stands for "west." Quoting them, Reynold adds: "Their excuse is that they lived in a time when it was still believed that Adam had spoken *bas-breton,* at least after his expulsion from the earthly paradise."

c) A semitic etymology derives Europe from *Ereb*,[20] a term denoting "evening" or "sunset"—apparently in the interests of . . . *orient*ation! Thus, the Rumanian historian Nicolas Jorga wrote in 1932:

For the ancient eastern nations which lived in the land where the sun rises, i.e., in Asia, the term Europe denoted the land

[20] The *Encyclopédie* (1777) derives "Europe" from the Phoenician *uroppa,* which denotes in that language "white face." Similarly, Moreri's *Grand Dictionnaire Historique* (1674) cites Bouchart's opinion that Europe is derived from the Phoenician *chur-appe,* "white face," which recalls the much-vaunted whiteness of Agenor's daughter.

where the sun sets. On their side, light; on ours, obscurity, darkness, *Arip*, a word that brings to mind the dark Erebus of Greek mythology. Since it was impossible to move the setting sun any farther west, one could only make it sink underground into the absolute darkness of departed shades and eternal doom.

From the historical point of view, everything mentioned so far on the "Phoenician" origins of the myth of Europa makes the etymology *ereb* more plausible. But in addition there is an argument drawn directly from phonetics. As is well known, only the consonants matter in Hebrew; the vowels are variable and are often supplied by way of reconstruction. Now, the consonants *r* and *b* invariably denote the sunset both in Hebrew and in Arabic. The Algarve is the westernmost province of Portugal, and Alga*rve* = El Gha*rb* = land of the setting sun in Arabic. The same consonants are found in Magh*reb* = e*reb;* in Hebrew, in M'a*rab*, maa*rab*, and maa*rab*ah, which are variants of the same name.

The series: eReB
          aRaBe [21]
          magReB
          euRoPe

thus seems extremely plausible.

Gonzague de Reynold favors the Greek etymology, yet he supplies a futher reason for preferring the Semitic one:

We no longer believe in the affinity between Ereb and Europe, in the sense of a direct connection such as that of brother and sister. There is, however, an indirect link, once again from mythology:

Erebus, in mythology, was the son of Chaos and the brother of Night. Chaos—the Abyss in Hesiod's *Theogony*—begot Night. Night bore terrible children: Woe, Doom, Death, the Fates, Nemesis, all that distresses and disturbs mortal men. She also bore, "though she lay with none," Sleep and Dreams; but also, by her brother Erebus, she bore Aether and Day, the light which is to triumph over her. Erebus then took on a derived

[21] Concerning the name "Arab" G. Rawlinson (*Notes to Herodotus*, II, 71) writes: "No doubt that the name of the Arabs was . . . given from their living at the westernmost part of Asia; and their own word *Gharb*, the West, is another form of the original Semitic name Arab."

meaning—the dark underground pit, "the depths of the dead," in Hesiod's words. Erebus is derived from the verb *erepho*, "to cover, to shade," or from *era*, a poetic term denoting the earth. It is thus possible that it was derived, directly or indirectly, from the Semitic *ereb*, "evening."

d) There is, finally, our Greek name, that of Agenor's daughter. Here we shall once more cite Gonzague de Reynold: [22]

Europe in its first meaning is a feminine adjective: *eurôpé*. This adjective corresponds to the masculine form *euruopa* or (more rarely) *euruopè*, one of the Homeric epithets for Zeus. *Euruopa* occurs several times in the Iliad and the Odyssey; *euruopé* appears twice only in works by relatively recent mythographers. These are vocative forms. The form *euruopa* also appears as an Aeolian nominative or accusative. By the rules, the nominative should be *euruopès* or *euruops*, but these two forms are hypothetical; i.e., they are not found in the texts, are merely to be inferred from the declension. As for the etymology, that is easy. What we have here is a compound of two other Greek words: the adjective *eurus*—broad, ample, spacious; and the noun *ops*, a poetic term for "eye," "glance," and by extension "face." *Zeus euruopè* is "far-seeing Zeus." *Eurôpé* is thus a woman with large eyes, a lovely way of looking, a beautiful face. The kinship between Europe and the Homeric epithet for Zeus is thus obvious.

Eurôpé, for its part, was not long in producing its masculine, *eurôpos*. "Zeus the far-seeing" has his divine city on Olympus; the river Paeneus has its source in the Olympus range, and the Europos is one of its tributaries.

The fact that *europe* served as one of the epithets for Zeus raises the question of whether we are not dealing with a duplication—whether the adjective was not separated from the noun and later became a noun itself. And so we are obliged to consult mythology.

e) Do these explanations exhaust the subject? Not quite, for Greek etymology in turn affords various possibilities. One of them was explored by Robert Graves [23] in his notes to the myth of Europa and Cadmus. The abundance of the etymological correspondences noted by this author will give some idea of the extreme complexity of the theme:

[22] *Op. cit.*, I.
[23] *Op. cit.*, I, 196–97.

Europe means "broad-face," a synonym for the full moon, and a title of the Moon-goddesses Demeter at Lebadia and Astarte at Sidon. If, however, the word is not *eur-ope* but *eu-rope* (on the analogy of *euboea*), it may also mean "good for willows"— that is, "well-watered." The willow rules the fifth month of the sacred year,[24] and is associated with witchcraft and with fertility rites throughout Europe. . . . Zeus's rape of Europa, which records an early Hellenic occupation of Crete, has been deduced from pre-Hellenic pictures of the Moon-priestess triumphantly riding on the Sun-bull, her victim; the scene survives in eight molded plaques of blue glass, found in the Mycenaean city of Midea. This seems to have been part of the fertility ritual during which Europe's May-garland was carried in procession. Zeus's seduction of Europe in eagle-disguise [25] recalls his seduction of Hera in cuckoo-disguise; since (according to Hesychius) Hera bore the title "Europia."

Europe's Cretan and Corinthian name was Hellotis, which suggests Helice ("willow"); Helle and Helen are the same divine character. Callimachus in his *Epithalamion for Helen* mentions that the plane-tree was also sacred to Helen. Its sanctity lay in its five-pointed leaves, representing the hand of the goddess. . . .

Need we recall that Hellen—the masculine form of Helen and the eponymous ancestor of all the Hellenes—was the son of Deucalion? Or that the latter is the Noah of Greek mythology, he and his wife being the only survivors (thanks to the Ark shaped like a half-moon which he built on order of Prometheus his father) of a flood the end of which was heralded by a dove? Hellen is thus the great-grandson of the Greek Iapetus, as Japheth was the son of the Biblical Noah. Hellen's mother Pyrrha would be the same as the goddess Ishtar, who according to Babylonian mythology provoked the deluge in the third millennium B.C., and who was also worshiped by the Philistines, a people which came from Crete to Palestine *c.* 1200 B.C. (Ishtar = Esther = Astarte.)

Dizzying mutations of symbols and myths! One could go on

[24] Cf. R. Graves, *op. cit.*, I, 182–84. The sacred year of the Celts, which seems to have been common to the sacred traditions of all Europe, began the day after the winter solstice and was divided into thirteen months, each designated by a letter and a tree.

[25] This refers to another, far less well-known legend of Europe.

endlessly defining them more closely, distinguishing them, contrasting them—until perhaps there would appear to be as many truthful accounts of the same event as there are different witnesses.

6: The Geographical Concept

IT IS CUSTOMARY to attribute to Paul Valéry the observation that Europe is no more than a cape or "an appendix" of Asia. Here is his most often quoted text in this connection: [26]

Will Europe become *what it is in reality*—that is, a little cape on the continent of Asia? Or will Europe remain *what it seems*—that is, the elect portion of the terrestrial globe, the pearl of the sphere, the brain of a vast body?

Elsewhere Valéry calls Europe "a kind of cape of the old continent, a western appendix to Asia."

Not so very long ago this statement caused a sensation. In fact, it has been commonplace among the geographers for centuries. Let us quote a few of their observations, as Gonzague de Reynold collected them:

Europe is a great peninsula.[27]
This narrow peninsula which figures on the globe only as an appendix to Asia has become the metropolis of the human race.[28]
Properly speaking, Europe is no more than a big peninsula, the western termination of the vast Asiatic continent.[29]
Europe does not, properly speaking, constitute an independent whole. It is but a peninsula of Asia, the westernmost point or extremity of the Asiatic continent.[30]

The same terms have been used by Elisée Reclus, Auguste Himly, and Raoul Blanchard, all of whom are authors of atlases

[26] Paul Valéry, "The Crisis of the Mind," in *History and Politics,* trans. Denise Folliot and Jackson Matthews (Bollingen Series XLV, X, 31).
[27] Noblot, 1725.
[28] Brun, 1816.
[29] Lapie *père et fils,* 1829.
[30] Schrader, Prudent and Antoine, 1890.

and textbooks. A no less traditional comparison describes Europe as a bigger Greece:

It has often been said that Europe is to the earth what Greece once was to Europe. Greece has a moderately fertile soil, a varied and accidented surface, and natural boundaries; surrounded by seas, washed by deep bays, she enjoyed a happy mean between Scythia's severe winters and Egypt's summer heat. At that time it dominated the best known seas. The parallel between Greece and Europe, however, must include nobler similarities than those of a physical nature. The interplay of several different and even opposed national characters, the spirit of freedom, civic as well as political—these are the major points of similarity.[31]

Yet it was not the Greeks who "discovered" Europe. It was the Phoenicians who set up trading agencies and extended their piratical explorations throughout the Mediterranean and beyond to the Pillars of Hercules, the Canary Islands, Brittany, the British Isles, and the North Sea where the world ends. From Carthage, a Tyrian colony (founded, as we have seen, by Phoenix, one of Europa's brothers), Hanno had been as far as Senegal in the fifth century B.C. And according to Pliny, another Carthaginian admiral, Himilco, a century later, was assigned the mission of sailing up the Atlantic coast of Europe: *Sicut ad extera Europae noscenda missus eodem tempore Himilco.*

About 370, Rusius Festus Avenius, a poet of the decadent period, celebrated the periplus of Himilco in Latin verse:

Beyond the Columns, on the beaches of Europe, the Carthaginians once had establishments and cities. It was their custom to construct flat-bottomed ships, suitable for gliding over shallows. Himilco reports that outside the Pillars, to the west of Europe, extends a boundless sea; there the ocean stretches on to horizons without end. No one has ever penetrated those unknown waters. No one has ever steered his ships there. A propitious wind will never lift their prows; never will the wind of heaven swell their sails. For the air is as though enveloped in a mantle of fog; a thick mist hides the waves at all times, and dark vapors veil the light of day.

However, it was the Greeks who first named this continent for

[31] Brun.

the princess whom their god stole from the Phoenicians. To be exact, according to Eustathius, a Byzantine writer who lived in the twelfth century, it was the learned Hippias of Elias, alleged inventor of mnemotechnics, who first named the continents after the Oceanids Asia and Europa. Hippias lived in the fifth century B.C. Before him, Hecataeus of Miletus, born *c.* 540 B.C., had written a "Description of the World in Two Books," one dealing with Europe, the other with Asia. What could he have meant by Europe? In *Prometheus Bound* (produced in 472) Aeschylus has the hero, describing a journey which involves the crossing of the Bosporus, say:

Thus thou wilt abandon the plain of Europe, and venture on the continent of Asia.

Anaximander made similar observations.[32] But from this point on, all the ancient authors down to Strabo give the same definition: *Europe extends from the Pillars of Hercules* (i.e., Gibraltar) *to the Phasis*—or Rioni—*a little river that flows into the Black Sea.* Thus Plato has Socrates say: [33]

I believe that it [the earth] is vast in size, and that we who dwell between the river Phasis and the Pillars of Hercules inhabit only a minute portion of it—we live round the sea like ants or frogs round a pond—and there are many other peoples inhabiting similar regions.

This is the place to recall that Socrates was the first philosopher to say that his fatherland was "the human race," and not merely his native city. What is more European that this universalism?

But let us look at the Greek texts. Gonzague de Reynold [34] distinguishes three stages in the transition from the mythical and geographical conception to the political and "cultural" plane —represented, respectively, by Hippocrates, Aristotle, and Isocrates. Here are the texts:

[32] The first map of the world, drawn by Anaximander (seventh century B.C.), divides the Earth into two halves: Asia situated to the east of the Hellespont and consisting merely of Asia Minor; to the west, Europe.

[33] *Collected Dialogues,* trans. Hugh Tredennick (Bollingen Series LXXI).

[34] In a letter he addressed to us concerning this Anthology.

Toward the end of the fifth century B.C., Hippocrates (or one of his disciples), in chapter 5 of his treatise *On Airs, Waters, and Places*, draws the first known parallel (or contrast) between Asia and Europe: [35]

I wish to show, respecting Asia and Europe, how, in all respects, they differ from one another, and concerning the figure of the inhabitants, for they are all different, and do not at all resemble one another. To treat of all would be a long story, but I will tell you how I think it is with regard to the greatest and most marked differences. I say, then, that Asia differs very much from Europe as to the nature of all things, both with regard to the productions of the earth and the inhabitants, for everything is produced much more beautiful and large in Asia; the country is milder, and the dispositions of the inhabitants are also more gentle and affectionate. . . .

And with regard to the pusillanimity and cowardice of the inhabitants, the principal reason why the Asiatics are more unwarlike and of more gentle disposition than the Europeans is the nature of the seasons, which do not undergo any great changes either to heat or cold, or the like; for there is neither excitement of the understanding nor any strong change of the body by which the temper might be ruffled, and they be roused to inconsiderate emotion and passion, rather than living as they do always in the same state. It is changes of all kinds which arouse the understanding of mankind, and do not allow them to get into a torpid condition. For these reasons, it appears to me, the Asiatic race is feeble, and further, owing to their laws; for monarchy prevails in the greater part of Asia, and where men are not their own masters nor independent, but are the slaves of others, it is not a matter of consideration with them how they may acquire military discipline, but how they may seem not to be warlike, for the dangers are not equally shared, since they must serve as soldiers, perhaps endure fatigue, and die for their masters, far from their children, their wives, and other friends; and whatever noble and manly actions they may perform lead only to the aggrandizement of their masters, whilst the fruits which they reap are dangers and death; and in addition to this, the lands of such persons must be laid waste by the enemy and want of culture. Thus, then, if any one be naturally warlike and courageous, his disposition will be changed by the institutions. . . .

[35] Hippocrates, *Ancient Medicine and Other Treatises*, trans. Francis Adams (Chicago: Henry Regnery Co., 1949), pp. 36, 39 f., 46 f.

And the same may be said of their [the Europeans'] dispositions, for the wild, and unsociable, and the passionate occur in
such a constitution; for frequent excitement of the mind induces
wildness, and extinguishes sociableness and mildness of disposition, and therefore I think the inhabitants of Europe more courageous than those of Asia; for a climate which is always the
same induces indolence, but a changeable climate, laborious
exertions both of body and mind; and from rest and indolence
cowardice is engendered, and from laborious exertions and
pains, courage. On this account the inhabitants of Europe are
more warlike than the Asiatics, and also owing to their institutions, because they are not governed by kings like the latter,
for where men are governed by kings there they must be very
cowardly, as I have stated before; for their souls are enslaved,
and they will not willingly or readily undergo dangers in order
to promote the power of another. . . .

The essential passage on Europe by Aristotle (384-322 B.C.)
is in *Politics*, Book VII, chapter 6: [36]

Those who live in a cold climate and in [northern] Europe
are full of spirit, but wanting in intelligence and skill; and therefore they keep their freedom, but have no political organization,
and are incapable of ruling over others. Whereas the natives of
Asia are intelligent and inventive, but they are wanting in spirit,
and therefore they are always in a state of subjection and slavery. But the Hellenic race, which is situated between them, is
likewise intermediate in character, being high-spirited and also
intelligent. Hence it continues free, and is the best governed of
any nation, and, if it could be formed into one state, would be
able to rule the world.

After this "hegemonic" stage comes the stage of "adoption."
It is characterized by the famous words of Isocrates, a contemporary of Plato (fifth to fourth century B.C.) and the ancestor
of all subsequent European "federalists" and "unionists": "The
man who shares our paideia is a Greek in a higher sense than
he who only shares our blood." [37]

We shall now go back to tracing the geographical descriptions
of Europe, from Herodotus to St. Augustine.

[36] Trans. B. Jowett (Oxford University Press).

[37] *Panegyricus*, 51. Cf. Georges Mathieu, *Les idées politiques d'Isocrate*
(Paris, 1925). The author has some reservations concerning Isocrates' universalism.

Herodotus, writing in the fifth century B.C., defines Europe as
a northern region not too clearly distinguished from Scythia
(which we think of today as the Russian plain). According to
him, its axis is the Danube, which he calls the Ister:

The Ister is of all the rivers with which we are acquainted
the mightiest . . . it receives the waters of several tributaries.
. . . For the Ister flows through the whole extent of Europe,
rising in the country of the Celts . . . and thence running across
the continent till it reaches Scythia, whereof it washes the flanks.

However Herodotus wonders "why the earth being one is
given three different names, which are names of women."

Indeed, according to Strabo:

In the time of Homer, neither Europe nor Asia had been given
their respective names; the *oikoumene* or inhabited world had
not yet been divided into three distinct continents. This fact is
too important for him to have failed to mention it.

And yet it seems that Homer had some notion of Europe. In
the *Iliad* (Book XIV) we read that Hypnos and Hera "over the
continent fared, and under their feet waved the tops of the
forests."

Strabo, a Greek native of Pontus, who wrote under Augustus
and Tiberius, gives us the earliest detailed geographical description of Europe, a continent superior to the two others, he says,
because

it is admirably adapted by nature for the development of excellence in men and governments. . . . Of the inhabitable part of
Europe the cold mountainous regions furnish by nature only a
wretched existence to their inhabitants, yet even the regions of
poverty and piracy become civilized as soon as they get good
administrators.

There follows a theory of climate which brings to mind the
school of Hippocrates, and which remained influential down to
the nineteenth century, for we find it in Taine:

Take the case of the Greeks: though occupying mountains and
rocks, they used to live happily, because they took forethought
for good government, for the arts, and in general for the science

of living. The Romans, too, took over many nations that were naturally savage, owing to the regions they inhabited, because those regions were either rocky or without harbors or cold or for some other reason ill-suited to habitation by many, and thus not only brought into communication with each other peoples who had been isolated, but also taught the more savage how to live under forms of government. But all of Europe that is level and has a temperate climate has nature to co-operate with her toward these results; for while in a country that is blessed by nature everything tends to peace, in a disagreeable country everything tends to make men warlike and courageous; and so both kinds of country receive benefits from each other, for the latter helps with arms, the former with products of the soil, with arts, and with character-building. But the harm they receive from each other, if they are not mutually helpful, is also apparent; and the might of those who are accustomed to carry arms will have some advantage unless it be controlled by the majority. However, this continent has a natural advantage to meet this condition also; for the whole of it is diversified with plains and mountains, so that throughout its entire extent the agricultural and civilized elements dwell side by side with the warlike element; but of the two elements the one that is peace-loving is more numerous and therefore keeps control over the whole body; and the leading nations, too—formerly the Greeks and later the Macedonians and the Romans—have taken hold and helped. And for this reason Europe is most independent of other countries as regards both peace and war; for the war-like population which she possesses is abundant and also that which tills her soils and holds her cities secure. She excels also in this respect, that she produces the fruits that are best and that are necessary for life, and all the useful metals, while she imports from abroad spices and precious stones—things that make the life of persons who have only a scarcity of them fully as happy as that of persons who have them in abundance. So, also, Europe offers an abundance of various kinds of cattle, but a scarcity of wild animals. Such, in a general way, is the nature of the continent.[38]

Could it be, as many historians maintain, that all these Greek authors confused Europe with the province of Thracia—which

[38] Strabo, *Geography* II, 5, 26, trans. Horace Leonard Jones (The Loeb Classical Library [Cambridge, Mass.: Harvard University Press; London: William Heinemann, Ltd.]).

indeed bore that name—or, as in Aeschylus' case, with Greece? If so, it would be hard to explain why they felt the need for a more general term if they really had only Greece in mind. We have seen, in the passage from Victor Bérard's book quoted above, that from the earliest times there had existed a "utopian" view of continental Europe, very much like the dream that inspired Christopher Columbus when he mistook the first islands he reached for a vast unexplored continent. A few centuries later Greece was clearly considered no more than "a small part" of Europe. Thus Cicero (*Pro Flacco* xxvii), referring to Greece: *Parvum quendam locum Europae tenet.*

St. Augustine, in *The City of God,* says that the world is divided into two halves, Asia constituting one, and Europe and Africa the other. Paulus Orosius, his disciple and continuator, delimits and describes a Europe which is fairly close to the Europe of today:

And now I shall rapidly sketch Europe in so far as it is known by men. It begins at the Ripheus mountains, then at the river Tanais [today the Don] and at the Maeotis swamps, which are to the east. It extends along the coast of the northern ocean as far as Belgian Gaul and the river Rhine, which comes down from the west, then continues as far as the Danube, also called the Ister, which flows from south to the east in the direction of Pontus Euxinus [the Black Sea]. To the east lies the country of the Alani, in the middle that of the Dacians and the Goths, and finally Germany, a large part of which is occupied by the Suebi. And all this together represents fifty-four nations.

Let us jump now to the fourteenth century. In his *Commento alla Comedia* (canto XIV), Giovanni Boccaccio (A.D. 1313–1375) adopts the tripartite division of the world, and significantly insists on the central position of Greece, where Zeus made Europa a queen:

There is no part of the world that may be said to be common to all nations unless it be the island of Crete . . . The ancients liked to divide the inhabited world of our upper hemisphere into three parts, which they named Asia, Europe, and Africa . . . And the island of Crete seems to be situated at the borders of these three continents.

According to the geographers who defined the boundaries of Europe, on the side of the rising sun these boundaries pass through the extremity of the Aegean Sea, the Hellespont [the Dardanelles], the sea called Propontis [Marmora] and the course of the river Tanais [the Don]; on the Tramontane side [the north] they pass through the northern ocean, which washes Norway, England, and the western parts of Spain down to where the Mediterranean sea begins; as for the southern side, they said that Europe was bounded by the Mediterranean sea, which is continued by the sea that we called the African Sea; this why the geographers named it the European Sea, which extends as far as the island of Crete.

Sebastian Münster wrote in his *Cosmography:* [39]

Europe is a marvelously fertile area and it has a naturally temperate air, a mild sky, and there is no lack of wine or fruit trees. In addition, it is a beautiful place, studded with cities, castles, and villages, and it has a virile population. It surpasses Asia and Africa. It is entirely populated except for a small part to the north where, because of the cold, no one likes to dwell. There are also arid mountainous regions where it is hard to dwell. But the flatlands are rich and everything grows there in such abundance that their inhabitants can help the people in the mountains.

In 1679 in Paris, Robbe, engineer and geographer to Louis XIV, published a *Method for Learning Geography Easily.* He says:

Undeniably Europe is the least extensive of the three parts that compose the old world; but it must be acknowledged at the same time that, small as it is, it is the greatest in quality . . . If Asia boasts of having seen the first man formed by the very hands of the Creator of heaven and earth, and of having been honored by the birth and presence of the Savior of the world during his mortal life: Europe will say that indeed it is a singular grace which it received from eternal Wisdom; but that its glory is a borrowed one, for Asia received this gift only by luck or special favor. Whereas Europe, without such extraordinary favors, earns her own glory, and her children alone make her illustrious.

[39] *Cosmographia Universa* (Paris, 1511; Basel, 1559).

The same idea is expressed in Moreri's *Dictionary:* [40]

> Although Europe is the smallest of the three continental parts, it nonetheless has advantages which make her preferable to the others. The climate is extremely temperate and the provinces are very fertile, save for the underparts of the continent. It abounds in riches of all kinds, and its peoples are usually gentle, honest, civilized, and well fitted for the arts and the sciences.

We find the same idea, expressed almost in the same terms, in *Géographie universelle* by Mantelle and Malte Brun, published in Paris in 1816:

> As shaped by nature, our part of the world received no title to that glorious pre-eminence which distinguishes it today. A small continent, the least well-endowed with territorial riches, . . . we are rich only through borrowings. Such is nonetheless the power of the human spirit. This region, which nature adorned only with immense forests, has become populated with powerful nations, covered with magnificent cities, and enriched by the spoils of two worlds; this narrow peninsula which figures on the globe only as an appendix to Asia has become the metropolis of mankind.

Thus, from Herodotus and Hippocrates to our own day, physical Europe has continually been conceived of as a characteristic, highly diversified whole, and for this very reason distinguished from the more massive continents. Although divided, according to Orosius, into "fifty-four nations" (in another passage he found only thirty-four), and although its eastern borders are undetermined—as they still are today—Europe nonetheless constitutes "a single body" in the eyes of the geographers. All this is summed up by the historian we have taken for guide through this Cretan labyrinth, Gonzague de Reynold:

> Europe, which is the only articulated continent, seems even physically a product of intelligence rather than of nature. Europe is the continent that projects beyond itself, the continent of expansion and conquest, of discovery and colonization. Europe was born imperial. It was created to be the globe. See its line of force come out of Asia and stretch over the ocean toward the

[40] Louis Moreri, *Grand Dictionnaire Historique* (10 vols.; 1st ed., Paris, 1674; 20th ed., 1759).

infinite. The other continents are heavy and immobile. Even on the map Europe seems to be moving. Its shape is evocative. Strabo compared it to a dragon; Camoens, to a human body with the Iberian peninsula serving as head and Portugal as the face.

Others have represented her as a seated woman. In the article "Europe" of his *Dictionary*, Moreri tells us that in honor of Charles V Postel represented her as follows: "Spain was the woman's head; her neck, the provinces of Languedoc and Gascony; the rest of Gaul, her chest; her arms were Italy and Great Britain; her belly was Germany; Bohemia, her navel; and all the rest of her body, the remaining kingdoms and provinces.

But the most symbolically suggestive representation is still that of some of the older geographers, who saw in Europe the image of the Virgin, a crowned Virgin, with Spain as head, France as heart, and Great Britain and Italy as her arms and hands, one holding the globe, the other the scepter; a Virgin whose robe with vast and indeterminate folds was represented by the Russian plain, ending somewhere in inner Asia.

The Christian Virgin, who conceived by the Holy Spirit.

7: From Geography to History

FROM THE FOREGOING pages two conclusions can be drawn: the geographical concept of Europe is far more ancient, and the Greek and Semitic myths far less remote from reality, than is generally believed today.

No such clear-cut conclusion can be arrived at when it comes to Europe's awareness of itself as a political entity. It is harder to find in the ancient world a sense of the common fate of the peoples of Europe as it is described by Herodotus and Strabo, though there are traces in Hippocrates' and Aristotle's broad comparisons between the nations of Europe and those of Asia. These men were geniuses, however, and did not reflect current opinion, or anything like popular awareness. In their time, anything of this nature found expression only in myth and religious belief.

During the Roman era, any political concept of Europe was very naturally pushed into the background by that of the imperial unity of east and west, the two geographical and administrative halves of a single State: *utraque pars, pars orientalis et pars occidentalis.* Now and then "Europe" is used to denominate the western half of the Empire, and "Asia" the eastern half. There is, for example, an inscription of the year 7 B.C. which was discovered on the island of Philae in Egypt. Augustus is there described as "Lord of Europe and Asia." [41] Such usages, of course, were more allegorical in character than they sound today, when the terms are more exactly defined, both geographically and politically.

It would not be amiss to note here that the terms "East" and "West," over the centuries, have had far more ups and downs than the term "Europe." At times, they denoted the administrative halves of the Empire (Arcadius and Honorius), at other times the theologic divisions in the Church (Rome and Byzantium). There have also been a number of attempts at vast and vague mystical characterizations, the East summing up and symbolizing all the light-giving spiritual qualities, and the West the impenetrable darkness of materiality.

Listing the characteristics regularly attributed to this mystical East and this mystical West by the metaphysicians of pre-Socratic Greece, later by those of Avicenna's Persia, and still later by a number of European authors down to our own day (all of whom speak of a "Tradition"), Denis de Rougemont has drawn up the following table of fourteen antitheses: [42]

East: Dawn, morning, the high, the right side, extreme refinement, light, The Angel of Revelation, the final goal, the soul, initiation, wisdom, regeneration, knowledge freed by illumination, the original homeland.

West: Sunset, evening, the low, the left side, opaque thickness, twilight, the demon of utilitarianism and blind power, obliviousness to the aims of the spirit, body, and matter, disorderly activity, passion, degradation, knowledge gone astray and obscured by material and passionate bonds, the place of exile.

This unanimity of interpretation—entirely favorable to the East—of our two symbolical terms cannot fail to be impressive. It cannot be passed off as anything accidental, physical or anec-

[41] R. Cagnat, *Inscriptiones Graecae ad res Romanas pertinentes* (1906).
[42] *Man's Western Quest,* trans. Montgomery Belgion (New York, 1956).

dotal. For if the sun rises on the East for the Greeks, so it does for the Hindus, and these do not stand for the West in the sight of China [43] or Malaya, nor is Japan the West for America! The unanimity thus discloses a form of spirit, a tendency of the soul —it might even be said, an "orientation" of the Western psyche.[44]

We may add to all this the influence of many passages from the Psalms, the Prophets, and the Gospels, which celebrate the East as the place whence cometh salvation. For instance, Matthew 24:27: "For as the lightning cometh out of the east, and shineth even unto the west; so shall also the coming of the Son of man be."

This theme of *ex oriente lux* is so powerful that the Vulgate almost always translates by *oriens* words that our modern versions render by "sky" or "rising sun," or even by "germ"! (Zechariah 6:12). The glamor of the Biblical, metaphysical and occultist East long prevented Europe (more or less synonymous with the West) from taking on more than purely geographical sense, that is, from coming to mean a historical and spiritual entity such as might be set off against Asia, without troubling the apologists.

Not until the beginning of the fifth century after Christ do we find a reappearance—the first since Herodotus [45]—of the idea of Europe's historical autonomy. A Latin poem by Claudius Claudianus (born at Alexandria *c.* A.D. 365; he remained a pagan) designates the "enemies" of Europe—the Moor Gildo and the barbarian Alaric:

> . . . Duo namque fuere
> Europae Libyaeque hostes: Maurusius Atlas
> Gildonis furias, Alaricum barbara Peuce
> Nutrierat . . .[46]

[43] The author has simplified matters. Actually, to the Chinese, light comes from the west; this was the Indian doctrine of Buddha, and Chinese texts acknowledge it explicitly.

[44] We shall see (p. 244) how Hegel conceives of an "East in itself," which is Asia.

[45] According to a remark by J. Fischer, *op. cit.*, p. 41.

[46] Claudius Claudianus, *Paneg. de sext. consul. Honorii*, in *Monumenta Germaniae Historica*, AA, X, 293.

In the second century after Christ (that is, two hundred years after the inscription at Philae—note this long silence), it is an anti-Christian polemicist, Celsus, who for the first time uses the term "Europeans" in a passage where he declares that it is impossible that "the Asians, the Europeans and Libyans, the Hellenes and the barbarians should ever agree to recognize one and the same Law." [47] The "Law" in question was Christian monotheism which, according to Celsus, would destroy the political diversities of the nations of the Earth, which the pagan gods had willed and guaranteed! To this ancestor of nationalism, who was not lacking in lucidity, the sworn enemy was the universalism of the Christians. But this is only a parenthesis.

With Sulpicius Severus, an ecclesiastical historian who was born in Aquitania toward the middle of the fourth century and who died c. 410, Europe at last finds her place in "the economy of salvation," thanks to her saints. Sulpicius Severus wrote the biography of St. Martin of Tours, who was to be regarded as "the greatest ascetic of all Europe" for centuries to come. According to his panegyrist, this single saint was worth all the saints the East can boast of: "When you go to Egypt, although the latter is proud of the number and the virtues of her saints, it will not be a bad thing if you let her know that Europe does not yield to all of Asia, and this thanks to Martin alone." [48]

To Martin of Tours would soon be added many European saints: Vitale of Ravenna, Gervais and Ambrose of Milan, Eulalia of Rome, Cecilia of Sicily, and finally the saints of the "Theban Legion," with St. Maurice at their head, martyred for their faith at Agaunum after having (according to contemporary chroniclers) made the tour of almost all Europe: omne . . . fere Europa circuita.

Thus it was her saints that at last set Europe apart from a notion of "the West"—so disliked by the "spiritualists"—and invested her with a dignity closer to "the East" of the mystics.

[47] Quoted in E. Peterson, Der Monotheismus als politisches Problem (1935).
[48] Sulpicius Severus, Dial. II (III), 17, 7, in Corpus Scriptorum Ecclesiasticorum Latinorum, I, 215.

From that time onward the name of Europe and the concept of Europe will recur in ever more solemn contexts down to the Carolingian Empire, in apostrophes to the Pope, in ecclesiastical panegyrics, in prose and verse chronicles, and in the lives of the saints.

The Irish evangelist Colomban, *c.* 600, addresses Pope Gregory as "the flower of all Europe," and in 615, Pope Boniface IV as "the head of all the churches of all Europe" (*omnium totius Europae ecclesiarum capiti*).

In the Burgundian *Annals* of Avenches (middle of the seventh century) we repeatedly encounter the name "Eurupa," designating both the Frankish nations and the land mass watered by the Rhine and the Danube. Isidore of Seville, in his *History of the Goths,* speaks of "all the nations of Europe trembling before them" (*Hos Europae omnes tremuere gentes*).

The author of the *Life of Gertrude,* speaking of the daughter of Pepin of Landen, says that "everyone in Europe" (*quisnam in Euruppa habitans*) knows her name and the glory of her race; and the author of the *Life of Landibert* writes: "At that time Pepin was the prince of numerous regions and cities of Europe" (spelled Eoruppa).

But here is the capital text, which may be looked upon as the birth certificate of historical, political Europe: it is found in a sequel to the famous *Chronicle* of Isidore of Seville that had been written a century earlier. The anonymous continuator (Isidor Pacensis or Isidore of Badajoz or of Beja—the author's identity is uncertain, and this text is today referred to as the "Mozarabis Chronicle of 754") describes the battle of Poitiers, won by Charles Martel against the Arabs in 732. He was certainly closely involved in the event, which he reports in detail some years later, writing, it seems, in Spain. According to him the battle lasted seven days, at the end of which "the Europeans" (soldiers from various regions, ranging from Aquitania to Germania and forming the army of the majordomo) saw, at dawn, the tents of the enemy camp: *diluculo prospiciunt Europenses Arabum tentoria tabernaculorum ut fuerant castra locata . . .*

But the Arab tents are empty; after the looting, Charles Martel's warriors return, joyously, each to his country: *Europenses vero . . . spolias tantum et manubias decenter divisas in suas leti recipiunt patrias.*[49]

Thus the term "Europeans," for the first time in our era, denotes a continental community, one which includes the nations living north of the Pyrenees and the Alps, sharing the task of defense against the common enemy. The historians who reduce the battle of Poitiers to a "myth" or "an unimportant incident" may be right on the military level. It seems true that the Arabs attached little importance to the defeat of Abd-er-Rahman: according to their historians of the time, this defeat merely marked the unhappy end of another raid into Frankish territory. The regression of Islam after that date has been accounted for by an internal crisis of the Arab world, and above all by the defeat the Moslem fleet suffered before Byzantium as early as 718.[50] But there is the chronicle by the anonymous Spanish author, there is the word *Europenses* which alone suffices to make Poitiers a crucial date in our history. There is the fact that in the eighth century those who defended this continent found it natural to be described not as the defenders of a Romania which had become mythical, or of the West in general, or of the papacy, or of their particular "nation" or homeland, but as members of the same family of nations.

8: "Europa vel Regnum Caroli"

THIS SHARED AWARENESS of Europe—to an ever increasing extent supplanting the disparaged or disparaging concept of the "West" —was strengthened and defined more closely with the conquests of Charlemagne from 768 to 814.

According to the Venerable Bede (673–735), historian of the English and chronicler of the Six States of the World, Europe was essentially composed of Gaul, Germania, and Spain, Italy

[49] *Monumenta germ. Hist.*, Chronica Minora, AA, XI, 363, 20 and 30.
[50] Emmanuel Berl, *Les Impostures de l'Histoire* (Paris, 1959).

being added later. (We may note that England and Scandinavia, even at that early date, were excluded from Europe—by an Englishman!) Now Charlemagne conquered the Lombards, and added the title of King of Italy to that of King of Neustria, Aquitania, and Austrasia; he went far beyond the ancient *limes* on the east and on the north, as well as the Pyrenees in the west: what would be the name of the empire he founded, if not "Europe"? This was in fact the name given it by contemporary chroniclers and panegyrists, almost against Charles's will it would seem, for he remained faithful to the idea—both Roman and Christian, imperial and universalistic—of an impossible *imperium mundi.*

In 775 the priest Cathwulf praises Charlemagne for having been chosen by God to be raised to the rank of "the glory of the empire of Europe": *quod ipse te exaltavit in honorem gloriae regni Europae.*

In 799, Angilbert, the emperor's son-in-law and court poet, bestowed upon Charlemagne the titles of "head of the world . . . summit [or tiara] of Europe . . . supreme father"—these are a combination of the titles designating the *imperator* and *pontifex:*

> Rex Carolus caput orbis, amor populique, decusque
> Europae venerandus apex, pater optimus, heros
> Augustus . . .

A few lines below he hails him as "father of Europe": [51]

> Rex, pater Europae.

This "Europe or kingdom of Charles," *Europa vel regnum Caroli,* as it is named in the *Annals* of Fulda (end of ninth century) is thus a single Christian empire, born outside of Rome, under uncontested Frankish—we should say Franco-Germanic—domination. Thus it is no longer merely one of the three divisions of the traditional map of the world (Europe, Libya or Africa,

[51] *Monumenta germ. Hist.*, Poet. Carol., I, i, 368, 59.

Asia), but an autonomous entity, endowed with spiritual virtues. According to Alcuin (735–804), master at the palace school, educator, theologian, and court rhetorician, it is "the continent of the faith." As such, Charlemagne's Europe is closer to the "East," which is Jesus Christ, than to the classical "West," the bad part of the world. . . . We have here the first flowering of a true European idea, of a shared consciousness attested by innumerable exclamatory expressions and by common feasts.[52] Alas, a premature spring.

For soon after Charlemagne, the great image of a "European kingdom" became blurred. Already under Louis the Pious, his son—the division of the empire had been consummated—we note a very typical change in the formulas of the panegyrists. Instead of *regnum Europae*—a single empire—a poem by the Spaniard Theowulf (after 814) uses the expression *regna*, i.e., kingdoms of Europe: [53]

Tu pius Europae regna potenter habes.

The idea of the *regnum Europae* becomes divorced from that of an earthly empire—which even then is no more than a compound of *regna*, that is, a multiplicity of distinct kingdoms—and moves closer to the medieval idea of spiritual empire, that is, concretely, a papal Christendom. Instead of Charlemagne's united Europe, a kingdom both sacerdotal and imperial, there began to loom up a vague federation of Western princes in the shadow of pre-national intrigues, which became the battlefield for the "Roman" ambition of the emperors of "the Germanic nation," while the spiritual unity became the other pole, the papacy. As early as 843, Leo IV took a stand against the Patriarch of Constantinople, calling upon "all the churches of Europe" to combat the Byzantine Empire.

In the following centuries, which were to be our Middle Ages, the Empire and the Papacy filled the chronicles with their strug-

[52] Heinz Gollwitzer, *Europabild und Europagedanke* (Munich, 1951), p. 417, cites "a feast of the Saints of Europe" instituted in Ireland at that time. *See also* Rosenstock-Wittig, *Das Alter der Kirche* (Berlin, 1927).

[53] *Monumenta germ. Hist.*, Poet. Carol., II, 32.

gles, relegating the concept of Europe to the domain of myth
and allegory or nostalgia for the great Carolingian past.

However, occasionally the name of Europe comes to the surface and shines for an instant. Notker the Stammerer, commissioned (in 883) by Charles the Simple to compose the *Gesta
Caroli,* celebrates the building of the bridge of Mayence as a
demonstration of the power of the Europeans, "great and little,"
if they are united: ". . . As witnessed by the arches of the
bridge of Mayence, which all Europe built by joint efforts to be
sure, but thanks to a very well ordered division of labor [*ordi-
natissimae participationis*]."

Jürgen Fischer cites several dozen authors writing late in the
ninth century and throughout the tenth century who still speak
of Europe, but the meaning of the name is now no more than
rhetorical (a recollection of Charlemagne) or merely geographical; all this, most often in a questionable Latin.

After the turbulent reign of Otto III, imitation *imperator,* the
idea of a "European nation" was revived: expressions such as
populus Europae or *totius Europae populo acclamante* recur
over several years in the works of the annalists: this is because
the tenacious utopia of a restoration of the Roman Empire was
temporarily abandoned.

Under Henry II we see the last furtive rays—but they are most
moving—of the long Carolingian sunset. The Saxon emperor,
fleeing the plague that ravaged Italy in 1022, went back north
to Germany, escorted, we read in a contemporary account,[54] by
only a very few troops, that is to say: ". . . supported only by
those whom mother Europe had sent to his aid" (. . . *exceptis
his quos sibi mater Europa occurendo admiserat*).

Embroidered on the star-studded mantle of the Emperor was
this inscription: *O decus Europae Caesar Heinrice beate—An-
nuat imperii tibi rex qui regant in aevum.* ("O blessed Caesar
Henry, honor of Europe—may the king who reigns in eternity
increase thy empire.")

After the death of this prince who was to become St. Henry II,
a funeral chant, composed by a Rhenish poet, proclaimed the

[54] *Monumenta germ. Hist.,* SS, III, 80.

end of the Carolingian idea of Europe: "Europe, now beheaded, weeps!"

Ploret hunc Europa iam decapitata.

And there began the medieval eclipse of the European idea —not of European reality, to be sure.

It will take the Mongol and Turkish menace to reawaken, with Christendom, the idea of Europe.

This brings to a close our survey of the documented origins.

PART TWO
THE CONCEPT
OF EUROPE

From Pierre Du Bois to the

Abbé de Saint-Pierre

PART TWO

1: On Several Centuries of "European" Silence

FROM THE MIDDLE of the eleventh century to the Renaissance, and especially during the early Middle Ages, texts on Europe are few and far between. And yet, it is precisely this period—the twelfth and thirteenth centuries—that is singled out in the titles of so many recent works as representing the moment of "the Birth," "the Rise," "the Formation," or even "the Origins" of Europe.[1] Must we conclude that according to modern historians Europe attained its highest point in that very period in which our ancestors showed no awareness of Europe? Could it be that this period of exemplary unity was also the one in which the subject of this unity did not know that it existed? J. Calmette opens his book *L'Effondrement d'un Empire et la naissance d'une Europe*[2] with this paradoxical statement: "Western Europe was born of the disintegration of the Carolingian Empire." But the Carolingian Empire *was* a united Western Europe. Was, then, Europe born of the disintegration of her political unity?

Hundreds of essays and thick volumes deal with this subject. Let us try to simplify. Charlemagne's Europe was a sacerdotal empire. The conflicts over Investiture claims put an end to its spiritual unity. Thus it declined once more to the level of a purely geographical entity. What mattered now, what was the subject of passionate interest, was the struggle for primacy between Empire and Papacy. The two parties based their claims on the one and common idea of Christendom. Early in the fourteenth century the appearance of a third internal party, threatening simultaneously the two others, changed the situation. Then the idea of Europe staged a dim re-emergence, as the new

[1] We refer to the works by J. Calmette, Louis Halphen, Friedrich Heer, G. de Reynold, and H. Brugmans.
[2] (Paris, 1941). The date and place are to be kept in mind.

[53]

symbol of a unity that so far *had been taken for granted*. No more than the Pope did the Emperor intend to challenge it: he wanted merely to avail himself of it.

From the outside came another threat, which was also apt to awaken the consciousness of what, despite everything, remained common to Ghibellines and Guelphs.

Islam had separated the share of Japheth from those of Shem and Ham. Thus only two powers confronted each other, militarily and culturally—Christendom and the Infidels. Virtually driven back to the territory of Europe, Christendom defined the most visible, deepest, and most keenly felt unity of all nations inhabiting this continent. But its internal dissensions and its separation from Byzantium left it powerless and vulnerable. The last crusade, that of St. Louis, had just ended in failure. Marco Polo's recent rediscovery of China had added a new dimension to the known world. This situation could not fail to confront the European mind with two concrete problems: that of restoring peace among the Christian nations, and that of resuming the war against the Infidels. Most of the projects for pacification, and hence for the union of Europe, were thus linked organically —and this until the eighteenth century—to projects for the reconquest of the Holy Land, and later for a defensive coalition against the Turks.

Three great themes dominate these projects—peace, crusade, the struggle for or against the hegemony of one power within Europe. We see these themes combined in the jurist Pierre Du Bois and in King George of Poděbrad, in the soldier François de la Noue and in the humanist Vives, in Guillaume Postel and in the shrewd statesman Leo X, and even in the universal Leibniz. The theme of the crusade against the Turks is absent only from very few of the prominent authors we shall quote—such as Dante, who is primarily concerned with insuring the triumph of the imperial principle; Emeric Crucé, an integral pacifist, who hoped to include the Turks in his system; and William Penn, the Quaker.

But why were not the first appeals to the union of the Princes of Europe launched—incidentally, in vain—until the beginning of the fourteenth century? Could it not be because at that time there appeared the first *nation* that defied both the Empire and the Pope—the France of Philip the Fair? (The outrage at Anagni took place in 1303.) Until then the tensions within the Christian body had been "universal" in nature, or could appear as such. They concerned all men and all social classes. They would now become openly particularistic, nationalistic, and hence separatist. At the same time as the dynastic, regional, and soon national claims, there would now develop, as though by way of compensation, the yearning for unity. Dante was the first to give it virile, sublime, absolute expression.

Let us situate him in the century's debate, with respect to the Empire, the Papacy, and the nations.

2: The Earliest Plans for European Union

DANTE (1265–1321)

ACCORDING TO EGIDIO COLONNA (Gilles of Rome, thirteenth century), the Pope is a Prime Mover, something like God. He is the source of the cosmic order, of all movement, and of the legal rights of princes and nations. The Emperor receives his temporal power from him, just as the moon receives the light it reflects from the sun. All authority derives from the Pope (a pagan prince can be no more than a "brigand"); the same is true of property and inheritance rights, and the legitimacy of marriage. A sinner separated from the Pope is literally nothing.

Now, however, the Pope is opposed by the Emperor. According to Marsilius of Padua, the true repository of all authority is the people, which delegates it to the Emperor. The Emperor thus represents the fullness of jurisdiction. Apart from him, there is no authority. The Church can admonish, enlighten the souls; the Emperor rules the earth.

Then a third claimant appears: the king of France who will later call himself "emperor in his kingdom" and who refuses to recognize the supremacy of both the Holy Empire and the Sovereign Pontiff. Philip the Fair, opposing the Emperor and Boniface VIII, for the first time represents the "sovereign rights" of the national state.

What is Dante's position in this drama?

For him, the Pope is the only source of authority, the ninth sphere of the heavens which communicates its motion to the eight others. No leader gives orders without owing him his authority. However, the Emperor is the first cause of the social order, and no baron can give orders without holding his power from him. He is the principle of mankind's unity. And he is necessarily just, being all-powerful, hence without personal ambition, and hence virtuous. Moreover, he is the delegate of the Roman people, predestined by God to rule the world. He is the sovereign head of the bodies, and he leads the nations to temporal happiness, while the Pope leads the souls to Light, which is their only freedom. (*De Monarchia* III, XVI.)

In such a system there is no room for the absolute sovereignty of the states, which could result only in chaos. A single monarchy, governing (but without uniformizing) a universal Society of States [3] is therefore indispensable for the peace of mankind. And the monarch, the Emperor, must rule men in the name of the superior intelligence imparted to him by nature. (Is this not an equivalent, one writer [4] observes, of the modern power of science?)

It was (probably) in 1311, as a salute to the Emperor Henry VII about to set out for Rome to be crowned by Pope Clement V, that Dante wrote *De Monarchia*. (He was forty-six, and he had composed only the *Inferno* of his comedy.) The central paradox of this work, which has been looked upon as the first proclamation of the federal union of nations under "Roman" (read: "European") aegis, is that while glorifying Christian

[3] When Dante pleads for an Empire that would bring about the *ordinatio ad unum*, he never has in mind a centralized and unified state in the modern sense. His conception is specifically federalist: he aims at union in diversity, as is made clear in the excerpt quoted below. (I, 14.)

[4] B. Landry, in his introduction to the French translation of *De Monarchia* (Paris, 1933).

unity, a myth that is medieval par excellence, Dante strongly emphasizes the distinction between the spiritual and temporal: however, this was to lead to the triumph not of the *princeps unicus* he calls for, but, on the contrary, of the "many-headed monster" he denounces—nationalism.

It is quite clear that the task proper to mankind considered as a whole is to fulfil the total capacity of the possible intellect all the time, primarily by speculation and secondarily, as a function and extension of speculation, by action. Now since what applies to the part applies also to the whole, and since the individual man becomes perfect in wisdom and prudence through sitting in quietude, so it is in the quietude or tranquillity of peace that mankind finds the best conditions for fulfilling its proper task (almost a divine task, as we learn from the statement: "Thou hast made him a little lower than the angels.") Hence it is clear that universal peace is the most excellent means of securing our happiness.[5]

If we consider a village, whose purpose is mutual help in questions of persons and goods, it is essential for one person to be supreme over all others, whether he is appointed from outside or raised to office by the consent of the others; otherwise, not only would the community fail to provide mutual sustenance, but in some cases the community itself would be utterly destroyed through some members' scheming to take control. Similarly if we examine a city, whose purpose is to be sufficient unto itself in everything needed for the good life, we see that there must be one governing authority—and this applies not only to just but even to degenerate forms of government. If this were not so, the purpose of civil life would be frustrated and the city, as such, would cease to exist. Lastly, every kingdom (and the end of a kingdom is the same as that of a city but with a stronger bond of peace) needs to have a king to rule over and govern it; otherwise its inhabitants will not only fail to achieve their end as citizens but the kingdom itself will crumble, as is affirmed by the infallible word: "Every kingdom divided against itself shall be laid waste."

If this is true of all communities and individuals who have a goal towards which they are directed, then our previous supposition is also valid. For, if it is agreed that mankind as a whole has a goal (and this we have shown to be so), then it needs one

[5] *De Monarchia*, I, 4, in *Monarchy and Three Political Letters*, trans. Donald Nicholl (New York: The Noonday Press).

person to govern or rule over it, and the title appropriate to this person is Monarch, or Emperor.

Thus it has been demonstrated that a Monarch or Emperor is necessary for the well-being of the world.[6]

A dispute may arise between two princes, neither of whom is subject to the other, and . . . this may be their fault or their subjects'; therefore a judgment between them is indispensable. However, since neither can take cognizance over the other (neither being subject to the other—and equals do not rule over equals), there needs to be a third person enjoying wider jurisdiction who by right rules over both of them. This person . . . will be the Monarch . . .[7]

When we say "mankind can be governed by one supreme prince" we do not mean to say that minute decisions concerning every township can proceed directly from him (though even municipal laws sometimes prove wanting and need supplementing outside, as we see from the Philosopher's remarks in the fifth book of the [Nicomachean] Ethics, where he commends the principle of equity). For nations, kingdoms and cities have different characteristics which demand different laws for their government, law being intended as a concrete rule of life. The Scythians, for instance, live outside the seventh circle, experience extreme inequalities of day and night and endure an almost intolerably piercing frost; they require a different rule from the Garamantes who live in the equinoctial zone, where the days and nights are of equal duration and where the excessive heat makes it unbearable to wear clothes. But our meaning is that mankind should be ruled by one supreme prince and directed towards peace by a common law issuing from him and applied to those characteristics which are common to all men. This common rule, or law, should be accepted from him by particular princes, in the same way as the practical reason preparing for action accepts its major proposition from the speculative intellect and then derives from it the minor proposition appropriate to the particular case, and finally proceeds to action. It is not only possible for one movement to issue from a single source, it is necessary for it to do so in order to eliminate confusion about universal principles.[8]

If we survey the ages and condition of men since the fall of our first parents (the false step from which all our errors pro-

[6] *Ibid.*, I, 5.
[7] *Ibid.*, I, 10.
[8] *Ibid.*, I, 14.

ceeded) at no time do we see universal peace throughout the
world except during the perfect monarchy of the immortal Augustus. The fact that mankind at that time was resting happily
in universal peace is attested by all the historians and the illustrious poets. Even the recorder of Christ's gentleness has deigned
to bear witness to it. Finally Paul, also, described that blissful
state as "the fulness of time." The times were indeed full, and
temporal desires fulfilled because nothing that ministers to our
happiness was without its minister. But what state the world
has been in since that seamless garment was rent on the nail of
cupidity we may easily read—would that we could not behold it!
O humanity, in how many storms must you be tossed, how
many shipwrecks must you endure, so long as you turn yourself
into a many-headed beast lusting after a multiplicity of things!
You are ailing in both your intellectual powers, as well as in
heart; you pay no heed to the unshakeable principles of your
higher intellect, nor illumine your lower intellect with experience, nor tune your heart to the sweetness of divine counsel
when it is breathed into you through the trumpet of the Holy
Spirit: "Behold how good and pleasant it is for brethren to dwell
together in unity." [9]

After this sublime utopia of Peace by Empire—which was
flouted by centuries of steady progress of nationalism, but which
nonetheless has not ceased to influence the conscience of the
best men down to our day—here is the description, astonishingly
precise for the epoch, of a Europe that is not merely geographical but already "cultural," as our century would say. Its unity
in diversity is illustrated by its languages. Here is an excerpt
from the treatise *De vulgari eloquentia* (I, 8): [10]

On account of the Confusion of Tongues, related above, we
have no slight reason for thinking that men were at that time
first scattered through all the climes of the world and the habitable regions and corners of those climes. And as the original
root of the human race was planted in the regions of the East,
and our race also spread out from there on both sides by a manifold diffusion of shoots, and finally reached the boundaries of
the West, it was then perhaps that rational throats first drank of
the rivers of the whole of Europe, or at least of some of them.

[9] *Ibid.*, I, 16.
[10] *A Translation of the Latin Works of Dante,* trans. A. J. Ferrers Howell
(London: J. M. Dent & Son, 1934).

But whether these men then first arrived as strangers, or whether they came back to Europe as natives, they brought a threefold language with them, and of those who brought it some alloted to themselves the southern, others the northern part of Europe, while the third body, whom we now call Greeks, seized partly on Europe and partly on Asia.

Afterwards, from one and the same idiom received at the avenging confusion, various vernaculars drew their origin, as we shall show farther on. For one idiom alone prevailed in all the country which from the mouths of the Danube, or marches of Maeotia, to the western boundary of England, is bounded by the frontiers of Italy and France and by the ocean; though afterwards through the Slavonians, Hungarians, Teutons, Saxons, English, and many other nations it was drawn off into various vernaculars, this alone remaining to almost all of them as a sign of their common origin, that nearly all the above named answer in affirmation *iò*.

Starting from this idiom, that is to say eastward from the Hungarian frontier, another language prevailed over all the territory in that direction comprised in Europe, and even extended beyond. But a third idiom prevailed in all that part of Europe which remains from the other two, though it now appears in a threefold form. For of those who speak it, some say in affirmation *oc*, others *oïl*, and others *sì*, namely the Spaniards, the French, and the Italians. Now the proof that the vernaculars of these nations proceed from one and the same idiom is obvious, because we see that they call many things by the same names, as *Deum, celum, amorem, mare, terram, vivit, moritur, amat*, and almost all other things. Now those of them who say *oc* inhabit the western part of the South of Europe, beginning from the frontiers of the Genoese; while those who say *sì* inhabit the country east of the said frontier, namely that which extends as far as that promontory of Italy where the Gulf of the Adriatic Sea begins, and Sicily. But those who say *oïl* lie in some sort to the north of these last; for they have the Germans on their east and north; on the west they are enclosed by the English sea, and bounded by the mountains of Aragon; they are also shut off on the south by the inhabitants of Provence, and the precipices of the Apennines.

PIERRE DU BOIS (*c.* 1250–1320)

Contemporaneous with *De Monarchia* (1308–1311), the essay by Pierre Du Bois (1306–1308) is distinguished from it by a shameless empiricism, or, if you will, by greater political realism (though it was of no avail).

It is to Ernest Renan that we owe the resurrection of this project, which was buried undisturbed for five centuries in the archives of Christina of Sweden, and later of the Vatican. Since Renan, everyone has been quoting it, but few have read it. To give some relief to the strange figure of the Norman lawyer whom the French historian Charles Langlois characterized as "the leading publicist of his epoch," we quote a few excerpts from the chapter Renan devoted to him in his *Histoire Littéraire de la France:* [11]

Pierre Du Bois was certainly born in Normandy and very probably at Coutances or its environs. He studied at the University of Paris where he heard St. Thomas Aquinas deliver a sermon, and Siger of Brabant [12] comment on Aristotle's *Politics.* Considering that St. Thomas Aquinas died in 1274 and that Siger of Brabant must have taught about the same time, it seems reasonable to suppose that Pierre Du Bois was born around 1250.

Du Bois embraced the law career at the very moment the most important of revolutions was taking place in the French judicature. Secular justice was definitely gaining the upper hand over ecclesiastical justice, relegating the latter to an ecclesiastical tribunal which still had very broad powers, but which was nothing beside the immensity of the attributions that the clerical courts had arrogated to themselves until then. In 1300 we find Pierre Du Bois exercising the functions of royal advocate at Coutances. Even before that time he had doubtless been in contact with some members of the government. For the earliest of his writings that has come down to us, the *Traité sur l'abrègement des guerres et des procès,* dated with the utmost precision (the last five months of the year 1300), is addressed to Philip the Fair, and fully reflects the concerns which dictated the papal pronouncement of 1298 as well as the actions of the king's diplomats in 1300. This work is evidence of extensive knowledge of Europe's political affairs and the secrets of the House of France; an obscure provincial lawyer, unconnected with the court, could not possibly have been so well informed . . . Pierre Du Bois'

[11] Ernest Renan, *Histoire Littéraire de la France* (Paris: Firmin-Didot, 1873), Vol. XXVI.

[12] Siger of Brabant, condemned by the Church for spreading the doctrines of Averroes, was one of Dante's teachers.

dominant purpose was to resist the encroachments of the Church and to extend the powers of civil society. The struggle between Philip the Fair and Boniface VIII provided him with an excellent opportunity to give vent to his anticlerical passions. Throughout this struggle we see him at the king's side, receiving inspirations from him, supplying him with arguments, wielding his pen in defense of the crown's rights . . . Before 1306, for unknown reasons, and certainly without breaking his connections with the court of France, Du Bois entered the service of Edward I, king of England.

. . . In 1306 he wrote the most important of his works, the one in which he chose to bring together all his ideas on politics and social reform. It is a treatise addressed to Edward I, on the means for recovering the Holy Land.[13] It is permitted to think that Du Bois was not too interested in the distant goal he assigned to the activity of the Christian nations . . . Under the pretext of pointing out the best methods for conquering the Holy Land, Du Bois expounds a vast plan for reforms, which consists in destroying the Pope's temporal power, despoiling the clergy of its possessions, transforming these possessions into pensions paid by the secular powers, and making the king of France the leader of Christendom.

In 1307 we again find Du Bois in Normandy. In 1308 he seems to have achieved the maximum of his credit with Philip. In that year, the emperor Albert of Austria having been assassinated, and Clement V being in Poitiers in the hands of Philip the Fair, Du Bois proposed to the king to seize the opportunity to get himself elected emperor . . . Once named emperor, the king would put himself at the head of Christendom and march on Jerusalem by land, as Charlemagne and Frederic Barbarossa had done before him. Philip seems to have made no attempt to carry out this project.

"It would be fairly difficult to expound the ideas of Pierre Du Bois' treatise according to the author's own plan," writes Chr. L. Lange,[14] and continues:

His work is not at all systematic; digressions and repetitions are

[13] This is the work that will be quoted below: *De recuperatione Sanctae Terrae.* The first part of the treatise is addressed in the form of a circular to all the prices of Christendom, beginning with Edward I; it concludes with a letter to Philip the Fair.

[14] *Historie de l'Internationalisme* (Christiania, 1919), Vol. I, chap. iv: "Les précurseurs de l'Internationalisme Moderne." Vol. II (from 1648 to 1815), completed by Auguste Schou, appeared in 1954.

frequent; the ideas advanced by the author seem rather disparate and are hardly relevant to the principal subject: he holds forth on the education of women and the military organization of France, the reform of convents, and the usefulness of learning languages, on mixed marriages between Sarrasins and Christian women and the means of speeding up court proceedings. The last-named subject is particularly dear to him, and he regards it as closely related to that of the "shortening of wars."

We shall therefore follow here the analysis propounded by Chr. L. Lange in his monumental work.

For Pierre Du Bois, as for Dante or Marsilius of Padua, peace is the *summum bonum*. But it denotes above all peace among the Christian nations, an absolute prerequisite for the success of the Crusade. The Crusaders will not stay in the Holy Land if they learn that their country is under threat of war. However, it is not enough to preach peace:

Do we not see that the Holy Scripture, which detests wars, and the preachers who say this to the public are not sufficient, and have not been sufficient in the past? . . . If the saintliness the teachings and the prayers of the Holy Fathers could not put an end to inter-Christian wars and all the perils accompanying them, how can the Pope believe that the speeches and the teaching of the present and future ministers of the Church can put an end to wars and to greed from which they proceed?

Stronger and more radical remedies are needed; penal sanctions must be instituted, and hence it is necessary *to organize the Christian society*. But with this end in view, Pierre Du Bois rejects the solution accepted by the majority of his contemporaries: the universal monarchy, which he does not think practicable.

I do not think that a sensible person can regard as possible, after all these centuries, that everyone should be ruled in respect of temporal things by a single monarch, who would be in charge of everything, and whom all would obey as their superior; for as things developed in this direction, there would be endless wars, seditions, and dissensions; and it would be impossible for anyone to put an end to them, because of the multitude of nations, the distances and the diversity of lands, and the natural disposition of men to discord; it is true that some were generally called monarchs of the world; however I do not believe that, since the various regions were settled, there has ever been any-one whom all did obey . . . But it is probable that there can and should be a single prince who, in respect of things spiritual, would rule and direct from east to west and from north to south.

Pierre Du Bois conceives of his "Christian republic" as a kind of federation directed by a Council; the nations forming it pre-serve absolute independence *quoad temporalia*. However, he does not believe that peace is possible without a reform of the Church. On the strength of his new authority, the Pope would have to take the initiative of convoking a Council which would establish peace among Christians by organizing the international society with a view to reconquering the Holy Land. Above all, it is necessary to organize juridical agencies for the purpose of settling conflicts. At this point Pierre Du Bois develops a de-tailed project for international arbitration between sovereign princes—the fact that he recognizes them to be "sovereign" does not make things easier . . .

But if these cities and these numerous princes, who do not recognize any superiors entitled to exercise justice over them according to local laws and customs, desire to start conflicts, before whom are they to plead? . . . It might be answered that the Council should decree that ecclesiastical or other arbiters are to be named, prudent, expert, and loyal men, who, after being sworn in, [would elect] three judges from among the prel-ates and three others for each party, well-to-do men and of a condition such that it would be probable that they could not be corrupted by love, or hatred, or fear, or greed, or anything else; they would assemble at an appropriate place, and, having been sworn in as solemnly as possible, after receiving, prior to their meeting, brief and clear pleas of each party, they would be given the proofs and the instruments—after eliminating every-thing superfluous or inept—which they would study conscien-tiously . . . If one of the parties is not satisfied with the decision, the judges themselves must send the whole record of the trial, accompanied by the sentences, to the Apostolic See, that they may be amended and changed by the Sovereign Pontiff, if that be just; if not, they must be confirmed and registered in the archives of the Church *ad perpetuam memoriam*.

It is interesting to note that this champion of the national state proposes the Pope as supreme judge in litigations between princes *superioris in terris non recognoscentes*. However, ecclesiastical sanctions are insufficient; for, he observes, it is above all temporal punishments that are feared: "Temporal punishment though incomparably less severe than eternal punishment, is more dreaded; it will be more advantageous to the Holy Land; it will cause less harm to the parents and friends of the condemned."

In other words, he wants to profit from the warlike spirit of his epoch to advance his project for the conquest of the holy places: the warmongers will be deported to the East where they will have opportunities to develop their military skills by fighting the Infidels, whereas, if they stayed in Europe, they would destroy the peace of the Christian republic! But this measure is insufficient. Du Bois shows by a specific example—that of the Duke of Burgundy—how the expected opposition could be defeated in Europe itself: the recalcitrant country would be encircled, every import to it prohibited, and starvation would be more effective than weapons.

"The characteristic feature of this project," Lange observes,[15] is it realistic spirit. Du Bois is able soberly and perspicaciously to evaluate the elements of the political world in which he lives. He sees that the universal monarchy is no longer possible; that the problem to be solved is that of peaceful coexistence of sovereign states; he also sees that the proper way to settle litigations between sovereign states is arbitration. He recommends measures many of which were known at the time—a Council convoked by the Pope; international arbitration, which had often been resorted to since the twelfth century; sanctions imposed by the arbiters, which were also practiced in his epoch . . . If he found no echo, it is because few men saw reality as clearly as he did. He was too much of a realist for his time, which was anything but realistic.

However, Lange clearly shows the essential weakness of Du Bois' system—which also makes for its interest.

The starting point of his reasoning is the existence of the state, of the sovereign prince, *rex qui non recognoscit superiorem*

[15] *Ibid.*, I, 106.

in terris . . . Now, the absolute assertion of state sovereignty must, when carried to its ultimate consequences, lead to anarchy in international relations—an anarchy that, in principle, still prevails . . . We see that our own epoch is still confronted with the problem that confronted that of Philip the Fair and Boniface VIII. Du Bois was the first to formulate it, and to outline a possible solution.

PETRARCH (1304–1374)

Meanwhile anarchy kept increasing in Europe. The emerging virulent absolute sovereignties were tearing her apart. Is Europe the body of Christendom? Petrarch does not seem to think so when he laments the decadence of a Europe where "Christ is unknown or ignored" in several regions:

Transport yourself in your mind further away: all of Gaul, the extreme limit of our continent, and Great Britain, projected outside the continent, are frequently weakened by disastrous wars. Germany, no less than Italy, suffers from internecine struggles, and burns in its own fire. The kings of Spain take arms one against another. . . . Greece plows for herself, harvests for herself, grinds corn for herself, eats her fill alone, but unable to digest the food of salvation, deserts the manger. In the other regions of Europe, Christ is unknown or held in no esteem . . . The birthplace and the very sepulcher of the Lord, double haven of peace for Christians, are trampled by dogs, and those who go there find no free or sure access to them.
. . . Who could ever have thought that the king of the Gauls would live in a British gaol, and perhaps die there? And now we are certain that he is in this gaol and we fear that he may die there. Who could have imagined that the army of the English would advance to the gates of Paris? Yet now it is there.[16]

KING GEORGE OF PODĚBRAD AND ANTOINE MARINI

The king of France did not listen to Pierre Du Bois. One hundred and fifty years later, at the other end of Europe, another monarch took up a similar project, which was perhaps inspired by the first.

[16] *Epistula 7 del libro delle Familiari, a Stefano Colonna.*

George of Poděbrad (1420–1471), a poor Czech gentleman, joined the army of the Taborites, or radical Hussites, although he himself was only a moderate Hussite or Utraquist. Elected King of Bohemia in 1458, he took steps against the Moravian Brethren, although they had influenced him, and he himself was a heretic. He hoped in this way to obtain the support of the Pope and of the princes of Christendom, for his plan to become a partner of Emperor Frederick.

"It was probably in the very year of his accession to the throne," writes Lange,[17]

that George met Antoine Marini, a native of Grenoble, inventor and big industrialist, who had founded tile-works and lime-burning plants in Styria and Salzburg. Since 1456 Antoine had been very active in several German states, probably also in Bohemia; in one of his credentials the king refers to Antoine as *carbonista,* "coal-miner." We must suppose that it was this enterprising and resourceful man, who suggested to George a grandiose plan for European federation which was to pave the way for his projects for political alliances. Antoine presented the plan to foreign princes in the name of the king of Bohemia; he went to Venice, and he addressed himself to the Duke of Burgundy who refused to hear him. Finally, during the winter of 1462/63, he submitted the project to Louis XI. In 1464 he was a member of a large Bohemian diplomatic mission to Louis XI. This was his last appearance on the stage of history. It is known that later, in 1466, Pope Paul II excommunicated King George and declared him forfeit to his throne. But he held out to the end and died as king in 1471.

The project submitted to Louis XI in 1463 is written in Latin. In the *Memoirs* of Philippe de Comines, which reproduces it, it bears the following title in French: *Traité d'alliance et confédération entre le Roy Louis XI, Georges roy de Bohême et la Seigneurie de Venise, pour résister au Turc.* George of Poděbrad counted on the immediate participation of the kings of Poland and Hungary, as well as the Dukes of Burgundy and Bavaria; but the Emperor and the Pope were excluded from it. Thus it was on a new Europe, that of the states and the emergent nations—the Europe of Pierre Du Bois—that this federal plan was

[17] *Op. cit.,* I, 108.

based: it took cognizance of an existing situation, and sought to forestall the threat of anarchy arising from the existence of sovereign states.

Although it failed owing to the resistance of two popes, whose power it was intended to check, this project marks a date in the history of Europe: it outlined, for the first time, a continental federation, explicitly limiting the national sovereignties while guaranteeing the autonomy of the member states. It provided for the creation of an Assembly voting by simple majority, a Court of Justice, international arbitration, a common armed force and a budget financed at the expense of the ecclesiastical tithe. We shall translate here large excerpts from this text, which is very long, redundant, and flowery, in the style of the time. This seems to be justified by the numerous analogies its content suggests with our present circumstances:

In the name of Our Lord Jesus Christ, We, George, King of Bohemia, let it be known to all and sundry, so that perpetual memory may be preserved of it, that examining the writings of old historians, we find that in former times Christendom was extremely prosperous and happy, its peoples no less than its strength. Its extent was such that it held within its bosom 117 vast kingdoms, and obtained from them so many men that for a long time it held a great part of the pagans along with Our Lord's Own Sepulcher. At that time there was no people in the world that dared attack the dominion of the Christians. Now, on the other hand, we all see how Christendom is torn, reduced, weakened, divested of all its former brilliance and splendor. . . .

For Islam, and then the Turks, had come, "first subjugating the glorious empire of the Greeks, and later . . . deporting an almost infinite number of souls to non-Christian countries."

O golden Province! O Christendom, glory of the universe, how has all honor been withdrawn from thee? How has thy unrivaled brilliance vanished? Where is the vigor of thy people? Where the respect all nations had for thee? Where thy royal majesty? Where thy glory? What profited thee so many victories, if thou werest so soon to be led in triumph by thy conquerors? What served thee to have resisted the power of the heathen chiefs, if thou canst no longer withstand the assault of thy neighbors? O vicissitudes of fortune, what changes you bring to em-

pires! How swiftly are kingdoms transformed and powers turned
to nought!

What is the cause of such a change, such a ruin? It is not easy
to discern because the judgments of God are hidden. The fields
are no less fertile today than formerly, the herds are no less
fecund; the product of the vineyards fills the vats to the brim;
industrious men have discovered mines gold and silver, great
minds have proved their valor in many domains, letters are as
flourishing as ever. What is it, then, that has brought down
Christendom to such a point that of the 117 kingdoms we have
spoken of, only sixteen remain? Perhaps God is punishing certain
sins, as we read in the Old Testament happened from time to
time. Therefore we think that we must carefully examine our
souls, so that if a fault was committed, it may be corrected.

. . . Although at present the fate of the Greeks is miserable,
and although we have to deplore the loss of Constantinople and
other provinces, we should, if we aspire to glory, wish for this
occasion which may earn us the honor of being called the main-
tainers and defenders of the Christian name. This is why, in our
desire to see war, pillage, disorder [etc. . . .] stopped and done
away with entirely, we have decided upon—in full knowledge
of the matter, after mature deliberations, after invoking the
grace of the Holy Ghost, with the counsel and agreement of prel-
ates, princes, lords, nobles, and our doctors of divine and human
law—this act of alliance, peace, brotherhood, and concord destined to endure unshakeably, because of the respect for God and
the maintenance of the faith, for us, our heirs, and our future
successors, for ever and ever.

Under the first three articles of the Treaty, the contracting
parties undertake not to resort to war against one another; not
to aid or abet any conspiracy against any one of them; and to
help one another in repressing crimes committed by their subjects in the territory of any member country. The next article
deals with the all-important subjects of mutual assistance and
international arbitration:

In the fourth place, if one party or several parties outside of
this agreement which imposes on us love and brotherhood, without being attacked or provoked, should open hostilities against
one of us, or should it happen that they have been opened
(which seems little to be feared, considering friendship and
charity), the Assembly designated below must, in the name of
all who figure in this treaty, immediately send ambassadors at

our common expense, even without being requested to do so by our attacked colleague, with the mission to settle the litigation and restore the peace, at a place convenient to the parties; and there, in presence of the conflicting parties or their plenipotentiary ambassadors, to employ all zeal and diligence to bring the adversaries back to peace and concord, amicably if possible, or to induce them to choose arbiters and plead before a competent judge or before the Parliament or Consistory designated below. And if by the deed and fault of the aggressor, peace and union cannot be achieved by one of the above-mentioned means, all the others among us, by unanimous agreement, shall aid our ally attacked or forced to defend himself by giving him tithes of our kingdom every year for his defense, as well as the revenues, earning or emoluments of our peoples and our subjects which they will have paid at the rate of three days a year for the enjoyment of their houses and habitations . . .

The organs of the Federation are mentioned next: Court of Justice, or Consistory, Assembly, and common armed force, as well as the means for financing and employing it:

But since peace cannot be cultivated without justice, nor justice without peace . . . we have provided first for the organization of a kind of general Consistory which shall have its seat at whatever place the Assembly finds itself, and whence, as from a spring, the rivers of justice will flow everywhere. This tribunal shall be organized, in respect of the number and rank of the persons and the statutes, in accordance with the decisions of our Assembly designated below or its majority.

And in order that in this tribunal a term may be set to the proceedings so as to avoid their being endless, we desire that the judge himself and his assistants render judgment and justice to the plaintiffs, as the nature of the causes will require, simply and clearly, without the pomp and uproar of a trial, without subterfuge or dilatory maneuvers. . . .

. . . On the other hand, since this act of good understanding and charity is done and established above all for the glory and honor of the divine majesty of the Holy Roman Church and the Catholic faith, to protect and defend the Christian religion and all the oppressed faithful against the ignoble prince of the Turks by assessing and declaring the forces and resources we have in common; to accomplish and execute this task, we shall give and pay all tithes given and paid to churches, priests, and monks in our kingdoms, principalities, and lordly domains with our revenues, profits, and emoluments and those of our subjects, to be supplied, as has been said, at the rate of three days a year as long as there shall be need.

Furthermore, since everything must be foreseen with judicious zeal and care, in order that misfortune may not in the end punish improvidence, we resolve that by common agreement of our entire Assembly or the majority thereof, a moment shall be set at which to attack the enemy, with what land and naval force to wage the war, what military chiefs, machines, and war materials are to be employed, and at what place all the land armies will have to gather to undertake their campaign against the Turks.

Now, this is how the federal Assembly, cornerstone of the structure, is to operate under the Treaty:

Item, in order that what is written above and below be executed properly, as a whole and in detail, we promise and undertake in the above-mentioned manner that each of us shall gather his ambassadors, eminent men enjoying great authority, armed with the fullest powers and with his seal, on the Reminiscere Sunday of the year 1464 after the nativity of the Lord,[18] in the city of Basel in Germany. There they shall stay for the five years immediately following without interruption, and, in your name, and in the name of the other members, incorporated or to be incorporated, make, constitute, and represent a true body, community, or College. When these five years of the Basel Assembly have elapsed, this same Assembly shall gather and meet in a city of France for another five years, and for the third five-year period, in a city X in Italy, so that the Assembly shall meet in a new place every five years until the Assembly itself or a majority thereof decides to make other dispositions. The Assembly itself shall have a special council of its own, with a single president X as head and father, and we, kings and princes of Christendom shall be its members. The above-mentioned College shall have as well over us, over our subjects and those who will have prolonged its term, gracious and contentious jurisdiction, at the same time as maternal and joint empire, according as the above-mentioned Assembly or majority thereof shall have resolved and decided. Lastly, it shall have its own arms, its own seal, and its own common treasure, as well as its official archives, its syndic, its fiscal agent, its officials and all other rights that touch upon and concern in any manner whatsoever a legal and legitimate College.

[18] February 26, 1465 (New Style).

And in order that each country may preserve intact its own rights, we resolve that, in whatever land the Assembly may be sitting, the principal office of the Assembly shall be headed by men native of this same land who know and understand its customs and usages.

On the other hand we say and desire that we, King of France, with the other kings and princes of Gaul, shall have a voice in the Assembly itself, and we, kings and princes of Germany another, and we, Doge of Venice, with the princes and towns of Italy, a third; but that if the king of Castile and other kings and princes of Spain join in our union, friendship, and brotherhood, that they shall similarly have a voice in the Assembly, in its body and its College; but if, among the ambassadors of the kings and princes of one and the same nation, contrary votes are given and uttered on some matter, we resolve that what has been done and resolved by the majority will be upheld as firmly as if it had been judged and resolved by the unanimity of that nation . . .

One of the last provisions of the Treaty was the obvious reason for the final failure of the project: by a threadbare stratagem the princes resolve to ask the Pope to see to it that the tithes collected by the Church should henceforward be turned over to the Assembly, as the new defender of the Faith!

Politely rejected by Louis XI, explicitly condemned by the Pope, George of Poděbrad's project came to nothing and fell into oblivion.

AENEAS SILVIUS PICCOLOMINI (1405–1464)

The reader will have noted that Dante, Pierre Du Bois, and King George of Poděbrad, although their plans deal exclusively with Europe, as the *de facto* Christendom, never use the term "Europe" or the adjective "European." Strangely enough, it was a pope at the dawn of the Renaissance who first used again the legendary and pagan term "Europe" to designate that part of mankind whose earliest efforts to achieve unity, as we know only too well, had until then been directed precisely against the Holy See and its temporal claims.

Aeneas Silvius Piccolomini, one of the most famous humanists of his time,[19] was raised to the pontificate under the name of Pius II in 1458–the very year George of Poděbrad was elected king of Bohemia. Byzantium had just been conquered by the Turks.

Aeneas Silvius identified Europe with "our fatherland, our home," for everyone there shares the same threat: "Now it is in Europe itself, that is, in our fatherland in our own home, in our Seat, that we are being attacked and slain." [20]

Toward the end of his life he began to compose a general cosmography, but was able to finish only the chapters on Asia and on Europe. Here, for the first time after several centuries, Europe is described as a human and historical whole, not merely a geographical entity. It is unfortunately impossible to quote here significant excerpts from this work, for it is divided into chapters dealing separately with each country, including the Balkans and Byzantium. Aeneas Silvius describes not only the physical milieu and landscape, but also political, ecclesiastical, economic, and social conditions–we would say, briefly, "culture."

"No one knew Europe better than he [Piccolomini] did, and when he became Pope Pius II in 1458, it became his prime task to defend Christendom from the Turks by force of persuasion and by force of arms. For Pius, Christendom and Europe are one and the same." [21]

In his famous *Letter to Mohammed II,* he lists the resources of Christendom as those of Europe and denies the existence of true Christians outside of Europe:

We cannot believe that you are so ignorant of our affairs as not to see how great is the power of the Christian people, how

[19] In the famous mural by Benozzo Gozzoli ("The Departure of the Three Magi"), he is shown on horseback in a highly civilized landscape, on his way to the Council of Basel; the well-known painting by Pinturicchio shows him receiving the crown of the poets, from Frederick III, last of the Holy Roman emperors crowned in Rome. Great symbols!

[20] *De Constantinopoliana clade ac bello contra Turcos congregando.* The original reads: *Nunc vero in Europa, id est, in patria, in domo propria, in sede nostra, percussi caesique sumus.* This *id est* deserves to be underlined.

[21] Denis Hay, "On a Problem of Terminology: 'Europe' and 'Christendom,'" *Diogenes,* No. 17, 1957. Cf., by the same author, *Europe, the Emergence of an Idea* (Edinburgh: Edinburgh University Press, 1957).

valorous is Spain, how warlike France, how populous Germany, how strong Brittany, how fearless Poland, how energetic Hungary, and how rich, ardent, and skillful in arms is Italy.

As for the *non-European* Christians whom Mohammed boasts of having in his power, Pius II does not hesitate to exclude them as false Christians:

They are all steeped in error, although they worship Christ— Armenians, Jacobites, Maronites, and the others. The Greeks broke away from the Roman Church when you invaded Constantinople. They never accepted the agreements concluded at Florence and have remained in error.

Mohammed would quickly realize the power of the Christians, the Pope says, were he to come close to the "heart of Christendom," that is, to the heart of Europe. Whereas, if Mohammed is willing to become a Christian (like another Constantine), the Pope promises him "the admiration of all Greece, of all Italy, of all Europe." At the end of his life, when he prayed for the success of the Crusaders, he said: "Grant us victory over Thy enemies, so that, having finally retrieved Greece, we may sing Thy praises throughout Europe."

Let us note the significant triad: Greece, Italy, and Christendom, used here to designate "all Europe": the first attempt to define our culture in terms of its three principal sources, Athens, Rome, and Jerusalem, a definition that Valéry was to popularize in the twentieth century.

However, the heads of the new states into which the body of Europe was divided turned a deaf ear to the Pontiff's appeals, as they had earlier done to those of his rival, the king of Bohemia. In vain did he join to his prayer the announcement— which he thought would suffice—of the gift of his sacred person, promising to lead a new Crusade himself: "Who could refuse his participation, when the bishop of Rome is ready to sacrifice his own life?" His appeals went unheeded. At Ancona where he had summoned the Christian princes in 1464—the very year George of Poděbrad had proposed for the meeting of the first federal Assembly at Basel—he found only a crowd of adventurers without arms or leaders. He died a few weeks later, bitterly dis appointed. He must have foreseen this failure, however, since ten years earlier, shortly before becoming Pope, he had written:

Christendom has no leader whom all would obey. Neither the Sovereign Pontiff nor the Emperor is given his due. There is no more respect or obedience. We regard the Pope and the Emperor as names, as fictions. Every city has its king, every house has its prince.[22]

3: The Problem of War and the Rise of National States

IN THE SIXTEENTH CENTURY, three major events transformed the image of the world, and the image of international relations as seen by contemporary thinkers and statesmen: the great discoveries and the beginnings of colonialism, the Reformation, and the failure of Charles V's grandiose imperial scheme. Their repercussions on the "image of Europe" were diverse and contradictory.

The great discoveries did not result in a new conception of Europe's unique position in the world (this did not come about until the eighteenth century); nor did they raise doubts about the excellence of our own civilization, which on the contrary the discoveries seemed to confirm. They inaugurated the era of an adventurous economic imperialism at a moment when the ideal of a continental Holy Empire came to grief. They shifted the creative centers of our civilization to the Atlantic coast. They laid the foundations of capitalism and of the primacy of the national State. But contemporary awareness of these transformations is discernible only in the utopias of Thomas More and Campanella with their references to the New World.

The best minds of the day took Europe for granted. It was something like the air they breathed. They knew it well, they moved about it freely, they carried on a continual exchange of

[22] *Opera omnia, Epist.* CXXVII.

ideas, conversations, erudite letters, and indulged in polemics both dignified and not. "Europe as a single body," as Guillaume Postel calls it,[23] remains at the center of the world, now enlarged as a result of the Spanish and Portuguese discoveries. Its universal, uncontested rule was threatened only by the Turks outside it: they alone, occasionally, awakened the realization of a need for some sort of union, but this union was invariably conceived of as a coalition among the sovereigns.

The deep crisis of the Reformation was felt to be dividing not so much Europe as Christendom alone. (On this point, therefore, our modern judgments are anachronistic.) If we confine ourselves to the testimonies of the day, we see that in fact *the concept of Europe was never invoked by the two contending parties in support of their theses*.[24] Calvin, Luther, and Loyola are very great European figures, but none of them ever spoke of Europe as such, still less of European unity.

By contrast, the political ideal of a Europe united under the crown of the Holy Empire seemed closer than ever to being translated into a grandiose reality. On his accession to the throne, Charles V found himself master of the German states, the Spanish states, the Low Countries, Naples, Milan, and a part of present-day France, that is, three-quarters of continental Europe: the conquistadors added to his titles that of Sovereign of India and the Mainland of the Ocean Sea, and that of Ruler of Africa and Asia. And yet, on his death in 1558, what was left of this great dream of a universal monarchy whose center was to have been the united Europe? Everything had fallen apart, had been perverted and dislocated. The unity of the Church had been broken for centuries to come, France had allied herself with the Turks against the rest of Europe, Spain had lost most

[23] In his *Abrégé de Cosmographie;* as quoted by Moreri.

[24] The only exception, as far as we know, is Tomasso Campanella (1568–1639) who thought at the end of the century that the Reformation had broken "the unity of peoples and princes" in "a Europe formerly wholly Catholic" (*Discorsi IV*). He concluded that Europe could no longer resist the Turks, and that in order to be saved Christendom would have to be transferred to America, which had been discovered thanks to "the universal king," Ferdinand the Catholic.

of her old communal and regional freedoms, Bohemia and Hungary had been routed at Mohacs, Rome had been sacked and Italy enslaved, the German states were in complete anarchy, and the New World, whose resources might have been developed in common by the shipowners and bankers of all Europe, was instead being ruinously exploited under the Iberian monopoly. An immense failure, in the eyes of History more than in the eyes of contemporaries, who seem not to have realized its extent.

The imperial ideal, this Platonic idea which had continually fascinated the great monarchs, from Charlemagne to Charles V, including Otto III and Frederick II, and which, for Dante, was the foundation of the Christian Peace, entered into an eclipse which was to last several centuries.

On the other hand, the rise of national states with their claims to absolute sovereignty brought to the fore the problem of war and the rights of belligerents. At the same time, the expansion of trade to other continents raised the problem of an international law, which was founded early in the seventeenth century by Hugo Grotius, on the basis of maritime law; and the problem of the law of nations (*jus gentium*), which had arisen out of the new colonies. The unity of the human race—a metaphysical and religious idea, and a profoundly European one, was exalted in noble statements: but the union of the Europeans, as an urgent political measure, was never so much as mentioned.

We shall quote two pages on war by Francisco de Vitoria (1480–1546), Dominican, professor at Salamanca, famous author of *De Indis,* and one of the founders, with Suarez, of the law of nations.

No war is legitimate if it is evident that it is waged to the detriment of the Commonwealth, rather than for its profit and advantage . . . And since a State is only a part of the whole world, and since, a fortiori, a Christian province is only a part of the whole Commonwealth, it is my opinion that even if a war is useful to a province or a State, but detrimental to the world or to Christendom, then that war is unjust for this very reason. For instance, if Spain started a war against France for just motives, and if it were otherwise useful to the kingdom of Spain, but if for all that it were waged with greater injury to Christendom and exposed it to dangers (if, for instance, the Turks seized this opportunity to occupy Christian provinces), then Spain would have to refrain from such a war.[25]

We cannot help thinking that Montesquieu's famous statement which ends with the words, "If I knew of something that would serve my nation, but would be harmful to Europe and to mankind, I should look upon it as a crime," [26] is a paraphrase of Vitoria.

In a letter to the High Constable of Castile, Vitoria takes up again the idea that wars can be justified only if they are beneficial to the nations waging them. But he observes that in fact they never are; thus they are implicitly condemned in toto:

Now, I shall not ask of God a greater favor than that of making these two princes [Charles V and Francis I] brothers in will as in kinship: for then there would no longer be heretics in the Church nor Moors to harass it, and the Church would be reformed, whether the Pope wanted it or no; and before I see this, I shall not give a maravedi for the Council nor for all the remedies and devices that can be imagined. We must not look for the culprit in the person of the king of France, still less in that of the Emperor. May God forgive the princes and their opponents; but He will not forgive them wars; wars are not invented for the good of princes but for the good of peoples; and this being the case, judge for yourselves, O upright men, whether our wars profit Spain or France or Italy or Germany, or rather whether they bring destruction to all these countries.[27]

It is interesting to note that the great sixteenth-century pacifists did not propose a system of supra-national law as the means for combating the principal cause of wars—the arrogant and anarchic sovereignty of the states.[28]

Notably less advanced than Dante and Pierre Du Bois, who had seen the need to set up a power superior to the national sovereigns, they contented themselves with railing against war and ridiculing the pretexts for it (see Erasmus, below) in the

[25] *Relectiones theologicae tredecim* (Venice edition, 1626).
[26] The full text of this passage by Montesquieu will be found on p. 144.
[27] To the High Constable of Castile, November 19, 1536.
[28] "One might add religion to these causes of war," writes Emeric Crucé, "if experience had not taught us that most often it serves as a pretext."

name of reason and Christian morality. As for the jurists, they scarcely mentioned the possibility of arbitration, which had been customary during the Middle Ages. And as for the political thinkers, far from the idea of contesting or limiting absolute state sovereignty, they sought to legitimate it (as Jean Bodin did) or confined themselves to describing its hard necessities (as Machiavelli did).

To be sure, Jean Bodin (1525–1596), in his *Method for Facilitating the Study of History*, published in Paris in 1566, says that the human race constitutes a single whole. Thanks to world trade, which Europeans had made possible, "all men are linked to one another and share wonderfully in the universal Commonwealth." But this universality remains purely spiritual, if not purely rhetorical; no political consequences can be drawn from it, neither for the world, nor for Europe, which remains ineluctably the prey to the anarchy of the rival sovereignties:

All the kingdoms, empires, tyrannies, and republics on earth are united by a bond which is none other than the authority of reason and the law of nations. Hence it follows that this world is like a great city and that all men are cast, as it were, into the mold of a single law, in order that they may understand that they are all of the same blood and under the protection of an identical reason. But because this empire of reason is devoid of constraint, it is impossible to unite all the existing nations in a single Commonwealth. This is why princes have recourse to arms and treaties.

Thus we are brought back to reality, the reality of the states and their fratricidal struggles, "senseless," endless, merciless. For, as the same Jean Bodin says in his *République:* "Properly speaking, the greatness of a prince is nothing but the ruin or diminution of his neighbors: and his strength is nothing but the weakness of others."

Would, then, "sacred egotism" be the last word in political wisdom? This is indeed the case if we accept the principle of unlimited sovereignty arrogated by a prince or a republic.

In contrast to this text which is Machiavellian in tone, we may quote a famous passage by Francisco Suarez (1548–1617). The great Spanish Jesuit does not confine himself to exalting the community of the human race; he also suggests and implies the idea of a law of nations which would impose its real *authority* on the alleged *potestas suprema* of the states: [29]

The human race, howsoever many the various peoples and kingdoms into which it may be divided, always preserves a certain unity not only as a species, but also, as it were, a moral and political unity called for by the natural precept of mutual love and mercy, which applies to all, even to strangers of any nation.

Therefore, although a given sovereign state, commonwealth, or kingdom, may constitute a perfect community in itself, consisting of its own members, nevertheless, each one of these states is also, in a certain sense, and viewed in relation to the human race, a member of that universal society; for never are these states, when standing alone, so self-sufficient that they do not require some mutual assistance, association and intercourse, at times for their greater welfare and advantage, but at other times also of some moral necessity or lack, as is clear from experience.

Consequently, such communities have need of some system of law whereby they may be directed and properly ordered with regard to this kind of intercourse and association; and although this law is in large measure provided by natural reason, it is not provided in sufficient measure and in a direct manner, with respect to all matters; therefore, it was possible for certain special rules of law to be introduced through the practice of these same nations.[30]

In all the immense intellectual activity that went on during the sixteenth century we have thus found only a few pages testifying to an awareness of Europe as an entity. Two other texts, however, deserve to be quoted. They show to what extent the vision of the thinkers of that time was naturally European, in the sense that they never stop comparing our diverse nations with one another as parts of an implicit whole. But they also show to what extent contemporary speculation on war and peace remained abstract in some, cynical in others, and unconcerned with a positive policy aimed at checking the anarchy of the states.

[29] *Tractatus de legibus ac de Deo legislatores*, II, XIX, 9. The treatise was written at Coimbra at the end of the sixteenth century, and published at Antwerp in 1694.

[30] Trans. James Brown Scott, in *The Catholic Conception of International Law* (Georgetown University Press, 1934).

Here are, first of all, little-known pages by Machiavelli (1469–1527), taken from *L'arte della guerra*,[31] in which he develops a thesis outlined by Aristotle in his parallel between Asia and Europe (quoted above):

You know, then, there have been many renowned warriors in Europe, but few in Africa, and fewer still in Asia; the reason of which is, that the two last mentioned quarters of the world have had but one or two monarchies, and but few republics in them; and that Europe, on the contrary, has had several kingdoms, but more republics in it. Now men become great and excellent, and shew their abilities accordingly as they are employed and encouraged by their sovereigns, whether they happen to be kings, princes or republics; so that where there are many states, there will be many great men; but where there are few of one sort, there will not be many of the other. In Asia, there were Ninus, Cyrus, Artaxerxes, Mithridates, and some few others like them. In Africa (without having recourse to the early times of the ancient Egyptians) we read of Massinissa, Jugurtha and some Carthaginian commanders of eminent note; the number of whom, however, is very small in comparison of that which Europe has produced; for in this quarter of the world, indeed, there have been numbers of great men that we know of, and many more, without doubt, whose memories are now extinguished by the malevolence of time; because every state being obliged to cherish and encourage men of merit and abilities, either out of necessity or for other reasons, where there are many different states, there must of course be many great men. Asia, on the contrary, has not produced many extraordinary men; because that quarter of the globe being subject, in a great measure, to one monarchy alone, of so large an extent that most parts of it languish in continual inactivity, cannot form any considerable number of men to great and glorious enterprizes. The same may be said of Africa; though indeed there have been more able commanders in that country than in Asia, which was owing to the republic of Carthage. For there will always be a greater number of such men in republics than in monarchies; because merit is generally honoured in the former, but feared in the latter; from whence it comes to pass, that able men are cherished and encouraged in one, but discountenanced and suppressed in the other.

If we consider Europe in the next place, we shall find that it

[31] Book II. On the European idea in Machiavelli, cf. the essay by C. Curcio in *Macchiavelli nel risorgimento* (Milan, 1953).

was always full of principalities, kingdoms, and republics, which lived in perpetual jealousy of each other, and being obliged to keep up good discipline in their armies, were under necessity of honouring and encouraging military merit. For in Greece, besides the Macedonian monarchy, there were several republics, every one of which produced many great and eminent men. In Italy, there were the Romans, the Samnites, the Tuscans, and the Cisalpine Gauls. France, Germany and Spain abounded with republics and principalities; and if we do not read of so many great men in any of them as amongst the Romans, that is owing to the partiality of historians, who generally follow the stream of fortune, and content themselves with praising the conqueror. It is but reasonable, however, to suppose there were a great many illustrious men amongst the Samnites and Tuscans, as they supported themselves against the Romans a hundred and fifty years. The same may be supposed of France and Spain; but the merit which most authors are so shy of allowing in particular men, they are forward enough to celebrate in whole nations, when they tell us, with what bravery and resolution they exerted themselves in defence of their liberties. Since it is manifest, then, that where there are many states there will always be many able men, it is certain, that when the number of those states is diminished, the number of such men will likewise decrease by degrees, as the effect must cease when the cause is taken away.

Thus, when the Roman empire had swallowed up all the kingdoms and republics in Europe and Africa, and most of those in Asia, merit and abilities met with no countenance anywhere but at Rome; so that great men began to grow scarcer and scarcer in Europe, as well as in Asia, till at last there were hardly any to be found: for as all manner of spirit and worth was extinguished, except amongst the Romans, so when they became corrupt, the whole world in a manner was corrupted, and the Scythians poured by swarms into an empire, which having extinguished the virtue of most other nations, was not able to preserve its own. And though that empire was afterwards dismembered by those barbarians, yet the several parts of it into which it was cantoned, never recovered their pristine vigour; for, in the first place, it is a very difficult matter, and requires a long course of time, to revive good order and discipline when it is once abolished; and in the next, the christian religion has wrought such a change in the manners and customs of mankind, that they are no longer under the necessity of defending themselves with such a degree of obstinacy and despair as they did in former times:

For then, all such as were vanquished in battle, were either put to death, or carried into perpetual slavery in the enemy's country, where they spent the remainder of their lives in labour and misery. If a town was taken, it was either demolished, or the inhabitants were stripped of their goods, dispersed all over the world, and reduced to the last degree of poverty and wretchedness; so that the dread of these evils obliged them to keep up good discipline in their armies, and to honour all those that excelled in the art of war. But at present, those terrible apprehensions are in a great measure dissipated and extinguished; for after the army is defeated, those that fall into the hands of the conqueror are seldom or never put to death, and the terms of their ransom are made so easy, that they do not long continue prisoners. If a town has changed sides an hundred times, it is not demolished, nor are the inhabitants either dispersed or stripped of their possessions. The worst they have to fear is being laid under contribution. So that men now no longer care to submit to the rigour and continual hardships of military discipline, to ward off evils which they are but little afraid of. Besides, the provinces of Europe are subject to few heads at present, in comparison to what they were formerly. All France is under the dominion of one king; and there are not many principalities or republics in Italy; so that the petty states find protection under the wings of the strong, and those that are more powerful are not afraid of utter ruin, even if they should be conquered, for the seasons already given.[32]

This is a far cry from Sulpicius Severus who praised Europe for her saints, and who, on the basis of their merits alone, placed her above the nations of the Near East. (For the "Asia" referred to in the foregoing passage is, needless to say, confined to the Near East.)

ERASMUS (1466–1536)

In striking contrast to the author of *The Prince*, for whom force alone in the last analysis defines reason and freedom, here is the author of *In Praise of Folly* and the treatise *Dulce bellum inexpertis* ("War Is Sweet to Those Who Do Not Know It"). It is not he who would call the man at arms "excellent"; rather

[32] Machiavelli, *The Art of War.* Printed by Henry C. Southwick (Albany, 1815).

he holds him to be a monstrous apparition, repugnant to nature: "Look at yourself, if you can, raging warrior . . . I had imagined you as an animal of a certain divine character." [33]

Erasmus is the very type of the sixteenth-century great men who do not speak of Europe because, all told, they see nothing but Europe. Born in Holland, he lived in Brussels, in Paris, in England, and in Switzerland; he spent time in Italy and Germany. It has been said of him that "if he had a homeland, it was Europe" (Lange). In all his life and works, in every fiber of his being, he well deserved to be called "the first European," if not in intention, at least in fact.

Here are a few excerpts from his *Querela pacis*,[34] which sums up his ideas on war, on the stability of the European states, on the Turks, and on the nationalism just beginning to make itself felt:

XXXIV. . . . I blush to record, upon how infamously frivolous causes the world has been roused to arms by Christian Kings. One of them has found, or forged, an obsolete musty parchment, on which he makes a claim to a neighbouring territory. As if it signified a straw to mankind, thus called upon to shed blood, who is the *person*, or what the *family* of the ruling Prince, *whoever he be*, provided he governs in such a manner as to consult and promote the public felicity.

Another alleges that some punctilio, in a treaty of a hundred articles, has been infringed or neglected. A third owes a neighbouring King a *secret* grudge, on a *private* account, because he has married some Princess whom he intended to be his consort, or uttered some sarcasm that reflects upon his royal person and character.

And what is the basest and most flagitious conduct of all, there are Crowned Heads, who, with the mean cunning that ever characterizes the Despot, *contrive* (because they find their Own Power weakened by the People's union, and strengthened by their *divisions*) to excite War, without any substantial reason for a rupture; merely to break the national union at home, and pillage the oppressed people with impunity.

XXXV. . . . Unanimous in nothing but in defrauding and oppressing the public! Yet . . . they are called Christians, and

[33] *Dulce bellum inexpertis*, No. 3101 of the *Adages* (1515).
[34] *Querela pacis undique genitum ejectae profligataeque*, written in 1515.

have the impudence to go with a face of piety to church, and dare even to kneel at the altar. Pests of mankind, worthy to be transported out of civil society, and carried with *convicts,* to the remotest islands, in exile for life. If it be true, that Christians are members of one body, how happens it that every Christian does not sympathize and rejoice in every other Christian's welfare?

XXXVI. Now, however, it seems to be cause enough to commence a *just and necessary* war, that a neighbouring land is in a more prosperous, flourishing or free condition, than your own. For if you can but prevail upon yourselves to speak the real truth, what, I ask, has excited, and what continues at this very day to excite, so many *combined Powers,* against the kingdom of France, unless it be, that it is the finest and most flourishing country in Europe? Nowhere is there a more extensive territory; nowhere a more august public Council; nowhere greater unanimity, and on all these accounts united, nowhere greater power.

Nowhere are the laws better applied, and in the matter of religion, nowhere is the integrity of the Dogma more respected. France is not corrupted by the trade of the Jews, as is the case with the Italians; nor is she poisoned by the proximity of the Turks or the Moors, as is the case with the Hungarians and Spaniards. Germany, not to mention Bohemia, is divided into a large number of kingdoms, and yet not a shadow of authority is to be seen there. France alone, intact flower of Christ's kingdom, is its safest refuge. If by accident some storm occurs, she will be attacked in every possible way, assaulted by all the ruses of those who devastate her, for the sole pleasure of congratulating themselves on the storm they have unleashed. And after that, can one say that these men possess the tiniest speck of the Christian spirit? . . .

LV. . . . A measure most dangerous to the existence of a State as a War must be, should not be entered into by a King . . . but by the full and unanimous consent of the whole People. The causes of War are to be cut up, root and branch, on their first and slightest appearance. . . .

LVII. . . . But if there is a fatal propensity in the human heart to War, if the dreadful disease is interwoven with the constitution of Man, so that it cannot abstain from War, why is not vent given to the virulence in exertions against the common enemy of Christianty, the unbelieving Turk? . . . It were far better to *allure* him by gentle, kind, and friendly treatment, by exhibiting the beauty of our Christian religion in the innocence of our lives, than by attacking him with the Drawn Sword, . . . never-

theless, if we must of *necessity* go to War . . . it is certainly a
less evil to contend with an infidel, than that Christians should
mutually harass and destroy their own fraternity. If Charity will
not content their hearts, certainly one common enemy may unite
their hands . . .[35]

LIX. . . . Thus for instance, an Englishman, say they, is the
natural Enemy of a Frenchman, because he is a Frenchman. A
man born on this side of the river Tweed must hate a Scotchman, because he is a Scotchman. A German *naturally* disagrees
with a Frank . . . O villanous depravity! The name of a place
or region, in itself a circumstance of indifference, shall be enough
to dissever your hearts more widely than the distance of place,
your persons! . . . How happens it, that such a frivolous thing
as a *name*, avails more with you than the tender ties of nature,
the strong bonds of Christianity? *Place,* local distance, separates
the *persons* of men but not their *minds.* . . . The river Rhine
once separated the Frenchman from the German, but it was beyond its power to separate the Christian from the Christian. The
Pyrenean mountains divide the Spaniard from the French, but
they break not that invisible bond that holds them together in
defiance of all partition, the Communion of the Church. A little
gut of a sea divides the English from the French; but . . . it
could not disjoin them as Men united by nature; and while they
mutually retain the Christian religion, still more indissolubly
cemented by Grace.

The Apostle Paul expresses his indignation that Christians,
separating into sects, should say, "I am of Apollos; I am of
Cephas; I am of Paul"; nor would he suffer the unnatural distinctions of a *name* to parcel out Christ, who is one with all his
members; and who has formed All into one inviolable Whole.
And shall we think the common name of a native country cause
sufficient why one race of Men should hunt down another race
of Men, even to extermination . . . ?[36]

How can we avoid applauding these sarcastic remarks on "the
causes of war" put forward by the various "Princes"? But at the
same time how can we fail to see that by making himself the
champion of firm frontiers and of a kind of "nationalizing" of

[35] In his *Institutio principis Christiani* (1515), dedicated to the young
Charles V, whose councillor he had just been named, Erasmus wrote, not
without profound irony: "Let us first become sincere Christians ourselves;
once we have done this, let us make war on the Turks."

[36] *The Complaint of Peace,* translated from the Latin of Erasmus (London, 1795).

the princes as well as by proposing that war be waged only
"with the consent of the whole nation," Eramus, far from abolishing the causes of war, plays into the hands of the collective
regressive forces whose future was to reveal that they could only
ravage Europe first by national, later by total, wars?

He was better inspired when in 1530, in his "Consultation on
the War Against the Turks," he finally arrived at the idea of a
supra-national Power. However, he could imagine it only in the
guise of Dante's "Monarchy," which seemed to him ideal, though
utopian; consequently he resigned himself to some sort of more
or less federal balance of power:

> Some are frightened by the word "universal Monarchy" which
> others seem to aspire to . . . To be sure, the Monarchy would
> be the best thing if it were possible to find a prince resembling
> God; however, men being as they are, states of moderate size
> [*moderata imperia*] are the safest, if they are united by Chris-
> tian pacts.

Meanwhile, at the other end of Europe, in Scandinavia, Machiavellian praise of warlike *virtù* was condemned in the name of
plain common sense by Olaus Petri (1497–1552), the Reformer
of Sweden, who was chancellor to King Gustavus Vasa, and
Stockholm's leading clergyman.

> Our Swedish chronicles greatly honor our ancestors for their
> glorious exploits in foreign lands. But if we look more closely,
> there is little honor in it all . . . Let those who will, praise the
> ancient Goths; those who had to deal with them did not praise
> them, but branded them a horde of bandits and tyrants, for hav-
> ing pillaged and burned villages and cities, and deprived hun-
> dreds of thousands of men of their lives and possessions. Such
> was their so highly vaunted courage, as the chronicles show
> clearly. Likewise, they did so much harm to the Latin language
> and to the works of scholars that it can never be made good.
> He who intends to acquire honor by arson, murder, and war
> must be able to do so in the name of a just cause, otherwise it
> will be seen that he is animated by the grossest brutality, not by
> courage.[37]

[37] From the Swedish sixteenth-century chronicle by Olaus Petri.

4: The Turk as Bogeyman

WE HAVE SAID that the sixteenth century contributed nothing new to the idea of European union: had it not been for the Turks it would have contributed even less. To be sure, the Turks besieged Vienna in 1552, spreading alarm throughout Christendom. However, Don Juan of Austria defeated their navy at Lepanto in 1571. Did no one see that Europe was being harmed more by its own internecine wars than by the Turks? At all events, union was proposed only in the mythical name of a Crusade, the traditional rallying cry, and one heard with favor by the princes.

Thus the Spanish humanist Juan Luis Vives (born at Valencia in 1492, died at Bruges in 1542; he was at Louvain with Erasmus, and later went to England where he was employed by Henry VIII) reached the conclusion that in order to pacify Europe, it would be enough to enlist the support of a few princes and their advisers. To this end, he wrote to the Pope: "What is above all expected of you is to make peace among the princes . . . Say that war between Christians is criminal; condemn it absolutely, as a quarrel between members of one and the same body . . ." [38]

This exhortation having been of no avail, he resorted to the Turkish argument, in a letter to the king of England: "There are two or three of you in the Christian world: the victories of the Turk have put us in extreme danger: and you would quarrel among yourselves! What God is going to give you His protection?" [39]

His best known work bears the significant title of *De Europae dissidiis et bello Turcico dialogus*. In it, Vives goes back, follow-

[38] Letter to Pope Adrian VI, October 12, 1522.
[39] Letter to Henry VIII, January 13, 1531.

[88]

ing Machiavelli and so many other Renaissance writers, to the old Greek theme of the opposition between Asia and Europe:

Aristotle, great votary of wisdom, and with him many other great men who dedicated themselves to the strenuous study of Nature and the causes of things, all testify that the most vigorous, most courageous, and hardiest race is that which populates Europe; that the Asians are timorous and unsuitable for war, being more like women than men. Indeed, Europe produces not only men superior to others in courage and strength, but the same is true of her wild animals. The lions born in Europe are more courageous than Punic lions; the same is true of dogs, wolves and other animals, although those of Africa seem to be more ferocious . . .

The disunity of Europe, particularly the one that broke out among the princes of Constantinople, delivered Asia into Turkish hands; it opened the gates of Thracia to them. Later, the dissensions among the kings of Europe, and the wars arising Hydra-headed one from the other, encouraged the Turks to penetrate even deeper into Europe . . . Anyone can keep a firm hand on the rudder as long as seas are calm. But by your fault so many successes further emboldened the Turks. Occasionally art succeeds in correcting some defects of Nature, but does not destroy their roots; and when art withdraws, Nature always comes back, gradually, into her own, and when art is suppressed or proves impotent, Nature demands imperiously what is hers. If the wind abated a little and if you turned your hatred and your fury against the Turk, you would know at once what the temple of the Asians is worth. Adversity would reveal what an uninterrupted series of successes had hidden, and would show most clearly that the Turks had not been victorious because of their own strength and courage, but because of your errors.

. . . The Christians are still in possession of the most solid part of Europe—Germany. Let them stop fighting one another, or else they are lost. Let them fortify Germany, yes, let them fortify it by walls and citadels, but first of all, let them work in common to prevent the Turk from laying hands on Germany; otherwise there is no hope that the whole West will not fall to the Turkish power, and that those who refuse to live under this yoke will not be safe from the attacks of this tyrant goaded by the gadfly af avidity and ambition. What redoubt could we provide to stop him if the Turk seized Germany? Any other obstacle would be a house of cards. It is painful to have to say that only weakness could be set against the sovereign of Germany and so many races and kingdoms. It is true that Europe is very strong; but what use would this be to her, if the Turk held the best part of Europe?

Vives here agrees with another champion of resistance to the Turks, Kaspar Peucer (1525–1602), German scholar, son-in-law of Melanchthon, whose belief that Europe could be saved only by the *pulchra coniuncto* of Germany, France, and Italy he shared. According to these Lutherans, it was primarily the support of the German states that was needed for the creation of a *respublica cristiana* in Europe, that is, a federation that was to be both antipapal and anti-imperial.

For his part, Vives, in a work complementary to the one just quoted, *De concordia et discordia in Humano Genere*,[40] advances the need for "a general reconstruction of Europe," but does not indicate the means to be used to this end. The "grand designs" were not to appear until a hundred years later:

Thereafter, in many wars which were begotten one on the other with extraordinary fertility, all Europe suffered gigantic damages, so that it needs a great and almost universal reconstruction in nearly every domain: but nothing is more urgent than an immediate reconciliation and concord, communicated to and extended over all human activities.

Finally, we find the conceptions of the Catholic Vives and the Lutherans Peucer and Melanchthon taken up and developed by a Calvinist. In *Political and Military Discourses*, written in captivity in the Spanish Low Countries, by the great Huguenot soldier François de la Noue, known as Bras-de-Fer, "Iron Arm" (1531–1591), we read: "The Christian Princes acting in close unity can drive the Turks from Europe in four years." La Noue proposes a federation of the Christian princes, to be convoked at Augsburg, the Emperor presiding: "Having set up such a federation, it would be useful to go further and to find effective means to continue it for at least the span of four years."

For all its moderation, this project had no more results than the others.

Finally, we may quote in this context Guillaume Postel (1510–

---

[40] *Opera*, II, 501, 59.

1581), an eccentric and polyglot humanist. (He wrote in French, Italian, and Latin, and translated the Scriptures from the Hebrew and the Greek into Arabic.) Postel believes in the universal monarchy, but differently from Dante. Having lived a long time in the East, he wants first to convert the Moslems or "Ismaelians" by propagating "a sensible Christianity." Then, once all are sharing the same religion: "Let us, if possible, give the whole world a single prince . . . the best image of the only God from whence proceeds the order of the universe."

This universal monarch can be only the king of France, since the king is a direct descendant of Japheth's eldest son, Gomer, who according to Josephus founded the Gallic race. . . . However, Postel is far from considering himself a "Gallic" imperialist. In one of his books, *La République des Turcs* (1560), he repeatedly calls himself *cosmopolite*. He is today looked upon as the inventor of this term, which was subsequently destined to have a very checkered career.

5: The "Grand Designs" of the Seventeenth Century

IT WAS THE seventeenth century that drew certain constructive conclusions, both philosophical and specifically political, from the welter of ideas advanced during the Renaissance and the Reformation.

Four plans of vast scope contributed to this effort to "put things in order" which seems to have been the motto of the century. Today we discover in them several rather profound similarities. All of them are utopias, presented as such—even though Sully's plan is to some extent inspired by political realism, and William Penn's by shrewd economic considerations. All four plans vigorously stress the need for a European federation, as well as the unavowed fear of the epoch in the face of the absolutist claims of the states All of them are the works of profoundly religious, but "ecumenical" minds, in the sense the latter word has assumed in our own day: their aim is to bring together the Christian denominations and achieve the unity ordained by the Gospels. All four, finally, having been so to speak unnoticed at the time, have survived the contemporary "realistic" treaties that were quickly obliterated by the movement of history, and have not ceased to act upon the imaginations of institutional creators down to the present day. We shall quote them in the chronological order: Crucé (1623), Sully (1638), Comenius (1645), and William Penn (1692).

EMERIC CRUCÉ's *Le Nouveau Cynée*

Little is known about this author of the earliest plan providing for the union not only of Christian Europe but of the whole world known at the time. He was born in the last quarter of the sixteenth century and died in 1648. He was a monk, master in some college in Paris, where he taught mathematics, and he published a few ponderous works, on the basis of which German scholars called him "a little Paris schoolteacher." [41] This obscure individual nonetheless had the courage to address himself to all the princes of Europe, in the dedication of his great treatise which was published in Paris: *Le Nouveau Cynée ou discours d'Estat représentant les occasions et moyens d'établir une paix generalle et la liberté du commerce par tout le monde. Aux monarques et princes souverains de ce temps.* ("The New Cyneas or Political Discourse Expounding the Opportunities and Means for Establishing General Peace and Freedom of Trade Throughout the World. To the Monarchs and Sovereign Princes of Our Time.") Its 249 big pages are not divided into chapters, and the entire text consists of only two paragraphs!

Peace is a trivial subject I confess, but it is only half searched for. Some exhort the Chirtsian Princes to it, in order that by their union they should fortify themselves against their common enemy; and even a famous personage has shown the means to exterminate the Turks in four years or thereabouts, and several

[41] Ernest Nys, "Emeric Crucé," *Etudes de Droit International,* Vol. I (1896).

other beautiful conceptions that are very easy to write out. There are those who limit even more their style, they give inventions to police and enrich their countries, and think so little of strangers, that they consider it a prudent policy to sow among them dissensions, in order to enjoy a more assured quiet.[42]

But I am of a very different opinion, and it seems to me that when you see the house of your neighbor burning or falling, that you have a cause for fear, as much as for compassion; since human society is one body, of which all the members are in sympathy in such a manner that it is impossible for the sicknesses of the one not to be communicated to the others.

Must it be that the monarchs establish themselves by massacres and butcheries? . . . But supposing that war were necessary to found monarchies. Now that they are established, it is no longer necessary for those who enjoy them to fill the world with carnage.

Later Crucé will insist on this idea of preserving the status quo, which was dear to Erasmus, as we have seen. War is "profitless" because it pulls down thrones, even that of the Great Turk.

On the other hand the Christians do not advance their affairs better: And besides they have this misfortune, that if they obtain a victory, they do not enjoy it for any long time, on the contrary the Turks maintain themselves, and do not easily let themselves be dispossessed of their possessions. I compare these two peoples, since they are so to speak natural enemies, and have divided almost all the world into two parts, because of the diversity of their religions, so much so that if they could agree, it would be a great step forward for universal peace.

There is no need to emphasize the analogy with our own "two blocs." According to Crucé, the surest means for preventing war is arbitration, an idea taken over from the Middle Ages:

Before resorting to arms [the Princes should] resort to the arbitration of the sovereign Potentates and Lords: which doing they will gain the friendship of their fellow beings, to turn to account against their enemies, in case they did not wish to submit to the judgment of a third party. Now if a Prince receives a judge who wished imperiously to meddle in arranging differences, that truly would debase his grandeur; but to accept voluntarily arbitrators is a thing formerly practiced and which is

[42] An allusion to Jean Bodin, quoted above.

practiced still among Monarchs . . . And for this the general assembly of which we speak hereafter would serve admirably. . . . How is it possible, some one will say, to bring in accord peoples who are so different in wishes and affections, as the Turk and the Persian, the Frenchman and the Spaniard, the Chinese and the Tatar, the Christian and the Jew or the Mahometan? I say that such hostilities are only political, and cannot take away the connection that is and must be between men. The distance of places, the separation of domiciles does not lessen the relationship of blood. It cannot either take away the similarity of natures, true base of amity and human society. Why should I a Frenchman wish harm to an Englishman, a Spaniard, or a Hindoo? I cannot wish it when I consider that they are men like me, that I am subject like them to error and sin and that all nations are bound together by a natural and consequently indestructible tie.

The same tolerance must be extended to the sphere of religion:

Is it necessary to wage war for the diversity of ceremonies, I will not say religion, since the chief object of these lies in the adoration of God, who demands rather the heart of men, than the exterior worship and sacrifices, of which so much parade is made: Not that I wish to conclude to the disdain of ceremonies; but I say that we should not persecute those who do not wish to embrace ours. . . . Piety is too good a tree to produce such bad fruits, as are revenges, hatred and scandals . . . while we try to go up to heaven by the means of religion, let us take care not to fall into a stupid and inhuman brutality . . . All these religions are based on evidence, alleging their miracles, and each one presumes that his is the best. I have not undertaken to solve this difficulty. A more knowing one than I would be confused: only I will say that all the religions tend to the same end, namely, the recognition and adoration of the Divinity. And if some do not choose the good road or the legitimate way, it is more from simplicity and ill teaching than from malice, and therefore they are more worthy of compassion than of hatred. . . . [Only the simpleton thinks that] all are held to live like him, and only prizes his customs, according to the way of those simpletons of Athens, who thought the moon of their country better than that of others. Sage and divine souls see much further, and consider that the harmony of the world is composed of diverse opinions, and that which is praiseworthy in one place, is not found good everywhere . . . [We must recognize] that men are very variegated, and that what is honored in one place, is abominated or mocked in another.

Crucé imagines a permanent Assembly or Senate of the States:

Suppose for instance that peace is signed to-day, that it is published to the whole world: how do we know that posterity will ratify the articles? Opinions are changeable, and the actions of the men of the present time do not bind their successors . . . Nevertheless, to prevent the inconvenience of this, it would be necessary to choose a city, where all sovereigns should have perpetually their ambassadors, in order that the differences that might arise should be settled by the judgment of the whole assembly. The ambassadors of those who would be interested would plead there the grievances of their masters and the other deputies would judge them without prejudice.

He proposes that the seat of the assembly be in the territory of Venice,

because it is practically neutral and indifferent to all Princes; added thereto that it is near the most important monarchies of the earth, of those of the Pope, the two Emperors, and the King of Spain. It is not far from France, Tatary, Moscovy, Poland, England, and Denmark.

Concerning the grave matter of precedence, Crucé goes into lengthy considerations. "Being Catholic and French," he has many ideas on the subject, but he has made up his mind "not to think of himself only," but on the contrary to speak as though he had been born "in Plato's imaginary republic or in the region of his Ideas." And so, he ends up by proposing that the Pope "be given precedence, out of respect for ancient Rome," but— an almost unthinkable revolution!—the Turkish Sultan should come right after him, "considering that he holds the seat of the eastern empire." Next would come "the Christian emperor," then the King of France, "considering that he heads the most renowned nation in the world," and then the King of Spain.

The sixth place can be contested between the Kings of Persia, China, Prester John, the Precop of Tatary and the Grand Duke of Moscovy . . . And the kings of Great Britain, Poland, Denmark, Sweden, Japan, Morocco, the Great Mogul, and other monarchs as well from India as Africa, must not be in the last ranks, all brave Princes, who maintain themselves and do not depend on anyone . . . And to give more authority to the judgment, one would take advice of the big republics, who would have likewise their agents in this same place. I say great Republics, like those of the Venitians and the Swiss, and not those small lordships, that cannot maintain themselves, and depend upon the protection of another. . . . This company therefore would judge then the debates which would arise not only about precedence, but about other things, would maintain the ones and the others in good understanding; would meet discontents half way, and would appease them by gentle means, if it could be done, or, in case of necessity, by force. . . . That if anyone rebelled against the decree of so notable a company, he would receive the disgrace of all other Princes, who would find means to bring him to reason.

In the first part of his treatise, Crucé asks what the nations would do if they no longer had war as "exercise." He proposes a plan for educating the nations (to begin with, sciences, medicine, and mathematics), a plan for developing handicraft industries and a plan for organizing the territories—rivers are to be made navigable, canals are to link "the two seas," agricultural methods and trade are to be renovated, new lands put under cultivation, swamps drained, etc. And he exclaims:

What a pleasure it would be, to see men go here and there freely, and mix together without any hindrance of country, ceremonies, or other such like differences, as if the earth were as it really is, a city common to all.

Toward the end of his work he takes up again and develops this theme of the free circulation of goods and persons:

Those are the means to maintain peace especially in each monarchy. There are others more universal, which concern the good relations of all sovereigns respectively one with the other, of which the first and most important is, that they content themselves with the limits of their lordship, which shall be prescribed to them by the general assembly, of which we have spoken. This point being settled it will be necessary to agree how the individuals of diverse nations can meet and trade together in safety, and that if some trial or dispute arises between them, that the magistrate of the locality will promptly bring them into accord without favors or orders from anyone. For since it is a question of a universal peace, justice must be rendered to foreigners, and they must not be permitted to be harmed in any way by natives of the country, when they come there for their business or even for their pleasure.

Crucé saw clearly that this freedom of trade—diametrically opposed to the national protectionism which was beginning to weigh upon European economic life—required other measures:

. . . it is necessary that Princes of a common consent reduce the money to one similar standard, so that each person may make a contract everywhere without damage.

And he advocates the uniformity of weights and measures . . .

But in order to begin this affair properly, it would be necessary that a powerful Prince should exhort all the others to follow the regulation described above, in order that the passages being free and commerce being open by means of peace, one can trade everywhere without damage. There is no one more capable of that than the Pope. It is his duty to bring about a general concord between the Christian Princes. And as regards the Mahometans, who form a notable part of the world, the King of France, on account of the credit and reputation that he has among them, will more easily make them condescend to peace. . . .

As for me I can in this bring only wishes and humble remonstrances, which perhaps will be useless. I have wished, nevertheless, to leave this testimony to posterity. If it serves nothing, patience. It is a small matter, to lose paper, and words. I shall protest in that case like Solon of having said and done what was possible for me for the public good, and some few who read this little book, will be grateful to me for it, and will honor me as I hope with their remembrance.[43]

Crucé's dissertation met with no more success than the projects of his predecessors. But those who scorned it are forgotten, while he is not. He has quietly made his way through a series of works many of which are famous. The young Leibniz read and remembered him: later he wrote about him to the Abbé de Saint-Pierre, who via Rousseau, Kant, Saint-Simon, Proudhon, Hugo, Renan, and Coudenhove, comes close to the position of

[43] *The New Cyneas of Emeric Crucé,* trans. Thomas Willing Balch (Philadelphia: Allen, Lane and Scott, 1909).

Briand and the League of Nations, Churchill, The Hague Congress, and the great debates of our own day.

THE DUC DE SULLY'S "GRAND DESIGN"

For three centuries everyone has referred to it, but almost no one has read it. Can we even be sure it exists? During the last war, the Atlantic Charter, too, had a great moral influence, although neither Churchill nor Roosevelt had ever been able to produce its text: the Charter existed only in their heads and in the statements they made to journalists from a few scribbled notes.

Nor is it possible to *quote* the Grand Design: its elements are scattered in the thousands of pages of Sully's *Memoirs,* of which moreover we have several versions. The first two parts dated 1638 were not "put in circulation"; the third part was published in 1662 with the two others; an elegant digest of the three parts by the Abbé de l'Ecluse (1745) gave the public at large a heavily revised work; finally, there are modern editions, in which the original text is more or less faithfully restored and often "improved." These *Memoirs* [44] were actually written by four anonymous secretaries on the basis of a gigantic hodgepodge of documents, copies of letters, rough drafts of speeches, financial statements, notes, recollections, dictations, balance sheets, etc. The secretaries tell the story of his life to the old minister confined in his château after the death of the king his master, and they address the minister in the second person plural—which is not without producing a singular effect!

Sully, who hoped to influence Richelieu, ascribes the Grand Design to Henry IV, more than twenty years after the king's death. The successive stages of the plan he reveals to us (in the form of apocryphal letters or speeches) defy quotation by the

[44] Here is the beginning of the original title: *Mémoires des sages et royales (Economies d'Estat, domestiques, politiques et militaires de Henry le Grand, l'Examplaire des Roys, le Prince des Vertus, des Armes et des Loix, et le Père en effet de ses Peuples François, et des servitudes utiles, obéissances convenables et administrations loyales de Maximilien de Béthune . . .*

length of the sentences and the disorderly presentation. However, here is a rather short fragment in which, by rare good
luck, the Design is summed up, though only partially. Sent on
mission to James I, Sully seeks to win over England to Henry
IV's projects against the Hapsburgs:

In accordance with the message sent you by the king of England, you went to Greenwich on the following day at 1 P.M. You
were received, as seems to us, by the Count Derby, and brought
to the king of England, who immediately took you by the hand,
and commanding that no one should follow him, even his own
councillors, he led you into his galleries. Having closed the
doors he embraced you twice, then praised the king's virtues
and your frankness, and reiterated that he considered himself
very much obliged to the king his good brother for having thus
sent him his oldest and most trusted servant, the one in whom
he himself could have the greatest confidence. Whereupon seeing, as it seemed to you, that the occasion was very opportune
to broach some of the secret instructions and most important
proposals that the King had ordered you to make to him, but
speaking as though in your own name only, you replied to him
as follows:
"Sire, I wish you to know that however I might appear to you
involved in wordly affairs, I nonetheless put the glory of God,
my salvation, and maintenance of the true religion that I profess
above the King my master, my fortune, my wife, my children,
my country, and all other human considerations. Now, I have
recognized that the Pope, the Emperor, the king of Spain, the
archdukes, the ecclesiastical princes of Germany, and all other
lords and Catholic communities, have no stronger passion in
mind than to form a powerful union aimed at the ruin and destruction of every faith contrary to the Roman. They had to
delay working openly to that end only because they have not
yet been able to obtain the adherence of the king my master to
the same design. But it is to be feared that should I fall from
his favor (for the favor of princes is subject to change), and
being exposed to continual solicitations, he might let himself be
persuaded in the end, if he is not kept from such a course by
other ways and means acceptable to his generous mind (for it
is this virtue of magnanimity which holds first place in his soul),
which ways and means are those I wish to communicate to Your
Majesty, and which you will also find capable of increasing your
own power and authority, of enlarging your dominions, of con-

tributing to the happiness of your reign, of exalting your honor and your glory, and of perpetuating your renown, which is the second goal of my desires. Upon you alone depends the execution of the things I wish to propose, which consist in attempting to form, if I have the means of so persuading the king my master, an offensive and defensive alliance between him, you, and the United Provinces of the Low Countries: This alliance could also include all other kings, princes, and above all those of Denmark and Sweden, the Protestant states, republics, cities and communities, which are so to speak always obliged to oppose the Spanish and Austrian faction. The alliance could be further cemented by the union of your [and my king's] children, when they reach an age that will make them suitable for each other. If I see that after studying my proposals you approve of them and agree to carry them out, I hope to obtain my king's approval, and be able to offer advantageous terms to other rulers. We shall obtain the adherence of the Duke of Savoy, by playing on his fickle-minded, turbulent disposition, and on his ambition to wear a royal crown. The most powerful Catholic princes of Germany can be induced to join us by the promise of wresting from the House of Austria, the imperial crown as well as Bohemia, Austria, Moravia, Silesia, and Lusatia, whose ancient privileges would be restored. Even the Pope himself might be won over by granting him the property of those lands in which he only holds vain feudal titles."

The king of England showed himself pleased with these proposals, and even praised and approved them, although at first only in general terms. However he expressed the wish to be informed in greater detail; whereupon he made many objections, pointing out the difficulty of uniting so many different princes, whose interests in the pursuit of such a high design were of the most varied kinds.

Your conversation with the king, on this subject as well as on several other very important ones, kept you locked up with him for more than four hours.

However, the Grand Design, initially only a project for a Protestant Alliance (even though it provides for the adherence of Catholic princes and the Pope himself), in the end assumes vaster proportions, aiming at a reorganization of all Europe. We quote here the masterful exposition that the historian Carl J. Burckhardt succeeded in extracting from the *Sages et royales Œconomies*:

Europe will be composed of:

5 elective monarchies: the German-Roman Empire, the Papal States, Poland, Hungary, and Bohemia;

6 hereditary monarchies: France, Spain, England, Denmark, Sweden, and Lombardy (that is, Savoy plus Milan);

4 sovereign republics: Venice, Italy, Switzerland, Belgium (for the definition of these territories, see below).

All the provinces of which these states will be composed are named; if there is disagreement on the attribution of a territory, it will be submitted directly to the central European authority, that is to say, it will become a mandate territory.

In area and resources, these states are to be approximately equal, so as to secure among them the greatest possible balance; the Catholic, Lutheran, and Calvinist religions will be similarly balanced.

This confederation of states will be supervised by a Council of Europe composed of six provincial Councils and one General Council.

The seats of the provincial Councils will be: Danzig for the northeastern kingdoms, Nuremberg for the German states, Vienna for eastern Europe, Bologna for the Italian countries, Constance for Switzerland, Lombardy, etc., and a city to be designated in western Europe for France, Spain, England, and Belgium.

The seat of the General Council will be in a Central-European city, to be designated each year from among the following cities: Metz, Luxembourg, Nancy, Cologne, Mayence, Trier, Frankfort, Wurzburg, Heidelberg, Speier, Worms, Strasbourg, Basel, and Besançon. We see that the Rhine is the principal artery of this new political configuration.

The General Council will be composed of represenatives of each of the states of the Christian republic, 40 experienced men in all, that is, 4 representatives for each of the great states and 2 for each of the smaller states.

These Councils will be given the power to settle all differences, whether between a sovereign and his people or between different states. Their task will be to solve the problems of common interest and to deal with all projects concerning the Christian commonwealth as a whole.

The Council of Europe has the powers and duties of a Senate, its members to be elected every three years.

The Council's decisions must be regarded by all states as binding and final. In relation to the Council, the sovereignty of the states will be no more than a conditional sovereignty.

As the basis of the European republic, Sully demands freedom of trade, and even abolition of customs barriers.

The border states of the 16 sovereignties composing the Christian republic of Europe must be strengthened against external enemies.

The kingdom of Hungary (including Lower Austria, Styria, Carinthia, Croatia, Bosnia, Slovenia, and Transylvania) is to serve as a bastion against the Turk. The king of Hungary is to be elected by the Pope, the Emperor, and the kings of France, Spain, England, Denmark, Sweden and Lombardy; each of these sovereigns will have the duty to act as an ally whenever Hungary is attacked. The same eight sovereigns will name the king of Bohemia. Similarly the kingdom of Poland will serve as Germany's outpost against the Muscovites and Tatars.

Every difference between Venice and her neighbors will be subject to arbitration; such differences will be settled by the king of Spain and the Swiss cantons. [The eight sovereigns named above will also have the duty to act as allies in relation to Venice and the kingdom of Sicily.]

Finally, Sully's plan provides for the territorial adjustments required in this reorganization of Europe:

Spanish sovereignty is limited to the Iberian peninsula. The other existing hereditary kingdoms—France, Great Britain, Denmark, and Sweden—keep their status quo.

The kingdom of Lombardy is formed by Savoy, the Piedmont, Monferrat, and Milan.

The Helvetian republic receives territorial additions—the Franche-Comté, Alsace, and Tyrol.

The republic of Belgium is composed of present-day Belgium and Holland.

Finally, an Italian republic will be formed, encompassing all the states which are not attributed to the Pope, Savoy, or Venice. This republic, made of the remaining territories will be placed under the sovereignty of the Pope.

According to Sully, Russia must not be admitted as a member of the Christian community.

In conclusion, C. J. Burkhardt compares Sully's Grand Design with the other European projects for perpetual peace:

These attempts . . . renewed time and again can be reduced to the same three motives: the hope that man will surmount the fatality of war by his own efforts; the hope for a supra-national justice, and above all, the awareness of a unique, common patrimony, in spite of all differences and conflicts among Europeans.

What distinguishes Sully's writings from those of his prede-cessors and contemporaries is that in his capacity as a statesman he starts from an entirely concrete and specific political context, and that later, as he evolves, as he slowly matures his plan, his desire to secure the primacy for his own nation recedes more and more into the background, until, in his old age, and almost excluded from the French community as a Protestant, he ends up by ardently wishing for a supra-national supreme power, compared to which the power of allegedly sovereign states will become relative—all this, as he told James I of England, in order to give peace to this continent which had seen so many dearly-bought victories, so many defeats, and so many disastrous peace treaties that it could not stand many more . . .

After many years he had spent as a mere spectator of human affairs, he succeeded in surmounting in himself the strongest power of his epoch, that power which in his youth had exposed him to action, to risk, to battle—the power of nationalism, then still young and pregnant with the future.[45]

COMENIUS' *The Universal Awakening*

Amos Comenius (latinized form of Jan Amos Komenski) was born in Moravia in 1592; he died in Holland in 1670. His prin-cipal title to fame is that more than anyone else he contributed, with his *Great Didactic* and numerous special treatises, to the creation of the science of education in Europe. His philosophical and theological investigations (he was the last bishop of the Union of the Moravian Brethren), as well as his educational ac-tivity, were to find their culmination and the expression of their profound unity in a work he did not complete: the *Universal Deliberation on the Reform of Human Affairs.* The *Panegersia,* or "Universal Awakening," which Comenius wrote at Elbing in 1645 and which was not published until 1666, was to serve as the Introduction to this great "pansophic" work. It bears the fol-lowing subtitle: *De rerum humanarum emendatione consultatio catholica ad genus humanum, ante alios vero Eruditos, Re-ligiosos, Potentes Europae.*

[45] Carl J. Burckhardt, *Vier historische Betrachtungen* (Zurich: Manesse Verlag, 1953), pp. 25–29, 48–49.

With a view to carrying out his reform, Comenius proposes the following: (1) an improved school system headed by a kind of international academy which is to aim at unifying all knowledge; (2) the creation of international agencies charged with the task of political co-ordination; and (3) the creation of a world Consistory which is to reconcile the Churches. The gigantic project for a world federation at once cultural, political, and religious, makes Comenius one of the great forerunners of a European union as well as of the ecumenical movement.

Let us note once again that the "world" referred to by Comenius is actually no more than the Christendom of his day—that is, Europe. Indeed, Comenius calls himself a European. In the *Praefatio ad Europeos* with which his *Panegersia* opens, he speaks—perhaps the first to do so—of "our European fatherland":

In order that we may stop dissembling our projects and our efforts, and work each for himself, I shall serve as an example, for my supreme goal is to proclaim Christ to all nations. This light must be brought to the other nations in the name of our European fatherland: and this is why we must first be united among ourselves; for we Europeans, we must be looked upon as travelers embarked on one and the same ship. I cannot be silent, for my hope is to allay the evils of war by my message, as though by an entirely harmonious music, otherwise I should be very guilty before God and before mankind. But I also see myself driven to this action by the efforts being made in our time, in Europe more than elsewhere, which carry the promise of great things.

Here are a few excerpts from the *Panegersia:* [46]

6. It is important, I say, to give the Scholars vigilant guardians as assistants; their task will be to exhort and instruct them in their principal mission, which is to eliminate all remnants of ignorance and error in the human mind. Similarly, guardians should be given to the Priests, in order to help them drive out whatever still survives of atheism, Epicureanism, and impiety. And guardians should assist the Powerful lest the seeds of discord sprout again through excess of zeal; or, should this happen, to extirpate it in good time.

[46] They are taken from John Amos Comenius, *Pages choisies,* with an Introduction by Jean Piaget (UNESCO, 1957).

9. . . . But guardians of men's salvation must be appointed; Christ Himself, in His eternal wisdom urges us to do just this in the famous passage, Matt. 23:8–10, when He tells us not to establish among men the government of a single chief, the dominion of one master or the wisdom of one sage. For he forbids that anyone in the world should have himself called Master, Father, or Leader, names that must be reserved for ecclesiastical scholars and statesmen.

This means that no other thing should be introduced save the teaching common to all of us, who are united by brotherly bonds, according to which all of us obey only our Father in Heaven and the Christ who was given us as our sole Master and Leader.

10. Consequently, in each of the three states there shall be instituted a guiding body. The supreme chief of each of these bodies will be that Hermes Trimegistes [47] (the thrice great interpreter of God's will for man—the supreme prophet, the supreme priest, the supreme king,) that is to say, Christ who alone has the power to direct all things. However, in the interest of order, everywhere the ones will be subordinated to the others, so that, thanks to this graduated subordination, the school of Christ, the temple of Christ, and the kingdom of Christ may be firmly established. . . .

12. It will be useful to adopt different names for these tribunals: the tribunal of the Scholars might be called the *Council of Light;* the ecclesiastical tribunal, the *Consistory;* and the political tribunal, the *Court of Justice.*

13. The Council of Light will see to it that there is no need anywhere in the world for one man to give instruction to another—every man should possess some useful knowledge—and that all men are instructed by God. Which means, that this Council, by creating favorable occasions, will make it possible for all men in the world to turn their eyes toward that light in which all will see, of themselves, the truth unmarred by errors and chimeras.

14. The World Consistory will see to it that all the bells of the horses and all the pots (Zech. 14:20) are dedicated to the Eternal, and that Jerusalem is not delivered to destruction but is henceforth safe (Zech. 14:11); that is to say, that all the earth in its fullness is dedicated to God; that there is no scandal, nor scandalous writings, engravings, paintings, etc., but that there is

[47] Hermes Trimegistes is the Hellenistic Greek name for Toth, the Egyptian god of weights, measures, numbers, and inventor of hieroglyphics. The Greeks identified him with their own Hermes.

everywhere a profusion of holy symbols, so that each man, wherever he turns, may find matter for holy reflection.

15. Finally the Court of Peace will see to it that nowhere does a nation rise against another nation, and that no one dares come forth to teach methods of making arms and using them; that all swords and lances be turned into ploughshares and scythes (Isa. 2:4, etc.).

16. Consequently, all the learned bodies (as at present the *Academia dei Lincei* in Italy, the Académie des Jeux floraux in France, Société fructifère in Germany, etc.), will do well to unite into a single Council of Light; for it is the eternal Father of Light himself who invites them to form a union and community of light . . .

17. And all the consistories or councils of elders of the Christian churches (such as there are among the Romans, the Greeks, the Ethiopians, the Reformed, etc.) will do well to merge into a single Consistory of the Church, such as is prefigured by the Jerusalem "marvellously builded," the only city where are set the thrones of judgment, the thrones of the house of David (Ps. 122:3,5).

18. And all the tribunals of the world will do well to become a single tribunal of Christ; for, once all the kingdoms of the world are handed over to him (Ps. 72:11; Dan. 7:14; Rev. 11:15), the king will reign according to justice, and the princes will govern with equity (Isa. 32:1).

WILLIAM PENN'S *Essay*

We have seen the plans proposed by a French monk, a Huguenot duke, and a Moravian bishop. Here now is the plan of an English dissenter, who unlike his predecessors had already founded a state. Montesquieu called him "the modern Lycurgus."

Son of a rich and noble admiral who sent him very young to France to learn the profession of arms, William Penn turned Quaker on his return to England, and for this reason was imprisoned several times in the Tower of London. In quittance of a claim on Charles II which his father bequeathed him, Penn obtained from the Crown the vast American territory which was to take his family's name. This took place in 1681, Louis XIV being king of France, and William Penn being thirty-seven years of age. He gave Pennsylvania the most tolerant, most democratic, and most peace-minded constitution Western history had ever known.

It was during a brief interruption in his career as governor (1692–1694) that he wrote his *Essay Towards the Present and Future Peace of Europe,* as well as other moral and historical works. He returned to England in 1701 leaving the government of his state to his descendants, and died in 1718.

The situation in Europe at the time William Penn wrote his *Essay* is well known: Louis XIV's aggression against the Palatinate provoked the Grand Alliance of 1689, under the leadership of William III of Orange, who had become king of England. The war spread. It was this spectacle of "the bloody Tragedies of this War, in Hungary, Germany, Flanders, Ireland, and at Sea" that moved the pacifist Quaker and pioneer legislator from the vantage point of the New World to write, "I have undertaken a Subject that I am very sensible requires one of more sufficiency than I am Master of to treat it, as, in Truth, it deserves, and the groaning State of Europe calls for." These are his opening words. The first three sections are devoted to showing why peace is desirable: that the true means to bring it about is justice, not war. "Thus Peace is maintained by *Justice,* which is a Fruit from Society, and *Society* from Consent."

The fourth section, excerpts from which are given below, introduces a project for a federation of princes, similar to that of Crucé, although it cites Henry IV (i.e., Sully's Grand Design) and the example of the United Provinces of the Low Countries.

. . . If the *Soveraign Princes of Europe,* who represent that Society, or Independent State of Men that was previous to the Obligations of Society, would for the same Reason that engaged Men first into Society, *viz: Love of Peace and Order,* agree to meet by their Stated Deputies in a *General Dyet, Estates,* or *Parliament,* and there establish Rules of Justice for Soveraign Princes to observe one to another; and thus to meet Yearly, or once in Two or Three Years at farthest, or as they shall see Cause, and to be stiled, *The Soveraign or Imperial Dyet, Parliament or State of Europe;* before which Soveraign Assembly, should be brought all Differences depending between one Soveraign and another, that can not be made up by private Embassies, before the Sessions begin; and that if any of the Soveraignities that Constitute these Imperial States, shall refuse to submit their Claim or Pretensions to them, or to abide and perform the Judgment thereof, and seek their Remedy by Arms . . . all the other Soveraignties, United as One Strength, shall compel the Submission and Performance of the Sentence, with Damages to the Suffering Party, and Charges to the Soveraignties that obliged their Submission. To be sure, *Europe* would quietly obtain the so much desired and needed Peace, to *Her harassed Inhabitants* . . .

SECT. VII. OF THE COMPOSITION OF THESE IMPERIAL STATES.

The Composition and Proportion of this *Soveraign Part,* or *Imperial State,* does, at the first Look, seem to carry with it no small Difficulty what votes to allow for the Inequality of the Princes and States. But with Submission to better Judgments, I cannot think it invincible; For if it be possible to have an Estimate of the Yearly Value of the several Soveraign Countries, whose Delegates are to make up this August Assembly, The Determination of the Number of Persons or Votes in the States for every Soveraignty will not be impracticable. Now that *England, France, Spain,* the *Empire,* &c., may be pretty exactly estimated, is so plain a Case, by considering the Revenue of Lands, the Exports and Entries at the Custom Houses, the Books of Rates, and Surveys that are in all Governments, to proportion Taxes for the Support of them, that the least Inclination to the *Peace of Europe* will not stand or halt at this Objection . . .

I suppose the *Empire of Germany* to send Twelve; *France,* Ten; *Spain,* Ten; *Italy,* . . . Eight; *England,* Six; *Portugal,* Three; *Sweedland,* Four; *Denmark,* Three; *Poland,* Four; *Venice,* Three; the *Seven Provinces,* Four; *The Thirteen Cantons,* and little *Neighbouring Soveraignties,* Two; Dukedoms of *Holstein* and *Courland,* One; And if the *Turks* and *Muscovites* are taken in, as seems but fit and just, they will make *Ten apiece more.* The *Whole* makes Ninety. A great Presence when they represent the *Fourth and now The Best and Wealthiest Part of the Known World; where Religion and Learning, Civility and Arts have their Seat and Empire.* . . . The Place of their First Session should be Central, as much as is possible, afterwards as they agree.

SECT. VIII. OF THE REGULATIONS OF THE IMPERIAL STATES IN SESSION.

To avoid Quarrel for Precedency, the Room may be Round, and have divers Doors to come in and go out at, to prevent Exceptions. If the whole Number be cast in Tens, each chusing One, they may preside by Turns, to whom all Speeches should be addressed, and who should collect the Sense of the Debates, and state the Question for a Vote, which, in my Opinion, should be by the *Ballot* after the Prudent and Commendable Method of the *Venetians:* Which, in a great Degree, prevents the ill Effects of Corruption; because if any of the Delegates of that High and Mighty Estates could be so Vile, False, and Dishonorable, as to be influenced by Money, they have the Advantage of taking their Money that will give it them and of Voting undiscovered to the Interest of their Principles, and their own Inclinations; . . . A Shrewd Stratagem and an Experimental Remedy against *Corruption,* at least Corrupting: For who will give their Money where they may so easily be Cozened, and where it is Two to One they will be so; for they that will take Money in such Cases, will not stick to Lye heartly to them that give it, rather than wrong their Country, when they know their Lye cannot be detected.

It seems to me, that nothing in this *Imperial Parliament* should pass, but by Three Quarters of the Whole, at least seven above the Balance. . . . All Complaints should be delivered in Writing in the Nature of *Memorials* and *Journals* kept by a proper Person, in a *Trunk or Chest,* which should have as many differing Locks, *as there are Tens in the States.* And if there were a *Clerk for each Ten,* and *a Pew or Table for those Clerks in the Assembly;* and at the End of Every Session *One out of each Ten* were appointed to Examine and Compare the *Journal of those Clerks,* and then lock them up as I have before expressed, it would be clear and Satisfactory. . . .

I will say little of the *Language* in which the *Session of the Soveraign Estates should be held,* but to be sure it must be in *Latin* or *French;* the first would be very well for Civilians, but the last more easie for Men of Quality.

SECT. IX. OF THE OBJECTIONS THAT MAY BE ADVANCED AGAINST THE DESIGN.

. . . The Second is, *That it will endanger an Effeminacy by such a Disuse of the Trade of Soldiery; That if there should be any Need for it, upon any Occasion, we should be at a Loss as they were* in Holland in 72.

There can be no Danger of Effeminacy, because each Soveraignty may introduce as temperate or Severe a Discipline in the Education of Youth, as they please, by Low Living, and due Labour. Instruct them in Mechanical Knowledge, and in Natural

Philosophy, by Operation, which is the Honour of the *German* Nobility. This would make them Men: Neither *Women* nor *Lyons:* for *Soldiers* are t'other Extream to Effeminacy. But the Knowledge of Nature, and the useful as well as agreeable Operations of Art, give Men an Understanding of themselves, of the World they are born into, how to be useful and serviceable, both to themselves and others: and how to save and help, not injure or destroy. The Knowledge of Government in General; the particular Constitutions of *Europe;* and above all of his own Country, are very recommending Accomplishments. This fits him for the *Parliament,* and *Council at Home,* and the *Courts of Princes and Services* in the *Imperial States abroad.* At least, he is a good Common-Wealths-Man, and can be useful to the Publick, or retire, as there may be Occasion.

The Third Objection is, *That there will be great Want of Employment for younger Brothers of Families; and that the Poor must either turn Soldiers or Thieves.* I have answer'd that in my Return to the Second Objection. We shall have the more *Merchants and Husbandmen,* or *Ingenious Naturalists,* if the Government be but any Thing Solicitous of the *Education of their Youth:* Which, next to the present and immediate Happiness of any Country, ought of all Things to be the *Care* and *Skill* of the Government. For such as the Youth of any Country is bred, such is the next Generation, and the Government in good or bad Hands.

I am come now to the last Objection, *That Soveraign Princes and States will hereby become not Soveraign; a Thing they will never endure.* But this also, under Correction, is a Mistake, for they remain as Soveraign at Home, as ever they were. Neither their Power over their People, nor the usual Revenue they pay them, is diminished: It may be the War Establishment may be reduced, which will indeed of Course follow, or be better employed to the Advantage of the Publick. So that the *Soveraignties* are as they were, for none of them have now any Soveraignty over one another: And if this be called a lessening of their Power, it must be only because the great Fish can no longer eat up the little ones, and that each Soveraignty is *equally defended* from Injuries, and disabled from committing them. . . .

SECTION X. OF THE REAL BENEFITS THAT FLOW FROM THIS PROPOSAL ABOUT PEACE.

I am come to my last Section, in which I shall enumerate some of those many real Benefits that flow from this Proposal, for the Present and Future *Peace of Europe.*

. . . So that besides the Loss of so many lives, of Importance to any Government, both for Labour and Propagation, the Cries of so many Widows, Parents and Fatherless are prevented, that cannot be very pleasant to the Ears of any Government, and is the *Natural Consequence of War in all Government*.

There is another manifest Benefit which redounds to *Christendom*, by this *Peaceable* Expedient, *The Reputation of Christianty will in some Degree be recovered in the Sight of Infidels*, which, by the many Bloody and unjust *Wars of Christians*, not only with them, but *one* with *another*, hath been greatly impaired. For, to the Scandal of that Holy Profession, *Christians*, that glory in their *Saviour's Name*, have long devoted the Credit and Dignity of it to their worldly Passions, as often as they have been excited by the Impulses of Ambition or Revenge. They have not always been in the Right: Nor has the Right been the Reason of *War:* And not only *Christians* against *Christians*, but the same sort of *Christians* have embrewed *their Hands in one another's Blood;* Invoking and Interesting, all they could, the *Good* and *Merciful God to prosper their Arms to their Brethren's Destruction*. . . .

The third Benefit is, that saves *Money*, both to the Prince and People; and thereby prevents those Grudgings and Misunderstandings between them that are wont to follow the devouring Expenses of *War;* and enables both to perform Publick Acts for *Learning, Charity, Manufactures, etc.* The Virtues of Government and Ornaments of Countries . . . I might mention *Pensions* to the *Widows* and *Orphans* of such as dye in Wars, and of those that have been *disabled* in them; which rise high in the Revenue of some Countries.

Our fourth Advantage is that the *Towns, Cities and Countries, that might be laid waste by the Rage of War, are thereby preserved:* A Blessing that would be very well understood in *Flanders* and *Hungary*, and indeed upon all the *Borders of Soveraignties*, which are almost ever the *Stages* of Spoil and Misery. . . .

The fifth Benefit of this Peace, is the *Ease and Security of Travel and Traffick:* An Happiness never understood since the *Roman Empire* has been broken up into so many *Soveraignties*. But we may easily conceive the Comfort and *Advantage* of travelling through the Governments of *Europe* by a *Pass* from any of the *Soveraignties* of it, which this League and State of *Peace* will *naturally make Authentick:* They that have travel'd *Germany*, where is so great a Number of *Soveraignties*, know the Want and Value of this Privilege, by the many *Stops and Exam-*

inations they meet with by the Way: But especially such as have made the *great Tour of Europe.*

THE CONCLUSION

. . . I confess that I have the Passion to wish heartily, that the Honour of Proposing and Effecting so Great and Good a Design, might be owing to England, of all the Countries in *Europe*, as something of the Nature of our Expedient was, in Design and Preparation, to the Wisdom, Justice, and Valour, of *Henry the Fourth of France*, Whose Superior Qualities raising his Character above those of His Ancestors, or Contemporaries, deservedly gave him the Stile of *Henry the Great.* [48]

The Abbé de Saint-Pierre's *Perpetual Peace*

These four great seventeenth-century projects were followed by that of the Abbé de Saint-Pierre, first published in 1712. Though it has become the most spoken of, it is far from the best of these projects. Its fame is due first to the fact that it struck his contemporaries with greater force than the earlier writers' projects had struck theirs, and, second, to the fact that the author was more roundly jeered than any other modern writer has been. Needless to say, neither this excessive honor nor this excessive indignity are justified.

Charles-Irénée Castel de Saint-Pierre (1658–1743) was born in the Cotentin, of a very old family of slender means. He entered the minor orders, but was never ordained priest. In Paris his career was launched under Fontenelle's auspices and he frequented the Marquise de Lambert's salon. He was admitted to the French Academy in 1695. Shortly before he had purchased the office of Almoner to Madame (the King's sister) which enabled him to frequent the Court. As secretary to the Abbé de Polignac, he was the French delegate to the peace congress at Utrecht (1712), where he could see at first hand how unsatisfactory the peace-making machinery was. Expelled from the Academy in 1716 for having spoken unfavorably of Louis XIV

---

[48] *An Essay Toward the Present and Future Peace of Europe* [By William Penn. *First published in 1693/94. John Bellows, Eastgate, Gloucester.*] (1914).

(who died in 1715), he founded the *Club de l'Entresol,* a club for free discussions, which got him into more trouble. "He had wit, learning, and indulged in wild fancies," Saint-Simon wrote in his *Mémoires.* Gentle and unassuming, forever devoting his energies to good causes, rather than in his own interest, "a public advocate," as he liked to call himself, famous for his conversation but no gossip, he died untroubled by the sarcastic reactions to his *Project.* The story goes that the last word in his life was "Hope."

The *Project for Perpetual Peace* was first published in Cologne without the name of the author, in 1712. Next year at Utrecht an enlarged version in two volumes appeared, to which a third was added in 1717. Finally an abridgment, this time signed, and dedicated to Louis XV, was published in Rotterdam in 1729. These works are rather poorly written, badly organized, and full of repetitions, and it is not easy to extract passages from them which do justice to the Abbé's constructive and original thinking. However, because of their historical, if not intrinsic, interest, we give below a number of passages from the Preface and the twelve principal articles of the *Project* of 1713. But let us first relate the unusual circumstances which inspired the good Abbé's *Project.*

During a trip in Normandy in the winter of 1706/7 his carriage turned over on a road which was in poor repair. This induced him to write a short *Mémoire sur la Réparation des chemins.* At the end of this book, without any transition, he adds:

I was making my last changes in this memoir, when the idea came to me for an institutional project which struck me as very fine. For two weeks it has absorbed me entirely. I feel the more inclined to go into it thoroughly because the more I consider it from different angles, the more advantageous I find it to the sovereigns. I propose the establishment of permanent arbitration among them, in order to settle their future differences without recourse to war, as well as in order to maintain perpetual intercourse among all nations. I may be mistaken, but there is reason to hope that a treaty may eventually be signed. . . . This hope fills me with joy and ardor at the loftiest undertaking the human mind can conceive. I do not know where all this will lead me, but I know what Socrates said: That a man goes far who has the courage to walk straight ahead for a long time.

Let us look now at the new trail the Abbé tried to blaze:

[*From the author's Preface.*]

About four Years ago, after having finish'd an Essay useful for the interiour Commerce of the Kingdom, being both an Eye-witness of the extreme Misery to which the People were reduc'd by the heavy Taxes, and also inform'd, by divers particular Relations, of the excessive Contributions, the Forragings, the Destructions, the Violences, the Cruelties, and the Murthers which the unhappy Inhabitants of the Frontiers of Christian States daily suffer; in short, being sensibly touched with the Evils which War causes to the Princes of *Europe,* and their Subjects, I took a Resolution to penetrate into the first Sources of this Evil, and to find out by my own Reflections, whether It was so inseparable from the Nature of Sovereignties and Sovereigns, as to be absolutely without Remedy; I applied myself to examine this Affair, in order to discover whether it was not possible to find out some practicable Means to terminate their future Differences *without War;* and so to render the Peace perpetual amongst them. . . .

I thought it necessary to begin, by making some Reflections upon the Happiness it would be, as well to the Sovereigns of *Europe,* as to private Men, to live in Peace, united by some permanent Society; and upon the Necessity they are at present in to have continual Wars with each other, about the Possession or Division of some Advantages; and finally upon the Means which they have hitherto used, either to avoid entering upon those Wars, or not to sink under them, when once they Have entered upon them.

I found that all those Means consisted in making mutual Promises, either in Treaties of Commerce, of Truce, of Peace, wherein Limits of Dominion, and other reciprocal Pretentions are regulated; or else in Treaties of Guarantie, or of League offensive and defensive, to establish, to maintain, or to re-establish the *Equilibrium* of Power between the Principal Houses; a System which hitherto seems to be the highest degree of Prudence, that the Sovereigns of *Europe,* or their Ministers, ever carried their Policy to.

I soon perceived, that so long as they contented themselves with such Methods, they would never have any sufficient Security for the Execution of Treaties, nor sufficient Means for terminating equitably, and above all *without War,* their future Differences. . . . 'Tis these Reflections that are the Subject of the first Discourse. I have reduced them all into two Heads, or two Propositions, which I propose to my self to demonstrate.

1st. *The present Constitution of* Europe *can never produce any thing else but almost continual Wars, because it can never procure any* sufficient Security *for the Execution of Treaties.*

2dly. *The* equilibrium *of Power between the House of* France, *and the House of* Austria, *cannot procure any* sufficient Security *either against Foreign Wars, or against Civil Wars, and consequently cannot procure any* sufficient Security *either for the Preservation of Territory, or for the Preservation of Commerce.* . . .

I afterwards consider'd, whether Sovereigns might not find some *sufficient Security* for the execution of mutual Promises, by establishing a permanent Arbitration; and I find, that if the eighteen Principal Sovereignties of *Europe,* in order to maintain the present Government, and to procure the Advantages of an uninterrupted Commerce between Nation and Nation, would make a Treaty of Union, and a Perpetual Congress, much after the Model, either of the seven Sovereignties of *Holland,* the thirteen Sovereignties of the *Swisses,* or the Sovereignties of *Germany,* and form an *European Union,* from what is best in those Unions, and especially in the *Germanic Union,* which consists of above two hundred Sovereignties: I found, I say, that the weakest would have a *sufficient Security,* that the great Power of the strongest could not hurt them; that every one would exactly keep their reciprocal Promises; that Commerce would never be interrupted, and that all future Differences would be terminated *without War,* by means of Umpires, a Blessing which can never be obtain'd any other Way. . . .

In examining the Government of the Sovereigns of *Germany,* I did not find that there would be more Difficulty in forming the *European Body* now, than formerly there was in forming the *Germanick Body,* in executing *in great* that which has been already executed *in little;* on the contrary, I found that there would be fewer Obstacles, and more Facility, in forming the *European Body;* and what greatly persuaded me that this Project was no Chimera, was the Information I received from one of my Friends, soon after I had shewn him the first Sketch of this Work: He told me that *Henry IV* had form'd a Project, which, in the main, was much the same; and so I found in the Memoirs of the Duke of Sully, his Prime Minister. . . .

I know the Weight of Prepossessions, and that they make more Impressions upon the Generality of Minds, than true Arguments, fetch'd from the very Bottom of the Subject, and from necessary Consequences of the first Principles; but I plainly foresee they will never be sufficient entirely to determine Spirits of the first Order; that They will be continually finding out Differences and Inequalities between the *European Society,* which I propose, and the Societies I quote as Models; that *Henry IV,* might after all be deceived in thinking That *possible,* which was in reality *impossible.* Thus I find myself obliged to demonstrate every Thing strictly. . . .

As for *practicable and sufficient Means,* which consist in the articles of a Treaty of Union, made to be to every one a *sufficient Security* for the Perpetuity of the Peace, I have spared no Pains to invent them, and I believe I have done it. . . .

The whole Project then is contain'd in this single Argument.

If the European Society, *which is propos'd, can procure for all the Christian Princes a* sufficient Security *for the Perpetuity of the Peace, both without and within their Dominions, there is none of them that will not find it more advantageous to sign the Treaty for the Establishment of that Society, than not to sign it.*

Now the European Society, *which is propos'd,* can procure, *for all the Christian Princes, a* sufficient Security *for the Perpetuity of the Peace both within and without their Dominions.*

Therefore there will be none of them but what will find it much more advantageous to sign the Treaty for the Establishment of that Society, than not to sign it.

The Major, or the first Proposition, contains the *Motives,* and the Proof of it may be found in the third Discourse after the Preliminary Discourses, which I thought necessary, in order to dispose the Mind of the Reader to conceive the Force of the Demonstration. The Minor, or the second Proposition, contains the Means; the Proof of it may be found in the fourth Discourse. As for the last Proposition, or the Conclusion, that is the End that I propos'd to my self in this Work. . . .

[Excerpts from the Fourth Discourse.]

ARTICLE I.—The present Sovereigns, by their under-written Deputies, have agreed to the following Articles. There shall be from this Day following a Society, a *permanent* and perpetual Union, between the Sovereigns subscribed, and if possible among all the Christian Sovereigns, in the Design to make the Peace unalterable in *Europe;* and in that View the Union shall make, if possible, with its Neighbours, the *Mahometan* Sovereigns, Treaties of League offensive and defensive, to keep each of them in Peace within the Bounds of his Territory, by taking of them, and giving to them, all possible reciprocal Securities.

The Sovereigns shall be perpetually represented by their Deputies, in a perpetual Congress or Senate, in a free City. . . .

ARTICLE II.—The *European* Society shall not at all concern itself about the Government of any State, unless it be to preserve the Fundamental Form of it, and give speedy and sufficient Assistance to the Princes in Monarchies, and to the Magistrates in Republicks, against any that are Seditious and Rebellious. . . .

ARTICLE IV.—Each Sovereign shall be contented, he and his Successors, with the Territory he actually possesses, or which he is to possess by the Treaty hereunto joyned. . . .

The Sovereigns shall not be suffered to make an Exchange of any Territory, nor to sign any Treaty among themselves, but with the Consent and under the Guaranty of the Union by the three fourths of the four and twenty Voices, and the Union shall remain Guarantee for the Execution of reciprocal Promises. . . .

ARTICLE VII.—The Deputies shall incessantly labour to digest all the Articles of Commerce in general, and of the different Commerces between particular Nations; but in such a manner as that the Laws may be equal and reciprocal towards all the Nations, and founded upon Equity. . . .

The Union shall establish in different Towns Chambers for maintaining of Commerce, consisting of Deputies authorized to reconcile, and to judge strictly and without Appeal, the Disputes that shall arise either upon Commerce, or other Matters between the Subjects of different Sovereigns, in value above ten thousand Livres; the other Suits of less Consequence shall be decided as usual by the Judges of the Place where the Defendant lives: Each Sovereign shall lend his Hand to the Execution of the Judgments of the Chambers of Commerce, as if they were his own Judgments. . . .

ARTICLE VIII.—No Sovereign shall take up Arms or commit any Hostility, but against him who shall be declared an Enemy to the *European* Society: But if he has any Cause to complain of any of the Members, or any Demand to make upon them; he shall order his Deputy to give a Memorial to the Senate in the City of Peace, and the Senate shall take care to reconcile the Differences by its mediating Commissioners; or if they cannot be reconciled, the Senate shall judge them by Arbitral Judgment by Plurality of Voices provisionally, and by the three fourths of the Voices definitively. . . .

The Sovereign who shall take up Arms before the Union has

declared War, or who shall refuse to execute a Regulation of
the Society, or a Judgment of the Senate, shall be declared an
Enemy to the Society, and It shall make War upon him, 'till he
be disarmed, and 'till the Judgment and Regulations be executed; and he shall even pay the charges of the War, and the
Country that shall be conquered from him at the time of the
Suspension of Arms, shall be for ever separated from his Dominions. . . .

ARTICLE IX.—There shall be in the Senate of *Europe,* four and
twenty Senators, or Deputies of the united Sovereigns, neither
more nor less; namely, *France, Spain, England, Holland, Savoy,
Portugal, Bavaria* and Associates, *Venice, Genoa* and Associates,
Florence and Associates, *Switzerland* and Associates, *Lorrain*
and Associates; *Sweden, Denmark, Poland,* the Pope, *Moscovy,
Austria, Courland* and Associates, *Prussia, Saxony, Palatine* and
Associates, *Hanover* and Associates, Ecclesiastical Electors and
Associates. Each Deputy shall have but one Vote. . . .

ARTICLE X.—The Members and Associates of the Union shall
contribute to the Expenses of the Society, and to the Subsidies
for its Security, each in Proportion to his Revenues, and to the
Riches of his People. . . .

ARTICLE XII.—None of the eleven fundamental Articles above-
named shall be in any Point altered, without the *unanimous*
Consent of all the Members; but as for the other Articles, the
Society may always, by the three fourths of the Voices, add or
diminish, for the common Good, whatever it shall think fit.[49]

Replying to objections raised mostly to the "utopianism" and
the "chimerical" nature of his *Project,* the Abbé wrote soberly:
"I grant it may well happen that European arbitration will only
develop but gradually, and may take two hundred years."

And he added: "At present my sole aim is to launch the
league with a Congress, to be held at The Hague or elsewhere."

Two hundred years later the first League of Nations was actually inaugurated in Geneva. But not until 1948 did a Congress
meet at The Hague, precisely for the purpose of "launching" the
European union. . . .

We have said that the *Project* owed its celebrity chiefly to
the jeers it provoked: it is a fact that they were not so much

[49] *A Project for Settling an Everlasting Peace in Europe* . . . [*By the
Abbot St. Pierre of the French Academy. London: Printed for J. Watts.*],
(1714).

forthcoming from the "reactionaries" of the period, as from "enlightened" minds. Men like Voltaire and Frederick II were writing at the good Abbé's expense; even champions of a federated Europe, such as Leibniz and Rousseau, expressed alarm at the Abbé's *Project*, fearing it might harm their cause.

Voltaire, speaking of military art:

> Je vous l'avoue, je formais des souhaits
> Pour que ce beau métier ne s'exerçat jamais
> Et qu'enfin l'équité fît régner sur la terre
> L'impraticable paix de L'Abbé de Saint-Pierre.

> [I must confess, I should have liked it,
> Were this noble profession never practiced
> and for equity at last to realize on earth
> the Abbé de Saint-Pierre's impracticable peace.]

Frederick II, in a letter to Voltaire: [50]

The Abbé de Saint-Pierre, who thought well enough of me to honor me with his correspondence, has sent me a fine work on how to re-establish peace in Europe. The thing is very practicable: all it lacks to be successful is the consent of all Europe and a few other such small details.

Leibniz, in connection with a plan for a European Catholic Tribunal: [51]

These are projects which are as likely to succeed as the Abbé de Saint-Pierre's, but since there is no law against novel-writing, why should we condemn his fiction, considering that it would bring back the golden age?

Rousseau, in his *Extrait du Project*:

If the Project is not carried out, it will not be because it is fantastical, but because men are stupid, and because it is a kind of folly to be wise when all around are mad.[52]

[50] Frederick II, *Œuvres*, XIV, 247.
[51] Letter to Grimarest, 1712. We shall quote it at greater length p. 129.
[52] "It is a great folly to want to be wise all by yourself."—*La Rochefoucauld*.

Bluntschli, Swiss international jurist of the nineteenth century:

This insipid chatterbox so feebly presented his idea as to make it ridiculous in statesmen's eyes.

The opinion of Cardinal Dubois is more often quoted: "It is the dream of a good man." To which Théodore Ruyssen adds: "But it is a dream that will go on haunting the conscience of mankind."

6: Some Utopians of the Period

BESIDES THE FIVE major projects published between 1623 and 1713, we have several dozen politico-mystical utopias, plans for federation and early pacifist tracts: often the titles alone would be worth quoting, in so far as they refer to Europe as an entity, but this would take up too much space. We shall confine ourselves to a few scattered examples from various parts of the continent.

In 1614, an anonymous work appeared in Cassel. The title was ten lines long. It begins thus: *Allgemeine und General Reformation der ganzen weiten Welt. Beneben der Fama Fraternitatis des löblichen Ordens des Rosenkreuz, an alle Gelehrten und Haüpter Europae geschrieben . . .*

Its author was a young Lutheran theologian, Valentin Andreae. It was inspired by the *Riforma generale dell'universo* by the Italian satirist Trajano Boccalini. Serious historians think today that the order of the Rosicrucians would never have existed were it not for this hoax; they claim that Descartes and Leibniz never met a single member of this society in the course of their travels, although they spared no effort to find one. However, it has been established that at the age of twenty Leibniz was secretary to a Rosicrucian confraternity at Nuremberg. . . .

In 1691, Goudet, a Swiss merchant, published in Holland a work that cannot be found today, and that is known only because it gave rise to a dispute between Jurieu and Pierre Bayle. Entitled *Eight Conversations between Irene and Ariste*, this work suggested that the Europeans should unite to divide the Ottoman Empire among them.[53] Perpetual peace was to be secured "by an army of 40,000 Swiss, equipped and kept under arms under an agreement among all the countries of Europe, as well as by 30,000 men recruited in other European nations." [54] Jurieu having wrongly denounced Bayle as the author of the tract, the latter was dismissed from his chair of philosophy at Rotterdam.

The Abbé de Saint-Pierre's *Project* was to give rise to a number of more or less similar works in the course of the eighteenth century.

In Italy appeared the *Progetto del Cardinal Alberoni per riddure l'Impero Turchesco all'obbedienza dei Principi Christiani e per dividere tra di essi la conquista del medesimo*.[55] The cardinal wanted to include in his project the Protestants and the Orthodox, but not the Pope! A European Congress, with headquarters at Regensburg was to be the instrument of permanent arbitration among the princes. In other words, he went back to the plans that had been advanced by the Abbé.

In Germany, Dr. Eobald Toze took up the idea in *Die allgemeine Christliche Republik in Europa* (Mecklemburg, 1752). He reviewed the projects of "Henry IV" (Sully), Goudet, and the Abbé, and judged them to be unrealistic, because incompatible with the triumphant principle of state sovereignty. He pins his hopes only on a slow development of "the spirit of justice, love for one's fellow man, and self-control, both among the princes and among the peoples." [56]

In a manuscript discovered at Nancy (dating from 1748), King Stanislas Leczinski criticizes the Abbé's *Project*, and proposes that the King of France should head a "union of European republics." With generous optimism he says, "no republic has ever waged war for self-aggrandizement."

[53] This is one of the *Hundred Projects for the Partition of Turkey* listed by Djuvara in a book of that title (Paris, 1914).
[54] Cf. Chr. L. Lange, *op. cit.*, II, 183.
[55] Text in *Rivista di diretto internazionale*, Series II, Vol. II (Rome, 1913).
[56] Cf. Chr. L. Lange, *op. cit.*, II, 269 f.

A French adventurer, author of a work on economics, Ange Goudar, brought out an essay entitled *La paix de l'Europe ne peut s'établir qu'à la suite d'une longue trêve: par le Chevalier G.* (Rotterdam, 1757). According to him, the situation in Europe is rather unfortunate: "There is talk only of machines of war, and the most destructive are always the most favored. A private individual who would discover a means for exterminating an entire Nation at one stroke would today be looked upon as a great statesman." Moreover it is the Europeans, he observes, who bring the scourge of war to the other continents, and they have done so as a result of their economic expansion. The economic weapon has become decisive: "Today it is no longer armies that wage war, but industries, because they produce the riches which are the sinews of war." This very modern and sober thinker sees hope only in a twenty-year truce, which according to him would pacify the war fever of the European sovereigns.

A Livonian aristocrat, J. H. Lilienfeld, published a thick book entitled *Neues Staats-Gebäude* (Leipzig, 1767). He too proposes a Congress of Christian powers, but adds two important innovations to the earlier plans: (1) the sovereignty of the member states would be transferred to the Congress, and (2) a "sovereign Tribunal" would judge differences between states in accordance with a code of international law, and in the event the Congress imposed sanctions on a recalcitrant state,[57] would support troops to enforce them. Needless to say, once this had been accomplished, the united Europe would show the Infidel what it could do.

Thus we see everywhere the same argument advanced in favor of the same type of union: *always to secure the peace, and thereby to throttle the sovereign states.* Our authors seek to unite the Christian powers by some sort of legal federal bond. And invariably, the apparently indispensable motive for such a federation is supplied by the Ottoman threat. Not until the last years of the Century of Reason was the Turkish threat replaced

[57] Cf. Jacob Ter Meulen, *Der Gedanke der Internationalen Organisation 1300–1800* (The Hague, 1917), pp. 263–70.

with another bogey. We shall skip ahead for a moment here, to record the end of an epoch.

There is, for instance, the *Plan d'une pacification générale en Europe* by the *citoyen* Delaunay, Consul of the Republic (Paris, 1794). The author begins with the warning that "when we are daydreaming for the public good, we must guard against falling asleep, and allowing our judgment to be ruled by our feelings." Our purpose is to create a "European Convention," but, he goes on to say, we must not count on popular uprisings, for the peoples are most ofen ignorant of their own rights. Nor should we try to dictate a program to future deputies; *we must confine ourselves to formulating ways and means to achieve such a Convention.* Above all, we must not resort to the myth of a crusade against the Turks: on the contrary, we must have the Turks on our side and we must help them . . . against the Russians! Without a firm European organization, there is everything to be feared from Russian influence: "Those who reflect on the amazing increase of Russia's power during the last century, on what she may develop into, and on her ambitions, will agree that it is necessary to check the only power in Europe capable of starting great revolutions there."

Hence the idea of two major groups: a "Western federation" comprising France, England, and Spain, and an "Eastern federation" comprising Russia, Austria, and the German states. As for Switzerland, she would be *entirely neutral* and would become the headquarters of the Western federation, while Danzig would be the headquarters of the Eastern federation.

In addition, we must not imagine that economic uniformity is a factor of union, quite the opposite:

It is because the soil of Europe is not the same everywhere, is not equally fertile, produces different fruits and contains riches of different kinds, that the Europeans are destined to unite and to live in harmony, in order to obtain, by easy exchanges, everything they may need, whether for use or luxury.[58]

[58] Cf. B. Mirkine Gurtzevitch, "La Révolution française et les projets d'union européenne," *La Révolution Française* (Paris), LXXXIV (1931), 321–35.

PART THREE

THE ERA OF THE
PHILOSOPHES

From Leibniz to Condorcet

1: Broadened Perspectives

Leibniz

Gottfried Wilhelm von Leibniz (1646–1716) was a mathematician, physicist, alchemist, naturalist, psychologist, logician, metaphysician, historian, jurist, philosopher, diplomat, theologian, councillor to princes, and traveler; in addition he carried on what might be called a universal correspondence. He had two dominant passions: to know everything, and to unite everything. *Utique enim delectat nos varietas, sed in unitatem reducta:* we delight in variety, particularly if it is reduced to unity. He lived in most of the European countries, he was distressed by their dissensions, he wanted the union of Europe without destroying her diversity, he made a plan for achieving it, and he proposed it to Louis XIV: *federalism.* He studied all the sciences and made contributions to all of them, but he wanted to harmonize them: *encyclopedism.* A convinced Lutheran, but a sincere admirer of Roman Catholicism and Russian Orthodoxy, he worked indefatigably to reconcile them, hence his famous correspondence with Bossuet: *ecumenism.* A European conscious of European values, he saw the world growing larger and was pleased: *universalism.* He tried to discover a method for writing in all languages, which he called *ars combinatoria,* and his most famous mathematical discovery, the infinitesimal calculus, too, serves as an instrument to pass from the discontinuous to the continuous: *harmony* . . . "The Academies he sought to found in various countries were in his mind but the scattered and provisional fragments of a vast European Academy,

[127]

of a federation of the learned, of which the local academies were to be merely separate colleges." [1]

How can we quote this proteiform genius? For three centuries no one has as yet succeeded in publishing his complete works, written in Latin, German, and French. We shall confine ourselves to a few specifically European themes, which he treated in his correspondence and in a pseudonymous work.

To begin with, the "citizen of the world":

I am not one of those who are fanatic adherents to their countries or even a particular nation; but I want to serve all mankind: for I regard Heaven as the Fatherland, and all men of goodwill as fellow citizens in that Heaven: and I would rather accomplish a great deal of good among the Russians than a little good among the Germans or other Europeans . . . For by inclination and by taste I am for the general good. [2]

As early as 1670 Leibniz, fearing the ambitious designs of Louis XIV, had sought to divert them toward the East. Hence the draft plan he submitted to the King, entitled *Consilium Aegyptianorum*. The idea was, once again, to turn against the Turks, to conquer Egypt, and to cut a canal through the isthmus of Suez. In this way Leibniz hoped to pacify Europe and to bring about its union. Louis XIV summoned the young man to Paris, but did not receive him: the difficulties between France and the Sultan had in the meantime been smoothed out. . . .

In 1676, when the Peace of Niemegen had asserted Louis XIV's threatening predominance in Europe, Leibniz published a Latin treatise under the pseudonym of Caesarius Fursterinus, in which he came out in defense of the autonomy of the princes of the Holy Roman Empire. He recalls that in the Middle Ages the double authority of the Emperor and the Pope respected the freedom of the federated sovereignties:

In this kingdom of Christ which had Christ himself as Chief and Lord, it was commonly accepted that two supreme magis-

[1] L. Couturat, *Logique de Leibniz* (Paris, 1901), pp. 527-28. It may be noted here that Campanella had before this dreamed of a "European Academy."

[2] Letter to Peter I, January 16, 1716. Leibniz had become Councillor to the Czar.

trates, the Pope and the Emperor, should exercise power in His name, one the spiritual power, the other the temporal power. And it was obviously in the interest of all that the Christians should be united under a common authority, so as to enable them to safeguard the peace by their common efforts, and at the same time make themselves more feared by enemies to the faith . . . And because, clearly, in the Christian world the sacred majesty of the Roman Emperor rests upon this foundation, it follows that it must not be contested but defended by our princes . . .

Thus, if one acts in accordance with the law, the Emperor must be invested with power in a large part of Europe, as well as with a kind of supreme sovereignty corresponding to that of the Church; and just as, with a view to keeping the universal peace, common contributions are required in our Empire for the war against the infidel, and justice is made to prevail among the princes, so the universal Church settles differences between princes, convokes them to councils, settles questions of precedence during those councils, and the latter, in the name of Christ, declares war on the enemies of Christianity.

We recognize here the fundamental theses of Dante's *De Monarchia*. The sympathy this Lutheran felt for the papacy was expressed repeatedly on other occasions, though it was sometimes tinged with a degree of irony. For instance, in a letter concerning a project by the prince of Hesse-Rheinfels for setting up a "European Catholic Tribunal" to be located at Lucerne, Leibniz wrote:

If there existed a permanent council or Senate created by this Council to look after the general interests of Christendom, what is done now by alliances and by so-called mediation and guarantees could be decided by a public authority empowered by the Pope and the Emperor in their quality of heads of Christendom: in other words, by means of a friendly understanding and in a more practical and convenient manner than at present.

. . . As for me, I would recommend to set it up in Rome itself and to make the Pope its president; indeed, formerly he used to act as judge between Christian princes. But at the same time the clergy would have to reassume their old authority, and kings and kingdoms would have to be held in check by the threat of interdict or excommunication, as in the time of Nicholas I or Gregory VII. And to obtain the consent of the Protes-

tants, His Holiness would have to be asked to restore the form
of the Church as it was in the epoch of Charlemagne, when he
held the Council of Frankfort; and to renounce all subsequent
Councils, which cannot be regarded as ecumenial. Moreover
the Popes would have to resemble the first bishops of Rome.
These are projects which are as likely to succeed as the Abbé
de Saint-Pierre's, but since there is no law against novel-writing,
why should we condemn his fiction, considering that it would
bring back the golden age.[3]

A little later Leibniz expressed himself concerning the Abbé
de Saint-Pierre with his usual courtesy, but not without skepticism. In 1715 he wrote to the Abbé:

I have at last managed to get off by myself to read your excellent work with care. I found it solid and pleasing; and after
I understood your system, I took special pleasure in the variety
of the objections to it, and in your precise and straightforward
way of replying to them. Men lack only the will to rid themselves of an infinity of evils. If five or six persons wanted it, they
could end the great Schism of the West, and put the Church in
good order. A Sovereign can preserve his states from the plague,
if he wants to; the House of Brunswick has been fairly successful in this, thank God; the plague stopped at its frontiers in my
time. A Sovereign could also preserve his states from famine.
But to bring an end to war, another Henri IV with other Princes
of his time would have to favor your Project. Unfortunately it
is difficult to explain it to the great Princes. Today no minister
would propose to the Emperor that he should renounce the
Spanish succession and the Indies. The sea powers and so many
others could not get anywhere with this. Most often there are
fatalities that prevent men from being happy . . .

Leibniz, as councillor to Peter the Great, held that Russia
should serve as a Christian bridge between Europe and China,
with a view to a higher synthesis of civilizations.

It also seems that by a singular fatality or rather by an act of
Providence, the three greatest Monarchs in the north, the east,
and the south should all have the same, very peculiar intentions.
For in addition to the Czar Peter Alexeevich, sovereign Lord
of the Russians and almost the entire north, we learn that

[3] Letter to Grimarest, Hanover, June 4, 1712. *Opera*, ed. Dutens (Geneva, 1768), V, 65–66.

Cam-hi, Amalogdo-Khan, monarch of China and the easternmost Tatars, and Jakso Adjam-Saugbed, king of the Abyssinians, who also won great victories over his barbarian neighbors, have all conceived designs which far surpass those of their ancestors, as we learn both from new reports from China, where Christianity has recently been authorized and supported by a royal edict, and from the Abyssinian embassy to Batavia in 1692. The Czar and the King of the Abyssinians are both Christians, enemies and neighbors of the Turk, though very distant from each other. But the Czar and the monarch of China have common frontiers, and both are marvelously inclined to attract to their countries the sciences, arts, and good manners peculiar to our Europe, and they can help and oblige each other in this respect.[4]

Leibniz hoped that Protestants would, like the Jesuits, send out missionaries:

I suggest that it would be to the glory of God and to the honor of the Protestants to take part in this great venture in the Lord's vineyard in order that the purified religion may be carried to that country no less than the Roman superstitions.[5]

I think that these missions are the greatest thing in our time, for the glory of God and for the propagation of the Christian religion, for the general good of mankind and for the development of the sciences and the arts, in our own lands as well as among the Chinese: for it is an exchange of lights that can give us at one stroke their works of several thousand years . . . and double, so to speak, our true riches here and there.[6]

And finally this touch: in a Latin fragment entitled "The State of Europe at the Beginning of the New Century," Leibniz wrote: *Finis saeculi novam rerum faciem aperuit.* ("At the end of the century, a new face of things was disclosed.")

IN DISCOVERING THE WORLD EUROPE DISCOVERS HERSELF

These last quotations from Leibniz are important. They are evidence of a spiritual revolution that took place at the end of

[4] Letter to Lefort, 1697, in Ernst Benz, *Leibniz und Peter der Grosse* (Berlin, 1957).
[5] Letter to Morell, 1697.
[6] Letter to the Reverend Verjus, Dec. 2, 1697.

the seventeenth and the beginning of the eighteenth century. Everyone who counted for something in Europe began to travel, even more than in the heyday of the Renaissance, and above all, much more extensively. This time it was not only the elites who learned to discover the diversity of Europe; it was Europe as a whole that discovered herself, comparing herself with the overseas peoples.

At the beginning and at the end of this vast investigation, let us place, as mottoes, four postcards from the epoch:

Miguel de Cervantes Saavedra (1547–1616):

I left our nation to enter France, and although we were well received there, I wanted to see all the rest. And so I went to Italy, and then to Germany, and there, it seemed to me that one could live in the greatest freedom.[7]

Balthasar Gracian (1601–1658), famous author of *The Courtier:*

Europe is the world's admirable face: grave in Spain, pretty in England, elegant in France, delicate in Italy, fresh in Germany, precious in Sweden, affable in Poland, indolent in Greece, and somber in Muscovy.[8]

Montesquieu (*c.* 1730):

Germany is made to be traveled in, Italy to be visited, England to think in, and France to live in.

Carl von Linné (1707–1778), "Europe's first botanist," also zoologist, and in this quotation anthropologist:

> Homo Europaeus. Albus sanguineus, torosus
> Pilis flavescentibus prolixis; oculis caeruleis.
> Levis argutus, inventor.
> Tegitur vestimentis arctis. Regitur ritibus.[9]

Louis Moreri's *Grand Dictionnaire Historique*, published in 1674, contains a brief description of Europe, in which we find, at that early date, all the clichés on the psychology of nations that have survived down to our own day:

[7] *Don Quixote de la Mancha*, II, liv.
[8] *El Criticon*, III, 4.
[9] Quoted in H. Gollwitzer, *Europabild und Europagedanke.*

It is said that the French are polite, clever, generous, but quick and inconstant; the Germans are sincere, hard-working, but ponderous and too much given to wine; the Italians are pleasant, subtle, gentle in their speech, but jealous and treacherous; the Spaniards are secret, prudent, but boastful and too formalistic; the English are courageous to the point of rashness, but proud, contemptuous, and fierce to the point of ferocity. The nations of Europe, by their skill and their courage, subdued those of the other parts of the world. Their spirit is shown in their works, their wisdom in their government, their strength in their armaments, their behavior in their trade, and their magnificence in their cities. Europe also surpasses the other parts of the world in everything, whether in sacred and secular edifices, or in the diverse geniuses of the nations inhabiting it. We must furthermore add to the advantages of Europe the fact that almost all of it is illumined by the light of the Gospels.

This is followed by a "list of authors who speak of Europe" (the first summary for a European anthology!) from Strabo and Ptolemy to modern geographers, like Rabbe.

The historian of culture Paul Hazard has described better than anyone in our day this phenomena of Europe's self-discovery: [10]

When Boileau was at Bourbon, taking the waters, he felt as if he was at the other end of the earth: Auteuil was world enough for him. So was Paris for Racine; and both of them, Racine and Boileau, were terribly put about when they had to accompany the King on one of his expeditions. Bossuet never went to Rome, nor did Fénélon. Nor did Molière ever revisit that barber's shop at Pézenas. The great classics were not given to moving about; for the wanderers we must wait for Voltaire, Montesquieu, Rousseau. But, in between, some obscure forces had been at work, preparing the way for the impending change.

The fact is that by the end of the seventeenth century and the beginning of the eighteenth, the Italians had revived their taste for travel; and that the French were as mobile as quicksilver. If a contemporary observer speaks the truth about them, they were so enamoured of novelty that they even took care not to keep a friend too long. According to the same authority, they brought out a new fashion every day, and finding nothing but drabness

[10] Paul Hazard, *The European Mind* (1680–1715), trans. J. Lewis May (London: Hollis and Carter, 1953).

and boredom at home, packed up their traps and set out for Asia, or it might be Africa, to get a little change of scene, and something to break the monotony.[11] The Germans travelled as a matter of habit; indeed the thing was in their blood; a sort of mania with them. There was no keeping them at home. "We are born travellers, every mother's son of us, like our fathers before us, and nothing, no business, however urgent, ever keeps us back." So says the German that Saint-Evremond brings on in that amusing comedy of his, *Sir Politick Would-be:* "As soon as we have got hold of a bit of Latin, we prepare to start on our travels. The first thing we do is to procure an Itinerary, showing the various routes we have to take; next, a handbook mentioning all the things that ought to be seen in the different countries. When our travellers are of a literary turn of mind, they invariably take with them a book consisting solely of blank pages, nicely bound, which they call an *Album Amicorum.* Armed with this, they make a point of calling on the various learned men of the locality they happen to be visiting, and beg them to inscribe their names in it . . ."

The English travelled as a way of putting the finishing touch on their education. Young gentlemen just down from Oxford or Cambridge, liberally furnished with funds, and attended by a staid and sober-minded tutor, crossed the Straits and set out to make the *grand tour.* They were birds of every feather, these young men. Some thought they had done all that was expected of them when they had sampled the wines of Frontignan and Montefiascone, of Ay and Arbois, of Bordeaux and Xeres. Others, bent on self-improvement, conscientiously examined every cabinet of natural history specimens, every collection of antiques. Every man to his taste! "The French usually travel to save money, so that they sometimes leave the places where they sojourn worse off than they found them. The English, on the other hand, come over with plenty of cash, plenty of gear, and servants to wait on them. They throw their money about like lords. It is reckoned that in Rome alone there are, in the ordinary way, upwards of six hundred English gentlemen, all with people in their pay, and that taking everything into account, they spend at least two thousand crowns per head every year, so that Rome alone derives from England a yearly revenue of thirty thousand pistoles, good and sound." . . . It is Gregorio Leti, adventurer and globe-trotter, who tells us that: Gregorio

---

[11] Giovanni Paolo Marana, *Lettre d'un Sicilien à l'un de ses amis, contenant une agréable critique de Paris et des Français, 1700 et 1710.*— Hazard.

Leti [12] who had at least five countries he could call his own. Born at Milan, he turned Calvinist at Geneva, became Louis XIV's panegyrist in Paris, England's historian in London, and government pamphleteer in Holland, where he died in 1701. Men of learning added to their stores of erudition, as they journeyed from city to city, like that Antonio Conti, for example, a native of Padua, who, in 1713, was in Paris, and two years later

[12] Gregorio Leti, *Historia e Memoria sopra la vita di O. Cromvele* (Amsterdam, 1692; French trans. 1694). It may be amusing to quote here a passage from Rousseau's *Emile* (Vol. IV, edition of 1762) which freely paraphrases Saint-Evremond and G. Leti, as P. Hazard quotes them:

"The French travel the most of any people in the world; but prepossessed with their own customs, they confound every thing that deviates from them. There are Frenchmen in all parts of the globe. In no country will you meet with greater numbers of persons who travelled, than in France. And yet they who see most nations, know them the least. The English are also travellers, but in a different taste; for these two nations must be opposite in every thing. The English nobility go abroad, which is not the case of the French: the common people in France ramble a great deal; in England the vulgar are not travellers. The difference seems to be in favour of the English. The French have always some interested view in going abroad; but the English do not go to seek their fortune among other nations, except it be to trade, and with a proper stock: when they travel, it is to spend their money, and not to live upon their industry; they are too proud, to creep and cringe out of their own country. And this is also the reason, that they gain better instruction among foreigners, than is usual for Frenchmen, who have quite a different object in view. Yet the English have also their national prejudices, nay they have them stronger than any other people; but these depend more on passion than on ignorance. The Englishman's prejudices are founded in pride, the Frenchman's in vanity.

"As the nations least polished are generally the wisest; those who go least abroad, improve most by their travels: because as they have not made so great a progress as we in frivolous researches, and are less employed about the objects of our idle curiosity, their whole attention is directed towards matters of real utility. I know none but the Spaniards, who travel in this manner: while a Frenchman runs after the polite artists, while an Englishman busies himself about the designing of an antique, and a German carries his *album* to shew to the learned; the Spaniard silently remarks the government, the manners, and the police of a country; and out of the four, he is the only one who brings back with him any observations of public utility."

And Rousseau concludes: "There is a hundred times more connexion at present between Europe and Asia, than there was formerly between Gaul and Spain. There was a greater separation between the different countries of Europe alone, than there is at present in the whole globe."—*Emilius; or, an Essay on Education.* [*By John James Rousseau, citizen of Geneva. Translated from the French.*], (London, 1763).

in London, where he took part in the controversy concerning the infinitesimal calculus. After that, he went to Hanover to confer with Leibniz, and on his way through Holland, did not fail to pay a visit to Leuwenhoeck. Philosophers went abroad, not to go and meditate in peace in some quiet retreat, but to see the wonders of the world. Such were Locke and Leibniz. Monarchs, too, indulged in foreign travel; Christina of Sweden died at Rome in 1689; and Peter the Great set out for Europe in 1696.

Travel literature, with its indeterminate frontiers, provided a reservoir for the most diverse material, from the dissertations of the learned, to museum catalogues and love stories, and so it came to the fore. . . . There is one alluring title that makes you feel as if you were already glimpsing the fair scenes which it promises and that you really must book your seat on the coach. "Delight" is the operative word. The "Delights" or the "Charms" of this country and of that—of Italy, of Denmark and Norway, of Great Britain and Ireland, of Switzerland. And finally, when all these "Delights" are rolled into one, we have "The wonders of Europe."

Attractive as these things were, the "Wonders of the World" outdid them. Indeed, from that time forth Europe never ceased to explore and exploit the world at large; the seventeenth century thus resuming the task which the sixteenth had bequeathed it. As far back as 1619, an obscure writer, P. Bergeron by name, and a little later, in 1636, Tomasso Campanella were putting forth this sort of thing: "The exploration of the globe having resulted in discoveries that have destroyed many of the data on which ancient philosophy reposed, a new conception of things will inevitably be called for." This idea, which at first gained ground but slowly, received a marked impetus when the Dutch not only opened up trade with the East Indies, but gave picturesque accounts of the strange things they found there; when the English not only displayed their flags in all the oceans of the globe, but described their voyages in the most marvellously circumstantial literature of the kind that the world had ever seen; when Colbert told the French people of rich territories and treasures in lands beyond the seas, and recommended them as fitting fields for enterprise. How many were the glowing reports and stirring tales, compiled by order of the king, that came to France from "over younder"! How little did His Majesty dream that from those very tales would spring ideas calculated to unsettle some of the beliefs he held most dear, beliefs essential to the maintenance of his royal authority.

. . . It is perfectly correct to say that all the fundamental concepts, such as Property, Freedom, Justice, and so on, were brought under discussion again as a result of the conditions in which they were seen to operate in far-off countries, in the first place because, instead of all differences being referred to one universal archetype, the emphasis was now on the particular, irreducible, the individual; in the second, because notions hitherto taken for granted could now be checked in the light of facts ascertained by actual experience, facts readily available to all enquiring minds. . . . Of all the lessons derived from the idea of space, perhaps the latest had to do with relativity.

Jesuit missionaries, Huguenots driven from France after the Revocation of the Edict of Nantes, "dissenters" embarked for New Amsterdam (the future New York), explorers, colonizers, merchants, sailors, and soldiers—the "Relations" they sent from the antipodes gave a new vision primarily of . . . Europe. A relativized Europe, to be sure, but seen more distinctly as a whole and in its unity.

Moreover, more than one of these men imagined that he had found among the "barbarians" the ideal he had nursed in his heart when he was fleeing the intolerance of Europe. The praises showered upon the far-off Primitive served at first as arguments against some neighbors. Hence the numerous compensatory myths developed in the eighteenth century—the Noble Savage, the Candid Huron, the Tolerant Hindu, and above all the Philosophical Chinese. Hence also the "utopias" (a term coined by Thomas More in the sixteenth century) and the imaginary travels: Savinien de Cyrano de Bergerac's *States and Empires of the Moon* (and later of the Sun), Swift's *Gulliver's Travels*, Giovanni Paolo Marana's "Great Lord's Hope," Montesquieu's *Persian Letters*, Voltaire's *Ingénu*, Rousseau's "Naturally Good" Man. And many pamphlets, many political and philosophical ventures, many critical appraisals of Europe's role in the world. Thus the eighteenth century marks the effect of her "Great Discoveries" on her own mind.

VICO

Giovanni Battista Vico was born in Naples in 1668 and died there in 1744. A sublime, universal mind, often disorderly, a

historian with vast and poetic views but little given to exactitude, a baroque metaphysician often anticipating later physical
science and sociology, in the eighteenth century, he was the last
of the Renaissance men and the first of the Moderns, the continuator of Pico della Mirandola, Giordano Bruno, and Cardan,
and the forerunner of Hegel and Croce. It is from his main
work, the *Scienza Nuova* that we borrow the following "Description of the Modern World," which gives the view of Europe
and its place in the world, entertained by a great mind of the
period.

Today a complete humanity seems to be spread abroad
through all nations, for a few great monarchs rule over this
world of peoples. If there are still some barbarous peoples surviving, it is because their monarchies have persisted in the vulgar wisdom of imaginative and cruel religions, in some cases
with the less balanced nature of their subject nations as an
added factor.

Beginning with the cold north, the Czar of Muscovy, although
Christian, rules over men of sluggish minds. The Khan of Tartary dominates an effeminate people, like to the ancient Seres,
who formed the larger part of his great empire, a part which
is now united with that of China. The Negus of Ethiopia and
the powerful kings of Fez and Morocco reign over peoples too
weak and sparse.

In the mid-temperate zone, however, where the nature of men
is better balanced, to begin with the Far East, the Emperor of
Japan practices a humanity similar to that of the Romans at the
time of the Carthaginian wars. He imitates their ferocity in
arms, and, as learned travelers observe, his language has a Latin
ring about it. Yet, through a religion of fierce and terrible imagination with dreadful gods all armed with deadly weapons, he
retains much of the heroic nature. For the missionary fathers
who have been there report that the greatest difficulty they have
encountered in converting the people to Christianity is that the
nobles cannot be persuaded that the plebeians have the same
nature as themselves. The Emperor of the Chinese, who reigns
under a mild religion and cultivates letters, is most humane. The
Emperor of the Indies is rather humane than otherwise, and
practices in the main the arts of peace. The Persian and the
Turk have mingled the rude doctrine of their religion with the
softness of Asia, which they rule; and thus both, and particularly

the Turk, temper their arrogance with magnificence, pomp, liberality, and gratitude.

But in Europe, where the Christian religion is everywhere professed, inculcating an infinitely pure and perfect idea of God and commanding charity to all mankind, there are great monarchies most humane in their customs. It is true that those situated in the cold north, such as Sweden and Denmark until a hundred and fifty years ago, and Poland and even England still today, although they are monarchic in constitution yet seem to be administered aristocratically; but if the natural course of human civil institutions is not impeded in their case by extraordinary causes, they will arrive at perfect monarchies. In this part of the world alone, because it cultivates the sciences, there are furthermore a great number of popular commonwealths, which are not found at all in the other three parts. Indeed, by the recourse of the same public utilities and necessities, there has been a revival of the form of the Aetolian and Achaean leagues. Just as the latter were conceived by the Greeks because of the necessity of protecting themselves against the overwhelming power of the Romans, so the Swiss cantons and the united provinces or states of Holland have organized a number of free popular cities into two aristocracies, in which they stand united in a perpetual league of peace and war. And the body of the German empire is a system of many free cities and sovereign princes. Its head is the emperor . . .

. . . Sovereign powers uniting in leagues, whether perpetual or temporary, come of themselves to form aristocratic states into which enter the anxious suspicions characteristic of aristocracies. Hence, as this [confederation] . . . is the last form of civil states (for we cannot conceive in civil nature a state superior to such aristocracies), this same form must have been the first, which . . . was that of the aristocracies of the fathers, sovereign family kings, united in reigning orders in the first cities. For this is the nature of principles, that things begin and end in them.[13]

Now to come back to our subject, in Europe today there are only five aristocracies: namely, Venice, Genoa, and Lucca in Italy, Ragusa in Dalmatia, and Nuremberg in Germany. Almost all of them have small territories. But Christian Europe is everywhere radiant with such humanity that it abounds in all the good things that make for the happiness of human life, minister-

[13] Vico has in mind: confederation. In his *Scienza Nuova prima* (*Works*, III, i, 56) he had imagined no less than a federation including all nations united as though in a great world city.

ing to the comforts of the body as well as to the pleasures of mind and spirit. And all this in virtue of the Christian religion, which teaches truths so sublime that it receives into its service the most learned philosophies of the gentiles and cultivates three languages as its own: Hebrew, the most ancient in the world; Greek, the most delicate; and Latin, the grandest. Thus, even for human ends, the Christian religion is the best in the world, because it unites a wisdom of [revealed] authority with that of reason, basing the latter on the choicest doctrine of the philosophers and the most cultivated erudition of the philologists.

Lastly, crossing the ocean, in the new world the American Indians would now be following this course of human institutions if they had not been discovered by the Europeans.[14]

2 : The Europe of the Enlightenment

IN ALMOST PERFECT contrast with the somber, tense genius of Vico, we turn now to a hedonistic, self-indulgent skeptical mind: that of Bernard Le Bovier de Fontenelle (1657–1757). Having taken the most detailed inventory of his domain, and having studied with an open mind the "relations" sent from far-off lands, and having sympathetically considered the cosmos, he also opted for Europe. In his famous *Entretiens sur la pluralité des mondes*, he is the distinguished and quite involuntary ancestor of the immense literature which culminates in the science fiction of our own day. During the Sixth of his conversations with his Marquise, after he explained in detail all that is known or imagined by astronomers about the other worlds, she says that according to what she had read, the Chinese described the simultaneous fall of a thousand stars. Fontenelle doubts it. The Marquise insists:

But have I not always been told that the Chinese are very great astronomers? True, I said; but the Chinese have the advantage of being separated from us by a long stretch of land, just as the Greeks and Romans have the advantage of being separated from us by a long succession of centuries; distance is always apt to deceive us. In fact, I believe more and more firmly that there is a

[14] *The New Science of Giambattista Vico,* trans. Thomas Goddard Bergin and Max Harold Fisch (Anchor Books, Doubleday & Co., 1961).

certain genius that has not yet existed outside our Europe, or at least that has never moved too far away from it. Possibly it cannot spread simultaneously over a large expanse of land, and some fatality keeps it within rather narrow boundaries. Let us enjoy it while we possess it; what is best about it, is that it is not confined to sciences and arid speculations; it extends just as successfully to pleasant things in which I doubt that any people is our equal.[15]

Montesquieu (1689–1755)

Charles-Louis de Secondat, Baron de Montesquieu, is not only the greatest theoretician of liberal government, but also the most reliable witness to the Europe of his day, which he had traveled over extensively.

He used the device of the "intelligent barbarian" merely as a way of expounding his own sociological observations. One of his Persians is explaining how he intends to conduct his own investigation into European diversity: [16]

I am learning about the secrets of trade, the interests of the princes, the forms of their governments. I do not neglect even the superstitions of the Europeans; I am applying myself to medicine, to physics, to astronomy; I am studying the arts; in short, I am emerging from the clouds that veiled my vision in the country of my birth.

We shall quote, with no more system than is found in Montesquieu's notes and short essays, a few results of this method.

On the interdependence of European nations:

A prince believes that he will become greater through the ruin of a neighboring state. The opposite is true. The condition in Europe is such that all states depend on one another. France needs the opulence of Poland and of Muscovy, just as Guyenne needs Brittany, and Brittany needs Anjou. Europe is a state composed of several provinces.[17]

[15] B. de Fontenelle, *Entretiens sur la pluralité des mondes* (1686), "Sixième Soir," conclusion.

[16] *Lettres Persanes*, Letter XXXI, from Rhedi to Usbek, dated from Venice.

[17] *Cahiers*, "On the Power of States." This is a refutation of Jean Bodin (cf. p. 79). See also *Réflexions sur la Monarchie universelle en Europe*: "Europe is no more than a nation composed of several provinces."

On the power of the spirit and the trump card that Europe holds by virtue of her culture:

It cannot be said that letters are no more than a diversion for a certain number of citizens; it must be looked upon from a different angle. It has been observed that their prosperity is so closely linked with the prosperity of empires that it is an infallible sign or even cause of the latter. And if we cast a glance on what is taking place in the world today, we shall see that just as Europe dominates the other parts of the world and prospers, while the rest groans in slavery and poverty, so Europe is more enlightened and the other parts are correspondingly enveloped in darkness. And if we cast a glance on Europe, we shall see that the states where letters are most cultivated are proportionately more powerful.[18]

On the position of Europe in the world:

A consequence of the discovery of America was the connecting Asia and Africa with Europe; it furnished materials for a trade with that vast part of Asia known by the name of the East Indies. Silver, that metal so useful as the medium of commerce, became now as merchandise the basis of the greatest commerce in the world. In fine, the navigation to Africa became necessary, in order to furnish us with men to labor in the mines, and to cultivate the lands in America.

Europe has arrived at so high a degree of power that nothing in history can be compared with it, whether we consider the immensity of its expenses, the grandeur of its engagements, the number of its troops, and the regular payment even of those that are least serviceable, and which are kept only for ostentation.

Father Du Halde says that the interior trade of China is much greater than that of all Europe. That might be, if our foreign trade did not augment our inland commerce. Europe carries on the trade and navigation of the other three parts of the world; as France, England, and Holland do nearly that of Europe.[19]

On the parallel between Europe and Asia:

In Europe, on the contrary, the temperate zone is very extensive, though situated in climates widely different from each other: there being no affinity between the climates of Spain and Italy

[18] *Cahiers,* "Sur les ouvrages de l'esprit."
[19] Montesquieu, *The Spirit of Laws,* trans. T. Nugent (New York, 1899), Book XXI, chap. xxi.

and those of Norway and Sweden. But as the climate grows insensibly cold upon our advancing from south to north, nearly in proportion to the latitude of each country, it thence follows that each resembles the country joining it; that there is no very extraordinary difference between them, and that, as I have just said, the temperate zone is very extensive.

Hence it comes that in Asia the strong nations are opposed to the weak; the warlike, brave and active people touch immediately upon those who are indolent, effeminate, and timorous; the one must, therefore, conquer, and the other be conquered. In Europe, on the contrary, strong nations are opposed to the strong; and those who join each other have nearly the same courage. This is the grand reason for the weakness of Asia, and of the strength of Europe; of the liberty of Europe, and of the slavery of Asia: a cause that I do not recollect ever to have seen remarked. Hence it proceeds that liberty in Asia never increases; whilst in Europe it is enlarged or diminished, according to particular circumstances.[20]

The nations in the north of Europe conquered as freemen; the people in the north of Asia conquered as slaves, and subdued others only to gratify the ambition of a master.

The reason is, that the people of Tartary, the natural conquerors of Asia, are themselves enslaved . . .

. . . Hence it follows that the genius of the Getic or Tartarian nation has always resembled that of the empires of Asia. The people in these are governed by the cudgel; the inhabitants of Tartary by whips. The spirit of Europe has been contrary to these manners; and in all ages, what the people of Asia have called punishment those of Europe have deemed the most outrageous abuse.

The Tartars who destroyed the Grecian Empire established in the conquered countries slavery and despotic power: the Goths, after subduing the Roman Empire, founded monarchy and liberty.

I do not know whether the famous Rudbeck, who in his *Atlantica* has bestowed such praises on Scandinavia, has made mention of that great prerogative which ought to set that people above all the nations upon earth; namely, this country's having been the source of the liberties of Europe—that is, of almost all the freedom which at present subsists amongst mankind.

Jornadez the Goth called the north of Europe the forge of the human race. I should rather call it the forge where those weapons

[20] *Ibid.*, Book XVII, chap. iii.

were framed which broke the chains of southern nations. In the North were formed those valient people who sallied forth and deserted their countries to destroy tyrants and slaves, and to teach men that, nature having made them equal, reason could not render them dependent, except where it was necessary for their happiness.[21]

In Asia they have always had great empires; in Europe these could never subsist. Asia has larger plains; it is cut out into much more extensive divisions by mountains and seas. . . .
Power in Asia ought, then, to be always despotic: for if their slavery was not severe they would make a division inconsistent with the nature of the country.
In Europe the natural division forms many nations of a moderate extent, in which the ruling by laws is not incompatible with the maintenance of the state: on the contrary, it is so favorable to it, that without this the state would fall into decay, and become a prey to its neighbors.
It is this which has formed a genius for liberty that renders every part extremely difficult to be subdued and subjected to a foreign power, otherwise than by the laws and the advantage of commerce.
On the contrary, there reigns in Asia a servile spirit, which they have never been able to shake off, and it is impossible to find in all the histories of that country a single passage which discovers a freedom of spirit; we shall never see anything there but the excess of slavery.[22]

Finally, this most famous text of all:

If I knew of something that could serve me but would be harmful to my family, I would dismiss it from my mind. If I knew of something that could serve my family but would be harmful to my country, I should try to forget it. If I knew of something that would serve my nation but would be harmful to Europe and mankind, I should look upon it as a crime.[23]

VOLTAIRE (1694–1778)

One man who was not taken in by utopias, whether set in the past or projected into the future, was Voltaire. "It is the condi-

[21] *Ibid.*, Book XVII, chap. v.
[22] *Ibid.*, Book XVII, chap. vi.
[23] *Pensées diverses* ("Self-portrait"). Cf. *supra* the quotation from Vitoria, p. 78.

tions in which we find ourselves we have to study, not conditions in which we can never find ourselves." He failed to be impressed by either Rousseau or the Abbé de Saint-Pierre.

In 1769 he devoted an essay to the Abbé de Saint-Pierre entitled *De la Paix perpétuelle, par le Dr. Goodheart,* in which he says:

The only possible perpetual peace among men is tolerance. The peace a Frenchman named the Abbé de Saint-Pierre has in mind will no more be realized than among elephants, rhinoceroses, wolves, or dogs. Carnivorous animals will always tear one another to pieces at the first opportunity.

Concerning Rousseau and all who argued in terms of the Noble Savage, the Wise Egyptian or the Philosophical Chinese—not to mention the Candid Huron whom Voltaire himself put to such good use!—a character in one of Voltaire's *Dialogues* referred to as A. and who seems to be English (C. defends the Ancients and B. the Primitives) says: [24]

C.: Would you be rash enough to maintain that you English are better than the Athenians or the Romans? That your cockfights and boxing matches—held indoors in dilapidated premises —surpass the spectacles of the Colosseum? Are the cobblers and clowns in your tragic drama superior to the heroes of Sophocles? Have you orators who put Cicero and Demosthenes in the shade? Is London better policed than ancient Rome?
A.: No, but London is a thousandfold better than it was in Roman times, and so is the rest of Europe.
B.: Please, aren't you forgetting that Greece is under the yoke of the Great Turk, and there is a wretched portion of Italy under that of the Pope?
A.: No, I am not. But bear in mind that Paris, today only smaller than London by one-tenth, was in those days a tiny barbarian city. Amsterdam was a swamp, Madrid a desert, and the whole of the territory from the right bank of the Rhine to the Gulf of Bothnia a wilderness. The inhabitants of these climes lived as the Tartars still live, in ignorance, want, and barbarism.
Aren't you discounting the fact that today there are philosophers on the throne in Berlin, in Sweden, in Poland, and in

[24] Excerpt from *Dialogues et anecdotes philosophiques* (1768), Seventh Conversation: "That modern Europe is better than ancient Europe."

Russia, and that the discoveries of our great Newton have become a catechism to the Moscow and Petersburg nobility?

C.: But you know the same cannot be said of the lands along the Danube and along the Mazanarès. The light has come from the north, and in relation to me you are northerners—I was born below the forty-fifth parallel. Do you think people are any happier today than they were when Caesar landed on your island, where you were running around half-naked?

A.: Yes, I am sure of it: good houses, good clothing, good food, with good laws and freedom are better than want, anarchy and slavery. Anyone who does not care for London can always go to the Orkneys and live just as we lived in London in Caesar's day —eat oaten bread, and fight to the death with one's neighbor over a bit of dried fish or a mean hut of straw. Uncivilized life may have its charms; but those who preach it do not practice it.

B.: Ah, but at least uncivilized people live under natural law! Nature in her purity has never known parliamentary debates, the prerogatives of the crown, the East India Company, or land-taxes three shillings on the pound, plus a shilling per window.

It's very possible that you have corrupted nature; in the Orkneys and among the Topinambus nature has not been adulterated.

A.: But I could argue that it is the savages who corrupt nature and we who are following it.

C.: You astonish me: are you following nature when you install an archbishop of Canterbury? When you address "Your Majesty" a German you have transplanted to your own country? When you are permitted but one wife, and pay more than a quarter of each year's income in taxes? Just to mention a few of the ways you depart from nature?

A.: No, I can prove my point, if I am not altogether mistaken. Do not judgment and instinct, nature's eldest sons, alike teach us to strive for our own well-being in all things? To work for the well-being of others, at least when it serves our own? If two starving cardinals met by a plum tree wouldn't they automatically help each other to climb the tree and get the fruits? Two ragamuffins in the depths of the Black Forest would do the same, and so would two Chicachas.

B.: Well, what does that prove?

A.: It proves what they all learned in this situation, both the learned doctors and the savages, namely, that in this situation we have to help one another. Therefore, those who help society are those who follow nature most closely. Inventors of the arts (which are the gift of God) and men who give us laws (their task is infinitely easier), are necessarily those who have best complied with nature's law; consequently, the more the arts are cultivated and the more secure is property, the better nature's law is being followed. So, when we agree to pay three shillings on the pound for the right to enjoy the other seventeen shillings in safety; and when we choose a German as our king to preserve our liberties, to act as arbiter between the lords and the common, to be the head of our commonwealth; and when we take only one wife for reasons of thrift, and to have peace and quiet at home; and when (because we are rich) we allow an archbishop of Canterbury to draw twelve thousand guineas to help the poor, to preach virtue (if he happens to be a good preacher), to keep peace among the clergy, etc., etc.—when we do all these things, we are not just bringing nature's law to perfection, but accomplishing something more.

Your savage brute, who lives unsocially (if any such animal exists, as I very much doubt) from morning to night, is perverting the natural law by being of no use to himself or to mankind.

A bee that produces neither honey nor wax, a swallow incapable of building a nest, a hen that never lays an egg—such would be corrupting nature's law, which is simply their own instinct. Men who live unsocially corrupt the instinct of human nature.

C.: So you are saying that it is the naked Brazilian who is the artificial man, not the one we know who covers himself with the wool of sheep and the secretions of silkworms, invents powder and shot to blow himself up, and travels two thousand leagues just to catch the pox? You are saying *he* is the natural man?

A.: No, I am not. But the Brazilian is a sort of animal which has not yet reached the end of its development. He is like a bird whose feathers have not appeared yet, a caterpillar as yet shut up in the chrysalis, still far off from becoming a butterfly. One day there may be Brazilian Lockes and Newtons, and when there are, then your Brazilian will have achieved full human stature. But the Brazilian's organs must be strong and adaptable to reach his goal, for everything depends on the organs. And anyway, what is the character of a Brazilian or the feelings of a Topinambu to me? I am neither the one nor the other, I can only be happy in my way. It is the conditions in which we find ourselves we have to study, not the conditions in which we can never find ourselves.

Thus Voltaire occupies a position midway between those who systematically disparage Europe and those who offer their own systems of how to turn it into a paradise. He occupies a position midway between Hobbes's pessimism and Leibniz's optimism, and between enlightened despotism and integral pacifism. Seeing Europe as it actually was, full of wrongs and intolerance, but also with its new "lights" and great geniuses such as Newton, he wrote in 1767: "I see with pleasure that an immense republic of cultivated minds is taking shape in Europe."

Thus it is "cultural Europe," as we would say today, the society of emancipated minds that seems to him to constitute our most praiseworthy element of unity. Beyond that, we have to be content with the bit of civilization that Christianized Europe has been able to introduce into the jungle of nations. In 1752, in his Introduction to *The Age of Louis XIV*, he wrote:

[Europe surpasses the other parts of the world.] The Christian part of Europe (excepting Muscovy) had long been in such a situation, that it might be considered as one great republic, divided into several states, some monarchical, and others mixed; some aristocratical, others popular; but all corresponding with one another; all having the same foundation for their religion, though divided into several sects; and all having the same principles of political and natural law, unknown in the other parts of the world. It is upon these principles, that the European nations never make their prisoners slaves, that they respect the embassadors of their enemies; that they are agreed touching the preeminence and particular rights of certain princes, as the emperor, the kings, and other inferior potentates; and that, more especially, they are unanimous in regard to the wise policy observed in preserving, as near as possible, an equal balance of power; incessantly employing negotiations, even in the midst of war, and reciprocally maintaining embassadors, or less honourable spies, in their several courts, who may warn all the others of the designs of any one, give at once the alarm to Europe, and preserve the weaker from those invasions which the stronger are continually meditating.[25]

ROUSSEAU (1712–1778)

"Rousseau invented nothing, but set everything on fire," Mme. de Staël said. This is one of those judgments that tell more about

[25] *The Age of Lewis XIV*. [*Translated from the French of M. de Voltaire. Printed for R. Dodsley, in Pall-mall.*], (London, 1762).

the author than the subject. For Rousseau actually believed that he himself invented federalism, "something entirely new," he wrote, "the principles of which are still to be formulated"; he may have been right. He intended to expound the federal system in a sequel to the *Contrat Social*. This sequel, if he ever wrote it, has been lost or destroyed.[26] But he spoke at length of the advantages of a European union in *Extrait,* and of the federal principle itself in a less known, but far more original work, *Le Gouvernement de Pologne.*

A certain Madame Dupin had entrusted Jean-Jacques with the education of her son. She asked him to make a "condensation" (a genre much favored at the time) of the Abbé de Saint-Pierre's *Project.* Rousseau made it, but did not publish it until 1761, at Amsterdam, under the title *Extrait du Projet de paix perpétuelle de M. l'Abbé de Saint-Pierre, par J. J. Rousseau, citoyen de Genève.*

In the opening pages he praises the *Project* enthusiastically, though he does not propose to lose his critical sense:

> Since no greater, nobler, more useful project has ever occupied the human mind than that for a perpetual and universal peace among all the nations of Europe, no author deserves more attention than one who proposes ways of realizing this project. . . .
> I could not help devoting these opening lines to the emotion that filled me. Let us consider it more coolly now.

> What is Europe's actual situation? So far, no one has been able to prevent local wars from becoming general wars; so far limited alliances have led to new conflicts.

> If there is any means to do away with these dangerous contradictions, it can only be a form of federal government, which, uniting the nations by bonds resembling those uniting individuals, subject all to the authority of law. Such a government moreover seems preferable to any other, in that it includes both big and little states. . . .
> Although this form seems new in certain respects, and although it has not actually been well understood in modern times, the

[26] Cf. *Du Contrat Social* (1762), Book III, chap. xv, note *in fine.* It is known that the *Contrat* is but a small part of a large treatise on Political Institutions which he long hoped to write.

ancients were not ignorant of it. The Greeks had their amphic-tyons, the Etruscans their *lucumonia*, the Latins their *feriae*, the Gauls their cities, and even expiring Greece achieved further fame within the Achaean League. But none of these federations came close, in respect of wisdom, to that of the Germanic union, the Helvetian League, and the States General.

In addition to these public federations, others, less apparent though no less real, can be formed out of the community of interest, common goals, similar customs, and other circumstances that further interrelations among divided peoples. Thus, all European powers form a kind of system which unites them in the same religion, the same law of nations, ways of life, letters, and trade, in a kind of balance which is the necessary result of all this, and which, without anyone actually intending to preserve it, could not be broken as easily as many people think.

This society of nations has not always existed: it is thanks to the Roman Empire and later to the Church of Rome that "the nations of Europe form a kind of closely knit society." But there is more than that:

Add to this all that makes Europe so special—the even distri-bution of the population, the equal fertility of the lands, its superior organization. There is a continual interdependence of the sovereigns' interests, which has resulted from ties of blood, from relations formed through trade, industry, and the colonies; the many rivers, which run in every direction, have made com-munication easy; the restlessness of the inhabitants has kept them continually on the move and they frequently visit other than their own countries; the invention of printing, along with a wide-spread love of letters, has created bonds between scholars and men of science; lastly, the fact that there are so many states, none of which is too big, combined with the need for luxury and the diversity of climates, makes every state necessary to every other state. All these causes taken together make Europe not only—as is the case with Asia or Africa—a collectivity of nations with only a name in common—but also a real society, which has its own religion, its own morality, its own way of life, and even its own laws. None of the nations composing it can depart from the society on any of these points without causing trouble at once.

On the other hand, when we also observe the things that divide and separate us—the differences of opinion, the acts of robbery and murder, the usurpation of power, the wars and the rebel-lions which day in and day out ravage this happy home of wisdom, of the arts and the sciences—when we reflect on the discrepancy between our fine words and our horrible ways—the humanity we profess and the cruelty we practice, the gentleness of our religion and the bloodthirstiness of our intolerance, a politics sound in theory but brutal in fact, our good and great leaders and the wretchedness of those who are ruled, governments so moderate and wars so atrocious—then it scarcely seems possible to reconcile such contradictions. What we took for fraternal bonds linking together the peoples of Europe seems now a cruel ironic euphemism for all that in fact sets them against one another.

In this, however, things are merely taking their natural course. Any society without laws and without leaders, any union set up and maintained by accident, must necessarily degenerate into quarrel and dissension at the first opportunity that brings change. The old union of the nations of Europe has complicated their interests and their rights in a thousand ways; they touch one another on so many points that the slightest motion made by one people cannot fail to disturb the others; their divisions are all the more alarming for the fact that their ties are so close, and so each quarrel very nearly takes on the ferocity of a civil war.

Let us now see whether a great work which was begun by chance can be completed by reason. Can a society constituted by the free and voluntary union of all the European states, by taking on the strength and solidity of a true political body, change into a real federation?

Up to this point Rousseau has been expounding his own ideas. Before passing to his digest of the *Project*, he speaks ironically of the hopes the Abbé pins on a Congress of nations:

From time to time general diets of a sort, under the name of Congresses, are convoked in Europe. Delegates from every state in Europe assemble in solemn attendance, and they disperse just as solemnly. They do not come together because they have anything to say: they discuss all public affairs in private; they deliberate on whether the conference table should be round or square, whether the chamber should have two doors or three, whether a given delegate should turn his face or his back to the window or should walk two inches more or less than another in the course of a visit. They devote their time to a thousand questions of similar importance, questions which have been vainly discussed for three hundred years, and which are still thought worthy of discussion in our own day.

It is not beyond the bounds of possibility that one of these assemblies might, for once, be informed by common sense; it is not impossible even that it might sincerely desire the public good, and for reasons which will be given below, it is conceivable that after smoothing out many difficulties, the delegates might be under orders from their respective sovereigns to sign a treaty of federation. Such a treaty might contain the following five articles.

There follows a long résumé of the *Project's* five main points, followed in turn by this justly famous conclusion:

The establishment of perpetual peace depends solely upon the consent of the sovereigns, and raises no other difficulty than their resistance to it. This is not to say, of course, that the sovereigns will adopt such a project (who can answer for another man's reason?), but only that they would adopt it if they consulted their true interests: for it must be noted that we have not assumed men to be what they ought to be, that is, good, generous, disinterested, humanely devoted to the public good; but we have assumed them to be as they are, that is, unjust, greedy, and ready to sacrifice everything to their own selfish interests. The only other thing we assume is that they are reasonable enough to see what is useful to them, and courageous enough to create their own happiness. If, despite all that, this project is not carried out, it is not because it is fantastical, but because men are stupid, and because it is a kind of folly to be wise when all around you are mad.

In *Jugement sur la Paix perpétuelle*, written at the same time as the *Extrait* but published only posthumously, Rousseau formulates severer criticisms. The Abbé expects the sovereign princes to convoke the European Congress; according to Rousseau, it is up to the peoples themselves to create their federation. For:

. . . can we hope to subject to a superior tribunal men who dare to boast that they hold power only by the sword, and who mention God only because he is in His heaven? Will the sovereigns agree to settle their differences by resorting to juridical means, when, despite the rigor of the law, private individuals have never resorted to those means to settle their quarrels? An ordinary gentleman, when he is insulted, does not run to the tribunal of the marshals of France; how can you expect a king to run to a European diet?

Continually taken in by the appearance of things, the princes would therefore reject this peace if they weighed their interests personally. What will happen if this is done by their ministers whose interests are invariably opposed to those of the people and very often to those of the prince? The ministers need war to make themselves indispensable . . .

And the public cannot fail to ask why, if this project is possible, they have not adopted it. The only thing the public finds impossible in this project is that the ministers should ever adopt it. What, then, will they do to oppose it? They will do what they have always done: they will turn it into ridicule.

Nearly twenty years after he wrote the *Extrait*, in 1771, Rousseau was approached by the Polish Confederates during a respite in the war they were waging against the Russians. On the eve of the tragic partition of Poland, these patriots asked the author of the *Contrat Social* to draw up a plan for a less bizarre and anarchic constitution than the one that had brought ruin to their country. Rousseau agreed to try, at the same time complaining that the state of his health had "scarcely left him the capacity to think coherently." He completed the work in 1773, the very year the treaty of partition was signed. He called it *Considération sur le Gouvernement de Pologne et sur sa réformation projetée en 1772.*

His primary concern throughout the essay is to persuade the Poles not to imitate "Europe," that is to say, the Western powers which "every day degenerate more and more because of the general tendency to adopt French tastes and French customs." To the cosmopolitanism then fashionable he opposed a resolute particularism, which he called "national," but which was in reality local or communal, as will be seen below.

Poland is a large state surrounded by even larger states, which, because of their despotism and military discipline, have great offensive power. Poland on the contrary is weak because of her anarchy, and despite her valor she is continually exposed to their assaults. . . . In the present state of affairs I see only one means for giving her the firmness she lacks: this is to instill, so to speak, the entire nation with the spirit of the Confederates, to implant the republican idea in the Polish heart so strongly that it will survive all attempts to destroy it. There, so it seems to me, is the only refuge where violence can neither affect nor destroy her. This has recently been proved in a manner forever memorable. Poland was enslaved by the Russians, yet the Poles have remained free. A great example, which shows you how to defy the power and ambition of your neighbors. You cannot stop them from swallowing you up; see to it at least that they cannot digest you . . .

It is the national institutions that form the genius, the character, and the way of life of a people, that makes it to be itself and not another. . . .

Today there are no more French, Germans, Spaniards, or even English, no matter what you may be told: there are only Europeans. All have the same tastes, the same passions, the same way of life, because none has received national form by virtue of a particular institution. . . . It does not matter to them what master they obey, of what state they observe the laws. Provided they find money they can steal and women they can corrupt, they are everywhere at home.

Therefore, the Poles should be themselves, and learn to love their own country, no other. Today we cannot read Rousseau's eulogy of "national education" without certain misgivings:

It is by education that minds are given a national form, that their opinions and tastes are guided in such a way that the people become patriots by inclination, by passion, by necessity. A child opening his eyes should see his country, and to the day of his death should see nothing else. Every true republican took in with his mother's milk the love that makes up all his existence: he sees his own country only, lives only for it; by himself he is nothing; the moment he no longer has his country, he no longer exists; and if he has not died, he is worse off.

National education belongs only to free men; only they have a life in common, only they are truly linked by the law. A Frenchman, an Englishman, a Spaniard, an Italian, a Russian are all more or less the same human beings; on leaving school they have all been fashioned for licentiousness, that is to say, servitude. By the age of twenty, a Pole should not be just another man, he should be a Pole. I want him, when he learns to read, to read books about his country; at the age of ten he should know all his country has produced, at twelve all his country's provinces, roads, and cities; at fifteen, he should know its entire history, at sixteen all its laws; in all Poland there should not be a noble action or a famous man who does not fill his heart and memory

and whose life he cannot recount at once . . . The law should
regulate the content, the order, and the form of his studies . . .
   All being equal under the state constitution, all should be
brought up together and in the same manner; and if it is impossible to set up a system of public education free to all, at least
education should cost no more than the poor can pay.

In such passages does not Rousseau seem a real forerunner of
twentieth-century totalitarian regimes? He does indeed, and he
certainly uses their language, but it is precisely the language that
is misleading in this case. For when he writes "national," Rousseau has in mind something entirely different from what this
adjective suggests to us. He has in mind a specific city, a small
state, the smallest and freest possible—he has in mind Geneva!
What he recommends to the Poles is actually the exact opposite
of modern nationalism—it is integral federalism, a return to the
spirit of the medieval free towns:

Almost all small states, whether republics or monarchies, thrive
solely because they are small, because all their citizens know and
respect one another, because the leaders can see for themselves
the evil that is done and the good that needs to be done, and
because their orders are carried out before their very eyes. All big
nations, crushed by their very mass, groan either in anarchy, as
you do, or under a hierarchy of subaltern oppressors whom the
rulers need to keep them in order. The first reform you need is
that of your territorial size . . . If you want to reform your government, begin by contracting your boundaries. Your neighbors
may be planning to render you this very service. This would no
doubt be very painful to the dismembered parts: but it would be
greatly beneficial to the body of the nation . . .
   I should like you, if possible, to have as many states as you
have provinces.[27] In each set up a local administration. Improve
the form of the little diets, extend their authority in their respective provinces; but carefully define their limits and see to it that
nothing can break the bond of common legislation which links
them, and their subordination to the body of the republic. In
short, apply yourselves to *extending and improving the system of
federal government, the only one that combines the advantages
of big and small states, and thereby the only one suitable for you.*

[27] At that time Poland was divided into thirty-three provinces ("voivod-
ships") each with its local, or "little," diet.

In this central part of his report, Rousseau explicitly recalls the means he advocated in *Du Contrat Social* for linking together the only kind of state he really tolerates: the free town. Here is the passage from the *Contrat* (III, 13) to which he refers his readers:

This might be good, I will be told, for a single town; but what are we to do if the state comprises several towns? Should the sovereign authority be divided? Or should it be concentrated in a single town, with the others subject to it?

My answer is that neither the one nor the other should be done. In the first place, the sovereign authority is one and indivisible, and cannot be divided without being destroyed. In the second place, a town just like a nation cannot be legitimately subject to another, because the essence of the body politic lies in the accord between freedom and obedience, and because the terms "subject" and "sovereign" are identical correlatives, the idea of which is combined in the single term "citizen" . . .

But how can small states be made sufficiently strong to resist the big ones? In the same way as the ancient Greek cities resisted the Great King, and as, more recently, Holland and Switzerland resisted the House of Austria.

If however, the Poles prefer national grandeur (in the modern sense of the term) to this integral federalism, let them follow the example of the rest of Europe, let them develop the arts, the sciences, trade, finance, and the army, and let them centralize the whole in the name of national power:

In this way you will form a nation like the others, ungenerous, greedy, servile, and knavish, unable to find a happy medium between the extremes of poverty and opulence, licentiousness and slavery, but you will be counted among the great powers of Europe, you will be part of the political systems: in every negotiation your alliance will be sought; you will be bound by treaties; there will be no war in Europe into which you will not have the honor of being plunged; with luck, you will be able to recover your former possessions, perhaps conquer new ones, and then you can say like Pyrrhus or the Russians, that is, like children: "When the whole world is mine, I'll have as much sugar as I want."

Glorious Europe

The Europe of Montesquieu, Voltaire, and Rousseau may occasionally criticize herself, make comparisons, and does so for the first time in the history of ideas; but she has no serious doubts about herself. It was a French Europe. France at the peak of her intellectual hegemony could not conceive any comparison that would turn to her disadvantage, though it might confound some opponent at the time not considered representative. (As Rousseau considered Voltaire, Voltaire considered Rousseau; the real France, and hence the real Europe, could scarcely be harmed by the downfall of opponents blind to her true genius!)

The three texts below will give an adequate idea of the pride and confidence that French Europe had in her destiny. All three proclaim the essential, quasi-absolute superiority of the European religion, the white race, and the French language.

Anne-Robert-Jacques Turgot, Baron de l'Aulne (1727–1781), was a seminarian before entering upon a civil service career which made him eventually one of Louis XVI's greatest ministers. In 1750, when he was still a very young man, holding the office of prior at the Sorbonne, he made a speech in Latin, a "First speech, on the advantages brought to the human race by the establishment of Christianity." From this long rhetorical exercise, we shall quote a prosopopoeia typical of the century:

. . . Proud Greece! Where are thy numberless cities that glittered with thy splendor? Hordes of barbarians obliterated the very traces of those arts by means of which thou hast formerly triumphed over the Romans, subjecting thy very conquerors. All was swept away in fanaticism with the rise of that destructive religion which consecrated Barbarism. Egypt, Asia, Africa, Greece, all disappeared as it advanced. When we look back on them today, all we see is the sloth, ignorance and brutal despotism that grew up on their ruins. Our Europe, too, did she not too fall prey to the barbarians from the north? What fortunate sanctuary could have kept burning the flickering torch of science amid howling storms? Who could believe it? The religion which had become established in Rome had attached itself to her despite itself, supported her, and secured her survival after her downfall! Yes, thanks to this religion alone did those ferocious conquerors, renouncing their pride, submit to reason, to the civilization of the vanquished, and carry its lights themselves back to their ancient forest, even into farthest north. Thanks to it alone have come down to us the immortal works from which we still draw precepts and examples of the purest taste, and thanks to which we could, with the revival of letters, venture on our own without great loss of time. It was thanks to Christianity alone, finally, that the genius which distinguished Greece and Rome from the barbarians is still alive today in Europe; and although many successive devastations, divisions among the conquerors, vicious government, the isolation of the nobility far from the towns, the absence of trade, the mixture of peoples and languages—although all these things long kept Europe in crass ignorance, and although it took time to efface the remnants of barbarism, at least the surviving monuments of this genius, the models of taste, though little consulted and rarely followed, were preserved in the hands of ignorance as in a storehouse waiting for happier days. Knowledge of the ancient languages was perpetuated through the needs of divine service. This knowledge long failed to produce visible effects; but it has survived, just as trees which lose their leaves in winter survive the frost, and bloom once again with the coming of spring.

The Abbé Fernando Galiani (1727–1787) was born in the Abruzzi. At the age of twenty-two he wrote a work on currencies. Marmontel described him as "the prettiest little Harlequin ever produced by Italy." Grimm was more enthusiastic: "Plato with Harlequin's ebullience and dash." Referring to Galiani's *Dialogues sur les blés* published in 1770, Voltaire wrote: "No one has ever written more amusingly on the subject of famine." His correspondence with Mme. d'Epinay reflects the opinions that were acceptable in the "advanced" salons of the epoch. Here are two excerpts from it: [28]

. . . Mankind too, has taken a very long time to begin to perfect itself; the peoples of California and New Holland, which are three to four thousand years old, are still true savages. Perfectibility began to make great progress in Asia, it is said, more than twelve thousand years ago; and God only knows how much time before then had been spent in vain efforts. If an Asiatic race had not migrated to Europe and Africa, and had not gone from Europe to America, and from there gone everywhere else, man would still be merely the most mischievous, cunning and clever of the monkeys. Thus perfectibility is not a characteristic of man-

[28] Fernando Galiani, *Correspondance inédite de l'Abbé F. G. conseiller du Roi, pendant les années 1765 à 1783* (Paris: I. G. Dentu, 1818), Vol. II. The two texts given below are excerpts from letters to Mme. d'Epinay, dated October 12, 1776, and November 22, 1777.

kind as a whole, but only of the bearded white race. The bearded swarthy race, the nonbearded swarthy race, and the black race have all made advances through intermarriage. Everything that is said about climates is silly, a *causa pro non causa*, the most common error in logic. Everything depends on race. The first and noblest of the races comes naturally from northern Asia. The Russians are closest to it, and this is why they have made so much more progress in fifty years than the Portuguese will make in a hundred.

. . . Instability is a physical law. . . . Without it, there is no fertility, no variety, no perfectibility. It is to the immense variety of the nations which have peopled Europe or intermarried that we owe the perfectibility of our race. The Chinese have become stagnant solely because they did not mix with others; and since the coming of the Tartars, they have advanced a great deal.

Antoine Rivarol (1753–1801), wit, and precursor of scandal sheet journalism, is known today almost exclusively for some cynical maxims on love and morals and for his *Discours sur l'Universalité de la langue française*, which was awarded a prize by the Academy of Berlin in 1784. It contains the following passage, which refers to the Renaissance:

In this epoch, the revival of letters, the discovery of America and of the route to India, inventions like gunpowder and printing changed the face of the empires. Those which had been brilliant were suddenly eclipsed; others, emerging from their obscurity, began to play their part on the world stage. Although the veil of religion was rent from north to south, an enormous expansion of trade has created new bonds among men. The American soil today is being worked by Africans, and we use the riches of America to traffic in Asia. Never before had the universe presented such a spectacle. Europe, especially, has achieved a degree of power unprecedented in history: the number of its capitals, the frequency and speed with which people move about, the development of public and private communications, have transformed it into one immense republic.

. . . Europe constitutes a federal republic composed of empires and kingdoms, the most formidable that has ever existed; it is impossible to foresee its end, and yet the French language will survive. States will be overthrown, but two anchors will hold the ship of this language—its literature and its clarity—up until the moment when, through one of those great revolutions which brings things back to the starting point, nature will renew her treaties with another mankind.

As though echoing these optimistic voices from France, here is a no less "philosophical" message from Spain by a champion of a Europe federated . . . by Education: Gaspar Melchor de Jovellanos (1744–1811), famous statesman and poet:

Who does not see that thanks to the progress [of education] the governments will work solely and effectively for the happiness of those they govern, and that the nations, instead of fighting and destroying one another for petty reasons of interest or ambition, will tighten the mutual bonds of love and brotherhood to which Providence has destined them? Who does not see that the progress of education will eventually lead, first the most enlightened nations of Europe, and then the rest of the world, into a general federation whose goal will be to secure to each of them enjoyment of the resources given them by God, as well as to maintain an inviolable and perpetual peace, and curb—not by means of armies and cannon, but by the strength of its voice, which will be more powerful and formidable than they—those foolhardy peoples who dare to disturb the peace and happiness of mankind? Who does not see, finally, that this federation of nations and societies which inhabit the earth is the only general society possible for mankind, the only one dictated to it by nature and religion, and the only one worthy of the high destiny for which God created it? [29]

3 : Evolution: Forward or Backward?

Already to Montesquieu, Rome as he studied it in *Considérations sur les causes de la grandeur et de la décadence des Romains* was a kind of organism subjected to immanent laws of development, or, to use his own words, to the action "of general causes" governing actual events, to the "main movement which carries along all particular accidents."

In the last third of the eighteenth century opened the era of general views of world history. The idea of an organic or "dialec-

[29] *Tratado teorice-practico de Enseñanza,* in *Works by Jovellanos* (Biblioteca de autores españoles), I, 251.

tical" development of civilizations was forcing itself gradually upon historians and philosophers. It has incalculable implications. For if "laws" of evolution exist, clearly each rise to greatness must be succeeded by a decline, just as maturity is succeeded by old age and death. In this way an anxious doubt slowly insinuates itself into the European consciousness: this accounts for the exactly simultaneous birth of the ideas of infinite Progress and of the West's inevitable total Decline.

Robertson set out to write a history of Europe conceived of as an organic whole. A few years later Gibbon treated Montesquieu's subject, but from a less moralistic, more historical point of view: his aim was to draw from the development of Rome instructive conclusions concerning the development of Europe, and these are just barely optimistic. But the problem of European decline was nonetheless raised from that moment on. Condorcet was well aware of it, but responded to the challenge by launching the idea of Progress. Volney, on the other hand, the first of the Romantics, succumbed to the dizzying vision of Decline. As for Wieland, the last of the "enlightened" philosophers, he was to believe to the very end, to the outbreak of the Revolution, and even after it, that the era of "cosmopolitan" reason had forever been instituted in Europe. . . .

William Robertson (1721–1793), royal chaplain for Scotland and head of the University of Edinburgh, may be looked upon as the first historian to have studied the whole of Europe treating it as an entity, not as the sum of regional chronicles. The reader of today will not fail to see this method as heralding Toynbee's thesis on "intelligible fields of historical study." In the Preface to his *History of the Reign of Emperor Charles V* (1769), Robertson states explicitly that he intends to confine the "study of history in detail chiefly to that period, in which the several states of Europe having become intimately connected, the operations of any one power are so felt by all as to influence their councils, and to regulate their measures." That is why he set out to write the history of Charles V. He says: [30]

[30] William Robertson, *The History of the Reign of Emperor Charles V* (Philadelphia, 1864).

An era should be pointed out, prior to which each country, little connected with those around it, may trace its own history apart; after which, the transactions of every considerable nation in Europe become interesting and instructive to all. With this intention I undertook to write the History of the Emperor Charles the Fifth. It was during his administration that the powers of Europe were formed into one great political system, in which each took a station, wherein it has since remained with less variation than could have been expected. . . . The age of Charles the Fifth may therefore be considered as the period at which the political state of Europe began to assume a new form.

Two passages from the Introduction, entitled "A View of the Progress of Society in Europe," cast light upon and define the European historiography initiated by Robertson:

During several centuries, the nations of Europe appear to have considered themselves as separate societies, scarcely connected together by any common interest, and little concerned in each other's affairs or operations. An extensive commerce did not afford them an opportunity of observing and penetrating into the schemes of every different state. They had not ambassadors residing constantly in every court, to watch and give early intelligence of all its motions. The expectation of remote advantages, or the prospect of distant and contingent evils, was not sufficient to excite nations to take arms. Such only as were within the sphere of immediate danger, and unavoidably exposed to injury or insult, thought themselves interested in any contest, or bound to take precautions for their own safety.

Whoever records the transactions of any of the more considerable European states during the two last centuries, must write the history of Europe. Its various kingdoms, throughout that period, have been formed into one great system, so closely united, that, each holding a determinate station, the operations of one are so felt by all as to influence their counsels and regulate their measures. But previous to the fifteenth century, unless when vicinity of territory rendered the occasions of discord frequent and unavoidable . . . the affairs of different countries are seldom interwoven with each other.

However, knowledge of Europe's diversities is for all that as essential to the historian as that of its unity:

While these institutions and occurrences, which I have mentioned, formed the people of Europe to resemble each other, and conducted them from barbarism to refinement, in the same path, and with almost equal steps, there were other circumstances which occasioned a difference in their political establishments, and gave rise to those peculiar modes of government, which have produced such variety in the character and genius of nations.

It is no less necessary to become acquainted with the latter than to have contemplated the former. The view which I have exhibited of the causes and events, whose influence was universal, will enable my readers to account for the surprising resemblance among the nations of Europe in their interior police, and foreign operations. But, without a distinct knowledge of the peculiar form and genius of their civil government, a great part of their transactions must appear altogether mysterious and inexplicable. The historians of particular states, as they seldom extended their views farther than to the amusement or instruction of their fellow-citizens, by whom they might presume that all domestic customs and institutions were perfectly understood, have often neglected to descend into such details with respect to these, as are sufficient to convey to foreigners full light and information concerning the occurrences which they relate. But a history, which comprehends the transactions of so many different countries, would be extremely imperfect without a previous survey of their constitution and political state.

In the end Robertson will thus be led to examine one after the other the national components of his "View," just as did Voltaire in his *Essai sur les Mœurs*, written shortly before, and Johannes von Müller, a little later. It was the frame of reference of the historian's judgments that had changed: when describing the evolution of a given nation, he mentions Europe on every page.

Edward Gibbon (1737–1794) hardly suspected that he was founding a tradition to reckon with when he titled his monumental work—which, as he said, "has amused and exercised near twenty years of my life"—*History of the Decline and Fall of the Roman Empire*. Down to our own day his example has not ceased to inspire writers attempting overall syntheses of the history of civilizations. Unlike Spengler and Toynbee, and like Schlegel, Hegel, and Comte, Gibbon, who wrote before Darwin and Marx, does not deduce the organic inevitability of a decline of Europe from the decline of the ancient world. Far from it! In "General

Observations on the Fall of the Western Roman Empire" (which follows chapter XXXVIII of his work), he examines the three major causes which, according to him, contributed to the ruin of Rome, and which now can justify belief in the security of Europe. In the light of our century's experience, the predictions he based upon observation of his own century can be reversed. But if he was overoptimistic, we may be overpessimistic, these two errors of appraisal changing nothing in the *facts* of civilization that Gibbon lists lucidly. "The ten thousand ships" ready to carry the treasures of Europe to America have already crossed the Atlantic more than once.

It is the duty of a patriot to prefer and promote the exclusive interest and glory of his native country; but a philosopher may be permitted to enlarge his views and to consider Europe as one great republic whose various inhabitants have attained almost the same level of politeness and cultivation. The balance of power will continue to fluctuate, and the prosperity of our own or the neighbouring kingdoms may be alternately exalted or depressed; but these partial events cannot essentially injure our general state of happiness, the system of arts and laws and manners which so advantageously distinguish, above the rest of mankind, the Europeans and their colonies. The savage nations of the globe are the common enemies of civilized society; and we may inquire, with anxious curiosity, whether Europe is still threatened with a repetition of those calamities which formerly oppressed the arms and institutions of Rome. Perhaps the same reflections will illustrate the fall of that mighty empire, and explain the probable causes of our actual security.

I. The Romans were ignorant of the extent of their dangers and the number of their enemies. Beyond the Rhine and Danube the northern countries of Europe and Asia were filled with innumerable tribes of hunters and shepherds, poor, voracious, and turbulent, bold in arms and impatient to ravish the fruits of industry. The barbarian world was agitated by the rapid impulse of war, and the peace of Gaul or Italy was shaken by the distant revolutions of China. The Huns, who fled before a victorious enemy, directed their march towards the West; and the torrent was swelled by the gradual accession of captives and allies. The flying tribes who yielded to the Huns assumed in *their* turn the spirit of conquest; the endless column of barbarians pressed on the Roman empire with accumulated weight; and if the foremost were destroyed the vacant space was instantly replenished by new assailants. Such formidable emigrations no longer issue from the North; and the long repose, which has been imputed to the decrease of population, is the happy consequence of the progress of arts and agriculture. Instead of some rude villages thinly scattered among its woods and morasses, Germany now produces a list of two thousand three hundred walled towns; the Christian kingdoms of Denmark, Sweden, and Poland have been successively established; and the Hanse merchants, with the Teutonic knights, have extended their colonies along the coast of the Baltic as far as the Gulf of Finland. From the Gulf of Finland to the Eastern Ocean, Russia now assumes the form of a powerful and civilized empire. The plough, the loom, and the forge are introduced on the banks of the Volga, the Oby, and the Lena; and the fiercest of the Tartar hordes have been taught to tremble and obey. The reign of independent barbarism is now contracted to a narrow span; and the remnant of Calmucks or Uzbecks, whose forces may be almost numbered, cannot seriously excite the apprehensions of the great republic of Europe. Yet this apparent security should not tempt us to forget that new enemies and unknown dangers may *possibly* arise from some obscure people, scarcely visible in the map of the world. The Arabs or Saracens, who spread their conquests from India to Spain, had languished in poverty and contempt till Mahomet breathed into those same bodies the soul of enthusiasm.

II. The empire of Rome was firmly established by the singular and perfect coalition of its members. The subject nations, resigning the hope and even the wish of independence, embraced the character of Roman citizens; and the provinces of the West were reluctantly torn by the barbarians from their mother country. But this union was purchased by the loss of national freedom and military spirit; and the servile provinces, destitute of life and motion, expected their safety from the mercenary troops and governors who were directed by the orders of a distant court. The happiness of an hundred millions depended on the personal merit of one or two men, perhaps children, whose minds were corrupted by education, luxury, and despotic power. The deepest wounds were inflicted on the empire during the minorities of the sons and grandsons of Theodosius; and after those incapable princes seemed to attain the age of manhood they abandoned the church to the bishops, the state to the eunuchs, and the provinces to the barbarians.

Europe is now divided into twelve powerful though unequal kingdoms, three respectable commonwealths, and a variety of smaller though independent states; the chances of royal and ministerial talent are multiplied, at least, with the number of its rulers; and a Julian or Semiramis may reign in the North, while Arcadius and Honorius again slumber on the thrones of the South. The abuses of tyranny are restrained by the mutual influence of fear and shame; republics have acquired order and stability; monarchies have imbibed the principles of freedom, or at least of moderation; and some sense of honour and justice is introduced into the most defective constitutions by the general manners of the times. In peace, the progress of knowledge and industry is accelerated by the emulation of so many active rivals; in war, the European forces are exercised by temperate and undecisive contests. If a savage conqueror should issue from the deserts of Tartary, he must repeatedly vanquish the robust peasants of Russia, the numerous armies of Germany, the gallant nobles of France, and the intrepid freemen of Britain, who, perhaps, might confederate for their common defence. Should the victorious barbarians carry slavery and desolation as far as the Atlantic Ocean, ten thousand vessels would transport beyond their pursuit the remains of civilized society; and Europe would revive and flourish in the American world, which is already filled with her colonies and institutions.

III. Cold, poverty and a life of danger and fatigue fortify the strength and courage of barbarians. In every age they have oppressed the polite and peaceful nations of China, India, and Persia, who neglected, and still neglect, to counterbalance these natural powers by the resources of military art. The warlike states of antiquity, Greece, Macedonia, and Rome, educated a race of soldiers; exercised their bodies, disciplined their courage, multiplied their forces by regular evolutions, and converted the iron which they possessed into strong and serviceable weapons. But this superiority insensibly declined with their laws and manners; and the feeble policy of Constantine and his successors armed and instructed, for the ruin of the empire, the rude valour of the barbarian mercenaries. The military art has been changed by the invention of gunpowder, which enables man to command the two most powerful agents of nature, air and fire. Mathematics, chemistry, mechanics, architecture, have been applied to the service of war, and the adverse parties oppose to each other the most elaborate modes of attack and of defence. Historians may indignantly observe that the preparations of a siege would found and maintain a flourishing colony; yet we cannot be displeased that the subversion of a city should be a work of cost and difficulty, or that an industrious people should be protected by those arts which survive and supply the decay of military virtue. Cannon and fortifications now form an impregnable barrier against the Tartar horse; and Europe is secure from any future irruption of barbarians, since, before they can conquer, they must cease to be barbarous. Their gradual advances in the science of war would always be accompanied, as we may learn from the example of Russia, with a proportionable improvement in the arts of peace and civil policy; and they themselves must deserve a place among the polished nations whom they subdue.

The Marquis Antoine de Condorcet (1743–1794), supporter and victim of the Revolution, wrote his *Esquisse d'un tableau historique des progrès de l'esprit humain* one year before his death; at that time he was a fugitive, sheltered by friends. His method of "calculation of life expectancy" makes him a precursor of social security; he was also a precursor of international scientific co-operation.[31]

We shall quote passages from *Esquisse* in which he lucidly foresees (but resolves overoptimistically) the problems that will be created in the world by the expansion of our concepts and technologies, or, as he puts it, that of "the lights and reason of Europe."

Will not every nation one day arrive at the state of civilization attained by those people who are most enlightened, most free, most exempt from prejudices, as the French, for instance, and the Anglo-Americans? Will not the slavery of countries subjected to kings, the barbarity of African tribes, and the ignorance of savages gradually vanish? Is there upon the face of the globe a single spot the inhabitants of which are condemned by nature never to enjoy liberty, never to exercise their reason?

Does the difference of knowledge, of means, and of wealth, observable hitherto in all civilized nations, between the classes into which the people constituting these nations are divided; does that inequality, which the earliest progress of society has augmented, or, to speak more properly, produced, belong to civilization itself, or to the imperfections of the social order? Must it not continually weaken, in order to give place to that actual equality,

[31] "I shall speak . . . of bringing together scientists from all over the world in one universal republic of the sciences, the only one of which the project and usefulness are not a puerile illusion."—*Fragment sur l'Atlantide, ou efforts combinés de l'Espèce humaine pour le Progrès des Sciences.*

the chief end of the social art, which diminishing even the effect of the natural difference of the faculties, leaves no other inequality subsisting but what is useful to the interest of all, because it will favor civilization, instruction, and industry, without drawing after it either dependence, humiliation or poverty?

. . . In fine, may it not be expected that the human race will be meliorated by new discoveries in the sciences and the arts, and, as an unavoidable consequence, in the means of individual and general prosperity; by further progress in the principles of conduct, and in moral practice; and lastly, by the real improvement of our faculties, moral, intellectual and physical . . . or of the improvement of our natural organization itself?

In examining the three questions we have enumerated, we shall find the strongest reasons to believe . . . that nature has fixed no limits to our hopes.

If we take a survey of the existing state of the globe, we shall perceive, in the first place, that in Europe the principles of the French constitution are those of every enlightened mind. We shall perceive that they are too widely disseminated, and too openly professed, for the efforts of tyrants and priests to prevent them from penetrating by degrees into the miserable cottages of their slaves, where they will soon revive those embers of good sense, and rouse that silent indignation which the habit of suffering and terror have failed totally to extinguish in the minds of the oppressed.

. . . Can it be supposed that either the wisdom or the senseless feuds of European nations, co-operating with the slow but certain effects of the progress of their colonies, will not shortly produce the independence of the entire new world; and that then, European population, lending its aid, will fail to civilize or cause to disappear, even without conquest, those savage nations still occupying there immense tracts of country.

Run through the history of our projects and establishments in Africa or in Asia, and you will see our monopolies, our treachery, our sanguinary contempt for men of a different complexion or different creed, and the proselytizing fury or the intrigues of our priests, destroying that sentiment of respect and benevolence which the superiority of our information and the advantages of our commerce had at first obtained.

But the period is doubtless approaching, when, no longer exhibiting to the view of these people corruptors only or tyrants, we shall become to them instruments of benefit, and the generous champions of their redemption from bondage.

. . . Then will the inhabitants of the European quarter of the world, satisfied with an unrestricted commerce, too enlightened as to their own rights to sport with the rights of others, respect the independence which they have hitherto violated with such audacity. Then will their establishments, instead of being filled by the creatures of power, who, availing themselves of a place or privilege, hasten, by rapine and perfidy, to amass wealth, in order to purchase, on their return, honors and titles, be peopled with industrious men, seeking in those happy climates that ease and comfort which in their native country eluded their pursuit. There will they be retained by liberty, ambition having lost its allurements; and those settlements of robbers will then become colonies of citizens, by whom will be planted in Africa and Asia the principles and example of the freedom, reason, and illumination of Europe.[32]

The Count Constantin-François Chassebœuf de Volney, born in 1757, visited Turkey, Syria, Egypt, and America. Orientalist, philosopher, and writer, deputy to the National Assembly, he was imprisoned under the Revolution, and appointed senator and peer of France under the Restoration. He owed his fame to a work entitled *Les Ruines* (published in 1791), which moved several generations to tears, and in which he shows himself to be not only a forerunner of Romanticism but also of the twentieth-century writers who have meditated on the end of Europe, "on the ashes of the nations and the memory of their greatness." (Paul Valéry no doubt recalled this when writing his famous pages on "The Crisis of the Mind.")

Here, said I, once flourished an opulent city; here was the seat of a powerful empire. Yes! these places now so wild and desolate, were once animated by a living multitude; a busy crowd thronged in these streets, now so solitary. Within these walls, where now reigns the silence of death, the noise of the arts, and the shouts of joy and festivity incessantly resounded; these piles of marble were regular palaces; these fallen columns adorned the majesty of temples; these ruined galleries surrounded public places. Here assembled a numerous people for the sacred duties of their religion, and the anxious cares of their

[32] *Outlines of an Historical View of the Progress of the Human Mind: [being a posthumous work of the late M. de Condorcet. Translated from the French. Baltimore: Printed by G. Fryer, for J. Frank.], (1802), pp. 210 ff.*

subsistence; here industry, parent of enjoyments, collected the riches of all climes, and the purple of Tyre was exchanged for the precious thread of Serica; the soft tissues of Cassimere for the sumptuous tapestry of Lydia; the amber of the Baltic for the pearls and perfumes of Arabia; the gold of Ophir for the tin of Thule.

And now behold what remains of this powerful city: a miserable skeleton! What of its vast domination: a doubtful and obscure remembrance! To the noisy concourse which thronged under these porticoes, succeeds the solitude of death. The silence of the grave is substituted for the busy hum of public places; the affluence of a commercial city is changed into wretched poverty; the places of kings have become a den of wild beasts; flocks repose in the area of temples, and savage reptiles inhabit the sanctuary of the gods. Ah! how has so much glory been eclipsed? how have so many labors been annihilated? Do thus perish then the works of men—thus vanish empires and nations?

And the history of former times revived in my mind; I remembered those ancient ages when many illustrious nations inhabited these countries; . . . This Syria, said I, now so depopulated, then contained a hundred flourishing cities. . . . whither vanished those brilliant creations of human industry? Where are those ramparts of Nineveh, those walls of Babylon, those palaces of Persepolis, those temples of Balbec and Jerusalem? Where are those fleets of Tyre, those dock-yards of Arad, those work-shops of Sidon, and that multitude of sailors, of pilots, of merchants, and of soldiers? Where those husbandmen, harvests, flocks and all the creation of living beings in which the face of the earth rejoiced? Alas! I have passed over this desolate land! I have visited the palaces, once the scene of so much splendor, and I beheld nothing but solitude and desolation. . . . At these words, revolving in my mind the vicissitudes which have transmitted the sceptre of the world to people so different in religion and manners from those in ancient Asia to the most recent of Europe, this name of a natal land revived in me the sentiment of my country; and turning my eyes towards France, I began to reflect on the situation in which I had left her.

I recalled her fields so richly cultivated, her roads so admirably constructed, her cities inhabited by a countless people, her fleets spread over every sea, her ports filled with the produce of both the Indies: and then comparing the activity of her commerce, the extent of her navigation, the magnificence of her buildings, the arts and industry of her inhabitants, with what Egypt and Syria had once possessed, I was gratified to find in modern Europe the departed splendor of Asia; but the charm of my reverie was soon dissolved by a last term of comparison. Reflecting that such had once been the activity of the places I was then contemplating, who knows, said I, but such may one day be the abandonment of our countries? Who knows if on the banks of the Seine, the Thames, the Zuyder-Zee, where now, in the tumult of many enjoyments, the heart and the eye suffice not for the multitude of sensations—who knows if some traveller, like myself, shall not one day sit on their silent ruins, and weep in solitude over the ashes of their inhabitants, and memory of their former greatness. [33]

Christoph Martin Wieland (1733–1813), writing on the eve of the Revolution, was the last to express the ideal of Montesquieu and Voltaire, symbolized by the "Cosmopolitan":

The cosmopolitan obeys all the laws of the state in which he lives, so long as they obviously reflect wisdom, justice and the general interest; as for the other laws, he submits to them because he must. He is of good faith where his nation is concerned, but also where other nations are concerned: he will never seek to base the well-being, glory, and grandeur of his country on wilful oppression and exploitation of other States.

This is why cosmopolitans never join any organization whose aims are incompatible with their ideal. They refrain from serving any government that follows principles contrary to their own maxims.

Therefore the cosmopolitan looks upon the different existing regimes as so many "scaffoldings for the building of the immortal temple of universal felicity toward which, in a sense, all past centuries have been laboring."

The text quoted below, taken from a work entitled Das Geheimnis des Kosmopoliten Ordens—which, by a tragic irony, appeared in 1788!—shows the full extent of the complacent blindness into which the Enlightenment had plunged the eighteenth-century intellectual elite:

Only few among the nations of the past knew the true value of freedom. The Greeks knew it, and it was thanks to the Greeks —whose merits can never be sufficiently appreciated by humanity —that Europe gradually became what she is and what she probably will always be, the true homeland of the arts and sciences,

[33] Volney, The Ruins, trans. J. Barlow (New York, 1890), chap. ii.

the continent where culture has reached its apogee, and which, even though it is the smallest continent, has conquered hegemony forever, thanks to the superiority which its inhabitants have been able to maintain over other peoples by an ever greater, and ever more advanced improvement of man's natural faculties.

This effect of well-known causes is equally well-known: despite the very rapid advances of civilization in the domain of particular arts and sciences, advances due to inventive genius, industry, stubborn zeal, and to the competitive spirit based on rivalry—the supreme art which surpasses all others, the royal art which consists in making and safeguarding the happiness of nations by legislation and responsible guidance of the affairs of government is by far the least advanced comparatively speaking. In the greatest and finest part of Europe, man's noblest energies are being stifled under weighty burdens, all that has been bequeathed to us by barbarian constitutions, and by the errors and uncertainties of a dark uncivilized millennium. And this is the case in Europe, in a century when art and science, taste, civilization, and refinement have climbed up, in a relatively short span of time, so many steps that it is not without a kind of dizziness that we look back on the preceding centuries.

But after these important stages, so essential for the happiness of nations, Europe now seems to be moving toward a beneficent revolution which will not be caused by insurrections and civil wars, but by a resistance both peaceful and stubborn, and unshakably faithful to the duties it has set for itself: a revolution that will not be caused by the baleful struggle of passion against passion, violence against violence, but by the gentle, persuasive, and ultimately irresistible power of reason; in short a revolution which, without drenching Europe in blood, nor setting it afire, will be beneficent by teaching men their true interests, rights, and duties, by giving purpose to their existence, and showing them the sure and infallible means to achieve this end.

In 1796 Wieland added the following note to this passage:

The extent to which cosmopolitans can be mistaken in their assumptions and disappointed in their hopes has become evident during the eight years that have elapsed since the writing of this essay. Our fellow citizens can no longer look upon man as wiser and more honest than they themselves were in the past, at least when they were acting together, en masse.

Wieland deserves our admiration for not letting the setback to the cosmopolitan ideal keep him from still urging a union of the European nations. Thus, in his *Gespräche unter vier Augen*, published in 1798, he has a Frenchman named "Frankgall" say:

What degree of accomplishment and prosperity the nations of Europe achieve, with us or independently of us, if they would renounce once and for all every shameful remnant of former barbarism—the bloodthirsty hatred of nation for nation, the vile attempts to secure one's happiness at the expense of others, all these grocer ruses and pickpocket tricks which were formerly called politics, and which no longer deceive anyone. They could achieve this result through a union of nations, and in constituting it, they need not take into account the actual variety of the forms of government, which is of little importance; thus would be created and organized a lasting European community of states.

Several years later, in 1806, Wieland proposed a plan for a European tribunal in his magazine, *Teutsche Merkur;* now he was looking to Napoleon to realize it. Once again, he was soon cruelly disappointed. . . .

4: Meanwhile in North America . . .

WHILE INTELLECTUAL EUROPE was asking itself what Europe's destiny was to be, America was deciding hers. She was on the way to become the future of Europe or at least of those Europeans who had lost hope in founding the necessary union in their native lands. This is what Benjamin Franklin (1706–1790) saw clearly and said in a series of letters written from Paris to his fellow countrymen:

All Europe is on our side of the question, as far as applause and good wishes can carry them. Those who live under arbitrary power do nevertheless approve of liberty, and wish for it; they almost despair of recovering it in Europe; they read the translations of our separate colony constitutions with rapture; and there are such numbers everywhere, who talk of removing to America, with their families and fortunes, as soon as peace and our independence shall be established, that it is generally believed we shall have a prodigious addition of strength, wealth, and arts, from the emigration of Europe; and it is thought, that, to lessen or prevent such emigrations, the tyrannies established here must relax, and allow more liberty to their people. Hence it is a common observation here, that our cause is *the cause of all mankind*, and that we are fighting for their liberty in defending our own. It is a glorious task assigned us by Providence; which has, I trust, given us spirit and virtue equal to it, and will at last crown it with success.[34]

Though the great statesmen paid no attention, intellectual Europe drew up countless plans for union. None of these was realized. America alone achieved federation.

Her people were European, without exception. And her ideas were European. She separated from the motherland only on the question of how these ideas were to be *realized*. This involved careful consideration of specific interests. Since the European statesmen showed themselves incapable of taking them seriously, the result was not to bring them closer together but to drive them further apart.

To be sure, the pioneers of American Union were guided by the principles that had been formulated by the European elites. These principles had in fact been rejected by every single European sovereign state. This is why the Englishman Penn, though unsuccessful as he had been in the remaking of Europe, contributed to the making of America. It must be noted that one of the reasons why the colonies found it desirable to put an end to their disunion was that they sought to become independent "of all European control and influence." We shall quote a page from *The Federalist*, which today will not fail to suggest the idea of a new reversal of things.

The Federalist is a collection of eighty-five newspaper articles written by Alexander Hamilton, John Jay, and James Madison in defense of the Constitution which the Federal Convention adopted on September 17, 1787. The influence of this collection has remained considerable down to our own day. American publicists, teachers, and students, and judges of the Supreme Court justly regard it as the earliest commentary on the federal Con-

[34] Franklin, *Collected Works* (Boston, 1839), VIII, 214

stitution, and a monument of political science. The text quoted here (chapter XI) is by Hamilton:

The world may politically, as well as geographically, be divided into four parts, each having a distinct set of interests. Unhappily for the other three, Europe, by her arms and by her negotiations, by force and by fraud, has, in different degrees, extended her dominion over them all. Africa, Asia, and America, have successively felt her domination. The superiority she has long maintained has tempted her to plume herself as the Mistress of the World, and to consider the rest of mankind as created for her benefit. Men admired as profound philosophers have, in direct terms, attributed to her inhabitants a physical superiority and have gravely asserted that all animals, and with them the human species, degenerate in America—that even dogs ceased to bark after having breathed awhile in our atmosphere.

Facts have too long supported these arrogant pretensions of the Europeans. It belongs to us to vindicate the honor of the human race, and to teach that assuming brother, moderation. Union will enable us to do it. Disunion will add another victim to his triumphs. Let Americans disdain to be the instruments of European greatness! Let the thirteen States, bound together in a strict and indissoluble Union, concur in erecting one great American system, superior to the control of all transatlantic force or influence, and able to dictate the terms of the connection between the old and the new world!

PART FOUR

THE ERA OF THE REVOLUTION

From Kant to Hegel

1: Europe and the French Revolution

WERE NOT WIELAND's illusions shared by the very men who touched off the most brutal upheaval Europe had suffered since Carolingian days? The "cosmopolitan" and philanthropic eloquence of a Mirabeau, of a Robespierre, was certainly sincere. But how quickly did its tone change when it became clear that its exalted ideal could enter history only by being identified with the nation's interests and military survival! The Revolution, which set out to establish world brotherhood and "the society of mankind," was very soon drawn into a succession of wars which gave rise to modern nationalism. This dramatic development was heralded in a statement by Mirabeau of August 25, 1790— note the significant admission at the end:

Will France need allies when she has no more enemies? Perhaps we are not far from the moment when freedom, reigning unchallenged in the old world and new, will realize the aspiration of philosophy, when it will absolve mankind of the crime of war, and proclaim universal peace. Then the happiness of nations will be the sole aim of legislators, the sole inspiration of the laws, the nation's sole glory; then private passions, replaced with public virtues, will no longer cause bloody quarrels and break the bonds of brotherhood that should unite all men and governments; then the pact of the federation of mankind will be consummated; but, let us admit it with regret, weighty as these considerations may be, they cannot of themselves at this moment determine our course.

The more immediate considerations which determined the Revolution were in fact dictated by the war, which it waged in the name of freedom and universal peace. Robespierre expressed this in a sentence of his speech of May 15, 1790 at the National Assembly:

It is in the interest of all nations to protect the French nation, because it is from France that the freedom and happiness of the world must stem.

Therefore the France which proclaimed universal peace and which represented Freedom must be protected by arms. Two years later, on November 9, 1792, the Convention decided to celebrate the victories of the army of Freedom by a *fête de l'Humanité,* which Vergniaud exalted in these terms:

Now let us hymn a victory that one day will be all Humanity's. Men have perished; but this is in order that men need never perish again. I swear it, in the name of the universal brotherhood that you are going to establish, every one of your battles will be a step toward peace, humanity, and the happiness of the peoples.

Earlier, on December 15, 1791, the *Patriote français* published this appeal to "holy war" in the name of anticlerical Reason:

War! war! this is the cry of every patriot, the wish of every friend of freedom from one end of Europe to the other. This is all they are waiting for, a pretext for attacking and overthrowing the tyrants. . . .

It is to this holy war that Anacharsis Cloots has come to invite the National Assembly, in the name of mankind of which he has never better deserved to be called the friend.

For it was Jean-Baptiste, called Anacharsis Cloots, a Prussian by birth, but of aristocratic Dutch lineage, who formulated the unitary ideal of the Revolution in the most theatrical manner, extending it to a mankind completely "leveled" by the laws of freedom. Cloots, too, was inspired by the cosmopolitan ideal. In his speech of June 13, 1790, he exclaimed:

There are to be no more provinces, armies, victors, or vanquished. . . . The Ocean is to be covered from shore to shore with ships forming one superb bridge of communication, and the highways of France are to be extended to the borders of China. We shall travel by stagecoach from Paris to Peking, as we do now from Bordeaux to Strasbourg, without anything to stop us, without customs, barriers, stone walls, officials, or hunting gentry. There will be no more deserts; the entire earth will have become a garden. The East and the West will embrace on the field of Federation.

And he added, in the same vein, on April 26, 1793:

We are not free as long as there is a single moral obstacle to our physical advance at a single point anywhere in the world. The Rights of Man are extended to the totality of men. A state that calls itself sovereign grievously wounds humanity, it is in full rebellion against common sense and happiness; it cuts the channels of universal prosperity; its Constitution, faulty at its root, is contradictory, uncertain, and ready to fall.

This universal liberalism, however, shifts without transition to totalitarian collectivism. For Cloots went on as follows:

We will have no other master than the expression of the general will, absolute and supreme. No, if I encounter on this earth a particular will which resists the universal instinct, I am against it; such resistance spells universal war and servitude, and mankind, the supreme being, will sooner or later treat it as it deserves.

On April 21, 1792, Cloots presented the Convention with a work entitled *La République Universelle,* in which he demanded the abolition of local Governments, and their replacement with a centralized world Republic:

A body does not make war upon itself, and mankind will live in peace when it forms a single body, one Nation, single and unique . . . The commune of Paris will be the central rallying point, the beacon of universal community.

He did not foresee difficulties in ruling the world from Paris:

When a Lama from Rome and a Lama from Mecca give laws to the Peruvians and the Malays; when the merchants of Amsterdam and London rule over Bengal and the Moluccas, I conceive how easily an Assembly whose seat is in Paris could steer the ship of mankind.

The federalist formula seemed reactionary to him:

A number of political writers have presented projects for perpetual peace, federations of states, of nations; but no one has risen to the true principle of sovereign unity, the federation of individuals.

In the name—paradoxical to say the least—of this "federation of individuals," Cloots, in conclusion proposed the following decree:

The National Convention, desiring to put an end to the errors, inconsistencies, and contradictory claims of states and individuals who call themselves sovereign, solemnly declares in the name of the Rights of Man:

ART. I.—There is no sovereign other than mankind.

ART. II.—Every individual, every commune that recognizes this luminous and immutable principle, will be fully entitled to become a member of our fraternal association of the Republic of Men, Brothers, Citizens of the World.

ART. III.—Distant communes and enclaves with which we are not in communication must await promulgation of the truth to be admitted.

Robert, however, a Dantonist, caused this fantastic proposal to be rejected. He adjured the Convention to come back to "reality":

Let us leave to the philosophers, let us leave to them the task of examining mankind in every respect: we are not the representatives of mankind. Therefore I want the French legislator to forget the universe for a moment and concentrate on his own country. I am demanding the kind of national self-interest without which we are unfaithful to our duties, without which we will make laws here for those who have not commissioned us, and not in favor of those for whose benefit we can make laws. I love all men; I love all free men in particular; but I love the free men of France more than all the other men in the world.

The Jacobin rejection of the federalist formula, both for France and for Europe, the mad enthusiasm for universal unity in the most leveled-down and centralized sense were to lead the Revolution, by a concrete necessity, to deny its own first principles. From "national self-interest" it moved gradually to aggressive nationalism.

The crucial importance for Europe of this development in French political thought and vocabulary cannot be stressed enough.

The Girondists who claimed to be partisans of federalism—and their enemy Robespierre was the first to use the term, if we are to believe Warburg's etymological dictionary—were denounced by the Jacobins as traitors to the Fatherland, the Nation, that is to say, as traitors to Freedom and the Revolution. To the Americans, the Dutch, and the Swiss, federalism meant freedom, to the members of the National Convention it meant the guillotine within forty-eight hours. This traumatism is still present—it is a conditioned reflex dating from the Terror—in the minds of Frenchmen and Europeans who continue to invoke the Revolution and the Jacobin tradition. Hence the permanent misunderstanding which has ever since set them against the empirical democrats of the Anglo-Saxon world and the small countries. A Frenchman of our day, if he wants to make sure of the meaning of this discredited word, consults the Littré dictionary, and under *Fédéralisme* reads the following:

Neologism; the doctrine of federal government. "Federalism was one of the most common political forms in use among savages." Chateaubriand, *America, Government.* During the Revolution, a project attributed to the Girondists for destroying national unity and transforming France into a federation of small states. "At the Jacobin club, the question of federalism was gravely discussed and the Girondins were denounced angrily." Thiers, *Hist. de la Rév.*

2: Plans for a European Union Contemporary with the Revolution

ALTHOUGH THE TERM "Europe" turned up repeatedly in speeches before the National Convention, not a single serious plan for continental union was produced by the Revolution, at least in France. This is not surprising. The emotional explosion drove its leaders from the utopia of "mankind" directly to the nationalist ideal; they skipped the realistic stage of a European federation. The concrete residue of this phenomenon was the "nationalization" of patriotic feeling all over Europe. Pascal's "who wants to act the angel acts the beast" was translated here as "who wants the abstract World gets the Nation in arms."

As early as 1790 Camille Desmoulins wrote:

We have torn down the divisive hedgerows that separated Frenchmen from Frenchmen, and there are no more provinces; let us hope that soon the division into kingdoms will disappear; there will be but a single nation, which will be called "mankind."

The leveling of regional diversity, which is advocated in this statement, must inevitably suppress European reality. It is true that when referring to "mankind," the speaker was really thinking of Europe, as pre-Renaissance writers had done when they referred to Christendom. This very lack of historical perspective prevented them from seeing the specific features of Europe. The farther one got from Paris, the more clearly these features were seen. The plans for union advanced by the Englishman Bentham, the Italian E. M. L'Aurora, and the Germans Kant and Gentz were explicitly European. Inspired by the great ideological upheaval of the Revolution, they sought to get back to the concrete realities more than ever clamoring to be organized.

Jeremy Bentham (1747–1832) was granted French citizenship by a decree of the National Convention on the occasion of a debate on colonialism. His name is not associated solely with utilitarianism; he also launched the idea of international legislation in his *Principles of International Law*, which he completed in 1789, but which was not published until after his death, in 1843. This work includes four essays on the Objects and Subjects of international law, War, and Peace. It is in the fourth essay, entitled "A Plan for an Universal and Perpetual Peace," that Bentham discusses the European question.

The field of his ambition is the world, he declares. But the measures he proposes concern Europe, and first of all Great Britain, for she alone matters, with France, and what he says of the one is applicable to the other.[1]

The object of the present essay is to submit to the world a plan for an universal and perpetual peace. The globe is the field

---

[1] Bentham, *Principles of International Law*, Essay IV.

of dominion to which the author aspires; the Press the engine, and the only one he employs; the cabinet of mankind the theatre of his intrigue. . . .

The following plan has for its basis two fundamental propositions:—(1) The reduction and fixation of the force of the several nations that compose the European system; and (2) the emancipation of the distant dependencies of each State. Each of these propositions has its distinct advantages, but neither of them, it will appear, would completely answer the purpose without the other.

As to the utility of such an universal and lasting peace, supposing a plan for that purpose practicable and likely to be adopted, there can be but one voice. The objection, and the only objection, to it is the apparent impracticability of it—that it is not only hopeless, but that to such a degree that any proposal to that effect deserves the name of visionary and ridiculous. This objection I shall endeavour, in the first place, to remove, for the removal of this prejudice may be necessary to procure for the plan a hearing.

What can be better suited to the preparing of men's minds for the reception of such a proposal than the proposal itself?

Let it not be objected that the age is not ripe for such a proposal. The more it wants of being ripe the sooner we should begin to do what can be done to ripen it. A proposal of this sort is one of the those things that can never come too early nor too late. . . .

The ensuing sheets are dedicated to the common welfare of all civilised nations, but more particularly of Great Britain and France.

The end in view is to recommend three grand objects—simplicity of government, national frugality, and peace.

Reflection has satisfied me of the truth of the following propositions:—

I. That it is not the interest of Great Britain to have any foreign dependencies whatsoever.

II. That it is not the interest of Great Britain to have any treaty of alliance, offensive or defensive, with any other Power whatsoever.

III. That it is not the interest of Great Britain to have any treaty with any Power whatsoever, for the purpose of possessing any advantage whatsoever in point of trade, to the exclusion of any other nation whatsoever.

IV. That is is not the interest of Great Britain to keep up any naval force beyond what may be sufficient to defend its commerce against pirates.

V. That it is not the interest of Great Britain to keep on foot any regulations whatsoever of distant preparation for the augmentation or maintenance of its naval force, such as the Navigation Act, bounties on the Greenland trade, and other trades regarded as nurseries for seamen.

VI, VII, VIII, IX, and X. That all these several propositions are also true of France. . . .

XI. That, supposing Great Britain and France thoroughly agreed, the principal difficulties would be removed to the establishment of a plan of general and permanent pacification for all Europe.

XII. That for the maintenance of such a pacification general and perpetual treaties might be formed, limiting the number of troops to be maintained.

XIII. That the maintenance of such a pacification might be considerably facilitated by the establishment of a Common Court of Judicature for the decision of differences between the several nations, although such Court were not to be armed with any coercive powers.

XIV. That secrecy in the operations of the Foreign Department ought not to be endured in England, being altogether useless and equally repugnant to the interests of liberty and to those of peace.

After a cursory discussion of the first twelve articles of his plan, Bentham observes, concerning the thirteenth:

Establish a common tribunal, the necessity for war no longer follows from difference of opinion. Just or unjust, the decision of the arbiters will save the credit, the honour of the contending party.

Can the arrangement proposed be justly styled visionary, when it has been proved of it that—

1. It is in the interest of the parties concerned.

2. They are already sensible of that interest.

3. The situation it would place them in is no new one, nor any other than the original situation they set out from.

Difficult and complicated conventions have been effectuated: for examples, we may mention—

1. The Armed Neutrality.

2. The American Confederation.

3. The German Diet.

4. The Swiss League.

Why should not the European fraternity subsist, as well as the

German Diet or the Swiss League? These latter have no ambitious views. Be it so; but is not this already become the case
with the former?

How then shall we concentrate the approbation of the people,
and obviate their prejudices?

One main object of the plan is to effectuate a reduction, and
that a mighty one, in the contributions of the people. The amount
of the reduction for each nation should be stipulated in the
treaty; and even previous to the signature of it, laws for the purpose might be prepared in each nation, and presented to every
other, ready to be enacted as soon as the treaty should be ratified
in each State.

By these means the mass of the people—the part most exposed
to be led away by prejudices—would not be sooner apprised of
the measure than they would feel the relief it brought them.
They would see it was for their advantage it was calculated,
and that it could not be calculated for any other purpose. . . .

Such a Congress or Diet might be constituted by each Power
sending two deputies to the place of meeting, one of these to be
the principal, the other to act as an occasional substitute.

The proceedings of such Congress or Diet should be all public.

Its power would consist (1) in reporting its opinion;

(2) in causing that opinion to be circulated in the dominions
of each State. . . .

(3) After a certain time, in putting the refractory State under
the ban of Europe.

There might, perhaps, be no harm in regulating, as a last resource, the contingent to be furnished by the several States for
enforcing the decrees of the Court. But the necessity for the employment of this resource would, in all human probability, be
superseded for ever by having recourse to the much more simple
and less burthensome expedient of introducing into the instrument by which such Court was instituted a clause guaranteeing
the liberty of the Press in each State . . .

The rest of the essay is devoted to a long polemic against secret diplomacy.

It is noteworthy that as early as the end of the eighteenth
century Bentham saw both the crucial importance of a free press
and its dangers when it is inspired only by national self-interest
hallowed as "patriotism":

The voice of the nation on these subjects can only be looked
for in newspapers. But on these subjects the language of all
newspapers is uniform: "It is we that are always in the right,

without a possibility of being otherwise. Against us other nations have no rights. If, according to the rules of judging between individual and individual, we are right, we are right by the rules of justice: if not, we are right by the laws of patriotism, which is a virtue more respectable than justice." Injustice, oppression, fraud, lying, whatever acts would be crimes, whatever habits would be vices, if manifested in the pursuit of individual interests, when manifested in pursuit of national interests become sublimated into virtues. Let any man declare, who has ever read or heard an English newspaper, whether this be not the constant tenor of the notions they convey. Party on this one point makes no difference. However hostile to one another on all other points, on this they have never but one voice—they write with the utmost harmony. Such are the opinions, and to these opinions the facts are accommodated as of course. Who would blush to misrepresent when misrepresentation is a virtue?

But newspapers, if their voice make but a small part of the voice of the people, the instruction they give makes on these subjects the whole of the instruction which the people receive.

Enrico Michele L'Aurora, who was called *"il bizarro agitatore,"* was one of the most eloquent Italian Jacobins. This can be seen from the title of the work he published in 1796: *All'Italia nelle tenebre L'Aurora porta la luce.* In it he called upon the Europeans to unite as a single Nation to inaugurate the era of freedom, equality, and brotherhood, which was to crown the epochs of history: the golden age, the age of barbarism, the age of justice, and the age of monarchy.

No, Europeans, our childhood, our ignorance, and our stupidity must come to an end! Unjust monarchists must at last respect our rights! And if they cling to their perverted and cruel system, let universal wrath come down upon the tottering heads of our persecutors, let the vicissitudes of bloody war strike our only enemies! And let the nations, united and liberated, be governed according to the principles of peace, virtue, and justice . . . Let all the nations of Europe look upon themselves as a single State, their interests held in common, and let Europe be looked upon as the universal mother of all her inhabitants!

He demanded the convocation of a "universal congress of wise and learned men," elected by the *"generalità del popolo."* It was to meet in Sicily or Majorca to deliberate on a "general constitution for all Europe" and on three pacts or codes regulating the moral, social, and military relations among the nations.

Bentham's plan was published a half-century after it was written, L'Aurora's was rediscovered by Italian scholars of our own century.[2] Kant's plan was far more famous (it appeared in 1795), but the greatest influence was exerted by Gentz, a political writer who took an active part in shaping the events of his day.

Emmanuel Kant (1724–1804) was seventy-one years old in 1795 when he published his treatise *Zum ewigen Frieden*. He left his native Königsberg only once in his lifetime, but he followed the great movements of the period closely: it is known that the news of the French Revolution made him change the direction of his daily walk from east to west. He knew the Abbé de Saint-Pierre's *Project* (which he quoted with approval as early as 1750) and Rousseau's digest of it. As early as 1760, under the influence of Rousseau, he conceived the idea of a *Völkerbund*. He defined its moral foundations in several works written on the eve of the Revolution. Then, in a short essay dating from 1793, *Über den Gemeinspruch: Das mag in der Theorie richtig sein, taugt aber nichts für die Praxis*,[3] he proves that the "anti-social" tendencies of the States (conquests, wars, increasingly burdensome taxes and armaments, higher prices) can be checked only if absolute sovereignty is taken away from the princes and transferred to the peoples: this is Rousseau's doctrine in all its purity.

The famous *On Perpetual Peace* takes up these ideas in systematic form, but with an obvious concern for political realism: thus, Kant refers (even in his outline) to the Peace of Basel, which had shortly before been concluded between Prussia and Spain on the one hand and the French Republic on the other. The essay is composed in the form of an international treaty divided into six preliminary articles, three "definitive articles," and two additional articles. The great philosopher's essential

[2] Cf. D. Cantimori, *Utopisiti e riformatori italiani* (Florence, 1943); C. Curcio, *Europa, Storia di un'idea* (Florence: Valecchi, 1958); and A. Saitta, *Dalla res publica christiana agli stati i uniti d'Europa* (Rome, 1948).

[3] *Sämtliche kleine Schriften* (Königsberg, 1797), pp. 67–113.

ideas on European federation are contained in the commentary
to the "Second Definitive Article."

When we see the attachment of savages to their lawless freedom, preferring ceaseless combat to subjection to a lawful constraint which they might establish, and thus preferring senseless
freedom to rational freedom, we regard it with deep contempt
as barbarity, rudeness, and a brutish degradation of humanity.
Accordingly, one would think that civilized peoples (each
united in a state) would hasten all the more to escape, the sooner
the better, from such a depraved condition. But, instead, each
state places its majesty (for it is absurd to speak of the majesty
of the people) in being subject to no external juridical restraint,
and the splendor of its sovereign consists in the fact that many
thousands stand at his command to sacrifice themselves for
something that does not concern them and without his needing
to place himself in the least danger. The chief difference between European and American savages lies in the fact that many
tribes of the latter have been eaten up by their enemies, while
the former know how to make better use of their conquered
enemies than to dine off them; they know better how to use
them to increase the number of their subjects and thus the quantity of instruments for even more extensive wars.
When we consider the perverseness of human nature which
is nakedly revealed in the uncontrolled relations between nations (this perverseness being veiled in the state of civil law by
the constraint exercised by government), we may well be as-
tonished that the word "law" has not yet been banished from
war politics as pedantic and that no state has yet been bold
enough to advocate this point of view. Up to the present Hugo
Grotius, Puffendorf, Wattel, and many other importune com-
forters have been cited in justification of war, though their code,
philosophically or diplomatically formulated, has not and cannot
have the least legal force, because states as such do not stand
under a common external power. There is no instance on record
that a state has ever been moved to desist from its purpose because of arguments backed up by the testimony of such great
men. But the homage which each state pays (at least in words)
to the concept of law proves that there is slumbering in man an
even greater moral disposition to become master of the evil principle in himself (which he cannot disclaim) and to hope for the
same from others. Otherwise the word "law" would never be
pronounced by states which wish to war upon one another; it
would be used only ironically, as a Gallic prince interpreted it

when he said, "It is the prerogative which nature has given the stronger that the weaker should obey him." . . .

The practicability (objective reality) of this idea of federation, which should gradually spread to all states and thus lead to perpetual peace, can be proved. For if fortune directs that a powerful and enlightened people can make itself a republic, which by its nature must be inclined to perpetual peace, this gives a fulcrum to the federative unification of other states so that they may adhere to it and thus secure freedom under the idea of the law of nations. By more and more such associations, the federation may be gradually extended. . . .

The concept of a law of nations as a right to make war does not really mean anything, because it is then a law of deciding what is right by unilateral maxims through force and not by universally valid public laws which restrict the freedom of each one. The only conceivable meaning of such a law of nations might be that it serves men right who are so inclined that they should destroy each other and thus find perpetual peace in the vast grave that swallows both the atrocities and their perpetrators. For states in their relation to each other, there cannot be any reasonable way out of the lawless condition which entails only war except that they, like individual men, should give up their savage (lawless) freedom, adjust themselves to the constraints of public law, and thus establish a continuously growing state consisting of various nations (*civitas gentium*), which will ultimately include all the nations of the world. But since, under the idea of the law of nations, they do not wish this, rejecting in practice what is correct in theory, if all is not to be lost, there can be, in place of the positive idea of a world republic, only the negative surrogate of an alliance which averts war, endures, spreads, and holds back the stream of those hostile inclinations which fear the law, though under constant peril of their breaking loose again. *Furor impius . . . intus fremit horridus ore cruento* (Virgil).[4]

The extensive and lively discussions that Kant's project provoked in Germany are accounted for by the recent interest among the Prussian elite in the plans of Sully and the Abbé de Saint-Pierre. The Abbé de l'Ecluse's edition of the *OEconomies royales* had appeared in 1745, and Rousseau's *Extrait* in 1762. As for the influence of Kant's ideas, which made itself felt very soon, it is illustrated by the publication, five years after *On Per-*

[4] Kant, *Writings in Moral Philosophy*, ed. Beck (Chicago, 1949).

petual Peace, of an important essay by Gentz, which bears a very similar title.

Friedrich von Gentz (1764–1832), minister to the king of Prussia, later close adviser to Austrian statesmen, Metternich's right-hand man and secretary to the Congress of Vienna, had been a pupil of Kant's, whose enthusiasm for the Revolution he shared as a young man. Edmund Burke's *Reflections on the Revolution in France,* which he translated one year after its publication in 1790, abruptly turned him into an uncompromising adversary of Jacobinism. His views on the European problem, as expressed in his writings and in his political career, shifted constantly back and forth between affirmation inspired by philosophical reason and negations suggested by political experience. Toward the end of his life he was weary and disillusioned. This man whom Czar Alexander dubbed "Europe's Knight-Errant" and "Europe's Presumptive Secretary-General" wrote in 1814: "My politics becomes every day more selfish and more narrowly Austrian. The word 'Europe' has come to inspire me with horror"; and "I have lost all desire to be a European."

What holds our attention in his essay of 1800, entitled *Über den ewigen Frieden,* is his lucid (though exaggeratedly pessimistic) criticism of the various "European" doctrines advanced under absolute regimes and during the Revolution—whether by the Abbé de Saint-Pierre or by Kant.

According to Gentz, three methods have been proposed for securing perpetual peace: a World State, a system of self-contained nations, and a Federation of States to be achieved either through arbitration or through a common constitution. Gentz emphatically rejects the Jacobin utopia of a single universal Republic, which is nothing but a new version of the frightening old myth of the universal Monarchy: "Europe subjected to a single government—the very thought of it is almost enough to make us shudder." And yet something must be done to prevent the return of the internecine wars that ruin Europe, this "twentieth part of the planet's dry land," which dominates the world only thanks to its culture. Will this hegemony last? Is not

America bound to contest it? Should we combine all our diverse
nations into a single continental State? Gentz did not believe so.
Nor did he believe in Fichte's solution proposed the same year:
the transformation of European states into commercial, political,
and cultural autarchies (see p. 203). That leaves the federal
solution. Gentz devotes the essential part of his essay to a critique
of this solution, which is at first sympathetic, and then becomes
more and more skeptical:

The proposed third means of securing or paving the way for
perpetual peace is to set up a "free federation" or to draw up a
very detailed "federal constitution" linking the various states.
This plan could be carried out under several forms. Thus, the
federated states could reserve for themselves the right to name
one or several arbiters in the event of litigation; or, they could
adopt the principle that the minority of the members must submit, whenever necessary, to the will of the majority: lastly a
"permanent congress" could be instituted, whose task it would
be to concern itself with the common affairs of the federated
states, to judge their differences, and to settle their disputes.

There follows a critique of Rousseau's *Extrait:*

If it were true, as Rousseau said, that this federation aiming
at peace cannot be realized because the rulers of the participat-
ing States would never accept a constitution preventing them
from "being unjust whenever they please"; if it were true, as he
claims later, that could it be realized "for a single day, this
would suffice for it to last forever," we should not give up the
hope of seeing it realized. There have been many moments in
recent European history when all governments would have
eagerly accepted the security of a lasting peace in preference
to the uncertainty of warfare; such a moment can and must occur
again and everything that, among men, depends upon a decision
of the moment, is possible and realizable in practice. The difficulty, or even the utter impossibility of this project, lies less in the
creation of the federation than in the conditions for making it
last. The conclusion of a free contract among the states can be
envisaged only if all signatories can never have the desire or
power to break it; or in other words, only if the peace, which
this contract is intended to secure, can last without it.

Therefore Gentz argues in favor of a return to the system of "European balance," thus heralding the policy of the

Holy Alliance of which he was to be one of the chief architects:

The purpose of this system has never been, as has wrongly
been charged, to make all the states equally powerful, but rather
to protect the weaker states as much as possible, by allying them
with the stronger ones, against encroachments by any one pre-
pondering state. The intention was to organize the kind of federal constitution that Europe has evolved of herself in such a
way that each weight within the overall political mass had its
counterweight somewhere else. Though it did not seek to make
wars impossible—something no general or partial alliance could
have achieved—the intention was at least to reduce their number
or scope. To do this, whenever necessary, the temptation to start
a war was checked by the great difficulties the war raised; or
else an effort was made to eliminate, by appeals to fear or interest, what, in the absence of any higher authority, neither law
nor morality could repress. In short, the intention was to obtain
by means of *separate pacts* what the Abbé de Saint-Pierre's project promised to bring about by means of a *general pact*.

As for the fourth possibility—federal Constitution—it is unfortunately, says Gentz, "an eternal chimera" for:

1. In order to realize the ideal of perpetual peace, it would
have to govern the entire earth. A federal system elaborated
down to the smallest details, but including only a part of the
world's states would in no way offer a sufficient guarantee of
peace. The state of nature which prevails among different countries will not truly come to an end over the world's entire surface
until the day when all nations are able to combine into one, something that is absolutely impossible.

2. Nor could one possibly set up a complete federal system,
including a considerable number of countries, especially big
countries. An association of small states, linked by a common
interest, can, to be sure, be viable and develop, if it has been
endowed with a constitution of this type.[5] But if the federal sys-

[5] "In this domain, the *successful* examples prove that only a federation
all of whose members form a country of small or average size has chances
to survive. It has been tried twice in very extensive regions—in Germany
and in North America. We know the outcome of the first of these; only
the future will enable us to judge the other. But unless very exceptional
circumstances preserve the unity of the independent state of North America,
the latter will find it very difficult to subsist even for as long as fifty years."
—Gentz.

tem were to be applied to great states—not according to the Abbé de Saint-Pierre's inadequate plan, but in the sense indicated here, the only valid one—the supreme Senate of this immense republic would have to be invested with an authority which would bear no comparison with that of its member States; again, something that is absolutely impossible.

3. Finally, even were it possible to imagine, in an immense federal state such as only Europe could form, an authority great enough to impose its decisions and verdicts on the private interests, perpetual peace would nonetheless fail to prevail among the nations—and this observation bears upon even the purely ideal aspect of the project. For it is impossible to assume that every state would submit of its own accord to the judgments of the Federation's High Court. Within individual states force is often needed to make justice prevail; the same would be true of differences between nations, where, perhaps more often than in the case of private litigations, the execution of the Tribunal's decisions would have to be backed up by coercive measures. Now, coercive measures against a state can only signify war; consequently, war remains inevitable, even should a European constitution come into being.

War, then, remains inevitable, and since the French Revolution has worsened the situation—here Gentz repeats the arguments advanced by Burke and De Bonald—all we can hope and work for is a system which "limits the evil":

The men of the Revolution intended to unite all the nations of the earth in one great cosmopolitan federation, but they succeeded only in unleashing the cruelest world war that has ever shaken society and torn it apart.

When the French Revolution broke out, Europe had in fact already taken several important steps toward a peaceful constitution in terms of international law. The most important step of all was incontestably the discovery of the true principles of political economy. An enlightened, liberal, and beneficent conception of the true needs and interests of nations was causing to regress the false system according to which the greatness and well-being of a state rest upon war and conquests. The governments were learning gradually that the very source of their power, which they had sought very far from home, was right in their own backyard. It became clear that the greatest gains any war might bring can never make up for the losses that war brings inevitably; and that the finest conquests are to be made at home. At the same time the relations between states appeared in an entirely new light. It was realized that industry, trade, and wealth were in fact common possessions, which, though unevenly distributed among the states, contributed more or less to the prosperity of all. Even the richest nation draws greater benefits from the opulence than from the poverty of its neighbors and all other nations. As for the ravages of war, whatever the regions afflicted, they are ultimately always a burden to society. These great and terrible truths could not be lost to makers of policy. Gradually taking possession of the best minds, argued in the works of the most skillful writers, adopted by the most perspicacious statesmen, they seemed to have found their way to more than one throne. Thus all Europe seemed to be embarking upon a new era of wisdom, humanity, and peace.

This terrible Revolution has in the end poisoned political life everywhere in Europe; for France alone could not gratify its enormous destructive power. Its ultimate consequences are far beyond human estimation. But at present one thing has become certain: far from having brought peace on earth, the Revolution has espoused warfare, providing more and more occasions for wars to break out, and more and more means for spreading them, and even disposing the human mind to greet them favorably.

To be sure, unforeseen and unforeseeable events may arise to counteract the dire fate which would seem to be in store for us. In the upheaval caused by wars, a new Constitution of international law may be born and develop more rapidly than we have the right to expect. A more peaceful order of things, founded on better principles, would then be established in a completely unexpected way for mankind's greater joy. But these are favors of fortune, on which no one can rely, especially when the building of the future is in question. In the present state of affairs, a single truth subsists: not only peace, but the mere possibility of peace is far removed from us; war is our earthly lot and unless extraordinary changes and revolutions come along to exorcise this evil fate, it will remain ours for a long time to come. This truth cannot be proclaimed loudly or too often in the antechambers of politics. Diplomats and statesmen must be made aware of the heavy task and great vocation which are now theirs; they must display twice as much will, courage, and energy if they are to achieve our salvation, or at the very least set a limit to the evil.

Edmund Burke (1729–1797), who has been called "the English Cicero," prolific writer on politics and brilliant orator in the House of Commons, was at once a prominent defender of American freedom and a leading adversary of Jacobin ideology. Heir to

Montesquieu, he inspired Gentz, and to us he appears as forerunner of "the moderates" whose voice continued to reverberate
throughout the nineteenth century. Guizot, Tocqueville, Ranke,
Blüntschli, Lord Acton, Burckhardt, and Renan all belong to the
tradition he founded. In our own day, clamorous with Leftist enthusiasm and Rightist anathematizing, Burke's voice is still influential in England and in the United States, where a revival of
conservativism invokes his measured realism. His style is vehe-
ment, and he is fond of paradoxes.

Unlike Kant, he believed war to be inevitable, but was far from
giving it a sacred character, as Joseph de Maistre did. Fully
aware of the difficulty of the task, he advocated a balance between the Christian ideal and political reality, between the European community and the claims of the Powers.

In his *Reflections on the Revolution in France* (1790), he
defines Europe as follows:

> . . . our manners, our civilization, and all the good things
> which are connected with manners and with civilization, in this
> European world of ours, depended for ages on two principles,
> and were, indeed, the result of both combined: I mean the spirit
> of a gentleman, and the spirit of religion.

But the spirit of chivalry is a thing of the past; we are witnessing the advent of the age of "philosophical barbarism," the age
of the economists and cynics. "The glory of Europe is extinguished."

Here is his classical description of European unity, contained
in *Letters on the Proposal for Peace with the Regicide Directory
of France* (1796).[6]

> The conformity and analogy of which I speak, incapable, like
> everything else, of preserving perfect trust and tranquillity among
> men, has a strong tendency to facilitate accommodation, and to
> produce a generous oblivion of the rancor of their quarrels. With
> this similitude, peace is more of peace, and war is less of war.
> I will go further. There have been periods of time in which com-
> munities apparently in peace with each other have been more

[6] Burke, *Selected Works*, ed. E. J. Payne ("Clarendon Press Series,"
[Oxford, 1874–1878]), III, 79–81.

perfectly separated than in later times many nations in Europe have been in the course of long and bloody wars. The cause must be sought in the similitude throughout Europe of religion, laws, and manners. At bottom, these are all the same. The writers on public law have often called this *aggregate* of nations a commonwealth. They had reason. It is virtually one great state, having the same basis of general law, with some diversity of provincial customs and local establishments. The nations of Europe have had the very same Christian religion, agreeing in the fundamental parts, varying a little in the ceremonies and in the subordinate doctrines. The whole of the polity and economy of every country in Europe has been derived from the same sources. It was drawn from the old Germanic or Gothic custumary, from the feudal institutions, which must be considered as an emanation from that custumary; and the whole has been improved and digested into system and discipline by the Roman law. From hence arose the several orders, with or without a monarch (which are called states), in every European country; the strong traces of which, where monarchy predominated, were never wholly extinguished or merged in despotism. In the few places where monarchy was cast off, the spirit of European monarchy was still left. Those countries still continued countries of states; that is, of classes, orders, and distinctions, such as had before subsisted, or nearly so. Indeed, the force and form of the institution called states continued in greater perfection in those republican communities than under monarchies. From all those sources arose a system of manners and of education which was nearly similar in all this quarter of the globe; and which softened, blended, and harmonized the colors of the whole. There was little difference in the form of the universities for the education of their youth, whether with regard to faculties, to sciences, or to the more liberal and elegant kinds of erudition. From this resemblance in the modes of intercourse, and in the whole form and fashion of life, no citizen of Europe could be altogether an exile in any part of it. There was nothing more than a pleasing variety to recreate and instruct the mind, to enrich the imagination, and to meliorate the heart. When a man traveled or resided, for health, pleasure, business, or necessity, from his own country, he never felt himself quite abroad.

All this was compromised or destroyed by Jacobinism on the continent, and England was shaken to the roots. For, according to Burke, the principles and the forms of the ancient common constitution of the European states, improved and adapted to the present situation of Europe, are now preserved in England only.[7]

But actually England was to be the implacable enemy of a con-tinent which had been won over to the ideas of the Revolution; and the policy of the balance of power, as applied by the Holy Alliance by Burke's disciple Gentz, opposed at best only a token resistance to the rise of nationalisms.

3: Historico-Philosophical Syntheses (1)

TWO GREAT ISOLATED FIGURES—Leibniz and Vico—had been able to look at Europe against the world background. Then came the French century par excellence, the century of France's influence on Europe, from Montesquieu, Voltaire the cosmpolitan and Rousseau the federalist to Condorcet.

There followed a Germanic age which fell astride the eight-eenth and nineteenth centuries, the French Revolution constitut-ing its midpoint. From Wieland to Schelling, from Herder to Hegel, from Kant to Goethe, Germany headed an intellectual and poetic revolution which took place on the fringes of the other revolution, was inspired by it, reacted to it, and in the end ex-tended far beyond it. Its theories of history, metaphysical systems, romanticism, the discovery of the unconscious, and the develop-ment of dialectics signaled the birth of modern thought.

We shall group here four writers and philosophers who, though their lives fell almost entirely within the eighteenth century, in-augurated in German universities and minor courts the great European process of re-examining values, which the fall of Napo-leon, after their deaths, seemed to touch off in Europe.

Johann Christoph Friedrich von Schiller (1759–1805), at the time he was writing his *History of the Thirty Years' War* (begun in 1790), finally settled at Weimar. His *Sturm und Drang* was a thing of the past; the author of *The Robbers* had become profes-sor at the University of Jena! It was then that the National Con-vention granted him the title of French citizen; indeed, his heart

[7] *Reflections on the Revolution in France.*

and temperament were with the Revolution whose great humanitarian hopes he shared.

Like Lessing, Herder and Kant, and like the orators of the Revolution, Schiller took his inspiration from Rousseau: and it is because he had read Rousseau's digest of the Abbé de Saint-Pierre's system that he wrote the famous stanza which Beethoven set to music.

> Seid umschlungen, Millionen,
> Diesen Kuss der ganzen Welt!
> Bruder, überm Sternenzelt
> Muss ein lieber Vater wohnen.

But he did not share the illusions of men like Cloots as to the neo-Roman style unity, which was to be imposed on all mankind. His conception of Europe was much more federalist than Jacobin. In his opinion, the real origin of the community of European nations lay in the supra-national bonds which had been forged by the Reformation. His ideas are in complete contrast with those of Schlegel, Novalis, and Görres, who were about fifteen years younger and who were soon to charge the Reformation with having broken up the ancient union and marked the beginning of the end of a German-Catholic Europe, that nostalgic utopia of German Romanticism.

On page 2 of *History of the Thirty Years' War* he expounds his thesis in rough outline:

It was the Reformation principally that first drew the northern powers, Denmark and Sweden, into the political system of Europe; and while, on the one hand, the Protestant League was strengthened by their adhesion, it, on the other, was indispensable to their interests. States which hitherto scarcely concerned themselves with one another's existence, acquired through the Reformation an attractive centre of interest, and began to be united by new political sympathies. And as through its influence new relations sprang up between citizen and citizen, and between rulers and subjects, so also entire states were forced by it into new relative positions. Thus, by a strange course of events, religious disputes were the means of cementing a closer union between the nations of Europe.

Fearful, indeed, and destructive was the first movement in

which this general political sympathy announced itself; a desolating war of thirty years . . . Yet out of this fearful war Europe came forth free and independent. In it she first learned to recognize herself as a community of nations; and this intercommunion of states, which originated in the thirty years' war, may alone be sufficient to reconcile the philosopher to its horrors.[8]

In another passage, Schiller speaks more specifically of the links created by the Reformation, between and among nations most removed from one another:

The differences of government, of laws, of language, of manners, and of character, which hitherto had kept whole nations and countries as it were insulated, and raised a lasting barrier between them, rendered one state insensible to the distresses of another, save where national jealousy could indulge a malicious joy at the reverses of a rival. This barrier the Reformation destroyed. An interest more intense and more immediate than national aggrandizement or patriotism, and entirely independent of private utility, began to animate whole states and individual citizens; an interest capable of uniting numerous and distant nations, even while it frequently lost its force among the subjects of the same government. With the inhabitants of Geneva, for instance, of England, of Germany, or of Holland, the French Calvinist possessed a common point of union which he had not with his own countrymen. Thus, in one important particular, he ceased to be the citizen of a single state, and to confine his views and sympathies to his own country alone. The sphere of views became enlarged. He began to calculate his own fate from that of other nations of the same religious profession, and to make their cause his own. Now for the first time did princes venture to bring the affairs of other countries before their own councils; for the first time could they hope for a willing ear to their own necessities, and prompt assistance from others. Foreign affairs had now become a matter of domestic policy, and that aid was readily granted to the religious confederate which would have been denied to the mere neighbor, and still more to the distant stranger. The inhabitant of the Palatinate leaves his native fields to fight side by side with his religious associate of France, against the common enemy of their faith. The Huguenot draws the sword against the country which persecutes him, and sheds his blood in defence of the liberties of Holland. Swiss is arrayed against Swiss;

[8] *The Works of F. Schiller,* translated from the German (New York, 1883).

German against German, to determine, on the banks of the Loire and the Seine, the succession of the French crown. The Dane crosses the Eider, and the Swede the Baltic, to break the chains which are forged for Germany.

Schiller was moreover one of the earliest writers to call attention to the great similarity of institutions and ways of life in medieval Europe, despite the absence of regular relations and intercourse among the various peoples. In a fragment on the Crusades in his *Universal-Historische Übersicht,* we read:

In the eleventh century, the West of Europe, although cut up into a number of states, affords a very uniform spectacle. Taken possession of by nations that stood upon the same level of culture at the time they made their conquests, that belonged to the same races of men, and lived in the same circumstances, it would have been necessary that the western countries should have offered a great variety of soil and climate to the new settlers, if, in the course of time, important distinctions were to develop among them. But the fury of desolation, which marked the conquests of these nations, reduced to the same level all the countries that were the theatre of their exploits, no matter what people inhabited them, or what a degree and extent of culture they had reached; for the conquerors trampled down and extirpated whatever they found, and realized a condition of things which changed the aspect of the conquered provinces so completely, that every trace of their past development had been utterly wiped out. Although the climate, the condition of the soil, neighborhood, and geographical position preserved a certain distinction; although the remaining traces of Roman civilization in the southern countries, the influence of the cultivated Arabs in the southwestern, the seat of the hierarchy in Italy, and the frequent intercourse with the Greeks in the same country could not fail to exercise some influence upon their inhabitants, yet these causes acted too imperceptibly, too slowly, and too feebly, to extinguish, or to effect perceptible changes in, the character of the nations that settled in these new homes. Hence it is that the historian discovers in the remotest corners of Europe, in Sicily and Britannia, on the Danube and Eider, on the Ebro and Elbe, a general uniformity of constitutions and customs, which is the more remarkable since it coexists with the greatest independence, and an almost entire absence of mutual intercourse. In spite of the centuries that have passed over the heads of these nations; in spite of the changes which so many new situations, a new religion, new languages, new arts, new objects of desire, new comforts and luxuries, must have occasioned in their internal condition, yet the same social structure that was erected by their forefathers has still been preserved in its main features. To this day, they have preserved their wild independence which they enjoyed in their Scythian country, and have extended throughout European provinces like a vast camp, prepared for attack or defense; even to this vast political arena they have transplanted their political system, carrying their northern superstition to the very bosom of Christianity.[9]

Like most of his contemporaries, who watched Europe being torn by conflict, and envisaged her possible decline, Schiller arrived at a new conception of her place in the world and her importance for the whole of mankind. In a letter to Goethe, dated January 26, 1798, he wrote:

In the meantime I have amused myself reading the travels of Niebuhr and Volney in Syria and Egypt, and I can only recommend these works to all who have been discouraged by recent political developments. For one really discovers for the first time what a blessing it was for us to have been born in Europe. It is truly incomprehensible that man's life-giving energy had only a little part of the world for its field of action, and that countless numbers of peoples count for absolutely nothing in respect of human perfectibility. I can scarcely conceive that all these nations, and all non-Europeans generally should be totally lacking in moral and aesthetic dispositions. Although both realism and idealism appear among them, these two dispositions never fuse in one humanly beautiful form.

Goethe confined himself to replying: "Therefore let us be content to live in this part of the globe, even if Europe must experience further upheavals."

Johann Gottlieb Fichte (1762–1814) may be looked upon as the first and most ruthless theorist of European nationalism. And yet this disciple of Rousseau and Kant, contemporary with the French Revolution (which he defended in 1793) and Napoleon (whom he was to attack violently), launched his series of great political writings with a project for a League of Nations and

[9] *Schiller's Complete Works,* ed. C. J. Hempel, M.D. (Philadelphia, 1861), II, 380, "Survey of the Condition of Europe at the Time of the First Crusade."

world citizenship. This was his *Grundriss der Völker und Welt-bürgerrecht,* 1796. It is up to reason and morality to bring about the worldwide triumph of the popular freedom won by the French Revolution. Fichte never deserted this ideal. But the methods by which he proposed to translate it into reality seem as aberrant as the methods by which Napoleon was to attempt to impose the Jacobin revolution on Europe. In either case, the means seem contrary to the professed ends: Napoleon wanted to bring freedom at the point of the bayonet; Fichte hoped to establish it by the coercive autarchic national State.

Starting from the idea of a society of free peoples, Fichte first of all declares that colonial expansion is Europe's great sin: it is useless and immoral—Bentham thought so too—and it is this expansion which has brought about Europe's anarchic dissolution into an unstable, bellicose collection of States. The trend cannot be reversed until all the States have been solidified, each reduced to its "natural frontiers," that is, to its economic optimum, and each made self-contained, without hope or need for aggrandizement. Then the most highly cultured State *(der auf der Höhe der Kultur steht),* which is of course Prussia, will become the true homeland of Christian Europeans. It will impose its culture, by war if necessary, on the rest of the world. In the end, it is Science which will unite mankind.

The steps in this argument—which often clearly foreshadows National Socialism and Communism—can be illustrated with the following excerpts, taken from the work entitled *Der geschlossene Handelsstaat* ("The Self-contained Commercial State"), published in 1800:

The peoples of the ancient world were rigidly separated from one another by many barriers. They looked upon strangers as enemies or barbarians. By contrast, the peoples of Christian Europe can be looked upon as forming a single nation. United in their common origin, customs, and the primitive beliefs that prevailed in the Germanic forests, they became linked as well, with their expansion into the provinces of the Western Roman empire, through a common religion, and common subjection to its visible head. The peoples of different races who came later were taught, at the same time as the new religion, the same fundamental Germanic system of customs and ideas . . .

It is not surprising that these peoples, united in every way, were not separated by what usually separates men, namely, state constitutions (since they had none). They looked upon themselves and acted as members of a single nation, freely mingling with one another, traveling, trading, and taking employment; they felt at home everywhere.

Not until Roman law was introduced and the Kings and the emperors began to model themselves on the Roman *imperators* (whereas the emperor was originally regarded as the chief of Christendom, and was to the Church as a whole what patrons were to bishoprics and monasteries)—not until then did specifically political ideas and institutions make their appearance . . .

The modern states did not come into being as a result of a compact among isolated individuals, as is maintained by theorists of the natural law; they actually were formed by the breaking up and division of a single loosely knit human mass. The various states of Christian Europe are fragments detached from the old whole; and the size of each fragment was largely determined by chance.

It was at the epoch of this unity of Christian Europe that the commercial system, which at least in its essential features has survived to this day, was developed. Every individual in every part of this great whole cultivated, manufactured, and sold or bought whatever he needed, according to his natural condition. He could travel within this whole without hindrance, and the prices of objects were fixed of themselves . . .

Citizens of one state naturally trade among themselves. Since Christian Europe formed a whole, the trade of Europeans among themselves had to be free.

In the light of this principle, it is easy to see that if Christian Europe, including her colonies and trading centers in other parts of the world, still forms a whole, the trade of all these parts with one another ought to remain as free as it was originally. But if, on the contrary, Europe is divided into several states under different governments, it must similarly be divided into several completely self-contained commercial units.

We have now come to the source of the greater part of the still existing abuses. In the new Europe there were no states at all for a long time. We are still in the period when attempts are being made to form states. Moreover, until now the mission of the state has been conceived in a onesided and half-complete manner, as an institution whose purpose is to maintain its citizens, by means of law, in the conditions of property in which they find themselves. The more fundamental duty of the State, which consists first of all in setting up each in the property due him, has hitherto been neglected. Now this is possible only if commercial anarchy is abolished, just as political anarchy is being gradually abolished, and if the state becomes self-contained in respect to trade, just as it has become self-contained in respect of legislation and judiciary functions.[10]

Should we deplore the division of Europe? No, says Fichte, it would be futile "to deplore the inevitable":

If we want to abolish war, we must abolish its cause. Every state must obtain what it plans to obtain by war, but only what it can reasonably plan to obtain, namely, its natural frontiers. After that it needs no longer ask anything of another state, for it has found what it had been looking for.[11]

Thus the Rousseauistic utopia of an innately good mankind finds its counterpart in Fichte's utopia of the innately reasonable State.

All that is left to be done is to draw the logical consequences from these premises: isolate the states, forbid trade among them, diversify their currencies, etc. We are witnessing the birth of the theory of absolute autarchy. What Fichte advocated is the exact opposite of the present-day Common Market:

All world currencies held by the citizens, that is to say, all gold and silver, will be withdrawn from circulation and exchanged for a new national currency, which will be exclusively used within each country . . .
The government must seize control of foreign trade in view of periodically restraining this trade and stopping it altogether after a specific lapse of time. . . .
Every year there must be fewer foreign imports. From year to year the public has less need of commodities which cannot be produced in their purity nor replaced by substitutes at home. The public must wean itself from them altogether, and be actively encouraged to do so by steadily rising prices. The importation of commodities which are sought after only because they are fashionable might even be prohibited at once. The need for such imports from abroad will decrease of itself if steps are taken to produce similar commodities at home. If domestic production and manufacture are rationally and methodically supervised,

[10] *Der geschlossene Handelsstaat,* II, 2.
[11] *Ibid.,* III, 3.

instead of being left to the mercies of blind chance, they will develop steadily, and foreign products will give way to domestic products.

Exports too must decrease . . . For the government will systematically decrease the number of factories producing for export, and the manpower which had previously worked for foreigners will now work for nationals. For the government does not aim at commercial preponderance, which is a dangerous tendency, but strives to make the nation entirely independent and autonomous.[12]

Not only trade is to be suppressed. Cultural exchange and travel will also have to go. The only exception allowed is scholarly travel. This last-named feature vividly brings to mind twentieth-century totalitarian practices:

Only the scholar and the superior artist need to travel outside the self-contained commercial state; those motivated by vain curiosity and search for diversion are no longer to be permitted to take their boredom abroad. The travels of scholars and artists are undertaken for the greater good of mankind and the State; far from stopping them, the government ought even to encourage them and let them travel at government expense.[13]

It is evident that a nation thus isolated, whose members live only among themselves and very little with foreigners, will in the course of time acquire its own way of life, its own peculiar organization and manner and will love the homeland and everything in it. Such a nation will rapidly develop a strong sense of national honor, as well as a clearly marked national character. It will be an absolutely new nation. The introduction of a national currency will truly create it. . . .

The only bond between the nations that will have to be allowed to remain is that of science:

Thanks to Science and science alone, men will unite in a lasting manner and they ought to do so, after their division into various peoples has been consummated in every other respect. Science alone remains their common possession after they have divided all the rest among themselves. The self-contained State will not abolish this bond, but will rather favor it, for enrichment of Science by the united power of the human race furthers even

[12] *Ibid.*, III, 4 and III, 6; II.
[13] *Ibid.*, III, 7.

specific earthly goals. The treasures of foreign literatures will be imported by paid Academies of professional scholars in exchange for those of the home country.

Once this system has become general, and perpetual peace is established among nations, no state on earth will have the slightest interest not to communicate its discoveries to another, since each state can use them only for itself, within itself, and can never use them to enslave others or to gain over them any kind of preponderance.[14]

It must be granted that Fichte's utopia, however fantastic it may appear to us, anticipates the historical realities of the 150 years that were to follow more accurately than any other similar work inspired by pre-Romantic philosophy. It would be unfair, however, to see in Fichte solely a forerunner of the anti-European totalitarian nationalisms. Though he followed a "dialectical" tortuous path, his ultimate goal was European unity. In his *Grundzüge des gegenwärtigen Zeitalters* (1804–1805), published five years after his manifesto on autarchy, he wrote:

. . . the Christian Europeans are essentially one people, they recognize this common Europe as their one true fatherland and from one end of it to the other they work toward the same goal. . . .
However unjust this scheme may appear in itself, it is nonetheless a rough draft for a world organization. The progress of universal culture is gradually gaining momentum: and in accordance with the same law, this progress will continue without respite until the whole of the human race has been united in a single Universal Republic of Culture.

Thus colonial expansion—responsible for splitting up Europe into hostile nations—followed by the total isolation of these political monads, will eventually result, according to Fichte, in the universal triumph of European culture, spread by Science and freed from all imperialism. In the second half of the twentieth century we are not perhaps so far off from achieving this.

However, the "dialectical" process was to cost Europe and the world more dearly than Fichte ever dreamed: we need only mention the latter-day collusion between the scientists and the national state . . .

[14] *Ibid.*, III, 8.

Johann Gottfried von Herder (1744–1803) inaugurated in Germany—as Vico had done in Italy, and Gibbon was doing in England—the era of sustained reflection on the rise and fall of civilizations. His work is exceptionally rich in insights into Europe's role in history, and fruitful though contradictory theories. As a precursor of romantic nationalism he celebrated "the soul of a people"; as a precursor of the Holy Alliance he advocated the "European balance"; as a precursor of racism he defended the Nordic virtues; as a precursor of modern theorists of "inevitable European decadence" he vaunted the spiritual superiority of the East. Now he sees Europe at the head of world progress, now he describes it as doomed to be justly punished by the other continents for colonizing and pillaging them. In these pendulum-like swings of his thoughts, let us single out a few of his more European-minded moments. To begin with, here is a European "Republic of the Learned," such as Voltaire might have described:

All of Europe is one Republic of the Learned, which, partly thanks to great internal rivalry, and partly, during the last centuries, to precious resources which she sought and found all over the earth, succeeded in giving herself an ideal form that only the scholar can perceive and the statesman make use of. This is why we cannot stop and just let things take their course: we are in pursuit of the magical image of a supreme Science and a universal knowledge, which we shall never attain to, but which keeps us moving, as long as the political Constitution of Europe shall endure. The States which have never taken part in this conflict are, so to speak, of no account.[15]

Next we shall quote one of those geo-historical-lyrical—typically Herderian—intuitions, which adumbrate such great "world-historical" systems as those of Schlegel, Hegel, and Spengler:

Was it the north or the south, the east or the west, which was the *vagina hominum?* Where did the human species come from, its invention, its arts, and its religions? Are we to believe that mankind left the east to reproduce its titanic strength in the cold northern mountains like those monstrous fishes preserved in the ice? Later, we are told, having invented a religion as cruel as the climate, it invaded Europe at the point of the sword, implanting

[15] *Gesamtausgabe,* ed. Stephan (1877–1913), 14, 36.

there its manners, customs and conception of justice. If it was so, I can see two currents: One, coming from the East, passes through Greece and Italy and deviates slightly to the south of Europe. To it we owe a gentle southern religion, a poetry of the imagination, a music, an art, a practical wisdom and a science all of which constitute the patrimony of the European southwest. As for the second current, it starts from Asia, reaches Europe in the north, and there overwhelms the other current . . . If it was so, will not the third current come from America and the last perhaps from the Cape of Good Hope and the regions beyond it.[16]

Concerning Europe's world function, Herder had prophetic views which have been confirmed by the anticolonialist nationalist movement of the twentieth century. As early as 1784, in his *Ideas for a Philosophy of History*, he predicted that the tool and techniques which Europe had invented to subjugate the other continents would eventually be turned against her: "We Europeans . . . are forging the chains with which you will drag us down, when your turn has come!" [17]

In Herder's view—even then—Europe was betraying her world mission. In the collection entitled *Adrastea*, we find the following dialogue between a European and an Asian:

The Asian: One day Providence put weights and measures in the hands of the Europeans; let them measure, let them weigh. If they measure everything by false standards solely to gain advantages, what will become of the great scales of fate, which were given them in charge for furthering the happiness of nations?

The European: No one ever thinks about that in Europe.[18]

Herder was one of the first to see that Europe cannot be conceived of as a closed entity, an autonomous monad. She is inseparably linked with the rest of the world. He says this in a crucial sentence which Hegel must have remembered: "The existence of a State can be considered in itself or in relation to other states; Europe finds herself obliged to use both yardsticks, the states of Asia have only one." [19]

[16] *Ibid*, 4, 351, 59.
[17] *Ibid.*, 14.
[18] *Ibid.*, 23, 503.
[19] *Ibid.*, 14, 37.

Johannes von Müller (1752–1809), historian of the Swiss, ful-filled Herder's wishes by giving his contemporaries a *Universal History* (1797), which was popular at the time. Though it is cen-tered on Europe, as is shown by its original title *(Vierundzwanzig Bücher allgemeiner Geschichte, besonders der europäischen Menschheit)*, the views expressed in it are pessimistic. According to Heinz Gollwitzer, Müller "was the first great German thinker to have expressed the emotional and intellectual implications of an awareness of European decline; his pessimism is akin to (but not identical with) that of the Christian vision of the world." [20] Like Rousseau, he saw "all the States of Europe rushing headlong to their ruin," and he anticipated that the future would belong "either to Russia or to America."

Here is his picture of the condition of the European states, as it could be seen at the close of the eighteenth century:

All powers can be divided into three groups: the maritime powers, which are subdivided into two—the Bourbon Princes who rule in France, Spain, and the two Sicilies; and Great Britain with the United Provinces which form together the Protestant interest in that part of Europe; some day armed neutrality will find its point of juncture there . . .

Among the powers of the second group, which hold the balance of European freedom, the Emperor, Russia, and Prussia, by vir-tue of the number and excellence of their troops, are naturally first. Others would dispute their rank if a new Gustavus Adolphus were to appear, who by his energy and heroism was able to transform a small nation into a great Power.

At the head of the barbarian powers is the Padishah; Europe has no relations with the courts of Asia. In Africa we may men-tion Algeria, Tunisia, Tripoli, and Morocco.

Switzerland and the kings of Sardinia and Portugal may be dealt with after the Bourbons, one of whom is regarded as an ally; the latter's connections alone can turn to account the rights or wishes of the Duke of Savoy concerning Lombardy. Scandi-navia, the Princes of the Empire, Poland, and several Italian states can be considered as coming after the three powers which hold the balance, because their alliance can contribute above all to obstructing or accelerating the advancement of one of these powers in relation to the others.

[20] H. Gollwitzer, *Europabild und Europagedanke* (Munich: C. H. Beck, 1951), p. 117.

Among the States governed by the Bourbons, France alone could be law-giver to the world by virtue of her size, situation, soil, and the character of her inhabitants, if a consistent policy, appropriate to the nature of a great power, turned her prodigious resources to account.[21]

One is struck by the complexity and fragility of these various groups of powers deemed "to be holding the balance of European freedom." They bring to mind the passage in which Kant, criticizing the idea of the European balance dear to Gentz and Burke, was reminded of Swift. The latter describes a house built in such perfect conformity to the principle of balance that when a sparrow perched on its roof, the house collapsed.

However, Müller is primarily interesting for his sweeping comparisons between whole civilizations. In this respect, his Résumé of the IXth Discourse is very typical. Here is dawning awareness of Europe's place in the world, so characteristic of Germanic thought in the period:

For eight centuries after the fall of the Roman Empire the East has remained what it was; an empire that rose as rapidly as that of Ninus or Cyrus has been growing weaker and weaker, breaking up, and new dynasties coming to power with the decline and collapse of the preceding ones; the Mongols, like the Scythians at the time of Cyaxares, invaded countless different tribes of mankind, and vanished quickly for lack of fresh troops. In the West, after a long period of unrest and the temporary ascendancy of the first Frankish emperor, the ancient Germans made the transition to a settled society. The nations, contained the ones by the others, were forced to draw upon their own resources, although they would have preferred to make war on others. From this labor came industry; next, among the burghers came the courage to be free, and lastly came the full development of the human mind. All the religions came from the East; feelings are more intense and more elevated there. Knowledge, both intuitive and based on sensory observation, took on a speculative force in the West; in the east, it serves conquerors; in the west it hastens the establishment of civil order.

We see more skillfulness and more preseverance in the politics of the Europeans; in that of the Orientals we see more spurts of

[21] Johannes von Müller, *Vierundzwanig Bücher allgemeiner Geschichte, besonders der europäischen Menschheit.*

energy. We are in the midst of the Drama that was begun by the Giants of the north, who swept down and destroyed the ancient Empire.

4: Europe and Napoleon

IN THE MEANTIME a new Empire was about to rise. Johannes von Müller himself, after successively serving Austria and Prussia and opposing every idea of European hegemony, concluded that the time had come "to replace the obsolete forms of old Europe with a new order of things" [22] and became minister to King Jerome of Westphalia. This was at a time when the *Gazette de France* (January 2, 1806) in an article titled "Tableau de l'Europe," said:

The time has past when equal opposing forces keep each other immobile; now a single preponderating power, too strong to be attacked, and too big to require expansion, will preserve the peace . . . From now on France will be the pivot around which all Europe remains quiet . . .

This was also the time when Laplace, advocating the decimal system and a general systematization of weights and measures, was saying:

What circumstance could more favor their adoption than this one? Napoleon the Great has brought half of Europe under his sway, his shining example exercises the most fortunate influence on the other half. Thanks to his Genius, all Europe will soon be one immense family, with one religion, one Code of laws, and one system of weights and measures. [23]

Several works were coming out in France and Germany which took up the old projects for European peace through a union of States, but this time under the aegis of the First Consul, and later the Emperor: *Die europäische Republik* by Niklas Vogt

[22] Cf. H. Gollwitzer, *op. cit.*, p. 117, from *Briefwechsel der Bruder J. Georg und J. v. Müller* (Fraunenfeld, 1893). The letter dates from 1804.

[23] Marquis de Laplace, *Exposition du système du monde* (Paris, 1813), I, 142.

(1802 and 1808), *De la Paix de l'Europe et des ses bases* by Delisle de Sales, *Du droit public et du droit des gens, suivi d'un projet de paix générale et perpétuelle* by Gondon (1807), *Das Urbild der Menschheit* by Karl Christian Friedrich Krause (1807–1811), and many others. . . . It is well known today how extraordinary was the prestige Napoleon enjoyed among the great minds of Weimar and Jena, such as Goethe, Wieland, and Hegel, the most "European" representatives of the Germanic world. Even so unpolitical a poet as Jean Paul (Johann Paul Friedrich Richter, 1763–1825) was enthusiastic. He praised the Emperor for having attempted to transform the whole continent into Fichte's "self-contained commercial state." Actually it is the image of a united mankind and a Europe opening to the world that inspire Jeau Paul's political writings, such as *Dämmerungen für Deutschland* and *Politische Fastenpredigten.* He often describes Europe as his true homeland, and Germany as its heart, for instance, in the following passage which curiously recalls the description of Europe as a single body asuch as Guillaume Postel and Renaissance engravers had circulated:

Not only does Germany occupy the geographical center of Europe, she also is its moral center. She is often represented—and rightly so—in the form of a heart on the effigy of a girl, while other parts of Europe are no more than the head or one clenched hand. This good, honest heart, which has been pierced with cannon balls in almost every European war! [24]

What was going on in the mind of the historical hero these utopians so admired, who embodied their hopes for Europe and had himself dreamed of conquering Asia, until failure in Egypt had put a check to his ambitions? Now he was turned back to the continent about which he is alleged to have said, "This old Europe bores me."

It has often been claimed that the Emperor did not disclose his intention to unite Europe until he was a prisoner on St. Helena, when it was too late. This is not exact. Even though the *Acte additionnel aux Constitutions de l'Empire*, composed on his return from Elba, was actually the work of Benjamin Constant,

[24] Jean Paul, *Sämtliche Werke* (Weimar, 1939), XIV, 6.

its preamble bears the imprint of the Emperor's thought and hand. It says:

At that time our aim was to organize a great European federal system, which we adopted as being in conformity with the spirit of the century and favorable to the advancement of civilization. In order to broaden, complete, and stabilize it we postponed the establishment of a number of internal institutions, especially destined to protect the freedom of the citizens . . .

It is clear that the deposed tyrant was able to form a coherent view of the motives which inspired his political action only thanks to his compulsory idleness on St. Helena. This accounts for the frequent statements he made to Las Cases on how he planned to organize Europe. Asked what would have happened if he had emerged victorious from the Russian compaign, Napoleon replied:

Peace concluded in Moscow would have been the consummation and the end of my military campaigns. It would have been, as far as the great cause is concerned, the end of risks and the beginning of security. New horizons, new tasks to be accomplished were opening up, calculated to bring well-being and prosperity to all. The European system would have been founded, and my only remaining task would have been to organize it.

Satisfied on these major points, and secure everywhere, I too should have had my Congress and my Holy Alliance. These ideas were stolen from me. In that assembly of all sovereigns, we should have negotiated our interests *en famille*, and settled our accounts with the peoples, as a clerk does with his master.

The Emperor, Las Cases adds in *Le Mémorial de Sainte-Hélène,*

then reviewed the proposals he would have made for the prosperity, the interest, the enjoyment and the welfare of the European confederacy. He would have aimed at the same principles, the same system everywhere. A European code, a European supreme court with full powers to review all wrong decisions just as our own court of appeals reviews those of the lower courts; money of the same value but in different coins; the same weights, the same measures, the same laws, etc., etc.

Thus Europe, he said, would soon have formed actually a single nation, and every traveler would have everywhere found himself in one common homeland. He would have opened all rivers to all; the seas would be held in common; the great standing armies would have been reduced to royal bodyguards, etc., etc.

In his mind, which has remained Jacobin—anything but federalist!—the condition of any European union lay in a "summary simplification" of codes, opinions, feelings, and interests, which had previously been unified inside the great nations:

One of my greatest ideas was the bringing together, the concentration of the same geographical peoples which had been dissolved, fragmented, by revolutions and by politics. Thus there are in Europe more than thirty million Frenchmen, fifteen million Spaniards, fifteen million Italians, thirty million Germans though widely scattered: I should have tried to turn each of these peoples into a single national body. To have achieved this would have been to go down to posterity gloriously and to be blessed by all the centuries to come. I felt equal to it!

This summary simplification would have made easier the realization of the noble ideal of civilization: more opportunities would have been found to establish everywhere the same codes, principles, opinions, feelings, views, and interests. Then, with the help of universal enlightenment, it might have been permitted to dream of introducing the American Congress or the Greek Amphictyons for the benefit of the great European family; and then what prospects of strength, grandeur, pleasures, prosperity! What a grand, what a splendid spectacle! . . .

However that may be, this union will come sooner or later. It is inevitable, it is already under way and I do not think that after my fall and the disappearance of my system there can be any balance possible except through union and federation of the great peoples. The first sovereign who, in the midst of the first great conflict, embraces the cause of the peoples in good faith, will find himself at the head of all Europe, and will be able to attempt whatever he pleases.

5: The Europe of the Emperor's Adversaries

NAPOLEON WAS RIGHT concerning the last point: the only "possible balance" in Europe after the fall of his Empire would have been Federation. Actually, the "impossible" balance of the Holy

Alliance was imposed by sovereigns who, very far from embracing "the cause of the peoples in good faith," were only able to form a precarious League of Monarchs in the name of stability. However, the European idea had gained sufficient strength and concentrated a sufficient number of diverse hopes for the negotiators of the peace treaties to feel obliged at least to pay it lip service:

Excerpt from the record of the meeting of February 5, 1814, at the Congress of Châtillon:

The plenipotentiaries of the allied courts declare that they do not attend the conference merely as delegates from the four courts for whom they are fully empowered to act, but as being entrusted with negotiating peace with France in the name of Europe, the latter forming a single whole.

Excerpt from the Treaty of Chaumont, March 1, 1814:

Because the present treaty of defensive alliance is aimed at preserving balance in Europe, securing peace and independence of the powers, and preventing invasions such as have for many years been ravaging the world, the High Contracting Parties have agreed to extend it for twenty years from date of signature.

Excerpt from the Vichy Declaration, March 15, 1814:

The march of events [has made] the allied Courts feel the full strength of the European league. . . . The peace will be a European peace, any other is inadmissible.

Excerpt from the Act of Recognition of Swiss Neutrality, 1814 and 1815:

The signatory powers . . . recognize . . . that the neutrality and inviolability of Switzerland . . . are in the true interests of all Europe.

And Metternich himself, one of the principal architects of these treaties, stated:

Europe has long been a fatherland to me.

Thus all Europe began to speak for Europe, in opposition to Napoleon, who had intended to create her. But this unanimity of the Intellectuals, like that of the Powers, was more apparent than real. Three principal groups may be distinguished: the liberals, the reactionaries (whether pessimistic or optimistic), and the authors of great systems (mystico-metaphysical or socio-economic).

French writers: two Swiss liberals—Benjamin Constant, and Mme. de Staël; one ultramontane from Savoy—Joseph de Maistre; and one pre-socialist economist—Saint-Simon.

German writers: a group of pro-Catholic Romantics—Novalis, Görres, Baader, and Adam Müller; and a group of philosophers whose views are profound, systematic, and universal, comparable to those of Fichte—the two Schlegels, Hegel, and Schelling.

Mme. de Staël serves as a bridge between the two language groups. And Goethe was to dominate them all, not by his influence, but by his stature.

Shortly after Napoleon escaped from Elba, Benjamin Constant (1767–1830) published his famous pamphlet, *De l'Esprit de Conquête et de l'Usurpation dans leurs rapports avec la civilisation européenne.* Although it does not contain a plan for union,[25] the idea of Europe as an entity is not just implied in the title, but pervades the whole work. Napoleon, who embodies the spirit of conquest and who would impose uniformity by arms, stands for the anti-European spirit. Benjamin Constant's polemic against war is linked with an attack on the Jacobin concept of the centralized nation. This makes Benjamin Constant a forerunner of the modern federalists, who champion a united Europe, but condemn the abstract, regimented self-contained national state, and favor the rebirth of local traditions that are destroyed by the latter, as well as the peaceful union of peoples.[26]

Remarkably enough, uniformity never met with greater favor than during the course of a revolution made in the name of freedom and the Rights of Man. The spirit of system begins with enthusiasm for the symmetrical. Love of power soon discovers the

[25] He had the opportunity to draft such a plan a few weeks later, when he wrote, at Napoleon's own request, the *Acte additionnel aux Constitutions de l'Empire,* in which the intention to create a European federation is explicitly asserted.

[26] *De l'Esprit de Conquête,* chap. xiii, "De l'Uniformité."

immense benefits it can derive from symmetry. Whereas true patriotism feeds on devotion to local interests, manners, and customs, our self-styled patriots declared war on all these things. They dried up the natural springs of patriotism and sought to replace it with a factitious passion for an abstraction, a general idea, devoid of everything that strikes the imagination or speaks to the memory. To build their edifice they began by grinding to dust the very building materials. They came close to replacing the names of cities and provinces with numbers, just as they had used numbers to designate legions and army corps, so much did they seem to fear that some spiritual meaning might be associated with their reforms!

. . . Even in old-established states, whose past aggressions and conquests had ceased to be felt as odious, we see a patriotism, which is reborn as though from its own ashes, the moment the pressure of central authority lightens. The magistrates of the smallest towns take pleasure in embellishing them, and devote much care to the local old monuments. In almost every village there is a learned man fond of telling over the annals of the region and he is listened to with respect. The inhabitants enjoy whatever gives them the appearance, however illusory, of being a community, united by particular bonds. We feel that if they were not prevented from developing this harmless and beneficent tendency, there would soon form in them a kind of communal honor, so to speak, a sense of pride in their city or province, which would be gratifying to them and conducive to virtue. But what happens is that the central authority watches them jealously, and frequently views with alarm and destroys the local seed before it has taken root.

Attachment to local customs is akin to all disinterested, noble, and pious feelings. How deplorable is a policy that treats such attachment as rebellion! What are its results? In every state where all local life is thus destroyed, a little state forms at the center; all interests gather in the capital; all ambitions seek to be gratified there; the rest remain inert. Individuals, lost in an unnatural isolation, strangers in the place of their birth, without contact with the past, living in a transitory present, and scattered like atoms over one vast level plain, become alienated from a fatherland which they see nowhere, and toward which they become indifferent, because their affections cannot be focused on any part of it.

Variety is organization; uniformity is mechanism. Variety is life; uniformity is death.

Benjamin Constant's pamphlet, a manifesto of political liberalism, appeared in 1814. The same year Fichte, theoretician of autarchic nationalism, died, Napoleon was deported to St. Helena, and Gentz, Europe's "Knight-Errant," found himself at the center of European politics. That year too, an obscure French aristocrat, the Count Henri de Saint-Simon-Sandricourt (1760–1825), ex-officer, ex-speculator, ex-prisoner of the Terror, economist, engineer, writer, and future founder of a religious sect, published a plan for a United States of Europe based on an entirely new conception. Here is the full title: *De la réorganisation de la Société européenne, ou de la nécessité de rassembler les peuples de l'Europe en un seul corps politique, en conservant à chacun son indépendance nationale.*

Even discounting the influence that Saint-Simon was later to exert on historiography through Augustin Thierry, on philosophy and sociology through Auguste Comte, on such engineering feats as F. de Lesseps' Suez Canal, and on French socialism through Enfantin, Fourier, and the Phalansterians, we must grant his European plan two major qualities. (1) He broke with the Du Bois–Sully–Saint-Pierre tradition of alliances among princes, which Metternich and Alexander were to make futile attempts to carry out, and he proposed the election of European deputies according to the "corporations" or professions they represent; (2) he put the European problem on the plane of "common interests and solid commitments." More than any author of earlier Plans, he bases himself on economic considerations. He is the true precursor of the institutionalizing tendency which in the twentieth century has produced the Common Market and the O.E.C.D. The reader may judge for himself:

The Treaty of Westphalia established a new order by a political device called the balance of power. Europe was divided into two confederations which were artificially kept in equilibrium, thus giving rise to war and legalizing it; for two leagues of equal power are necessarily rivals, and rivalry cannot persist without war.

Thenceforth each power concentrated on increasing its military strength. Instead of puny handfuls of soldiers levied for the occasion and soon discharged, everywhere appeared formidable armies on a permanent footing, nearly always actively, for since

the Treaty of Westphalia war has been the normal condition of
Europe. . . .

Formerly Europe consisted of a federal community united by
common institutions, subject to a common government which was
in the same relation to the different peoples as national governments are to individuals; a similar organization is the only one
which can effect a complete cure. Of course, I do not suggest
that this outworn institution which still encumbers Europe with
its useless remains should be raised from the dust—the nineteenth
century is too remote from the thirteenth century.

A constitution, strong in itself, based on principles derived
from the nature of things, independent of beliefs which lose their
force, and of ephemeral opinions—that is what Europe needs, and
what I now put forward . . .

With a union of peoples as with a union of individuals, common institutions and an organization are required. Without these
everything is decided by force. To seek peace in Europe by
means of treaties and congresses is to seek the maintenance of a
society by conventions and agreements. In both cases a compelling force is required which will unite wills, concert movement,
make interests common and undertaking firm. . . .

Europe would have the best possible organization if all the
nations composing it were to be governed by parliaments, recog-
nizing the supremacy of a common parliament set above all the
national governments and invested with the power of judging
their disputes. . . .

It is the same with the European government as with the national governments: there cannot be action without a will common
to all the members of the government.

Now this corporate will, which in a national government
springs from national patriotism, must come in the European government from a greater breadth of view, a wider sentiment, which
we may call European patriotism.

Montesquieu says that institutions mold men. Therefore this
tendency which fosters a patriotism beyond the limits of one's
own fatherland, this habit of considering the interests of Europe
instead of national interests, will be a natural development
among those who compose the European parliament, once it is
established.

This is true, but it is also the fact that men make institutions,
and an institution cannot take root if men are not adapted for it
beforehand, or a least in a condition to be adapted.

It is therefore essential to admit to the House of Commons of
the European Parliament, i.e. one of the two active powers of the

European constitution, only such men as by their wide contacts, emancipation from purely local customs, their occupations which are cosmopolitan in aim rather than national, are better able to arrive quickly at this wider point of view which makes the corporate will, and at the common interest which should be also the corporate interest of the European parliament.

Men of business, scientists, magistrates, and administrators are the only classes who should be summoned to form the House of Commons of the great parliament. It is a fact that whatever common interests exist in the European community can be traced to the sciences, arts, law, commerce, administration, and industry.

For every million persons in Europe who know how to read and write there should sit as their representatives in the House of Commons of the great parliament, a man of business, a scientist, an administrator and a lawyer. Thus, assuming that there are sixty million men in Europe who know how to read and write, the House will be composed of 240 members. The election of members will be made by the professional body to which they belong. They will be elected for ten years. . . .

Every question of common interest of the European community should be brought before the great parliament, to be considered and decided by it. It should be the sole judge of disputes arising between the different governments.

The European parliament should have a city and surrounding territory as its property in full sovereignty.

The parliament will have the right to levy from the Confederation such taxes as may be considered necessary.

All undertakings of common advantage to the European community will be directed by the great parliament; thus, for instance, it will link the Danube to the Rhine by canals, the Rhine to the Baltic, etc. Without external activity, there is no internal tranquillity. The surest means of maintaining peace in the Confederation will be to keep it constantly occupied beyond its own borders, and engaged without pause in great internal enterprises. To colonize the world with the European race, superior to every other human race; to make the world accessible and habitable like Europe—such is the sort of enterprise by which the European parliament should continually keep Europe active and healthy.

State education in the whole of Europe will be under the direction and supervision of the great parliament.

A code of general as well as national and individual ethics will be drawn by the great parliament, to be taught throughout Europe. It will demonstrate that the principles on which the

European Confederation rests are the best, the most solid, the only principles capable of making the community as happy as it can be, according to the nature of man, and the state of his enlightenment. The great parliament will allow complete freedom of conscience, and of worship; but it will prohibit religions with principles contrary to the great moral code which will have been drawn up. Thus the European people will be united by the essential bonds in any political association; uniformity of institutions, union of interests, conformity of principles, a common ethic and a common education. . . .

With great effort and labour I have reached the standpoint of the common interest of the European peoples. This standpoint is the only one from which it is possible to perceive both the evils which threaten us, and the means of averting them. If those who are in charge of affairs can reach the same level as I have done, they will be able to see what I have seen. . . .

There will come a time, without doubt, when all the peoples of Europe will feel that questions of common interest must be dealt with before coming down to national interests; then evils will begin to lessen, troubles abate, wars die out. That is the ultimate direction in which we are steadily progressing; it is there that the progress of the human mind will carry us. But which is more worthy of man's prudence—to hasten towards it, or to let ourselves be dragged there? [27]

The Count Joseph de Maistre (1754–1821), a native of Savoy, who served a long time as the King of Sardinia's minister at the court of St. Petersburg, represents outside of France—though he is a great French writer—the most fanatical opposition to the liberal and Jacobin Revolution, to Napoleon, to nationalism, and to democracy. Convinced that Europe (*audax Japeti genus,* as Horace wrote) was in the vanguard of mankind, he nonetheless expressed the gloomiest prophecies concerning her future. He could envisage salvation in only one way: all the peoples must return to the Roman fold, must unconditionally place themselves under the Pope, "civilization's great Demiurge," founder of "European monarchy," and "ultimate source of Europe's sovereignty." Could anyone really believe that so grandiose a theocratic dream might come true? It is doubtful whether its

[27] Henri Comte de Saint-Simon, *Selected Writings,* edited and translated by F. M. H. Markham (Oxford: Basil Blackwell, 1952.)

own author believed it. The fact is, on August 9, 1819, he wrote in a letter to the Count de Marcellus: "I am dying along with Europe, I am in good company."

In his book *Du Pape,* published in 1821, he nonetheless emphasizes the superiority of Europe and of freedom in relation to Asia and despotism:

The world is divided between two systems decidedly different. *The daring race of Japheth* has not ceased, if the expression may be permitted, to gravitate towards what is called *liberty,* that is to say, towards that State in which the governing power governs as little and the governed are as little governed as possible. Always on his guard against his masters, the European has sometimes expelled them and sometimes opposed the barriers of law to them. He has tried everything, he has exhausted all imaginable forms of government in order to dispense with rulers or to restrain their power.

The immense posterity of Shem and Cham have adopted another course. From primitive times till those in which we live, it has always said to one man: "Do whatever you please, and when we are tired of you, we shall put you to death."

Besides, it has never been willing or able to understand what is meant by a republic; it knows nothing about the balance of power, about all of those privileges or all those fundamental laws in which we glory so much. Among them the wealthiest of men, he who is most the master of his actions, the possessor of an immense moveable fortune, absolutely free to carry it wherever he pleases, sure, moreover, of complete protection on the soil of Europe, and already beholding the approach of the cord or the poniard, prefers them, nevertheless, to the misfortune of dying of tedium among us.

Nobody, doubtless, will take it in his head to prescribe for Europe the public law, brief and clear as it is, of Asia and Africa; but since in Europe power is always clamorous in discussion, attacked or beside itself—since there is nothing so intolerable to our pride as despotic government, the greatest problem Europe has to solve is, "How can sovereign power be restrained without being destroyed?" [28]

It has been asked whether the true purpose of the book was not to persuade Czar Alexander I to submit to Rome. For such an en-

[28] De Maistre, *The Pope,* trans. The Reverend Aeneas McDawan (London: C. Dolman, 1850), Book II, chap. ii, "Inconveniences of Sovereignty."

terprise De Maistre was poorly equipped. A rapprochement with the Orthodox Church or with the Protestants had been excluded in advance; it was for them to submit. For the Orthodox Church, a return to Rome is, according to him, the only way "to raise themselves to the highest level of European culture"; for the Protestants, it is a question of renouncing their "pride" and giving allegiance without qualifications. As he says, the Protestant "half of Europe has no religion." More than that:

The greatest enemy of Europe, which must be crushed by every means that is not criminal, the baleful ulcer that attaches itself to all sovereignties and corrodes them without respite, the son of pride, the father of anarchy, the universal disintegrant is Protestantism.

The Baroness de Staël-Holstein (1766–1817), daughter of Necker (Protestant in religion, a liberal in politics, a native of Geneva, minister to Louis XVI), was spiritually the antithesis of De Maistre. She was born to unite and to admire, as De Maistre had been to provoke and to cast anathemas; she exalts peace, whereas he insists on the sacred character of war; she sees in Catholicism and Protestantism two complementary needs of the human heart, while he saw the Reformation as the sworn enemy of unity. Could it not be because his conception of unity was as formal and implicit with coercion as that of the Jacobins he detested? Mme. de Staël belongs to the federalist school, which is also ecumenical:

There are two very distinct forces in the human mind: one inspires the need to believe, the other the need to examine. Neither of these faculties should be gratified at the expense of the other: Protestantism and Catholicism are not accounted for by the circumstance that there were Popes and that there was Luther; it is a poor conception of history, to see it in terms of accident. Protestantism and Catholicism exist in the human heart; they are moral powers which develop in nations, because they exist in each man.
. . . One day a cry for union may arise, and the universality of the Christians may aspire to profess the same theological, political, and moral religion; but before this miracle comes to pass, all men who have a heart and obey its dictates must respect one another. . . .

Futhermore, did not the Christian religion begin by uniting opposites, thus founding Europe?

The Christian religion was the link between the northern and the southern peoples; it fused, so to speak, opposite ways of life into a common opinion; and bringing enemies closer to each other, it transformed them into nations in which energetic men strengthened the characters of enlightened men. This mixture came into being slowly, no doubt. Eternal Providence lavished whole centuries on fulfilling its designs, and our transitory existence is annoyed and surprised by this; but after all the victors and the vanquished alike have in the end become a single people scattered over the diverse countries of Europe, and the Christian religion has powerfully contributed to this result.[29]

Mme. de Staël's historical role consisted far less in her ineffectual opposition to Napoleon than in the fruitful use she made of her exile. Thanks to her, Coppet became (this was held against her by later nationalists like Charles Maurras) the "point of entry" through which European-minded thought, initiated by the genius of such as Goethe and Herder, reached France. Her work *De l'Allemagne* is a European document, the consequences of which were more far-reaching than the diplomatic documents of the period:

In our modern times, one must be European-minded.
. . . The nations must serve as guide to one another, and it would be wrong of any of them not to take advantage of the light each can supply to the other. There is something very singular in the way one people differs from another with respect to climate, natural scenery, language, government, and above all history, a power more extraordinary than the others. No man, no matter how superior, can guess what develops naturally in the mind of one who lives on another soil and breathes another air; thus any country would do well to be hospitable to foreign ideas in any country; for in this order of things, hospitality enriches the host.
. . . Finally there remains something else that cannot be enjoyed by ignorance or frivolity: the close ties that exist among all thinking men from one end of Europe to the other. Often there is no contact between them; they often live at great dis-

[29] *De la Littérature* (Paris, 1820), in *Œuvres complètes de la baronne de Staël*, Vol. IV.

tances from each other; but when they do meet, they recognize each other at a glance. It is not a given religion, opinion, or intellectual pursuit that brings them together, but a common devotion to the truth. Now they dig deep into the earth, like miners, to penetrate the mysteries of the world of darkness in the bosom of eternal night; now they climb to the very top of Chimborasso to discover some unknown phenomena at the highest point of the globe; now they study the languages of the East to investigate man's primitive history; now they go to Jerusalem and explore the holy ruins, in search of some spark to revive religion and poetry; in short, they are truly God's people, these men who have not yet despaired of the human root, and want to preserve for it the empire of thought.[30]

No more distinguished service can be rendered to letters than to translate the masterpieces of the human mind from one language to another. There are so few productions of the first rank; genius, in any genre whatever, is a phenomenon so rare, that if each modern nation were confined to its own treasures, it would be forever poor. Moreover, of all the types of trade, the circulation of ideas is the one that results in the most certain benefits.[31]

We shall find echoes of this spiritual ecumenism or federalism in Goethe's statements on world literature.

6: Goethe

JOHANN WOLFGANG VON GOETHE (1749–1832) is beyond all labels: he deserves a chapter to himself. In the 143 volumes in octavo which contain the works of this "great European" we find little about Europe: for Europe is implicit in everything Goethe thought, and so deeply rooted in his personality that he scarcely finds an occasion to speak of it as an objective entity. Plans for union left him indifferent, as did all things political. However, it was as a European that he reacted to the first expressions of cultural nationalism, both in France and in his own Germany. But when he was led to compare Europe with other civilizations

[30] *De l'Allemagne, ibid.,* Vol. IX. This work, confiscated and destroyed by the imperial police when it appeared in 1810, could not be published in France until 1814.

[31] *De l'esprit des traductions, ibid.,* Vol. XVII.

—with the East for example in the *West-Östlicher Diwan* and
the young America in *Wilhelm Meisters Wanderjahre*—his attitudes may seem to be ambivalent. We have seen his evasive
reply to Schiller when the latter extolled the unique advantages
of Europe. We will quote contradictory passages where he compared the advantages respectively of an old culture like Europe's
and of a brand new culture like America's. We need not be surprised. These apparent contradictions are just as naturally part
of Goethe's vitality as of Europe's creativity. Nothing could be
less Goethean than a "European nationalism," nothing more contrary to Europe than a refusal to criticize her, to compare her
objectively with other civilizations and, if need be, to find her
wanting—though in the name of the same universal ideals she
was the first to conceive and propagate. . . .

Here, to begin with, are some passages in which Goethe takes
up ideas Mme. de Staël had expressed, sometimes in almost the
same terms:

The innate diversity of conceptions and sentiments . . . characterizing entire peoples as well as individuals, and resulting
from inclination, pride, erroneous views, and passionate exag-
gerations, come to be looked upon by the unthinking man as
impassable frontiers, like the seas and mountains that close a
country in. Hence the duty, for cultivated people, for the elite, to
exert a pacifying and reconciling influence on relations among
nations, similar to the influence which would consist in facilitating navigation and clearing roads across mountains. The free
exchange of ideas and manners of feeling increases the wealth
and general welfare of mankind just as much as the exchange
of products and foodstuffs. It has not taken place until now
solely because the international community still has no moral
laws and firm principles such as obtain in private relations,
capable of fusing the countless individual differences into a more
or less harmonious whole.[32]

It is pleasant to see that intercourse is now so close between
the French, English, and Germans, that we shall be able to correct one another. This is the greatest use of a world literature,
which will show itself more and more.[33]

[32] *Gespräche, zu Mickiewicz,* 1829.
[33] *Conversations with Eckermann* (Washington and London: Walter
Dienne, Publishers, 1901), July 15, 1827.

National literature is now rather an unmeaning term; the epoch of World literature is at hand, and everyone must strive to hasten its approach. But, while we thus value what is foreign, we must not bind ourselves to anything in particular and regard it as a model. We must not give this value to the Chinese, or the Servian, or Calderon, or the Nibelungen; but if we really want a pattern, we must always return to the ancient Greeks, in whose works the beauty of mankind is constantly represented. All the rest we must look at only historically, appropriating to ourselves what is good, so far as it goes.[34]

There is no such thing as patriotic art or patriotic science. The one and the other, like everything that is noble and good, belong to the entire world.[35]

. . . National hatred is something peculiar. You will always find it strongest and most violent where there is the lowest degree of culture. But there is a degree where it vanishes altogether and where one stands to a certain extent *above* nations, and feels the weal or woe of a neighboring people, as if it had happened to one's own. This degree of culture was conformable to my nature, and I had become strengthened in it before I had reached my sixtieth year.[36]

What has created Europe's true unity is her culture, and what destroys it is the ideological politics which has been adopted by the masses.

Technology however will increasingly further union:

Europe was formerly one of the most extraordinary Republics that had ever existed, and her ruin was brought about by the fact that one of her parts tried to become what the whole had been, namely, France which wanted to become the Republic.[37]

We then spoke of the unity of Germany, and in what sense it was possible and desirable.

"I am not uneasy," said Goethe, "about the unity of Germany; our good high roads and future railroads will of themselves do their part. But, above all, may Germany be *one* in love: may it

[34] *Ibid.*, January 31, 1827.
[35] *Wilhelm Meisters Wanderjahre.*
[36] *Conversations with Eckermann*, March 14, 1830.
[37] *Gespräche, zu Riemer*, May 14, 1808.

always be *one* against the foreign foe . . . *one,* so that my traveling chest may pass unopened through all the six-and-thirty states! . . . may Germany be one in weight and measure, in trade and commerce . . . Whence is Germany great, but by the admirable culture of the people, which equally pervades all parts of the Empire?" [38]

But Goethe fears that excessive political centralization might harm that cultural unity which can thrive only on diversity: everything he says of Germany here, applies as well to Europe.

Great technical feats—such as he celebrated at the end of the *Second Faust*—in his eyes also held the promise of a union of the peoples. He waxes enthusiastic over the project for the Panama Canal:

Would that I might live to see it—but I shall not. I should like to see another thing—a junction of the Danube and the Rhine . . . And, thirdly, and lastly, I should wish to see England in possession of a canal through the Isthmus of Suez. Would I could live to see these three great works! It would be well worth the trouble to last some fifty years more for the very purpose. [39]

America, in the eyes of the aged Goethe, becomes the symbol of the technological world, free from all traditional constraints, succeeding to the world of European culture. (Once again, the political stage has been skipped.) But he cannot make up his mind to choose between the two worlds. Occasionally he expresses his annoyance in the face of the complexity of personal relations and the lack of cordiality in Europe, as here:

There is something more or less wrong among us old Europeans; our relations are far too artificial and complicated, our nutriment and mode of life are without their proper nature, and our social intercourse is without proper love and good will. Everyone is polished and courteous; but no one has the courage to be hearty and true, so that an honest man, with natural views and feelings, stands in a very bad position. Often one cannot help wishing that one had been born upon one of the South Sea

[38] *Conversations with Eckermann,* October 23, 1828.
[39] *Ibid.,* February 21, 1827.

islands so as to have thoroughly enjoyed human existence in all its purity, without any adulteration.[40]

And here are his famous lines on America:

> Amerika, du hast es besser
> als unser Kontinent, der alte,
> hast keine verfallene Schlösser
> und keine Basalte.
> Dich stört nicht im Innern
> Zu lebendiger Zeit.
> Unnützes Erinnern
> Und vergeblicher Streit . . .
> Benutzt die Gegenwart mit Glück!

He warns, nonetheless, against what he called the "velociferousness" of his century which lets "nothing ripen," and which obliges us "to live from day to day without ever bringing anything to accomplishment." And he congratulates himself on having lived in the age of culture, as "one of the last men of an epoch the like of which will not come soon again." [41]

This ambivalence in his judgment is reflected in the fact that while some of the characters in *Wilhelm Meisters Wanderjahre* embark for the New World, one character came back to Europe after spending his childhood in America with his parents, first generation emigrants.

At the beginning of the eighteenth century America exercised a strong attraction on Europeans; all who felt more or less unhappy in Europe hoped to emigrate overseas to live in freedom. This attraction was increased by the prospect of desirable possessions which were to be had before the population had spread further westward. Entire so-called Counties could still be bought on the edges of settled territories, and our master's father had acquired a considerable tract of land in this way.

Sons often feel and think differently from their fathers, and this was also the case here. Our master who came to Europe as a young man discovered a new world here: this priceless culture, so many centuries old—which had grown up, been hampered

---

[40] *Ibid.*, March 12, 1828.
[41] Quoted by E. Ludwig, *Goethe, the Story of a Man*, III, 362.

and oppressed though never destroyed—now taking on new life, and, as it had done before, manifesting itself in countless activities, inspired him with very different ideas as to the destiny of mankind, He chose to share in these great advantages and to contribute to the regular activities of the masses as one of them rather than to go back several centuries and play the part of an Orpheus or a Lycurgus overseas. No matter where a man may find himself, he said, he needs patience; everywhere he must adjust himself to circumstances, and I would rather come to terms with neighbors to obtain certain freedoms in exchange for certain concessions, than make war on the Iroquois to repel their attacks or cheat them by treaties in order to drive them from their swamps where one suffers agonies from mosquito bites.[42]

7 : Historico-Philosophical Syntheses (2)

NOVALIS, WHOSE REAL name was Frederich von Hardenberg (1772–1802), as early as 1799 wrote an essay, *Christendom or Europe*, which he read to a number of friends (among them the brothers Schlegel and the young Schelling), the magazine *Athenaeum*, however, rejected it on Goethe's advice, as being too "pro-Catholic." It was not published until 1826, long after the author's early death. But even though he did not influence the first generation of the Romantics, he nonetheless expresses the Roman-Germanic ideal which was to become the common yearning of all his friends, philosophers, artists, and poets, born Catholics or neophytes like Novalis himself: Schlegel, Schelling, Görres, Baader, Adam Müller, Clemens Brentano. . . . Almost alone, Fichte and Hegel remained Protestant and progressive.

However, the *myth* of the Middle Ages—the theme of *Hymns to the Night* interpreted historically—which had always fascinated Novalis, is not merely a utopian vision of the past, flung in the face of the present, as in the case of Görres and Joseph de Maistre. It is also the anticipation of a religious rebirth and reconciliation, of a great "European Council" assembling Christians

---

[42] *Wilhelm Meisters Wanderjahre*, I, 7.

and libertarians, Protestants and mystics in a new Jerusalem to celebrate the *Liebesmahl,* the agape, the Feast of peace. The excerpts below recapitulate the arguments and lyrical themes evoked by this great poet.

Once there were fine, resplendent times when Europe was a Christian land, when one Christendom occupied this humanly constituted continent. One great common interest united the remotest provinces, of this broad spiritual realm. Without great worldly possessions, one Head guided and unified the great political forces. . . .

With good cause the wise Head of the Church countered insolent excrescences of human talents at the expense of the sacred sense, as well as untimely, dangerous discoveries in the area of knowledge. . . . At his court assembled all the clever and reverend men in Europe. All treasures flowed thither, Jerusalem destroyed had avenged itself, and Rome itself was Jerusalem, the holy residence of divine government on earth. Princes laid their disputes before the father of Christendom, willingly laid their crowns and their splendor at his feet. Indeed, they deemed it a glory to conclude the evening of their lives as members of that high guild in godly contemplation within solitary cloister walls. . . .

Such were the fine essential characteristics of the truly Catholic or truly Christian times. For this splendid kingdom mankind was not ripe, not developed enough. It was a first love, which died away amid the press of business life, whose memory was crowded out by selfish cares, and whose bond—afterwards cried down as imposture and illusion and judged in the light of subsequent experiences—was sundered forever by a large proportion of Europeans. This great inner cleavage, which was attended by destructive wars, was a noteworthy sign of the harmfulness of culture to the sense for the Invisible, or at least of the temporary harmfulness of the culture of certain stage. . . .

The insurgents rightly termed themselves Protestants, for they protested solemnly against the usurpation of the conscience by an inconvenient and seemingly illegal force. For the time being they reappropriated, as though it were free, their silently surrendered right to the examination, determination, and choice of religion. They also set up a number of right principles, introduced a number of praiseworthy things, and abolished a number of pernicious laws. But they forgot the inevitable result of their procedure, they separated the inseparable, divided the indivisible Church, and sacrilegiously wrenched themselves loose from the universal Christian community, through which and in which alone was possible the true, then enduring rebirth. . . .

With the Reformation Christendom came to an end. From then on there was no such thing any more. Catholics and Protestants or Reformed stood further apart from one another in sectarian division than from Mohammedans and heathens. The remaining Catholic states went on vegetating, not without imperceptibly feeling the harmful influence of the neighboring Protestant states. Modern politics first developed at this point in time, and individual powerful states sought to take over the vacant universal Chair, which had been transformed into a Throne. . . .

The Reformation was a sign of its time. It was significant for all Europe, even if it had openly broken forth only in truly free Germany. The good minds of all nations had secretly come of age and in the illusory feeling of their vocation revolted the more sharply against obsolete constraint. The erudite is by instinct the enemy of the clergy according to the old order. The erudite and the clerical classes, once they are separated, must war to the death, for they strive for one and the same position, This separation advanced ever further, and the erudite gained the more ground the more the history of European humanity approached the age of triumphant erudition, whereas knowledge and faith entered into more decisive opposition. It was to faith that people looked to find the cause of the general impasse, and this they hoped to obviate by keen knowledge. Everywhere the sense for the holy suffered from the manifold persecutions of its previous form, its former personality. The end product of the modern manner of thinking was termed "philosophy," and under that head was reckoned everything that was opposed to the old, hence primarily every objection against religion. The initial personal hatred of the Catholic faith passed gradually over into hatred of the Bible, of the Christian faith, and finally of religion in general. Still further, the hatred of religion extended itself quite naturally and consistently to all objects of enthusiasm. It made imagination and emotion heretical, as well as morality and the love of art, the future and the past. With some difficulty it placed man first in the order of created things, and reduced the infinite creative music of the universe to the monotonous clatter of a monstrous mill, which, driven by the stream of chance and floating thereon, was supposed to be a mill in the abstract, without Builder or Miller, in fact an actual *perpetuum mobile*, a mill that milled of itself.

One enthusiasm was generously left to poor mankind and, as a touchstone of supreme culture, was made indispensable to every shareholder in it—enthusiasm for this grand and splendid "philosophy" and more particularly for its priests and initiates. France was fortunate enough to become the womb and the seat of this new faith, which was pasted together out of pure knowledge. Yet, decried as poetry was in this new church, there were nevertheless some poets in its midst who, for the sake of effect, still made use of the old adornments and of the old light, though in so doing they ran the risk of setting the new world system on fire with the old flame. Shrewder members, however, knew how to pour cold water at once upon such listeners as waxed warm. The members were tirelessly busy cleaning the poetry off Nature, the earth, the human soul, and the branches of learning—obliterating every trace of the holy, discrediting by sarcasm the memory of all ennobling events and persons, and stripping the world of all colorful ornament. The Light, by virtue of its mathematical submissiveness and its insolence, had become their favorite. They rejoiced that it yielded to refraction sooner than to play with colors, and thus they took from it the name of their great undertaking: Enlightenment. . . .

Where no gods are, ghosts prevail, and the actual development time of European ghosts—and this fairly completely accounts for their forms—was the period of transition from Greek doctrines of gods into Christianity. Come, therefore, you Lovers of Mankind and encyclopedists, into the pacific lodge and receive the fraternal kiss, cast off the gray net, and with youthful love behold the wondrous splendor of Nature, of History, and of Mankind. I shall lead you to a brother, and he shall speak with you so that your hearts shall leap up, and so that you shall clothe your dead, beloved intuition with a new body, and so that you shall embrace again and recognize what hovered before you and what the sluggish earthly intelligence could not grasp for you.

This brother is the heartbeat of the new era. Whoever has felt him no longer doubts of the era's coming, and with sweet pride in his contemporaneity steps forth even from among the multitude to the new band of disciples. . . .

Now let us turn to the political spectacle of our time. The old world and the new world are engaged in battle. The defectiveness and shortcomings of the organization of states up to now have become apparent in dreadful phenomena. What if here, too, as in the branches of knowledge, closer and more multiple connections and contacts of European states were the primary historical goal of war? What if a new stirring of hitherto slumbering Europe were to come into play? What if Europe were to reawaken and a state of states, a political theory of knowledge, were to confront us! Might perhaps hierarchy, that symmetrical basic figure of states, be the principle of unification of states, as the intellectual concept of the political ego? It is impossible for secular forces to put themselves into equilibrium; only a third element, which is at once secular and superwordly, can solve that problem. Between the conflicting powers themselves no peace can be established. All peace is mere illusion, mere truce. From the standpoint of cabinets or the common consciousness, no unification is conceivable. Both parties have great and urgent claims and must make them, driven as they are by the spirit of the world and of mankind. Both are indestructible powers in the heart of man: on the one side reverence for antiquity, dependence upon historical system, love for the monuments of ancestors and of the ancient and glorious family of the state, and joy in obedience; on the other side delightsome sensation of freedom, unlimited expectation of tremendous provinces of activity, pleasure in things new and young, effortless contact with all members of the state, pride in the universal validity of man, joy in one's personal rights and in the property of the whole, and the powerful feeling of citizenship. Let neither of these two hope to destroy the other. All conquests are meaningless here, for the inner capital of every kingdom lies not behind earthwalls and is not to be taken by siege.

Who knows whether there has been enough of war? But it will never come to an end unless someone grasps the palm branch, which a spiritual power alone can proffer. Blood will wash over Europe until the nations perceive the fearful madness which is driving them about in a circle; until, arrested by holy music and soothed, they approach former altars in multi-hued fusion and undertake works of peace; until a great feast of love is celebrated as a festival of peace amid hot tears upon smoking battlefields. Only religion can awaken Europe again, and reassure the peoples, and install Christendom with new splendor visibly on earth in its old peace-establishing office. . . .

The other continents await Europe's reconciliation and resurrection in order to join with it and become fellow-citizens of the heavenly kingdom. Should there not be presently once again in Europe a host of truly holy spirits? Should not all those truly related in religion become full of yearning to behold heaven on earth? And should they not gladly join together and begin songs of holy choirs?

Christendom must come alive again and be effective, and, without regard to national boundaries, again form a visible church which will take into its bosom all souls athirst for the supernatural, and willingly become the mediatrix between the old world and the new.

It must once again pour out the cornucopia of blessing over peoples. From the holy womb of a venerable European Council shall Christendom arise, and the task of awakening will be prosecuted according to a comprehensive divine plan. Then no one will protest any longer against Christian and secular compulsion, for the essence of the Church will be true freedom, and all necessary reforms will be carried out under its guidance as a peaceful and formal state process.

When and when sooner? The question is not to be asked. Patience only! It will, it must come, that sacred time of endless peace when the new Jerusalem will be the capital of the world. Until then be cheerful and courageous amid the dangers of the time. Partakers of my faith, proclaim with words and deeds the divine Gospel, and to the veritable and everlasting Faith remain true unto death.[43]

Josef Görres (1776–1848) wrote more about Europe than any other political thinker of the period of Restoration and Romanticism. His style is obscure, his judgments are contradictory, immoderate, and arbitrary. It is not easy to quote him; he nevertheless must be mentioned in this work, were it only to take note of his main themes.

Like so many other Germans, he was at first enthusiastic about the Revolution. In 1795, in a work entitled *Der allgemeine Friede, ein Ideal*, he wrote: "As Sparta did one day in Greece, O France, you too will rise to liberate Europe from her despots!"

He proposes an international organization headed by republican France. But like so many others, immediately after Brumaire, 1799, he made a complete about-face—Bonaparte betrayed the Revolution. The Restoration found him a supporter of the Holy Alliance. In 1815 he published in his journal, *Der Rheinische Merkur*, a long unsigned article titled "The European Republic," in which Europe is described as a German creation. In 1819 he hailed the Holy Alliance as "the foundation of a European Republic worshiping the unknown God." At the same time, he proclaimed

[43] Novalis, *Hymns to the Night and Other Selected Writings*, translated, with an Introduction, by Charles E. Passage (New York: The Liberal Arts Press, 1960), pp. 45, 46, 47, 49, 51, 53–54, 59, 60–61, 61–63.

German greatness: if this nation is fortunate enough to find one day its Wallenstein, he says, he "will conquer all Europe, to the very borders of Asia!"

In 1821, in *Europa und die Revolution*, he attacks the Reformation, which he calls "the second original sin," and likens it to the other disasters that "ruined old fortress Europe": the Byzantine schism, Islam, the dismemberment of the Holy Empire, the rise of national Churches, the Revolution, and finally, "Satan's Empire," i.e., Napoleon's. As we can see, Joseph de Maistre's favorite themes (*Du Pape* had been published two years earlier) are taken up now in a German version.

Finally, in 1822, in a essay on "The Holy Alliance and the Nations at the Congress of Verona," he calls on Germany to become once again

the honorary Higher Authority of the European republic, the Court of conciliation for settling differences, because her position, her situation, her way of thinking, everything impels her toward peace and away from conquest; she is the great Authority which traces, defends, and stabilizes frontiers, she it is who separates the East from the West, the North from the South. She is the pivotal point around which the whole system of the European states revolves, the natural center of the new Germanic Holy Roman Empire, greater than the old one, founded with no constraint by the Holy Alliance in the form of a federation of states.

And who are to be the enemies of this restored German-Catholic Empire? Not Russia, "a colony of Europe," which will freely open herself to our culture, but Asia and America. . . .

Franz von Baader (1765–1841), Bavarian philosopher, theosophist and mystic, was for a long time a disciple of Claude de Saint-Martin. He, too, saw the only salvation for "European society" in a religious rebirth. But far from demanding the stamping out of Protestantism as a *preliminary condition*, and the return to the fold of orthodoxy, like Görres and De Maistre, he shared Novalis' ecumenical hope.

In an essay he addressed in 1814 to the emperors of Russia and Austria and to the king of Prussia he proposed a European

Christian federation, based upon "new and closer bonds between religion and politics," and upon the union of the three great denominations represented by these monarchs. The central idea seems to have been to draw Russia back into the European concert as a repentant heretic or a semibarbarian to be educated. Even a certain Russian Messianism begins to manifest itself, at that early date, in Baader and in several of his contemporaries: the first Slavophiles were not Russians, but Germans!

Frederich von Schlegel (1772–1829) edited the first European magazine, *Europa,* from 1803 to 1805. (He edited it from Paris, but it was printed in Frankfort.) In it he developed ideas which foreshadow his monumental *Philosophy of History.* Asia, more particularly India, is the homeland of every true religion, but Christianity made Europe what she is and can alone preserve her unity, in spite of the fundamental oppositions that divide, rend, and fertilize her: the oppositions between the North and South, between Romanticism and Classicism, between the moderns and the ancients, between Christianity and Hellenism. Charlemagne's Empire, then the Papacy (Schlegel was to become a Catholic in 1808), represented the highest institutions of the "European republic," and after that all was decadence. At the beginning of the nineteenth century we have not yet hit bottom. However, we would be wrong if we despaired of Europe, for she still is the crucial part of the world, considering

that it is here, by virtue of the very organization of the telluric energies, that the true seat of the conflict is situated; here the good fight is being fought out on earth with the greatest vehemence, and here the fate of Humanity will be sealed. . . . First of all the true Europe must see the light of day.[44]

Such professions of faith in Europe's future (to be compared with Hegel's conception of Europe as the "end of History") [45] recur many times in *Europa* and in *Lectures on Modern History.* They sharply distinguish Schlegel and the German Romantics, even those who are Romanized, from Joseph de Maistre and the

[44] *Europa* (Frankfort on the Main, 1803–1805), pp. 38–39.
[45] Cf. p. 244.

pre-Romantic French Catholics. This is to be remembered when we read Schlegel's famous pages on Europe's unity in the Middle Ages, which frankly echo the fervor and the illusions of Novalis:

The general idea of the Christian Empire was a universal protectorate over all Christian nations and countries—a mighty central dominion founded on justice, while the great connecting and pervading power of the whole system was supposed to reside in the perfect unity of religious principles. When this religious unity was destroyed, the whole political edifice fell to pieces; and, in the struggles of later times, the artificial relations founded on a mere mechanical balance of power, on a republican equality of states, without the foundation of Christian or any other principles, have furnished, as experience has shown, but a very bad substitute for that old Christian brotherhood of the European states and nations; and have, in the general subversion of Christian morality, produced a sort of polite disorder and refined anarchy.

In the partition of the Carlovingian Empire—a partition which was only in accordance with those principles of descent which regulated the inheritance of the great families—we can trace an almost heroic, and, if we might use the expression, a naive patriarchal confidence in the duration of that religious unity; for it was only on such a basis that men deemed it possible to combine the advantage of the domestic, internal government of a country, limited in extent, with the control of one general superintending monarch. . . .

In the primitive monarchy of the Germans . . . the existence of the four great national duchies, which were subordinate to the imperial crown, far more happily accomplished this union of a local, domestic, and paternal government with the control of one powerful and superintending monarchy; so long at least as internal union subsisted, and discord had not obtained the supremacy. There then existed, though most in a different form than afterwards, a division of powers in the state as well as in the church; but unity in this division, or with this division, was sought for only in Christian and National sentiments; and as long as these subsisted in their integrity, the body politic remained unimpaired. At no time has a political constitution or mode of government been devised, which could permanently supply the place of principle.

In the national meetings of the great and smaller states of that age, in their assembled councils of dukes and princes, bishops, counts and lords, nobles and freemen (to whom were added the commons of the cities, when by their rights and privileges they began to obtain importance), we must look for the first germ of all the succeeding parliaments and states-general of the European nations, and of the rights of the different orders of society, and the privileges and corporate immunities of the cities. All these rights and liberties were purely local—they grew up on the roots of national customs—they were founded on no speculative theory of universal equality, but on positive usage, and special laws. The union and stability of an empire was then sought for not in the balance of artificial forms, but in the holy heritage of ancient customs, in principle in short. . . .

Ecclesiastical power had then a real and substantial weight, and a very extended circle of operation; although its limits and relations with secular authority were not so rigidly circumscribed as afterwards. To be sensible that this division of power will not necessarily impair the unity of strength and spirit in the social frame, as long as principle remains pure, and religious concord is preserved, we need only call to our recollection the fact that all Christian states and kingdoms have sprung from this happy agreement between secular and ecclesiastical authority, and that this union was the sure foundation of their stability. And so long as both powers remained in harmonious accord, the times were prosperous, peace and justice ever increased, and the condition of nations was flourishing and happy. . . .

The Church was like the all-embracing vault of heaven, beneath whose kindly shelter those warlike nations began to settle in peace, and gradually to frame their laws and institutions. Even the office of instruction, the heritage of ancient knowledge, the promotion of science, and of all that tended to advance the progress of the human mind, devolved to the care of the church, and were exclusively confined to the Christian schools. If science was then of a very limited range, it was still quite proportioned to the exigencies and intellectual cultivation of the age; for mankind cannot transcend all the degrees of civilization by a single bound, but must mount slowly and in succession its various grades; and at any rate, science was not at that time unprofitably buried in libraries and in the closets of the learned, as was afterward the case in Europe, and even partly then among the Byzantines. The little knowledge which was then possessed, was by the more active spirit and the sound understanding and practical sense of the European nations, and their better priesthood, applied with general advantage to the interests of society. Society was not then, as in the later period of its proud ascendancy, in open hostility with the pure dictates of faith and the institutions of life. On that world so variously excited in peace, as in war, and by the different pursuits of art and industry, useful knowledge and wholesome speculation descended, not like a violent flood, but like the soft distillations of the refreshing dew, or the gentle drops of fertilizing rain, from the heaven of faith which overarched the whole.[46]

In his *Vorlesungen über die neuere Geschichte* (Lecture I) Schlegel evokes once more the classical contrast (already evoked by Aristotle) between Asia and Europe, especially in respect to their conceptions of freedom. After stressing the Unity of Europe, he speaks in glowing terms of her diversity:

Had this migration [of nations] not taken place; had the Germanic nations not succeeded in throwing off the Roman yoke; had, on the contrary, the rest of northern Europe been incorporated with Rome; had the freedom and individuality of the nations been here too destroyed, and had they been all transformed with like uniformity into provinces, then would that noble rivalry, that rich development of the human mind, which distinguishes modern nations, have never taken place. And yet it is precisely this rich variety, this manifoldness, that makes Europe what it is, that confers on it the distinction of being the chief seat of all human civilization. Instead of a Europe, thus free and richly diversified, there would then have been but one Rome, wherein all things would have been melted down and dissolved; and where, instead of the rich variety of European history, the annals of the single Roman empire would have presented us with a counterpart to the dull monotony of the Chinese year-books. . . .

Let us first cast a glance at the primitive state of the whole of Europe. It is a remarkable and attractive spectacle to contemplate men who were so richly endowed by nature, and gifted with such noble faculties, in a state so totally different from that to which we are accustomed. Before the passion for universal dominion had been transmitted from Asia to the Greeks, and had next taken possession of the Romans, the state of Europe was nearly everywhere the same. The rudiments of civilization were already known; agriculture was general; and some countries were proportionately thickly peopled. Towns were numerous, but there were likewise almost as many individual petty states as considerable towns. Everything was, for the most part, isolated

[46] Schlegel, *Philosophy of History* (New York: Appleton & Co., 1841), Vol. II, Lecture XII.

and unconnected. Europe was inhabited and peopled chiefly by three or four great nations; but none of these were united among themselves so as to form a whole. Each of them was split into numberless petty tribes and races, constituting as many distinct states. Each of these tribes had but a slender knowledge of the remoter ones, and often carried on war with the adjoining.

. . . Necessitous as the condition of these ancient nations may appear to us, they yet almost universally possessed one great good, which we have for the most part been obliged to sacrifice for other advantages—freedom, to wit. It was fostered and maintained by their isolation and universal subdivision into petty states and tribes. This original freedom must be considered the decided characteristic of Europe as contrasted with Asia. In Asia we find from the very beginning great masses of states, and nations, and universal sovereignty; in Europe everything was originally isolated; there was, for that very reason, a constant mutual rivalry, and each state developed itself in individual freedom. Asia may be called the land of unity, in which everything has been unfolded in great masses, and in the simplest relations; Europe is the land of freedom, that is, of civilization through the antagonism of manifold individual and isolated energies. This variety has been at all times the characteristic of European civilization; for even after great states and nations had sprung up within it, the essential qualities of that original character remained.[47]

In his discussion of Charles V (Lecture XIV), he deplores the end of the living synthesis between unity and diversity, which the Emperor dreamed of reviving:

Thus withdrew from the world a man . . . who, as emperor . . . had always aimed at the noblest objects with indefatigable effort; a man who in his mighty soul embraced all the relations of his age and of Europe; and, with the clearest intellect, saw through the complicated problems she had to solve, and discerned the formidable dangers that menaced her.

At his death all Christian nations rivalled each other in funeral festivals, of unexampled pomp, in honour of his name and greatness. Even in the capital of the Turkish empire, a noble-minded foe honoured by a funeral festival the memory of the great monarch who had left the world. Europe appeared to feel that the hero and champion of the age was no more; an age which, now that this last pillar of strength and union had also dis-

[47] Schlegel, A Course of Lectures on Modern History, trans. Lyndsay Purcell and R. H. Whitelock (London: H. G. Bohn, 1849).

appeared, was the more surely hurrying on to a century of war and anarchy.[48]

According to Georg Friedrich Hegel (1770–1831), world history reflects and embodies the dialectics of "the Idea that realizes itself," of the Idea of freedom, that is, "the actual coming-into-being of the Spirit." Hence it is in fact a theodicy. In Hegel's System, History is divided into three periods which correspond, in theological terms, to the Father, the Son, and the Holy Ghost; and in philosophical terms to what he calls the "In Itself," the "For Itself," and the "In and For Itself" (*an und für sich*). In his *Lectures on the Philosophy of History* (published posthumously) Hegel describes the evolution of Asia, classical times, and modern Europe, as though it actually were an evolution of the Spirit. The ultimate term of this grandiose process is none other than Europe, "truly the end of History," eminently represented by her Germanic component, and as will be specified by the right-wing Hegelians, by the Prussian state.

Two famous quotations (taken from the Introduction) will be sufficient to characterize Hegel's conception of Europe's role in world history:

I have said that the Oriental world knew only that *one* was free; that the Graeco-Roman world knew that *some* were free, but that we know that *all* are free, that *man* as *man* is free. These stages in the knowledge of freedom constitute the divisions that we shall make in world history and in accordance with which we shall study it . . .

World history moves from east to west, for Europe is truly the end of history, as Asia was the beginning. For world history there is an East in itself, *kat exochen*, the East for itself being entirely relative; for although the earth is a sphere, history does not describe a circle around it; rather, it has a specific East, which is Asia. There rises the physical, external sun, which sets in the west: this is why, here rises the inner sun of self-awareness, which shines with a loftier brilliance.

Wilhelm Josef von Schelling (1775–1854) was the longest-lived of the generation of great Romantic philosophers. The end of his career closes the cycle inaugurated by Herder, Kant, and

[48] *Ibid.*

Novalis, and this is why we quote him here, although his System bears the same date as Fichte's "self-contained state," and Gentz's essay on Europe.

A friend of Novalis in his youth and later converted, like him, to Catholicism, he was one of the most influential nineteenth-century European thinkers. He influenced not only his friends from the *Athenaeum* (mentioned above), but also Schopenhauer, Kierkegaard (who attended his lectures in Berlin), and later Bergson, and most of the Russian thinkers of his time, especially the Slavophiles.

At an early date, in the Introduction to his *System des Transzendentalen Idealismus* [49] published in 1800, Schelling defends the idea of an international federation and a Court of Justice. He views these as the inevitable culmination of the era of "Nature," coming after the era of "Fate," and heralding the era of "Providence."

History as a whole is a continuous and progressive revelation of the absolute.

We may distinguish three periods in this process, and consequently, three periods in history.

The first period is the one in which Fate is dominant; an absolutely blind power, it ruthlessly and unconsciously destroys what is greatest and noblest. This period of history, which we may call "tragic," is that of the decline of the splendor and marvels of the ancient world, and of the fall of the great empires of which only the memory has been preserved, and from the ruins of which alone we can infer their greatness: the decline of the noblest humanity that has ever flourished, and whose return on earth is no more than a perennial dream.

During the second period Fate, which during the first period appeared as a complete blind power, reveals itself as nature. . . . It seems to have begun with the expansion of the Roman republic, which, in its avidity for conquest and subjugation—expressions of the unbridled despotism that prevailed—at first united the peoples with one another, and brought about the contacts among customs and laws, arts and sciences, which until then had been the monopoly of a few isolated peoples; this republic was constrained, without being conscious of it and even against its will, to follow a natural plan whose completion will

[49] *Sämtliche Werke*, I, 3, pp. 586 f.

be marked by the universal union of peoples and the universal State.

In the third period the forces that in the preceding periods were attributed to fate or to nature will develop and disclose themselves as the work of Providence; thus even that which seemed to be brought about by fate or nature had only been the beginning of an as yet imperfectly revealed Providence. We cannot say when this period will begin. But when this period shall be, God shall be.

It is therefore impossible to envisage the lasting existence of a single political constitution—even if its form were perfect—without an organization superimposed on the individual State, without a federation of all States, in which each will guarantee the other's constitution. However, this general and mutual guarantee is itself possible only if, first, the states accept the principles of a true legal order, so that each State will have an interest in safeguarding the constitution of the others; and second, if they submit to a collective law.

In 1806 he wrote, referring to Napoleon:

I am praying for the complete reconciliation of all the European peoples and I want to believe that they will once again adopt a common policy toward the East. Whether he is conscious of it or not, it is toward this end that the Destroyer is working.

Later on, Schelling too came around to the view that Europe's only salvation lies in free co-operation between Church and State, sole basis of lasting union:

The study of modern history which essentially begins with the appearance of Christianity in Europe discloses two attempts by mankind to attain unity.

The first, aimed at creating spiritual unity in the bosom of the Church, was doomed to failure, for it tended at the same time to secure the external unity of the Church. The second sought to bring about this external unity through the State.

The error, which the Church committed in the epoch of ecclesiastical hierarchy, did not consist in encroaching on the domain of the State, but on the contrary, in allowing the latter to meddle in her own domain. Instead of keeping herself pure from all external elements, she surrendered to the State by espousing some of its forms. External violence can never serve the cause of the true and holy, and the Church departed from her true vocation the moment she began to persecute heretics.

The State became important with the overthrow of the ecclesiastical hierarchy, and it is evident that the yoke of tyranny always grew heavier to the very extent that it believed itself able to do without spiritual unity.

At all events, it is certain that whatever the ultimate goal may be, true unity can be realized only through religion. What is meant here is not the domination of the Church by the State or vice versa, but the necessity for the State itself to develop religious principles such that union of all peoples can be founded on common religious beliefs.[50]

Auguste Comte (1798–1857) was one of the few Frenchmen of his day to compose a grandiose historico-philosophical system like those we have been reviewing. But his system does not remotely resemble any of them. The favorite disciple of Saint-Simon, he replaced Augustin Thierry as his "adoptive son" and founded a sect of his own, the Positivist Religion. He is remembered chiefly, however, as the founder of modern sociology.

Like all Saint-Simonians (D'Eichtahl, Pierre Leroux, Feugueray, Considérant, Pecqueur, Littré, and many others, all of them authors of treatises on European unity), Auguste Comte was a convinced, almost mystical, champion of *européocentrisme*, of the privileged and formidable role Europe was to play in the world. Europe in the end was to become identical with humanity; she alone could unite it, after being unified herself. The title of one of his publications will give an idea of the kind of rational frenzy (but romantic too, though it called itself "positive") which generally characterizes the thinking of the Saint-Simonians about Europe: "Positivist calendar, or general system of public commemoration, destined primarily for the final transition to the Great Western Republic, composed of five advanced populations, French, Italian, Germanic, British, and Spanish, which have always been interdependent since Charlemagne" (Paris, 1850).

However, in his major work, *Cours de Philosophie Positive* (1830–1842), Comte sets out to give his Europeanism a solid

---

[50] *Aus dem Nachlass* (*Stuttgarter Privatvorlesungen*), 1810.

critical base, by concentrating his "scientific analysis" on a single "social series," the most accomplished that can be found: Europe. Therefore he proposes to

study exclusively the actual development of the most advanced populations, leaving out, scrupulously and persistently, all vain and irrational digressions on the various other centers of any independent civilization which has for any cause whatever been arrested at some more imperfect state; unless comparative investigation of these secondary series can cast a useful light on the main subject, as I have defined it in my discussion of sociological method. Our historical exploration will thus be almost exclusively confined to the elite or avant-garde of mankind, comprising the greater part of the white race, the European nations, and even restricting ourselves for the sake of greater precision, especially in the modern era, to the nations of western Europe. . . .

We certainly cannot expect to discover the true fundamental progress of human societies unless we concentrate first of all on the most complete and most clearly characterized evolution; all collateral observations concerning imperfect and less pronounced progressions must play a subordinate part. However, interesting the latter may be in themselves, their special evaluation must be systematically postponed until the main laws of social movement having been established in the case most favorable for their full expression, it will become possible, and even useful, to proceed to a rational accounting for the more or less important modifications they were subjected to in populations which, for one reason or another, have lagged behind such a type of development. Until that time, the puerile, inopportune display of sterile, ill-digested erudition, which tends today to obstruct the study of our social evolution by wrongly introducing historical considerations on the history of peoples who, like those of India, China, and others could exert no real influence on our past, must be emphatically pointed out as a source of inextricable confusion. If, in investigating the real laws of human society, we were to be obliged to consider simultaneously its basic progression and all its various modifications, the problem, in my opinion, would become essentially insoluble. In this respect, the genius of the great Bossuet, though doubtless guided solely by the purely literary principle of unity of composition, seems to me to have instinctively sensed in advance the logical conditions imposed by the nature of the subject, when he spontaneously confined his historical evaluation to the study of one homogeneous and continuous series, justly qualified as universal. Such limitation is eminently judicious, although so many anti-philosophical minds criticized him for it; today we are essentially led back to his approach by the careful analysis of the intellectual method proper to such study.[51]

That is why Auguste Comte confined his study to a "special explanation of the agent of the most complete social evolution," i.e. to Europe and the theater of its operation. In subsequent volumes he explained why "the white race possessed, to so pronounced a degree, the de facto privilege of being at the head of the main social development." Europe, meanwhile, "has been the essential, binding force in this preponderant civilization."

[51] *Cours de Philosophie Positive* (Paris, 1894), Vol. V.

PART FIVE

THE ERA OF NATIONALISM

From Mazzini to Georges Sorel

(1848-1914)

1: The System of the Sovereign States: Harmony in Theory, Anarchy in Practice

AROUND 1826, Théodore Jouffroy (1798–1842), a French liberal, spiritualist philosopher, in a work titled *The Present State of Mankind*, made the following statements which might well have been written today. In fact they were true as diagnosis at the time, though what was prophetic in them was largely ignored for a hundred years.

What matters today is not the balance of power in Europe, but the future of mankind. The civil wars in Europe are over, the rivalry of the European peoples becoming a thing of the past, just as the rivalry of the Greek city-states had become a thing of the past under Alexander . . . similarly, Europe has begun to become a single nation only since America, Asia, and Africa appeared on the scene. Man must now concern himself with the unity of Europe in the face of these masses, and with keeping balance among them.[1]

Like the Romantics, especially Hegel, Jouffroy thought that every nation, like every individual, has its own genius, and hence, its own historical vocation. To him Europe was the avant-garde of mankind, as a civilization; and France, the avant-garde of Europe, as a nation. As for individual interests within each nation, and national interests within each civilization, they would inevitably converge in the bosom of an admirable harmony of minds and creative energies.

For "France" read "Prussia," and you have Hegel.

It was a glorious ideal to expect that the one and the many would achieve worldwide harmony. However, at the very moment the great nations reached their highest degree of development, and peace should have followed, the First World War broke out, brutally to negate the ideal.

[1] Théodore Jouffroy, *De l'Etat actuel de l'humanité, mélanges philosophiques* (Brussels, 1834).

[253]

Romanticism, which had given the principle of nationality both lyrical and doctrinal justification, actually unleashed passions which men's minds were unable to control. "Nationality" had been celebrated as a necessary stage in a dialectical unfolding of the spirit. In fact the states exploited this principle and soon "nationalized" it, in the present-day sense of the term.

The poets of the generation of 1848, enthusiastic and deluded, were the first victims of this tragic misunderstanding. To them, "nation" = "freedom." They had all been inspired by the Messianism of the French Revolution: to liberate one's own nation from the yoke of domestic or foreign tyranny was to liberate Europe and mankind. . . . In actual fact, the freedom of the Nation, once it had been won, turned out to mean no more than the sovereignty of the State; and the States were not slow to recognize this. The anarchy of the divinized sovereignties, rejecting any authority superior to their "sacred egoism," led inevitably to war at the very moment when according to the great idealist Dialectics the reign of peace was to begin on earth.

Inaugurated by the trauma of the Revolution, imposed on all Europe by Napoleon's armies, the era of Nationalism succeeded the era of the cosmopolitan Elites. The Germans, especially, with their heritage of the *Reichsgedanke*, were readiest for great syntheses, and produced some inspired theoreticians. Later, the militant poets of 1848 translated the nationalist ideal into the popular lyrical language of freedom and patriotism. The stirring and improbable utopia of a "Holy Alliance of the Peoples" was proclaimed in the face of the short-lived "positive" policies of the Holy Alliance of the Kings. Then the last Saint-Simonians, the Fourierists, the Italian agitator Mazzini, the great poet Victor Hugo, and Proudhon, a champion of socialism, attempted to fill the vacuum left by the myth of the Holy Empire by proclaiming the myth of the "United States of Europe," a democratized substitute for an authority above the Nations. Unfortunately, history was moving in another direction. The building of the Suez Canal—a project worthy of Saint-Simon's organizational genius—was first opposed by the States, but once under way became an object of shameless political maneuvering. The great libertarian impulse of the men of 1848 survived only in elementary-school textbooks, to degenerate there into nationalism, i.e. the secular worship of the State. The Young Europe movement, which sought to harness the national feeling in the service of the federal idea, saw the exact opposite take place. Never had ideas been more completely negated by the facts, never more thoroughly used to other ends. Europe, which with the industrial revolution was creating the means for unifying the world, and which in the meanwhile with its arms was completing its subjugation, had never been less humanitarian and less united. Everything the states did remained within the framework of national sovereignty, and each state was shortsightedly intent solely on satisfying its immediate interests, to the detriment of the world balance whose conditions had been formulated by Jouffroy. This is why, at the end of the nineteenth century, great minds like Ranke, Renan, Nietzsche, and Sorel recorded this dissolution of the European ideal in a series of uniformly pessimistic prophecies concerning the future of civilization.

The texts quoted below may serve as landmarks in the evolution of ideas from Heine to Georges Sorel, and the parallel, radically divergent evolution of the events which led Europe to the war of 1914.

First let us quote one particularly typical expression of the revolution that went on in Europe between 1789 and 1898, which Herder had anticipated. The new humanism, such as inspired the founders of compulsory public education, had an anti-cosmopolitan, nationalistic cast.

Nicolas Grundtvig (1783–1872), was both a pioneer of public education in northern Europe, and the initiator of a religious movement (derived from Lutheranism) which long marked the life of his country. Poet, theologian, educator, and political leader, he admirably sums up—as is possible only in a small country—the thought and feeling of the period:

So-called "cultured" people fall victim to a serious error concerning human life and the conditions of its enlightened evolution, when they embrace the idea that, because we are all men, it is of little importance to what nation we belong and what language we speak; that no nation surpasses another or is distinguished by some particular feature which it is destined to develop; that all differences among men are purely fortuitous, stemming from habit and circumstance, so that we might just as well look upon them all as interchangeable and conclude that pure humanity manifests itself the more fully the more every particularity is disregarded.

Nothing falser can be imagined, for on this planet, where no leaf is like another, and where no two horses respond to the reins in the same way, it is demented to claim that all men can be treated alike, whereas on the contrary diversity is one of the greatest goods in human nature.

Nonetheless, the last century thought that the excellence of culture consisted in denying all differences between Englishmen, Frenchmen, Germans, and Scandinavians. As a result, the notion of what distinguishes a wise man from a fool, intelligence from feeling, and even man from woman has been lost sight of.

True culture, however, must hold to this truth: just as life developed starting from two elements, the male and the female, so mankind divided into very different peoples, each of them speaking its own language and displaying many features peculiar to itself. The more courageously a people defends its particularities, the more fully can life as a whole unfold in all directions, and the more fruitful will be the influence each people can exert upon the others.[2]

Henrich Heine (1799–1856) was the principal representative of the Young Germany literary group, which must not be confused with the German branch of Mazzini's Young Europe movement (of which more below). There is no systematic reflection on the subject of Europe in Heine, but only a series of alternating "insights"—lyrical diastole, sardonic systole. Omnipresent in his works, the idea of Europe crops up in contradictory observations, judgments, and prophecies; a few very dissimilar quotations will give the reader some idea.

At first Heine espoused the Herderian ideology of a Europe of "nationalities." He regarded it, a little like Fichte, as an indispensable stage in history:

All the peoples of Europe and the world will have to go through this agony, so that life may arise from death, and pagan nationality may be succeeded by Christian brotherhood.[3]

[2] To Gustav Kolb, Florence, November 11, 1828.
[3] *De la Pologne*, in *Œuvres complètes, Patries et Portraits* (Paris, 1868).

His conception of the union of peoples is clearly federalistic; as Goethe put it, "harmony but no unison":

Herder looked upon humanity as a great harp in the hands of a great master; each people seemed to him one string of the giant instrument, each with its own tone, and when all the different strings were sounded he heard a harmony.[4]

Such lyrical outbursts, however, never for long prevented him from lucidly seeing Europe as it was, threatened simultaneously (one might say) by its excess of self-awareness and its lack of vigilance. He likened Europe by turns to an old man and to a foolish virgin:

The spirituality at present dominant in European literature is perhaps a sign of an imminent death; just as some men are vouchsafed glimpses into the Beyond on their deathbeds. Or should we persuade ourselves that old Europe is becoming younger, and that the twilight spirituality displayed by her artists and writers is not so much the marvelous clairvoyance of the dying, but the disturbing presentiment of a rebirth, the spiritual breath of a new spring?[5]

Whatever the Virgin Europe may do—whether she stays prudently awake by her lamp or, like a very thoughtless young lady, has let her lamp go out—no joyful day lies in store for her.[6]

In his poem *Germania*, Heine has another surge of hope:

The virgin Europe is betrothed to the noble genius Freedom: they are lovingly holding out their arms to each other for their first kiss. . . .

But the poem opened with the wild assertion: "Yes, the whole world will be German!" This swinging backward and forward between Germanic nationalism and universal liberalism was already to be found in Herder and most of the German Romantics. In every case, it centers on the passion for a freedom conceived by turns as the freedom of a given people, as "nationality" shaking off the yoke of all despotisms, whether political or spiri-

[4] *Romantische Schule* (1833), Vol. II.
[5] *Salon*, 4, 73, quoted in H. Gollwitzer, *op cit.*, p. 308.
[6] *Ibid.*, H. Gollwitzer, *op. cit.*, p. 444.

tual, or as the universal embrace of the "millions" invoked by Schiller. When Heine makes the idea of the nation his own, he takes it in the Mazzinian sense of an "International of Nationalists." He is the defender of local freedoms and differences against "Europe's most terrible levelers" (*die furchtbarsten Nivelleurs Europas*), against "unifiers" à la Richelieu or Robespierre, and such "emperors of finance" as Rothschild. According to Heine, this deadly leveling, which would make our world unlivable, will be the inevitable result of a great Franco-German war, touched off by the revolutionary ideas of Paris:

What would be the end of this movement, for which Paris, as always, would give the signal? It would be war, the most horrible war of annihilation, which would send to the battlefield the two noblest civilized peoples and would mean the destruction of both: I refer to France and Germany. . . .
The second act will certainly be European revolution, even world revolution, an implacable duel between the proletarians and the property-owning aristocrats; then there will be no question of nationality or religion; there will be only one homeland, the earth, and only one religion, happiness on earth. . . . How will the show end? I do not know, but I think that in the end the head of the sea serpent will be crushed and the northern bear will be skinned. Then there will be only one shepherd and only one flock, a free shepherd with an iron crook and a human flock shorn uniformly and bleating in unison. Dark ferocious times are approaching, we can hear them rumble . . . The future has a strong smell of leather, blood, impiety, and the sound of flesh on flesh. I advise our grandchildren to come into the world with a very thick skin.[7]

This curious prophecy belongs with all those previously quoted. There will be more and more of them right down until the twentieth century—when they will all come true! Here is another version, in a letter Heine wrote two years earlier:

What Napoleon said on Saint-Helena—that in the near future the world will be an American republic or the Russian world monarchy—what a discouraging prophecy! . . . is not a soap bubble that can be blown away. It opens up a terrible prospect, which turn us to stone like Medusa's head. What a future! The

[7] July 12, 1842.

best we can hope for is to die of boredom as republicans! Poor posterity! [8]

We know what indignation the Russians aroused in Europe when they crushed the Hungarian and Polish insurrections of 1848. The situation was in every respect like that of 1956. Then, too, the governments were as if paralyzed, to all intents and purposes insensitive to a unanimous public opinion. Here are two brief texts on the subjects: one by the leader of the Hungarian uprising, Lajos Kossuth (1802–1894), who escaped to Europe, and the other by the soldier-poet Alexander Petöfi (1823–1849), aide-de-camp to the Polish general Bem, who was killed in action:

All I can say is that Hungary has been Hungary since the ninth century. Her glorious past and her hopes for the future, the memory of the incalculable services she rendered to Christendom and to civilization, the immense interest Europe has always taken in her vigorous existence—everything testifies to the fact that she was Hungary, and everything demands that she should remain Hungary. Take this away, and she means nothing more to Europe, less than nothing: all she can become is an outpost of the Russian world monarchy.[9]

Petöfi, in his poem of 1848 entitled *Silence of Europe,* wrote:

Europe keeps silent . . .
Shame on silent Europe
She has not won her freedom!
The cowardly nations have abandoned you
O Magyars! You alone keep fighting . . .
Freedom, lower thine eyes to look at us,
Recognize us! Recognize thy people!
While others dare not even shed tears
We the Magyars are shedding our blood.
What more dost thou need, O Freedom,
Before your grace deigns to descend upon us?

Adam Mickiewicz (1798–1855), the great Polish poet, then an exile in Paris, voiced the centuries-old complaint of East-

[8] Lutezia, June 3, 1840, in *Sämtliche Werke,* 6, 186.
[9] Lajos Kossuth, *L'Europe, L'Autriche, et la Hongrie* (Brussels, 1859).

European countries periodically "liberated" by the Russians. The following is an excerpt from his long prose poem *The Book of the Pilgrims:* [10]

When freedom is enthroned in the capital of the world, she will judge the nations.

And she will say to the first nation: Behold, I was attacked by brigands, and I called thee, nation, asking for a scrap of iron and a bit of gunpowder to defend myself, and you gave me a newspaper article. And the nation will answer: When didst thou call me? And Freedom will say: I called through the mouths of these pilgrims, and thou didst not listen to me; therefore thou shalt be enslaved, and thou shalt hear the whistling of the knout and the rattling of ukases.

And Freedom will say to the second nation: I was in pain and misery, and I asked thee, O nation, to give me assistance and the protection of your laws, and thou answeredst me with regulations. And the nation will answer, O Freedom, when did you come to me? And Freedom will say: I came to you under the guise of these pilgrims, and thou scornedst me; therefore thou shalt go into slavery and hear the whistling of the knout and the rattling of ukases.

Verily I say unto you, your pilgrimage will be a stumbling block to the Powers.

The Powers have rejected the stone you brought for the building of Europe. And lo and behold, this stone shall become the cornerstone and the keystone of the future edifice; and it shall crush him on whom it shall fall, and he who knocks against it, shall fall and be crushed, and he who knocks against it, shall fall and never rise again.

And of the great European political structure no stone shall be left standing. . . . And you will cry to the foreign despot as though to a deaf anvil: O despot, we have served thee, soften thy heart, open unto us that we may escape the hammer. And the despot shall turn his back on you, cold and hard, and the rod shall be struck and struck again until you recognize it not.

"Today, the West is dying of isms!" exclaimed the Polish poet, despairing of his fatherland. The Italians, who felt that they were about to gain their independence, took a far less pessimistic view of Europe.

One of them was Vincenzo Gioberti (1801–1852). Philosopher

[10] Chap. xxii, "The Cause of the Peoples' Freedom."

and theologian, liberal Catholic statesman, involved in the republican conspiracies of 1833, an exile in Paris and in Brussels, later prime minister of Piedmont, Gioberti was a neo-Guelph. He strove for the unification of Italy, but he also wanted the unification of Europe; to him the two were inseparable. In his eyes, Italy ("the East of the West") was to play the part of guide to other European nations, under the leadership of the Pope, and Rome was to become the capital of a world in which all political and cultural "nationalities," preserving their differences, would achieve a "dialectical" unification: "The dictatorship of the Sovereign Pontiff, charged with the political direction of Italy and with the organization of Europe, aimed at setting up the various national Christendoms," he wrote in 1843, in a widely read work published in Brussels under the title *On the Moral and Civil Primacy of the Italians* (known in Italy as *Il Primato*). In his treatise *Della nazionalità italiana*, he formulated the "dialectical" transition from city-state to nation, Europe, and the world:

Christ, who set civilization the ultimate earthly goal of unifying the great human family, suggested the dialectical idea of the nation which is, so to speak, the city-state enlarged, humanity in miniature . . . The concept of a united Europe, a kind of amphictyonic federation of the Christian states, and the final stage of the process of unification which is tending to encompass the entire human race, had no other origin.

He went further in *Rinnovamento*: "Every divided people that decrees a mass levy of its citizens speaks in the name of the country as a whole; every country that sounds the call to arms is really addressing Europe."

Moverover, he gave the classical definition of Europe, first formulated by the Greeks, who were, according to him, the true ancestors of the "European idea":

Europe is the leading part of the world because she is situated more advantageously than any other, at the dialectical crossroads of mankind, with respect to geographical location, climate, and race. This fact is clearly seen if we consider her physical makeup, crisscrossed with seas and great rivers, with temperature intermediate between that of the arctic circle and that of the blazing tropics, which, both for beings protected naturally and for beings who must clothe themselves artificially, is gentler than the temperature of other regions situated in the same latitudes. The same fact can also be deduced from the quality of the race, which is white, Japhetic, and which belongs to the main Indo-Pelagian branch: or again from her religion, which is Christianity, father of that adult civilization which is advancing with such great strides toward the conquest of world peace and concord.

Europe's superiority stems from the variety of and contrasts between her component parts, which are harmonized by the dominant unity of the race and the Christian rites, since the value of every created energy results from the interaction of two dialectical factors, namely, the opposition of contraries and their conciliatory nature.

Europe, in respect of constitutional law, is at the same stage Italy is at, due allowance being made; which amounts to saying that she is a composite of several states in need of unification (without losing their individuality thereby). But there is in the states no seed engendering unification: moreover, they are disunited and vie with one another because of hatred and mutual discord.[11]

Poland and Hungary were oppressed nationalities, which had lost their political independence; Germany and Italy were nations still to be born. It is understandable that for these four countries, the national idea was inevitably identified with the idea of freedom and in tune with the idea of a unified Europe. A nation in process of being born has, as yet, no "traditional" interests to oppose it to the greater whole. But what about France and Spain, those elder sisters, those models of the strong national state, which claim to owe nothing to anyone? The two cases are very different. The France of 1848 herself as a nation that had just been reborn, in a Europe renovated by the principles of her own revolution; whereas Spain saw in these principles, when extended to all of Europe, merely a diabolical threat to her very existence.

Let us first illustrate the position of the Europe-minded French. These include, besides Jouffroy (that forgotten philosopher), the best-known French writers of the mid-nineteenth century.

[11] *Prolegomeni al Primato.*

Alphonse de Lamartine (1790–1869) was not only the elegiac poet of the *Harmonies* and the *Méditations,* but also a historian (not too reliable) of the Revolution and an eloquent member of the provisional government of 1848. He favored a "sincerely progressive and vigorously conservative" regime. All his speeches, in which he stresses France's role as liberator in the two revolutions, refer to Europe as a vague and solemn higher entity, in the bosom of which the liberated Nations will naturally be in harmony, and before which they must prove their invariably special claims. In 1843, in a speech to the Chamber of Deputies, he said:

France, fortunately, is so placed in the world that none of her real interests is incompatible with the great European interests. She must negotiate with others and maintain harmony. . . . We have given the political, social, religious European world such a jolt, that there is no empire that has not trembled or crumbled as a result of it, not a single human nerve in the whole universe that has not felt it as a blessing or a curse, with joy or with terror, with hatred or with fanaticism.

Appointed minister of foreign affairs in the provisional revolutionary government (February, 1848), Lamartine addressed to French diplomats a *Manifesto to the Powers* [12] intended to reassure Europe concerning the intentions of the new France. In this document, the idea of harmony among Nations for the benefit of Europe as a whole is emphatically restated:

In 1792, France and Europe were not ready to understand or to accept the idea of harmonious coexistence among the nations for the benefit of the human race. The century that was coming to a close had not given it much thought, apart from a few philosophers. Philosophy today is of the people. Fifty years of freedom of thought, speech, and writing have had their effect. Books, newspapers, speeches all represent a European intelligence. A widely disseminated reason which is above all boundaries between nations, has created a great intellectual nationality, the consummation of the French Revolution, and the basis of global international brotherhood. . . .

[12] Sometimes called *Manifesto to Europe,* cf. H. Gollwitzer, *op. cit.,* p. 323.

By its intellectual heat, by the spectacle of order and peace it hopes to give the world, the Republic will practice the only kind of honest proselytizing, that which is based upon mutual respect and sympathy. We are not appealing to arms, but to nature. We are not trying to stir up Europe, but to live and let live. We are not trying to set fire to the world, we are lighting a beacon for the nation, we take the lead only to guide them.

In the same spirit, but with greater profundity, the historian Jules Michelet (1798–1875) exalted the "intimate harmony" that was to unite all the constituent parts of Europe, and all the patriotisms, however "unique" each of them might conceive itself:

What is least simple, least natural, most man-made, that is to say, what is least the result of blind fate, most human, freest in the world is Europe, and what is most European is my country, France.[13]

In the end, however, it was Victor Hugo who many years later effected "the transfiguration" of the ideals of 1848 into a sublime Europeanism and universalism, thus consummating— but in the realm of the imagination only—the nationalist dialectics of political romanticism. Because he cannot be suspected of narrowminded nationalism, and because he was the most enthusiastic prophet of European unity in the nineteenth century, his repeated statements on the European future of his country illustrate more than any others the grandiose ambivalence of the national idea. Must this generous and sincere aspiration to universality, this vision of France transfigured, a France that becomes Europe and the world, be interpreted in other countries as a secret desire to win over the whole world to the style of life and thought of a "mother nation"? When Hugo speaks of the "savages" from the French empire who came to Paris to see the World's Fair of 1867, he made some remarks that give the critic pause:

These eyes saturated with darkness have come to gaze upon the truth. . . . They know that there exists a people of reconciliation . . . an open nation that invites all those who are or want to be her brothers. As they see it, invasion; as France sees it, expansion.

[13] Jules Michelet, *Introduction à l'histoire universelle* (Paris, 1831).

Here are a few inspired passages on this inexhaustible dialectical theme:

What is admirable about France is this, that she is destined to die, but to die as gods die, by being transfigured. France will become Europe. Some people end by being sublimated, like Hercules, or by ascending to Heaven, like Christ. One might say that at a given moment a people forms a constellation: the other peoples, stars of the second magnitude, group themselves around it, and that is how Athens, Rome, and Paris are Pleiades. Immense laws! Greece transfigured became the Christian world; France transfigured, will become the human world. The revolution of France will be called the evolution of the peoples. Why? Because France deserves it; because she is unselfish, because she does not work for herself alone, because she is the creator of universal hopes, because she represents all human goodwill, because where other nations are merely sisters, she is mother. This motherhood of generous France is evident in all social phenomena of our time; the other nations make her misfortunes for her, she their ideas for them.[14]

In the twentieth century there will be an extraordinary nation. This nation will be great, which will not prevent it from being free. It will be illustrious, rich, thinking, peace-loving, cordial toward the rest of mankind. It will be gentle and grave like an elder sister . . . The capital of this nation will be Paris, and it will not be called France; it will be called Europe. It will be called Europe in the twentieth century; in the following centuries, even more transfigured, it will be called Mankind. Mankind, the definitive nation, whose coming is even now sensed by thinkers, who contemplate the shadowy future; but what the nineteenth century is witness to, is the formation of Europe.[15]

In his speech saluting the Paris World's Fair of 1867,[16] Hugo rises to peaks of eloquence. From these heights he sees Europe herself absorbed into immensity of the most modern humanity. Here is the exordium:

Let us welcome Europe.
May she feel at home here. May she take possession of this

[14] Article entitled "Le Droit et la Loi" (1875), in Œuvres complètes, Actes et Paroles (Paris: Hetzel et Cie et Quantin, 1882), I, 4–5.
[15] Article entitled "L'Avenir" (1867), ibid., IV, 289–95.
[16] Article entitled "Déclaration de Paix" (1867), ibid., IV, 349–50, 351, 365.

Paris which belongs to her, and to which she belongs! May she be comfortable, breathe deeply in this city of all and for all, which has the privilege of performing European deeds! It is in Paris that all the noble impulses of the nineteenth century spirit originated; it is in Paris that the council of minds, this magnificent contemporary spectacle, has been held during thirty-six years of freedom; it is here that all the great questions of our epoch were raised, debated, and given solutions on the side of freedom: rights of the individual, foundation and starting point for social justice, rights of labor, rights of women, rights of children, abolition of ignorance, abolition of poverty, abolition of the sword in all its forms, inviolability of human life.

Like glaciers which have a kind of grandiose chastity, and which, by imperceptible, yet irresistible and unknown motions cast out unwanted blocks on their moraines, so Paris has cast out all impurities, all refuse, the slaughter houses, the death penalty.

And here is the peroration:

O France, farewell! you are too great to be but a fatherland. One separates from one's mother when she becomes a goddess. A little longer, you will be lost from sight, transfigured. You are so great that you will be no more. You will be France no longer, you will be Mankind; you will be nation no longer, you will be omnipresence. You are destined to be entirely dissolved in radiance, and nothing is more sublime today than the visible disappearance of your frontier. Resign yourself to your immensity. Farewell, Nation! Hail, Mankind! Accept your inevitable and sublime enlargement, O my homeland, and just as Athens became Greece, just as Rome became Christendom, you, France, become the world.

Spain was in a markedly different position in the mid-nineteenth century from the oppressed or recently reborn nations that together made up most of continental Europe. Spain intended to remain as she was, even after losing her American empire. She did not look to Progress, Science, Social Democracy, the movement of history, or even to Freedom. She placed all her this-worldly political faith in a supernatural hope: the restoration of the Catholic order. Her most Europe-minded spokesman, the philosopher and diplomat Donoso-Cortés, marquess of Valdegamas (1809–1853), gave uncompromising anti-Jacobin and antiromantic form to the most haughty nationalism. To him sovereignty was not founded on a libertarian ideology, but on an authoritarian theology. His antitheses are as violent and oversimplified as Hugo's, but in the opposite sense. The following brief excerpts from two letters to Montalembert sum up the philosophy of the most implacable adversary of the political ideals of 1848:

I believe that the Catholic civilization contains the good without admixture of evil, and that the philosophical civilization contains the evil without admixture of good. . . .

When I consider the Catholic civilization in its historical reality, I shall say that since its imperfections originate solely in the fact that it is combined with human freedom, true progress would consist in subjecting the human element that corrupts it to the divine element that purifies it. Society has taken a different direction. By representing the empire of faith as dead, and by proclaiming the independence of human reason and will, it has rendered absolute, universal, and necessary the evil which was relative, exceptional, and contingent. The period of rapid regression began in Europe with the restoration of literary paganism. This led successively to the restoration of philosophical paganism, then religious paganism, and finally political paganism. Today the world is on the eve of the last of these restorations: the restoration of socialist paganism. . . . Even now history can formulate her judgment on these two great civilizations, one of which consists in subjecting man's will and reason to the divine element, and the other in discarding the divine element and in proclaiming the independence and sovereignty of the human element. . . . However, this great regression was part of the wise mysterious law by which God guides and governs the human race. If the Catholic civilization had followed a path of continuous progress, the earth would in the end have become man's paradise, but God willed the earth to be a vale of tears. God would have been socialist. And then, what would Proudhon have been? Everyone is where he should be: God in heaven and Proudhon on earth; Proudhon always seeking, without ever finding, a paradise in the vale of tears, and God placing this vale of tears between two paradises, so that man may always find himself between a great memory and a great hope.[17]

[17] Letters of M. Donoso-Cortés on the Future of the New Society, to M. le Comte de Montalembert, May 26 and June 4, 1849.

Such Hugoesque rhetoric does not in the least prevent Donoso-Cortés from making cruelly clear-sighted judgments on political Europe. In his famous speech "On the General Situation of Europe," delivered to the Spanish Chamber of Deputies on January 30, 1850, he does not, as Hugo will do later, prophesy the peace which men should strive for and believe they love, but realities men should fear, and which the ringleaders of History do nothing to stem:

The cause of all your errors, gentlemen [the speaker turns to the deputies of the Left], is your ignorance of the march of civilization and of the world. You think that civilization and the world are progressing, whereas civilization and the world are regressing. The world is marching with great strides toward the establishment of a despotism, the most gigantic and the most terrible mankind has ever seen. And to predict these things, I need be no prophet; it is enough for me to consider the totality of human events from the only true point of view, that is, from the height of the Catholic position.

I will tell you the truth, gentlemen. The truth is that we are today what we were yesterday, what we have been since the February revolution. Since this revolution of fearful memory, nothing solid, nothing sure is left in Europe. . . .

Look at the condition of Europe. It seems that all chiefs of state have lost the gift of judgment; human reason suffers eclipses, institutions suffer upheavals, and nations, great and sudden declines. Cast, gentlemen, cast with me your eyes on Europe, from Poland to Portugal, and tell me, in all conscience, tell me in good faith whether you find a single society capable of saying: I am firm on my foundations; or a single foundation capable of saying: I am firm in myself!

Do not object to me that the revolution was defeated in Spain, defeated in Italy, defeated in France, defeated in Hungary; no, gentlemen, this is not the truth. The truth is that all social forces concentrated and raised to their highest degree of power were hardly sufficient, were just barely able to contain the monster. . . .

There has been mention here, gentlemen, of the danger with which Europe is threatened by Russia, and I think that for today and for a long time to come I can set the assembly's mind at rest, by assuring it that it need not fear the least danger from that quarter.

The influence that Russia exerted in Europe, gentlemen, was exerted through the intermediary of the Germanic federation.

This federation was made against Paris, which was the revolutionary city, the accursed city, and in favor of St. Petersburg, which was then the holy city, the city of government, the city of the restoration tradition. What was the result? That the Federation was not an empire as it could have been at that time; it was not an empire because Russia could in no case afford to be confronted by an empire of the united German races. Thus the Federation was composed of microscopic principalities and two great monarchies. What was convenient in the hypothesis of a war in France? What was convenient to Russia was that these monarchies should be absolute, and these monarchies were absolute. That is how it came about that the influence of Russia, from the day the Federation was founded to the February revolution, extended from St. Petersburg to Paris. But since the February revolution the shape of things has changed; the revolutionary storm has overthrown monarchs, dragged crowns in the dust, humiliated kings; the Germanic federation is no more; Germany today is but a chaos. In other words, gentlemen, the influence of Russia which reached from St. Petersburg to Paris has given way to the demagogic influence of Paris, which reaches as far as Poland. . . .

It is not, however, my opinion that Europe has nothing to fear from Russia; I believe the very opposite; but for Russia to accept a general war, for Russia to seize Europe, three events must first take place, events which I will tell you and which—note this, gentlemen—are not only possible, but also probable.

To begin with, the revolution, after dissolving society, must proceed to dissolve the standing armies; second, socialism, by taking property away from its owner, inevitably extinguishes patriotism, because a proprietor stripped of his possessions is not, cannot be a patriot; for once things have been carried so far, so terribly far, patriotism is dead in men's hearts; third, the powerful federation of all the Slav peoples under Russia's influence and protection is inevitable. The Slav nations, gentlemen, comprise eighty million inhabitants. Very well, then, after the revoluton has destroyed the standing armies in Europe, after the socialist revolutions have extinguished patriotism in Europe, after the great federation of the Slav peoples has been formed in the east of Europe; after the West is left with more than two armies, that of the despoiled, and that of the despoilers, then Russia's moment will have come; then an armed Russia can walk unopposed right across Europe into our own country; then the world will witness the most appalling punishment ever recorded in history—the punishment of England.

2: A Compensatory Ideal: The United States of Europe

WHO COINED THE EXPRESSION? Cattaneo? Cobden? Mazzini? or Hugo? An obscure speaker during the pre-revolutionary "Banquets Campaign" in 1847? The anonymous writer of a piece in the *Moniteur* of February 26, 1848? [18] Historians hesitate and conclude wisely that the idea was in the air.

Exalting nations, even liberated nations, can lead after all to aggressive nationalism as well as to the harmony of spiritual collectivities. Mystical appeals to "Europe" such as Lamartine's become mere rhetorical exercises when governments in the name of their interests refuse to play the noble game of idealist dialectics. Hence the need for a new kind of sovereignty, an authority superior to the states, a federal Europe more explicit and more effective than the "Europe of the Nations." The latter might be celebrated by poets who took the long view, but it was shrewdly exploited by politicians who took the short view. Born of a premonitory fear, the slogan "The United States of Europe" was, all told, no more than a compensatory ideal. Except perhaps with Proudhon, it does not continue the plans for European Peace, quoted above, from Pierre Du Bois to Saint-Simon. Rather it seeks to forestall the anticipated crimes of national passions too lyrically extolled to be opposed otherwise with impunity.

Carlo Cattaneo (1801–1869) was a philosopher, historian, sociologist, geographer, linguist, and economist, and let the Milan uprising in March, 1848. What brought him around to a European point of view was neither a passionate impulse nor a logical idealism of the Hegelian type. He seems to have dis-

[18] Cf. P. Renouvin, *L'idée de fédération européenne dans la pensée politique du XIX siècle* (Oxford, 1949).

covered for himself the existence of an underlying European reality, sufficiently broad and yet clearly defined to account for how the complexes of interest he was studying arose and operated. (By an analogous process, Toynbee was to choose "civilizations," rather than nations or the world, as his intelligible field of study.)

However, Cattaneo does not envisage a unification of all our diversities. Variety, multiplicity, individuality, nationality, seem to him European essentials. They are what distinguish Europe from mother Asia, although she had inherited the elements of uniformity such as constitute any civilization. In thus posing the problem of the necessary tensions between the one and the many, Cattaneo reveals himself a federalist in the proper sense of the word. Europe's organic development, the logic of economic facts as well as historical facts lead us inevitably to a progressive federal integration: for Cattaneo, union is by no means a primitive golden age to be restored, as the Romantics had thought; on the contrary, it marks the end of the civilizatory process:

It would be vain to believe that Europe, in these centuries of savagery, has been different from the lands which have stayed just as they were down to our own day. The European found America and Australia in the same state as that in which the Asians seem to have found Europe. Here too, long before the great nations arose, there must have been little peoples, and before these peoples, isolated tribes. And each tribe, whether occupying an isolated valley or a grassland surrounded by marshes and crisscrossed by rivers, must at first have lived in isolation, each having its own way of speaking and clothing itself, within the narrow area to which it was confined by enemy tribes. It would be false and misleading to ask to which of the great nations that later developed over the centuries by a slow historical process, a given tribe belonged; this would be absurd, like asking from what river small streams flow, when in reality it is the other way around. Consequently it is high time to stop divagations on the subject of the posterity of the Celts, the Illyrians, or the Thracians; all these primitive populations had lived long before the eastern civilization came to Europe bringing its system of colonization, its religious rites, its trade, its superior weapons, as well as all the miseries of exile and servitude. On the other hand, the same civilization spreading along Europe's sea coasts and rivers propagated that mysterious unity of language which, to our great wonder, originated in India and Persia. It is this linguistic unity which, ever more ramified, gave birth to what we call the Celtic, Germanic, and Slavic races. If there is in Europe an element of unity which is certainly rooted in Asia, ancient mother of religions, empires, alphabets and arts, there is also an element of variety; the latter provides the foundation for the various nationalities and represents the surviving autochthonous element in the populations, including their ways of combining with and adjusting to the civilization that was disseminated from the centers of Asian influence in Europe. The multiple combinations between foreign unity and autochthonous variety came into being on European soil, not in Asia. The principal languages spread in lands and countries ever more extensively and among populations of different origin, even some who were each other's hereditary enemies. In this way they acquired a uniform aspect giving rise to the belief that they were of common descent . . . The farther we go back in time, the more clearly we see the original elements of which each nationality is composed; and if we discard the uniformities, that is, the alien and factitious components, the harsh vernaculars come back to life as independent self-contained languages, which were created by the conditions of life that the human race experienced at its beginnings.[19]

There is a sharp contrast between Cattaneo and Giuseppe Mazzini (1807–1872), the contrast between the cautious scientific spirit and militant eloquence, between sober sociology and enthusiastic propaganda. Both strove for the union of Italy within a unified Europe: both believed that "nationality" was an essential element in any living European union—the other element being Mankind. But while Cattaneo is a thinker, Mazzini is above all an agitator. Hence the different ways in which the two make use of ideas. The philosopher verifies concepts by confronting them with reality, which he studies closely by various methods; the agitator seeks to carry away realities in a mystical upsurge of an ideology, which is far less his individual creation than a turbulent summing up of the noblest illusions of his epoch.

Denounced by the aged Metternich as a public danger to the

[19] *Notizie naturali et civili sulla Lombardia,* chap. v.

whole of Europe, feared by Cavour, who suspected that he was a demagogue and a potential dictator, admired by the young Nietzsche, whom he met by chance on the St. Gothard Pass in 1871—a sacred spot, roof and heart of Europe—his views reflect the century's two most extreme positions: the reaction to Jacobin France and the hard historical pessimism which was to mark the end of the era of Nations. He believed all a man of his time could believe concerning freedom, love, and harmony, assuming them to be dear to the heart of the peoples. "The People," he said "the sacred word of the future . . ."

He was, to begin with, an apostle of Italianism, of Italian unity through republicanism; then, as though in consequence,[20] an apostle of European unity; but he conceived of it as a union of outlaws from all the monarchies, the Austrian, the French, and then the Italian (once it had been established). Unlike the precursors and utopians, quoted previously, he did not propose a plan for a union of princes or states; he wrote the first charter for a *movement of European militants*, a document dated 1843, which bears the signatures of seven Italians, five Germans, and seven Poles. At that time Mazzini was living in hiding in Switzerland. He had founded the Young Italy movement, which was opposed to the *carbonaria:* he thought the latter too amenable to obstructive French influences. After a number of defeats the movement had suffered in Italy (several uprisings had been crushed), Mazzini decided to broaden its scope of action. He created the Young Germany and Young Poland committees, and later Young Switzerland and Young France committees. The Charter given below was intended to seal the union of these national and republican groupings:

YOUNG EUROPE

Liberty—Equality—Humanity

Act of Fraternity

[20] In 1834 he wrote to his friend L. A. Melegari: "I love mankind religiously, but I love my country religiously and individually, like a lover! Was it not patriotic inspiration that gave us the courage to undertake this immense labor? Did we not seek to wreathe it with a crown of elements that would hail its first resurrection?" Cf. Dora Melegari, *La Jeune Italie et la Jeune Europe* (Paris, 1908), p. 241.

We, the undersigned, men of progress and liberty:

Believing—In the equality and fraternity of all men:

Believing—that humanity is destined to achieve, through a continuous progress under the dominion of the universal moral law, the free and harmonious development of its faculties, and the fulfilment of its mission in the universe:

That this can only be achieved through the active co-operation of all its members, freely associated together:

That true, free association can only exist amongst equals; since every inequality implies a violation of independence, and every violation of independence is the destruction of free agreement and consent:

That liberty, equality, and humanity, are all equally sacred— that they constitute the three inviolable elements of every positive solution of the social problem—and then whensoever any one of these elements is sacrificed to the other two, the organisation of human effort towards the solution of that problem is radically defective:

Convinced—That although the ultimate *aim* to be reached by humanity is essentially one, and the general principles destined to guide the various human families in their advance towards that aim, are identical for all; there are yet many paths disclosed to progress:

Convinced—That every man and every people has a special mission; the fulfilment of which determines the *individuality* of that man or of that people, and at the same time bears a part in the accomplishment of the general mission of humanity:

Convinced lastly—That the association both of individuals and peoples is necessary to secure the free performance of the individual mission, and the certainty of its direction towards the fulfilment of the general mission:

Strong in our rights as men and citizens; strong in our own conscience and in the mandate given by God and humanity to all those truly desirous of consecrating their energies, their intellect, and their whole existence to the holy cause of the progress of the Peoples:

Having already constituted ourselves in free and independent national associations as the primitive nuclei of *Young Poland, Young Germany,* and *Young Italy:*

Assembled together by common consent for the general good, this 15th April 1834, we, constituting ourselves, as far as our own efforts are concerned, securities and pledges for the future, have determined as follows:—

I. *Young Germany, Young Poland,* and *Young Italy,* being Republican associations, having the same Humanitarian aim in view, and led by the same faith in liberty, equality, and progress, do hereby fraternally associate and unite, now and for ever, in all matters concerning the general aim.

II. A declaration of those principles which constitute the universal moral law in its bearing upon human society, shall be drawn up and signed by the three national committees. It shall set forth and define the belief, the purpose, and the general tendency of the three associations. Any of the members who shall separate their own work from that of the association, will be regarded as guilty of culpable violation of this *Act of Fraternity,* and will take the consequences of such violation.

III. In all matters not comprehended in the Declaration of Principles, and not appertaining to the general interest, each of the three associations will be free and independent.

IV. An alliance—defensive and offensive—expressive of the solidarity of the Peoples, is established between the three associations. They will work together in harmony in the cause of the emancipation of their several countries. In matters peculiarly or specially concerning their own countries, they will each have a right to the assistance of the others.

V. An assembly of the National Committees or their delegates, will constitute the Committee of *Young Europe.*

VI. The fraternity of the three associations is decreed, and each of them is bound to fulfil every duty arising out of that fraternity.

VII. The Committee of *Young Europe* will determine upon a symbol, to be common to all the members of the three associations. A common motto will be inscribed upon all the publications of the three associations.

VIII. Any people desirous of sharing the rights and duties established by this alliance, may do so by formally adhering to this *Act of Fraternity,* through the medium of their representatives.

Berne, 15th April 1834 [21]

All the hopes of 1848 are contained in this text. When the February Revolution broke out in Paris, at a time when the Swiss cantons were planning to federate, when a German federal parliament met at Frankfort, and there were uprisings in Milan, Budapest, and Warsaw, it was possible to believe for a

[21] From *Life and Writings of Joseph Mazzini* (London, 1864–1870).

few months in the advent of Young Europe, or at least in the triumph of its ideals.

In 1850, as a refugee in London, where a more successful refugee—Karl Marx—ridiculed him, Mazzini was confronted with the defeat of libertarian revolts all over Europe, with the victory of governments over peoples and of nationalism over the free "association" of nationalities. He asked himself why this failure had come about, and found the answer in the disunion among the federalists themselves. He was the first European, as we have said, whose organizational plans took the form of a movement:

Yes, the cause is in ourselves, in our lack of organization, in the fragmentation produced within our ranks by systems, which are sometimes absurd and dangerous, always incomplete, premature, and yet advocated with the exclusivism and stubbornness of intolerance. It is in our suspicions, our perpetual petty vanities, in the total lack of discipline which alone can accomplish great things. Our forces are scattered into a multitude of little centers, groups, sects, cliques, powerful instruments of disintegration, but incapable of founding anything. It is in the worship of material interest which has gradually replaced in our schools the cult of sacred ideas, the great educational task which alone justifies our efforts, the feeling for Life and its mission. It is in our having forgotten God, his law of love, devotion, and moral progress within the great religious tradition of mankind, in having preferred prosperity, the Volney catechism, Bentham's principle of selfishness, indifference to super-terrestrial truths which are alone capable of transforming this world. It is in the spirit of nationalism that has everywhere supplanted the spirit of nationality; in the foolish claim put forward by every people that it can solve political, economic, and social problems within its own boundaries and by its own powers alone, forgetting this great truth, that the cause of all peoples is one and the same, that fatherland must rest upon humanity, that every revolution not explicity a cult of devotion to those who fight and suffer must lead to a vicious circle and end in failure; that the Holy Alliance of the nations is the goal of our struggles, the only force capable of crushing the league of the powers originating in privilege and selfish interests.

As for our enemies, they are at the mercy of our efforts. They are strong only because of our own mistakes. Now the skies are dark; but beyond the clouds is sunshine, God's own eternal, dazzling sunshine. They can for some time obscure it, screen it from our eyes; but erase it . . . never. Thank God, Europe is emancipated; she has been emancipated since Marathon. That day the *static* oriental principle was forever conquered; Europe began. Europe is still on the march; she will not be stopped by a few scraps of paper.[22]

The Young Europe movement had failed. But several Societies, of a less subversive cast, were founded in its wake, under the auspices of Frédéric Passy and later Camille Lemonnier, among others. Here we find the last disciples of Saint-Simon, Cobden, Bastiat, and Mazzini himself, anarchists, inspired pacifists, as well as General Garibaldi, who served as chairman at one of their congresses in Geneva, in 1867. Again and again, over a twenty-year period, surrounded by thunderous applause, we find Victor Hugo (1802–1885), the most lyrical of the champions of European union.

In his speech of July 17, 1851, to the legislative assembly, during a debate on revision of the Constitution, he for the first time uttered the words "The United States of Europe." Here is an excerpt from the official record:

M. Hugo: The first nation of the world made three revolutions —like the three steps taken by the gods of Homer. These three revolutions which are but one are not a local revolution, they are the human revolution; what we have here is not the selfish cry of a people, it is the sacred demand for universal equality, it is the liquidation of the general grievances of humanity that have existed since history began; it is, after centuries of slavery, serfdom, theocracy, feudalism, inquisition, despotism under every name, human torture under every form, the august proclamation of the rights of man!

After long trials, this revolution gave birth to the republic in France . . . the republic which for the people is a kind of natural law as freedom is for man. The French people has carved in indestructible granite, and set in the very midst of the old monarchic continent, the first foundation of the immense edifice of the future which will one day be called The United States of Europe!

[22] *Foi et Avenir* (Paris: Bureau du Nouveau Monde, 1850), pamphlet of 104 pages written in French.

M. de Montalembert: The United States of Europe! That's too much! Hugo is mad.

M. Molé: The United States of Europe! What an idea! How extravagant!

M. Quentin-Bauchard: Those poets! [23]

Earlier, on August 21, 1849, Hugo, appointed chairman of the Peace Congress (held in Paris that year), had proclaimed his faith in the "inevitable" coming of European union. The opening and the conclusion of his inaugural speech, given below, prefigure the great themes of hope and the noblest anticipations that were to inspire the eloquence of militants for a united Europe for a whole century:

Gentlemen, if anyone, four centuries ago, at a time when wars were fought between villages, cities, and provinces, if anyone had said to Lorraine, to Picardy, to Normandy, to Brittany, to Auvergne, to Provence, to the Dauphiné, to Burgundy: A day will come when you will no longer make war upon each other, a day will come when you will no longer raise armed troops against each other, a day will come when it will become impossible to say: The Normans attacked the Picards, the Lorrainers repulsed the Burgundians. You will still have many differences to settle, interests to discuss, litigation to resolve, but do you know what you will put in place of armed troops? Do you know what you will put in place of infantrymen and cavalrymen, cannon, falconets, lances, pikes, swords? You will have a little pinewood box which you will call the ballot box, and from this box there will emerge—what?—an assembly which all of you will consider your home, an assembly which will be like the soul of all of you, a sovereign and popular council which will decide, judge, resolve everything according to law, which will cause swords to drop from all hands, and justice to surge up in all hearts, which will say to each: There ends your right, here begins your duty. Drop your weapons! live in peace! . . .

If someone had said this at that time, gentlemen, all practical men, all serious people, all great statesmen of that time would have exclaimed: Oh, the dreamer! Oh, the impractical visionary! How little this man knows mankind! What a strange madness, what an absurd chimera! Gentlemen, time has marched on, and this chimera is a reality. . . .

[23] Hugo, *Œuvres complètes, Actes et Paroles* (Paris: Hetzel et Cie et Quantin, 1882), I, 425–26, 427 (note).

A day will come when your weapons too will drop from your hands! A day will come when war between Paris and London, between Petersburg and Berlin, between Vienna and Turin, will seem to you as absurd and as impossible as would today a war between Rouen and Amiens or Boston and Philadelphia. A day will come when you France, you Russia, you Italy, you England, you Germany, all of you, nations of the continent, without losing your distinct qualities and your glorious individualities, will merge tightly into a superior unity, and you will constitute the European brotherhood, exactly as Normandy, Brittany, Burgundy, Lorraine, Alsace, all our provinces have become fused into France. A day will come when there will be no battlefields other than markets opening to trade and minds opening to ideas. A day will come when cannonballs and bombs will give way to votes, with universal suffrage of the peoples, with true arbitration by a great sovereign senate which will be to Europe what Parliament is to England, what the diet is to Germany, what the legislative assembly is to France! . . . A day will come when these two immense groups, the United States of America and the United States of Europe will be seen facing each other, stretching hands above the seas, exchanging their products, their trade, their industry, their arts, their spirits, bringing the globe under cultivation, colonizing the deserts, improving the creation under the eyes of the Creator, and combining, for the welfare of all, these two infinite forces, the brotherhood of men and the power of God! [24]

In 1872 Hugo did not attend the Peace Congress, which that year was held at Lugano, but sent it a message that opens with these words: "My European fellow countrymen." The war of 1870 had once again put civilization in doubt. What lies in store for us—a Cossack Europe, a Vandal Europe, the European empire, or the European republic? And will this come about through war or revolution? Hugo does not know the answer, but he exclaims:

. . . there can be no doubt, this immense thing, the European republic, we shall have it. We shall have the great United States of Europe, which will crown the old world as the United States of America crowns the new. The spirit of conquest will be transfigured into the spirit of discovery; the generous brotherhood of nations will replace the ferocious brotherhood of emperors;

[24] *Ibid.*, I, 475-86.

we shall have a fatherland without boundaries, a budget without parasitism, trade without customs duties, circulation without barriers, education without stultification, young men without army barracks, courage without battlefields, justice without gallows, life without murder, forests without tigers, plowshares without swords, speech without the gag, conscience without servitude, truth without dogma, God without priests, heaven without hell, love without hate.

A few years later, the savage repression unleashed by Ahmed Pasha against the Serbian people, still under Turkish domination, moved the aged poet to write an appeal in a tone which the events at Budapest in our own century make tragically pertinent.

It becomes necessary to call the attention of European governments to a fact so insignificant, it would appear, that the governments seem not to notice it. This fact is: a nation is being murdered. Where? In Europe. Are there witnesses to this fact? One witness: the whole world. Do the governments see it? No.

Peoples have above them something which is beneath them, namely, their governments. At certain moments, this absurdity becomes obvious: civilization is in the peoples, barbarism is in the governments. Is this barbarism deliberate? No, it is merely professional. What mankind knows, the governments do not know. This is due to the fact that the governments see nothing except through the myopia of *raison d'état;* mankind looks at things with a different eye, the eye of conscience.

We are going to surprise the European governments by telling them one thing, namely, that crimes are crimes, that a government, just like an individual, has no right to be a murderer; that Europe is jointly responsible, that everything that is done in Europe is done by Europe; that if a government is a wild beast, it must be treated as such; that at this moment, very close to us, before our eyes, there are massacres, burnings, pillaging, extermination, that fathers and mothers are being killed, little girls and little boys are being sold; that children too little to be sold are cut in two by a stroke of the sword; that families are being burned alive in their houses; that a given city, Balak, for example, has been reduced from 9,000 inhabitants to 1,300 in a few hours; that the cemeteries are cluttered with more corpses than can be buried, so that to the living who organized their carnage, the dead send back the plague—just retribution. We are telling the European governments this, that pregnant women are slit open to have their unborn children killed in their wombs, that in public places there are piles of women's bodies bearing the marks of having been slit open; that dogs in the streets gnaw at skulls of girls who had been raped; that all this is horrible, and that one gesture on the part of the European governments would be enough to stop it, and that the savages who perpetrate these heinous crimes are dreadful, and that the civilized people who allow them to be perpetrated are even worse.

It is high time that civilization should issue a solemn warning to go no further. . . .

What is happening in Serbia proves the necessity for the United States of Europe. Let the disunited governments be succeeded by the united peoples. Let us put an end to the murderous empires. Let us muzzle the fanatics. Let us break the swords that are in the service of superstition, and the dogmas that wield swords. No more wars, no more massacres, no more carnages; free thought, free trade; brotherhood. Is peace as difficult as all that? The Republic of Europe, the continental Federation—there is no other political reality. Reasoning confirms this, events confirm it also. On this reality, which is a necessity, all philosophers are in agreement, and today the hangmen add their proof to the proof philosophers had given . . . What the Serbian atrocities establish beyond doubt, is that Europe needs a European nationality, a single government, an immense brotherly arbitration, democracy in peace with itself, all sister nations having as their city and center Paris, that is to say, freedom having light for its capital. In a word, the United States of Europe. That is our goal, that is our haven.[25]

We have just quoted a sociologist, a mystical agitator, and then a poet who believed he could spellbind History through the Word. Now let us examine a thinker who blazed a new trail.

Pierre-Joseph Proudhon (1809–1865) could justifiably boast of having been the first theorist of federalism, even though Rousseau—whom he had read, of course—could have claimed the title more or less in the same terms: for it must be recognized that Proudhon treated the subject in an exhaustive and realistic manner, with a kind of intellectual tenacity that was hardly Rouseau's strong point. Although Marx is incontestably superior to him in economic analysis, Proudhon is nonetheless the European ancestor of the democratic forms of socialism; not a single chief

[25] "Pour la Serbie" (1876), *ibid.*, IV, 3–5, 6–8.

of a slave labor camp, not a single totalitarian bully has ever been able to justify his crimes by invoking Proudhon's ideas. Until now Proudhon's federalist and libertarian socialism has met with practically no success whatever. Marx's collectivist, centralizing, and authoritarian socialism won out in the U.S.S.R., and holds sway over half of the world today. Doubtless their subsequent fate should not be allowed to reflect on either body of thought. But Marx has a hand in the distortion of his thinking, whereas Proudhon was a victim of such distortions. He believed in freedom, while Marx believed in the power of external circumstances, which can indeed be overwhelming unless man tries to change them. Marx is victorious despite himself in the very parts of the world that he deemed—like Hegel before him—to be far behind in the process of mankind's creative evolution. Proudhon will come into his own only after Europe has recognized that her good health, and her continued influence elsewhere in the world, both lie in federalism.

We have quoted Donoso-Cortés' virulent attacks on the young Proudhon, whom he equated (or almost equated) with the Antichrist. It is only fair to listen to what Proudhon says of himself:

I too have a tradition, a political pedigree which is as dear to me as the legitimacy of my birth: I am a child of the Revolution, which was itself the child of eighteenth-century Philosophy, which in turn had as its mother the Reformation, as its grandmother the Renaissance, and as its ancestors all the Ideas, both orthodox and heterodox, which followed each other over the centuries from the beginnings of Christianity to the fall of the Eastern Empire. Let us not forget, in this glorious lineage, the Communes, the Leagues, the Federations, down to that Feudalism, which, by virtue of its hierarchical constitution and its caste distinctions, was also a form of freedom in its day. And whose child is Christianity itself, which I do not exclude from this revolutionary pedigree? Christianity is the child of Judaism, Egyptianism, Brahmanism, Magism, Platonism, Greek philosophy, and Roman law. If I did not believe in the Church, St. Augustine says somewhere—he meant the tradition—I would not believe in the Gospels. I say with St. Augustine: Could I have confidence in myself and could I believe in the Revolution, if I did not know how far back it all goes? [26]

[26] Proudhon, Œuvres complètes, Vol. VIII, Du Principe Fédératif (Paris, 1868), p. 177.

The excerpts below are all taken from the major work which was published just before the author's death: *Du Principe Fédératif*. They are posthumous in the sense that they are written for our own day and age.

The political contract can remain advantageous and convenient to all only if the citizen, when entering the association, (1) receives from the State as much as he sacrifies to it, and (2) keeps all his freedom, sovereignty, and initiative, minus what is determined by the special purpose for which the contract is made, and which the State is required to guarantee. So drawn up and understood, the political contract is what I call a *federation*.

FEDERATION, from the Latin *foedus*, genitive *foederis*, i.e., pact, contract, treaty, agreement, alliance, etc., is an agreement by which one or several heads of families, one or several free towns, one or several groups of free town or States, bind themselves mutually and reciprocally to achieve one or several well defined aims, the responsibility for which falls then especially and exclusively on the delegates of the federation.

In short, the federative system is the opposite of centralized government or a hierarchized administration such as distinguishes, *ex aequo*, imperial democracies, constitutional monarchies, and unitary republics. Its typical fundamental law is this: In the federation, the attributes of central authority are specialized and restricted; they decrease in number, in immediacy, and if I may say so, in intensity, in proportion as the Confederation grows with the inclusion of new States. On the contrary, in centralized governments, the attributes of supreme power multiply, extend in scope, and become more direct in their effect, drawing the affairs of provinces, free towns, corporations and individuals under the competence of the prince, in direct ratio to the territorial extent and the number of inhabitants. Hence the oppression under which not only communal and provincial freedom disappears, but even national and individual freedom.

One consequence of this is that, the unitary system being the inverse of the federative system, a federation of great monarchies, and a fortiori, a federation of imperial democracies, is impossible. States like France, Austria, England, Russia, Prussia, can make treaties of alliance and trade agreements; federation is repugnant to them, first because it is contrary to their founding principle, because the federal fact would represent opposition; consequently they would have to give up some part of their sovereignty and recognize a higher arbiter at least in certain connections. Their nature is to give orders, not to obey or to back down on a single point. The princes who in 1813, supported by mass uprisings, fought for the freedoms of Europe against Napoleon, and who later formed the Holy Alliance, were not confederated: the absolutist nature of their power ruled out such a possibility. They were members of a *coalition*, as had been the case in 1792; history will never call it by another name.

. . . the idea of a universal confederation is contradictory. This once again shows the moral superiority of the federative system over the unitary system, for the latter is subject to all the inconveniences and all the vices of the indefinite, the unlimited, the absolute, the ideal. Europe would still be too large for a single confederation: she could constitute at best a confederation of confederations. It was with this in mind that in my last publication I recommended, as the first step in the reform of European public law, the restoration of the Italian, Greek, Batavian, Scandinavian, and Danubian confederations, as a preliminary to the decentralization of the great States, and subsequently to general disarmament. Then every nationality could regain its freedom; then the idea of a European balance could be realized. Many statesmen and publicists have looked forward to such an achievement, but it cannot be realized by great powers with unitary constitutions.

The *people*, in its unlogical way of thinking, sees itself as a gigantic and mysterious entity, and in its speech does everything to foster belief in its own indivisible unity. It calls itself the People, the Nation; that is to say, the Multitude, the Mass; it is the true Sovereign, Legislator, Power, Domination, Fatherland, State; it has its Assemblies, its Elections, its Assizes, its Demonstrations, its Pronouncements, its Plebiscites, its direct Legislation, sometimes its Judgments and its Executions, its Oracles, its thundering Voice—the very voice of God. To the same degree as it feels itself innumerable, irresistible, immense, it abhors divisions, schisms, minorities. Its ideal, its favorite dream is unity, identity, uniformity, concentration; it curses, as offensive to its own Majesty, everything that can divide its will, break up its mass, create within it diversity, plurality, divergence.

The federative system would put a term to the restlessness of the masses, would free them from demagogic agitation; it would do away with the rule of the street, with oratorical triumphs, and also with the attraction of the capital cities. Suppose within its own walls, Paris does make a revolution? To what point if Lyon, Marseille, Toulouse, Bordeaux, Nantes, Rouen, Lille, Strasbourg, Dijon, etc., all the separate self-governed departments, do not follow suit? The labors of Paris will have been for nothing. . . .

Thus the federation becomes the salvation of the people: for by dividing the people, it saves it both from the tyranny of its own spokesmen and from its own folly.

. . . The revolution in ideas must have for its legitimate consequence a revolution of interests. The twentieth century will see an era of federation if mankind is not to embark upon a thousand-years' purgatory.

About ten years after Proudhon's *Principe Fédératif,* two works appeared in German which are worth mentioning here. One, by J. K. Bluntschli, a Swiss, was *The Organization of a League of European States* (1878), and the other was by Constantin Frantz, a German, on Federalism (1879). Neither the Swiss jurist nor the Prussian diplomat seems to owe anything to the French socialist; they draw solely upon their respective professional experience. The problem of European federalism is thus brought down to the level of political practice and the study of political conditions from the heights where Hugo's eloquence and Mazzini's ideology had set it.

Johann Kaspar Bluntschli (1808–1881) was the author of the civil code of his native canton, Zurich; later, he became one of the best-known professors of international law of his time, in Heidelberg. His personal experience of Swiss federalism enabled him to formulate some fundamental distinctions which almost inevitably escaped the notice of the French and Italian heirs to Jacobinism and political romanticism. Among other things he tackled the problem of "nationality," the ambiguities of which, as we have seen, had undermined the generous impulses of 1848. How could one conceive a "European nationality" on the model of the sovereign and uniform Nations of which Europe was made up? The problem turned out to be insoluble, because it had not been properly formulated. However, the problem of a nation "international" by nature makes it possible to imagine what a European federal state might be:

Switzerland, a mountainous country in central Europe, where the great European rivers, the Rhine, the Danube, and the Po, have their principal sources, and which both separates and links such great nations as Germany, Italy, France, and Austria, possesses a very special character for these very reasons. Similarly, the Swiss people and the various Swiss republics—the little cantonal republics as well as the great republic which is the Confederation—are faced with great vital tasks, whose importance is not only local, but also European. These small democratic states are full of energy, because they enjoy complete political freedom inside a country where peace prevails. They can and must according to the natural characters of each ask themselves all the questions that fate and the development of humanity pose to the great nations. They have to solve them fully, in conformity with the circumstances of the moment. In this respect, these states can serve as an example to the other nations, and play a determining role in the evolution of mankind.

. . . As long as the Swiss people aspires courageously to fulfill these duties and to pursue these ideals, its bonds with Europe will not be threatened, and the Swiss nationality will not be arrested in its development.

. . . If a Swiss nationality exists, it possesses an international character to the highest degree. . . . The parts of which it is composed are linked indissolubly to the other great nations, forming with the latter a cultural community which has determined their spiritual life. For this reason the political nationality of the Swiss must preserve an international character in the domain of cultural relations. The more true nationality is indistinguishable from cultural community, the more this international character of the Swiss nationality will appear in its true light. It has become for Switzerland a vital principle, conferring upon it, within the family of the European states, an importance to which a population of three and half million inhabitants speaking one language could not lay claim today.

. . . For that very reason Switzerland has produced and realized ideas and principles which are a source of prosperity and development for the European states as a whole, and which will eventually insure peace in Europe. . . . If this ideal of the future comes true one day, the Swiss nationality whose character is international will have to become incorporated within the Greater European community. Thus it will not have lived in vain nor without glory.[27]

Thus the way is prepared for a federated Europe, a change Hugo and Mazzini described as a "transfiguration" of national vocation, though here it seems conceivable only in the case of a *nonunitary* nation, that is to say, a nation with a federal struc-

[27] Bluntschli, *Die schweizerische Nationalität* (1875).

ture. The "International of nationalisms," advocated by the prophets of 1848, brings to mind the idea of a universal Club of Misanthropes or a Friendly Society of Egoists. Such things may be written about, they cannot be done.

It is, however, interesting to note that Bluntschli, so conscious of the advantages of a true federation for the cantons that were formerly "sovereign states" within his country, shrinks from this solution when it is a question of applying to the whole of Europe. To the Scotsman James Lorimer, who had just published a project for a European federal state, Bluntschli opposed a plan that is far more cautiously confederative:

If a solution is to be found for the great problem of constituting a community of European states, the main condition to be met will be the scrupulous preservation of the independence and freedom of the member states.

The European States look upon themselves as sovereign persons, and they are all resolved to assert their sovereignty and not to submit to any influence due to the supremacy of another State. Although they can co-operate in carrying out common tasks, they will not voluntarily submit to the authority of a constitution that seems to them foreign. They will never renounce their own governments and their own armies; they will never tolerate a universal monarch above them or a single European parliament. This is why any European constitution setting up a single new European State, in which all previously sovereign States are to be incorporated, is unrealizable.

Therefore Bluntschli proposes a League of sovereign States (*Staatenbund*) under a Federal Council representing the States and under a Senate representing the peoples:

The preservation of peace among the peoples, deliberations and decisions taken with regard to European policy will be primarily in the hands of the Federal Council, under the control of the great powers. However, every more far-reaching measure of reorganization will require the Senate's approval.

Among the affairs pertaining to high policy, we must include all questions concerning the existence, independence, and freedom of the States, upon which the living conditions, security, and development of the peoples depend.

To settle all these questions, the only competent authority will be the community of the European States, which will be supplemented by a European popular representation—and the latter will be entitled to collaborate only under certain conditions. States in litigation will have to submit to the decisions of this authority. The latter will find the means to impose its resolutions only through collaboration between governments and peoples, and when possible, through close union between them, or at least through support of an important majority.

He concludes with typical Helvetian sobriety:

The new project for a European federal constitution is not too brilliant and has nothing extraordinary about it; it is modest and moderate; but considering that it is upon real forces that it relies, entrusting them to carry out the noble tasks envisaged by this ideal, it will be—or so I hope—more realizable and more effective than preceding projects.

Constantin Frantz (1817–1891), political philosopher, diplomat, and Prussian official (yet anything but a supporter of Prussian claims to hegemony), was not only one of the most zealous advocates of the federal type of German union but also drew up a plan for the union of the countries of central and northern Europe, a union which he regarded as the nucleus of a future world confederation on a Christian basis.[28] His primary concern was to hold in check the two imperialist powers—France in the west and Russia in the east; then, once the atmosphere had been cleared, to make them, as well as North America, join the union.

Constantin Frantz starts from his personal experience of a Germany only very recently unified, all the more fitted by her history to join with larger groupings. We may recall that Bluntschli had conceived a unified Europe on the Swiss model.

It leaps to the eye that in a country so constituted [Germany] no predominant center can oppose the natural development. . . . The very nature of things enables us to foresee that Germany is not suited to form a centralized unitary State, nor even, more generally speaking, to form a simple "self-contained" nation. This is because of the close relations which have always existed

[28] Frantz had in mind the following countries: Germany, Austria, Switzerland, the Scandinavian countries, Belgium, and Holland. An agreement was to be concluded with England concerning foreign policy.

between Germany and her neighbors, and which have been crucial to her development. . . .

If the German territory scarcely lends itself to the formation of a unitary State, this is even truer of the German nation, because it does not constitute a unified whole, but has always been, from its very beginnings—to use Schelling's words—"a people of peoples." [29]

Frantz saw clearly and stated that the unitary State could never serve as the basis of a federal union. So long as it keeps that form, union is impossible; only when its iron fetters have been broken, does union become possible—*tertium non datur:*

I pose the question: can a state of affairs be regarded as lasting when the facts are in flagrant contradiction with the written law? If it is admitted that the law turns its back on the facts, as things are at present, this means that the formation of a pure unitary state is close at hand. It is not impossible that we will witness this transformation; but assuming that the unitary State has been constituted and is developing to its ultimate consequences, the nation crushed by it would not tolerate it for long, and would quickly break out of the straitjacket forced upon it. This is one of the terms of our alternative. On the other hand, if we would escape from the present unitary current, we shall have to change the present state of affairs. *Tertium non datur.* . . .

If such a change came about, one could seriously envisage the possibility of a Central European federation. And every step taken in that direction would be an advance in two respects: such a federation would not only create a new market, whose importance would be measured by the size of the federation itself, it would also make possible the creation of such a mass of defensive forces that each member State could reduce its standing army, which would be a saving in the military budget and would release considerable manpower for more productive work. No power in the world would dare to attack such a federation which, at the same time, could in no wise display aggressive tendencies. Thus a system would be created for the maintenance of peace, a system such as Europe has never seen before. And what honor for Germany if she could be the basis of a federation

[29] This and the following excerpts are taken from C. Frantz, *Der Federalismus als das leitende Prinzip für die soziale, staatliche und internationale Organisation, unter besonderer Bezugnahme auf Deutschland, Kritisch nachgewiesen und Konstruktive dargestellt* (1879).

for peace, instead of being the creator of European militarism, which has been sucking our own blood ever since the system of 1866 went into force.

However great the real obstacle to the foundation of the Central European federation—and we are the last to indulge in illusions—they could be effectively surmounted with proper foresight, energy, and patience. The main difficulty resides rather in people's attitudes, in the narrow opinions and false ideas which have prevailed until now. For instance, the idea of the State, from which there is nothing to hope anyhow. . . .

He renders justice to the primitive libertarian impulses that animate nationalities, but he also observes that these impulses have been carried too far:

This accounts for the present vogue for the nationality principle. It is a reaction against the absolutism of the last century, which almost entirely ignored and often even trampled nationalities underfoot, by treating the peoples as a mere taxable and recruitable mass . . . Just as every reaction goes beyond its original goal, nationality too has become absolute. . . .

The stage of self-contained nations is marked by temporary alliances between great Powers. This system has become obsolete. The future Federation requires permanent institutions:

It has been well established that the final goal of the organization is not the universal State, but a federation of peoples, which of course can develop, grow strong, and spread only gradually. This is what we call "alliances," which clearly are preliminary to such a process. By alliances, we designate temporary associations entered into for a specific purpose; whereas the federation will have a definitive character from the outset: its constitution will be for all time to come and it will be given agencies designed to last.

From this point of view, the political system called the "European concert of the great powers" comes to mind at once. Taken in its proper sense this term originally denoted merely a system of alliances. . . . If the great power system is examined closely, the very name betrays that it is exclusively based on the idea of power, and that it disregards the principles of both history and morality, along with the lofty goals of civilizations. The only purpose is to be or to become a great power. And considering

that several of the great powers are situated next to one another,
what end will they pursue primarily, if not that of increasing
their military strength? It is striking to discover that the predominance of the military element goes hand in hand with the
rule of money, so that the whole development of the peoples in
the last analysis is determined in the Stock Exchange or in the
barracks.

. . . All the small States are thus threatened with decline,
where they have not already fallen into decay. . . . On the
other hand, history shows that the small States have done a great
deal more, on the average and proportionately, to secure the
liberty of citizens and their political rights, as well as to advance
civilization, than the big States have, especially the great military powers. . . .

Let us, then, go forward! since this system saw the light of day
solely as the result of a historical process, the notion of "the
great big power" comes down to a mere historical category,
bound to disappear at the next stage of evolution, just as it had
appeared one day and for a time prevailed nearly everywhere. . . .

Is not the principle of nonintervention, that has long since
been proclaimed, tantamount to recognition that the policy of
the European concert has gone bankrupt? For this very reason,
this policy has become, so to speak, an "asystem." And now the
important task is devolved upon us to create a new system, that
is, an order founded on reality, which will regulate relations between European States, and will reinstate the law of nations
upon positive foundations, such as have been totally lacking in
recent years.

According to Frantz, this new political system is in keeping
with the developments of the period. It must be based on the
model of the German union, which excludes the hegemony of
any one State. Thus the nationalism condemned by Frantz in
its limited "state" form, reappears irresistibly in the purified
form of Germany's "European mission." We are now familiar
with this process, having illustrated it with quotations from
Gioberti, Mazzini, Lamartine, Hugo, Donoso-Cortés, and even
Bluntschli. A German voice was lacking in this chorus, and here
it is:

Obviously, such a federation cannot be set up all at once. It
must first be established on a real basis, such as can eventually

provide the impulse. . . . If it is Germany, where the cleavage within the Church began, that has most contributed to the decline of the community of western nations, it would be proper for this country to regard it as a duty to take active part in the restoration of this community, and to devote itself to this task in such a way as to make it possible for us to look forward to the transformation of the European system as a whole. . . .

Federalism alone can truly lead to this result; it alone, however slight the part it plays in present politics, is the principle of the political evolution of the future.

3:   A Centuries-Old Problem:
Russia and Europe

Is IT UP to France, to Italy, or to Germany, or even to federalist Switzerland, to create Europe and to become one with it, thereby fulfilling a national, universal vocation? No, say the Russians, it is up to Russia! According to most nineteenth-century Russian thinkers, it was Russia that had the mission to regenerate and unify Europe, for only thus could Russia become European.

Whether Europe is united or not, France, Germany, Italy, and Switzerland are incontestably parts of it. But the case of Russia is different. She can choose to be or not to be a part of Europe, according to whether Europe will or will not correspond to the Russian ideas of humanity, Christianity, and the social order. Does this extraordinary claim have any basis in fact? Is it justified theoretically? Or is it merely a fantasy, a need to overcompensate for the fact that Russia lagged behind the West on the score of "progress"—a progress it both envied and reviled?

Since it is our intention, in this book, to present texts and let them speak for themselves, we shall first recall the West's contradictory attitudes to Russia, and then go on to the two antagonistic schools of thought which divided the Russian elite on the question of Europe. Lastly we will cite Dostoevsky, our leading witness, at some length.

European Opinions on Russia from Voltaire
to Karl Marx

We have seen that Sully excluded Russia from his Grand Design, that Leibniz attempted to include her (though not without reservations) in Europe's spiritual whole, that William Penn accepted her in his League of Nations, and that their utopian successors counted on Russian power to drive back the Turks. Then toward the end of the eighteenth century the trend was reversed. Russia suddenly became the danger, against which it would be desirable to unite and reach an agreement with the Turks.

Voltaire and his contemporaries still held that Europe ended at the river Don; beyond lay "Muscovy" and "Scythia," and these were in Asia. . . . To them, the enlightened Czarina Catherine *le* Grand (as the Prince de Ligne called her), far from being a menace, was a friend, almost a fellow conspirator. A little later, however, in 1790, Melchior Grimm, the first literary gazetteer in Paris, in one of his letters to the same empress, made this sensational prophecy, which so many men greater than he have kept repeating down to our own day:

Two Empires will divide between them . . . all the advantages of civilization, power, genius, letters, arts, armaments, and industry: Russia in the east, and America, which has become free in our own time, in the west. The rest of us, the peoples of the nucleus, will have become too degraded, too debased, to remember what we were, save for some vague and inexact traditions.

From that moment on, America and Russia were to haunt the historical imagination of the *"peuples du noyau."* America and Russia were looked upon as the "countries of the future" destined to succeed Europe after her wars and spiritual conflicts had utterly exhausted her.

In 1797, Johannes von Müller prophesied that "the future will belong either to Russia or to America."

Napoleon, in the *Mémorial de Sainte-Hélène,* foresees that the world will soon be "the American Republic or the Russian universal monarchy," and that Europe will not be able to stand up against any Russian leader worthy of the name:

Let there appear, he said, a valiant, impetuous, capable, emperor of Russia, in short, a Czar with guts [Napoleon, however, used a far more vigorous expression], and Europe will be his. He can begin his operations on the German soil, a hundred leagues from the two capitals, Berlin and Vienna, whose sovereigns will be his only obstacles. . . .

. . . If need be, he could, while crossing the Alps, throw a few firebrands down on Italian soil—ready to explode anyway—and keep on marching right into France, whose liberator he will once again proclaim himself. Assuredly, in his place, I should reach Calais on schedule, traveling by stages, and there I would find myself master and arbiter of Europe.

In 1823 the Abbé de Pradt, a contemporary of Metternich, published an essay, *Parallel Between English and Russian Power in Relation to Europe.* In it he proves that America ("that other England") and Russia are destined, the one to renovate the old world, and the other to attempt to dominate it. Anticipating Churchill in the use of the expression "Iron Curtain," he wrote:

Beyond the Vistula falls a curtain behind which it is hard to see clearly what is going on within the Russian empire. The Russian government which originated in the East, and has kept many of its customs, is concentrated in the ruler's private study. He alone speaks, hardly ever writes, and publishes nothing. With a country so constituted as to conceal everything from public knowledge, we are virtually reduced to conjecture; and it is only conjecturally that we may speak of the Russian army. . . .

. . . From Peter the Great down to our own day, Russia's politics has never stopped being one of conquest; it is as though for a whole century her government has consisted entirely of one man, always the same, so true it is that it has had only one idea, always the same, namely methodical aggrandizement.

Sainte-Beuve, commenting on and paraphrasing Thiers, noted in his *Cahiers,* in 1847:

There are only two peoples left. Russia is still barbarian, but big. . . . Old Europe will have to reckon with this *youth.* The other youth, is America. . . . The future of the world is there, between these two great powers. They will clash some day, and when they do, struggles will be seen of which the past can give no idea, at least in respect of mass and physical shock. . . .

Czarist Russia invariably represents Despotism and Autocracy, and the United States Democracy, even when they are not named. Thus:

Carlo Cattaneo, in 1848: [30]

The great prophecies are coming true, there is storm over the ocean, the waves are being whipped up by two cross currents: toward the Autocrat of Europe, toward the United States of Europe.

At about the same time Tocqueville (whom we shall presently quote at greater length) wrote in the same vein:

When I consider the stage already reached by several European nations, a stage to which they are all tending, I feel inclined to believe that soon there will be left room among them only for democratic freedom or Caesarian tyranny.

Jakob Burckhardt, in 1869: [31]

It is clear to me, and has been for a long time, that the world is moving toward the following alternative: either total Democracy or absolute Despotism.

Finally an American voice, Henry Adams, in 1900: [32]

The sum of my certainty is that America has a very clear century of start over Russia, and that western Europe must follow us for a hundred years before Russia can swing her flail over the Atlantic.

But the most famous and the most precise formulation of what I should like to call "the European myth of the two Great Powers" is to be found in *Democracy in America,* published in 1835 by the Count Alexis Clérel de Tocqueville (1805–1859):

[30] Cattaneo, *Considerazioni in fine del primo volume dell'Archivio triennale.*

[31] Burckhardt, *Historische Fragmente,* ed. W. Kaegi (Basel, 1942), p. 142.

[32] *Letters of Henry Adams (1892–1918),* pp. 347–48, quoted in Erik von Kuehnelt-Leddihn, *Freiheit oder Gleichheit?* (1953), which contains a remarkable chapter titled "The Russian Danger and Europe."

There are at the present time two great nations in the world, which started from different points, but seem to tend towards the same end. I allude to the Russians and the Americans. Both of them have grown up unnoticed; and while the attention of mankind was directed elsewhere, they have suddenly placed themselves in the front rank among the nations, and the world learned their existence and greatness at almost the same time.

All other nations seem to have nearly reached their natural limits and they have only to maintain their power; but these are still in the act of growth.[33] All the others have stopped or continue to advance with extreme difficulty; these alone are proceeding with ease and celerity along a path to which no limit can be perceived. The American struggles against the obstacles that nature opposes to him; the adversaries of the Russian are men. The former combats the wilderness and savage life; the latter, civilization with all its arms. The conquests of the American are therefore gained by the plowshare; those of the Russian by the sword. The Anglo-American relies upon personal interest to accomplish his ends and gives free scope to the unguided strength and common sense of the people; the Russian centers all the authority of society in a single arm. The principal instrument of the former is freedom; of the latter, servitude. Their starting point is different and their courses are not the same; yet each of them seems marked out by the will of Heaven to sway the destinies of half the globe.[34]

It will be noted that Tocqueville does not fail to stress his preference for America. As though the evolution he foretells implied not so much a double fatality as an alternative, which gives Europe the chance of a final choice; this choice, though inevitable, will nonetheless be her *choice*.

Most of the countless authors from the end of the eighteenth century to our own day who have tried to foresee the future of our continent think along similar lines; the very fact that they come out for or against one of the young successor empires proves that they have not given up all hope, although pessimism tends to prevail. If they had enough faith in the fate of Europe, they would say no to both empires, calmly and for perfectly

[33] The population of Russia increases proportionately more rapidly than that of any other country in the Old World.—*Tocqueville.*

[34] Tocqueville, *Democracy in America* (New York: Alfred A. Knopf, 1945), I, 434.

good reasons. If they thought, as Ernst von Lasaulx wrote in 1856, that Europe must inevitably be ground "between the two millstones," they would not be so passionately for or against one of the millstones. In fact, their choices reveals an anxiety of the imagination rather than an immediate horizonless anguish.

We have seen above that Turgot, Gibbon, and Condorcet, and later Goethe, Schlegel, and Hegel, saluted America as the great sanctuary for the freedoms and treasures of Europe. On the other hand, the virulent and contemptuous criticism of the "country of the dollar and its 'materialism,'" from Joseph de Maistre to Georges Sorel, skipping over Proudhon and Renan, was to keep mounting down to our own day, when it has become a commonplace among nationalists of both the extreme Right and the extreme Left.

Far rarer are authors who, like Jean Paul, Franz von Baader, and Schelling, chose to pin their hopes on Russia. Fear of pan-Slavism and "Russian despotism"—well before the Soviet era!—has never ceased to haunt conservatives, liberals, and socialists. Only a few Catholics of the extreme Right, like Joseph de Maistre, Ernst von Lasaulx, and the Spaniard Donoso-Cortés, by a seeming paradox betray, if not a tendency to minimize the Russian peril, at least a secret willingness to imagine the possibility of just punishment inflicted on our democracies by Moscow. . . .

With his customary calmness and sobriety, Leopold von Ranke said in 1824, in his earliest work:

> We must be on guard against opposing Europe and America; what is found over there is but a development from our own blood and our own way of life: in fact, New York and Lima are more important to us than Kiev or Smolensk.

To be sure, the Russians, says Ranke, rendered a great service to Europe by protecting her from the Mongols. But their way of westernizing themselves remains, in his eyes, "linked to the tendency to assimilate the material aspects of Western culture." [35]

[35] Ranke, *Geschichte der romanischen und germanischen Völker* (Leipzig, 1824).

On the Left, all the men of 1848 raised their voices against the Russian oppression of Poland and Hungary. Bruno Bauer, Gioberti, and Mazzini, and later Michelet, denounced pan-Slavism. Heine saw Russia as a Medusa's head, with arms extending from the Bosporus toward Asia, Africa, and Europe; Europeans will have to seek their salvation in the United States.

On the Right: The Marquis de Custine, in his famous account of a visit to Russia, *Russia in 1839*, foretells the frightening awakening of the Russian giant, whereupon "violence will put an end to the reign of the word":

An ambition inordinate and immense, one of those ambitions which could only possibly spring in the bosoms of the oppressed, and could only find nourishment in the miseries of a whole nation, ferments in the hearts of the Russian people. That nation, essentially aggressive, greedy under the influence of privations, expiates beforehand, by a debasing submission, the design of exercising a tyranny over other nations: the glory, the riches which it hopes for, consoles for the disgrace to which it submits. To purify himself from the foul and impious sacrifice of all public and personal liberty, the slave, upon his knees, dreams of the conquest of the world.

. . . Russia sees in Europe a prey which our dissensions sooner or later yield to it; she foments anarchy among us in the hope of profiting by a corruption which she favours, because it is favourable to her views: it is the history of Poland recommencing on a larger scale. For many years past Paris has read revolutionary journals paid by Russia. "Europe," they say at Petersburg, "is following the road that Poland took; she is enervating herself by a vain liberalism, whilst we continue powerful precisely because we are not free; let us be patient under the yoke; others shall some day pay for our shame."

The views that I reveal here may appear chimerical to minds engrossed with other matters; their truth will be recognized by every man initiated in the march of European affairs and in the secrets of cabinets, during the last twenty years.[36]

Lasaulx himself wonders whether one day "the Communist right wing will not be called Russia." And Constantin Frantz:

Just as the Macedonian influence contributed to the disintegration of Hellenism, so the Russian influence—even to a greater

[36] Marquis de Custine, *Russia in 1839* (London, 1954).

degree—has a dissolving and corrupting effect on the Western system.

The same opinion is expressed, with greater precision and a lucidity that today turns out to be prophetic, by Jakob Burckhardt:

The fate of Europe has been tragic because its perpetual changes and revolutions are determined by an almost mechanical external power, which is very little concerned with the Western nations' joys and sorrows, their spirit or their high aspirations, and which nonetheless constitutes the principal weight on the scales, and exerts a restraining or revolutionizing influence as it sees fit.[37]

However, the harshest judgments on Russia's policies, on her anti-European imperialism and Machiavellianism, are those expressed by the founders of communism, Marx and Engels.

Karl Friedrich Marx (1818–1883) all his life shared with his first master, Hegel, an absolute conviction that western Europe was the most "gifted" (*begabt*) part of the world, the most advanced, the most civilized, the most mature, the most capable of shaping the future of mankind. (He would have been embarrassed if he had been asked to state the reason for this paradoxical superiority, for he held that culture was merely a by-product of material and quantitative processes.) Like his friend Engels, he hailed the movements for national liberation among the Poles, Hungarians, and Germans (all of them crushed by Russia's interventions) as so many "dialectical" stages in the march toward the final union of Europeans, in a society without classes and without nations. He was, however, convinced that this union could never be brought about by the liberal bourgeoisie or by idealists like Mazzini, whom he ridiculed pitilessly, but only by the proletariat, which was to be victorious first in France:

The fall of the bourgeoisie in France, the triumph of the French working class, the emancipation of the working class in general, this is how the problem of European liberation will be solved.[38]

[37] Burckhardt, *Historische Fragmente*, ed. W. Kaegi (Basel, 1942), Fragment 190.
[38] Marx, *Aus dem literarischen Nachlass* (Stuttgart, 1913), IV, 131.

To be sure, bourgeois England would not fail to oppose this development, but a "world war" would compel her to assume "the leadership of the revolutionary movement."

Moreover, Marx believed that the United States was to form an integral part of the West and would intervene in Europe. He wrote in 1853:

The great event of the day is the appearance of American policy on the European horizon. Saluted by one party, detested by the other, the fact is admitted by all. . . . At Beirut the Americans have abstracted another Hungarian refugee from the claws of the Habsburg eagle. It is cheering to see the American intervention in Europe beginning just with the Eastern Question. . . . [The possession of Constantinople is] the hotly controverted and permanent subject of dispute between the East and the West—and America is the youngest and most vigorous representative of the West.[39]

But the great adversary of this liberation of Europe was—and according to Marx would always be—Russia, a power intermediate between progressive Europe and "Mongol barbarism," whose policy aiming at world hegemony would never cease to deceive the European nations:

Counting on the cowardice and apprehensions of the Western Powers, he [the Czar] bullies Europe, and pushes his demands as far as possible, in order to appear magnanimous afterwards, by contenting himself with what is immediately wanted . . .

Russian policy, with its traditional craft, cheats, and subterfuges, may impose upon the European Courts, which themselves are but traditional things, but it will prove utterly powerless with the revolutionized peoples . . .

In a speech delivered in 1867 Marx stated explicitly that the permanent objective of Russian policy, its "polar star," is world domination.

Now there are many people who are naive enough to believe that all that [Russian imperialism] has changed, that Poland has ceased to be "a necessary nation," as a French writer called it, and is now only a sentimental memory. . . . But I ask you, what

[39] Marx, articles in the *New York Tribune*, from 1853 to 1856, published in 1897 under the title *The Eastern Question.*

is there that has changed? Has the danger diminished? No, only the intellectual blindness of the ruling classes in Europe has reached its zenith . . . The policy of Russia is changeless, according to the admission of its official historian, the Muscovite Karamzin. Its methods, its tactics, its maneuvers may change, but the polar star of its policy—world domination—is a fixed star.

However, Marx foresaw the final fall of Russia's inborn despotism—as a result of the "progress of the masses" and the "power of ideas"—restoring the "power and unity of Europe." In one of the nearly five hundred articles which Marx published in the *New York Tribune* between 1851 and 1861, we find the following lines that appeared on December 30, 1853:

The people of the West will rise again to power and unity of purpose, while the Russian Colossus itself will be shattered by the progress of the masses and explosive force of ideas.

Needless to say, Marx could refer only to Czarist Russia, but his prophecy, though not quite confirmed by the events of 1917, has not lost its pertinence today.

RUSSIAN OPINIONS ON EUROPE FROM CHADAEV
TO TOLSTOY

In the Kiev era, Russia was oriented to the West. In the epoch of the Golden Horde, Russia was oriented toward Asia. Muscovite Russia, after she shook off the Tartar dominion, considered herself, in the words of the monk Philoteus (addressed to Ivan III), the political and spiritual "Third Rome": a Rome as theocratic as Byzantium, if we are to believe Ivan the Terrible's claim to have held not only political power but also the power of saving souls. Finally, Peter the Great forcibly opened Russia to Europe. During the reign of Catherine the Great, the French Encyclopedists ruled Russia by letters. At the beginning of the nineteenth century came the turn of the German philosophers— Baader, Görres, Hegel, and above all Schelling. The great debate between Slavophiles and Westernizers was to develop against this very complex background.

The Slavophile saw in it [Peter's work] the betrayal of the original national basis of Russian life, a violation and interruption of its organic development. The Westernizers saw nothing original and distinctive whatever in Russian history; they considered Russia as only a backwater in enlightenment and civilization. The Western European type of civilization was for them the only hope.[40]

After the Napoleonic wars, the Russia of Alexander (and later of Nicholas I) was still a country where the peasants were serfs, but her intellectual elite, her intelligentsia, as it was to be called, was reading Saint-Simon, Fourier, and the German Romantic philosophers. The question of the day was that of the relations between Russia and Europe. The first important answer to it was given by a convinced Westernizer.

Piotr Chadaev (1796–1856), ex-officer of the Guard, disciple of de Maistre, Bonald, and Schelling, in 1836 published the first of his *Philosophical Letters* (translated from the French into Russian) in a Moscow magazine. All the ambivalences we shall later find in his Russian friends, enemies, and successors, are present in germ in these letters: "He negates the history of his country," writes Berdyaev, "and his negation is the very type of the Russian negation." He wants Russia to become European, and he asserts that the Russian people alone is capable of solving the spiritual and social problems of the West. After the Czar had him declared insane, he published *Apology of a Madman,* in which he reiterates his condemnation of the Russian past, and at the same time his faith in the Messianic destiny of the Russian people. Here is the luminous definition of Europe which he contrasts with the pregnant darkness of Russia: [41]

The peoples of Europe have a common physiognomy, a family likeness. Despite the overall division of these peoples into a Latin and a Teutonic branch, into southerners and northerners, there is a common bond that unites them all in one cluster, very visible

[40] Nicolas Berdyaev, *The Origin of Russian Communism,* translated from the Russian by R. M. French (Ann Arbor: Ann Arbor Paperbacks [University of Michigan Press], 1960).

[41] Chadaev, *Lettres sur la Philosophie de l'Histoire,* ed. Gershenson (Moscow, 1913), pp. 81–88.

to anyone who has closely studied their history. You know that not so long ago all of Europe called itself Christendom, and this term had its place in public law. Apart from this general character, each of these peoples has a particular character, but all this is merely History and tradition. This constitutes the hereditary patrimony of ideas among these peoples. Every individual there enjoys its usufructs, picks without labor or fatigue these notions scattered in society, and turns them to his own profit. Make the parallel yourselves and see what we can pick in this way through the mere exchange of elementary ideas, so as to make what we can of them in the way of directing our own lives. And note that we do not refer here to study or reading, to anything literary or scientific, but only to the meeting of minds; to the ideas which take possession of the child in his cradle, which surround him in the midst of his games, which his mother whispers to him as she fondles him; which, in the form of various feelings, penetrate into the marrow of his bones with the air he breathes, and which shape his moral being even before he is handed over to society and the world. Do you want to know what these ideas are? They are the ideas of duty, justice, right, order. They derive from the very events which constituted society there: they are the integral elements of the social world in these countries.

That is the atmosphere of the West: it is more than history, more than psychology, it is the very physiology of European man. What is there to put in its place in our country?

All the nations of Europe advanced hand in hand over the centuries. No matter how they may diverge today each in its own way, they always find themselves again on the same road. To understand the family development of these peoples, it is not necessary to study history. Just read Tasso, and see them all prostrate before the walls of Jerusalem. Recall that for fifteen centuries they had but one language for speaking with God, but one single moral authority, but one faith. Think that for fifteen centuries, every year, the same day at the same hour, in the same words, all together raised their voices to the Supreme Being, to celebrate His glory in the greatest of His blessings.

However, Chadaev does not believe that Russia is of Europe, although she is destined to save Europe by adopting her forms of thought, her sense of time, continuity, unity. . . .

In his *Philosophical Letters* he goes back to the idea that Russia gave nothing to the world:

Alone in the world, we have given nothing to the world, we have taught the world nothing; we have not added a single idea to the mass of human ideas; we have not contributed anything to the progress of the human mind, and we have disfigured everything this progress gave us. We never took the trouble to imagine anything of ourselves, and of all that others have imagined, we have borrowed merely superficial appearances and futile luxuries.[42]

In a letter of 1835 he carries his self-criticism to a "dialectical" point where it "tilts over" into its opposite: from the Russian wilderness the Messiah of European culture is to emerge:

Therefore we must not run after the others, the Western Europeans: we must make a frank appraisal of ourselves, see ourselves as we are, leave all shams behind, and stand in the midst of the truth. When we have that we can begin to advance, and we shall advance more rapidly than the others, because we came after them, because we have all their experience and the labor of all the centuries that have preceded us. The people of Europe are strangely mistaken about us. There is M. Jouffroy, for instance, who tells us that we are destined to civilize Asia. This is fine; but let us ask him what peoples of Asia did we ever civilize, please? Apparently the Siberian mastodons and other fossil populations, the only races we have rescued from darkness, so far as I know, and even here we needed the help of Pallas and Fischer. They keep giving us the East; it seems to be a kind of instinct in the European nationality to push us back to the East so as not to run into us in the West. Let us not be taken in by their involuntary artifice; let us try to discover our future ourselves and not expect others to tell us what we have to do. The East belongs to the masters of the sea, this is obvious; we are farther removed from it than the English, and we are no longer in the epoch when all eastern revolutions started in Central Asia. The new Chart of the East India Company, that is the true civilizatory element in Asia now. On the contrary, it is Europe that we are destined to instruct in countless things she would never have dreamed of save for us. Do not laugh, you know this is my innermost conviction. A day will come when we will be in the thick of political Europe, more powerful by virtue of our intelligence than we are today by virtue of our material strength. Such will be the logical result of our long isolation: the great things of the world have always come out of the wil-

[42] *Ibid.*, p. 84.

derness. The powerful voice that has just resounded in the world will serve singularly to hasten the consummation of our destinies. Stricken with amazement and terror, Europe has rejected us angrily; the fatal page of our history, written in Peter the Great's own hand, has been torn up; thank God, we are no longer of Europe; from this moment forward, therefore, our universal mission has begun.

Chadaev is here very close to the fiercest critics of his *Apology of a Madman.*

A year later, in 1837, the first number of the Slavophiles' magazine appeared. The Slavophiles advocated cultural and spiritual nationalism, pure orthodoxy, and the ancestral ways of peasant Russia, such as the *mir.* Thus they were opposed to "Europeanism"—and yet the magazine was called *Europa!* Through the pen of Ivan Kireyevsky, its main contributor, it opposed to Europe the notion of enthusiasm, which according to him had remained the privilege of the Russians, and which the Western countries had lost; this notion, however, happens to be borrowed from Schelling. . . . In the face of a shattered, disunited, unreligious, revolutionary, materialistic, and smugly bourgeois Europe, Russia's authentic mission is to undo the work of Peter the Great; Europe's salvation will come from Russia. To Kireyevsky and his friends, the notion of organizational hegemony is essential:

To make sure that the unity of Europe will come about organically and harmoniously, a definite center must exist, a nation that dominates the others by virtue of its political and cultural superiority.

All great European nations have successively exercised this hegemony. But they are exhausted. America is merely a projection of them. Only Russia, though she is not European and perhaps for that very reason, remains capable of restoring Europe by bringing it into conformity with the Russian genius. At the same time, however, this can be done only with Europe's help. . . .

Our nationality has so far been a crude, barbarian nationality, as static as the Chinese. To civilize it, to elevate it, to give it life and the capacity for developing would be possible only through the mediation of a foreign influence. Since until now our whole civilization has been inspired by foreign countries, it is only from abroad that we can receive it, at least until such time as we are equals with the rest of Europe. Then, when the common civilization of Europe coincides with our own, there will arise a truly Russian civilization, expression of the spiritual life of an educated nation, a stable, deep, living civilization, full of fortunate consequences for Russia and for mankind.

Such are the premises of the debate that was to animate the intelligentsia down to the end of the century. It must be confessed that in the eyes of a European of today, the theses common to the two schools (European decadence, Russian Messianism in both the religious and the social sense) seem more striking than the points of disagreement (appraisal of the Russian past, stress on religion and its social consequences, or, on the contrary, on a socialism strongly marked by Byzantine dogmatism).

Nicolas Berdyaev, in a striking passage in *The Origin of Russian Communism*, gives a description of the Russian intelligentsia, which the recent history of the U.S.S.R. illustrates and confirms.

Russians possess a particular faculty for assimilating Western ideas and doctrines and giving them an original form. But the assimilation of Western ideas and doctrines by the Russian intelligentsia was for the most part a matter of dogma. What was scientific theory in the West, a hypothesis, or in any case a relative truth, making no claim to be universal, became among the Russian intelligentsia a dogma, a sort of religious revelation.

Russians are always inclined to take things in a totalitarian sense; the sceptical criticism of Western peoples is alien to them. This is a weakness which leads to the confusion of thought and the substitution of one thing for another, but it is also a merit and indicates the religious integration of the Russian soul. Among the Russian radical intelligentsia, there existed an idolatrous attitude to science itself. When a member of the Russian intelligentsia became a Darwinist, Darwinism to him was not a biological theory subject to dispute, but a dogma, and anyone who did not accept that dogma (e.g., a disciple of Lamarck) awoke in him an attitude of moral suspicion. The greatest Russian philosopher of the nineteenth century, Soloviev, said that the Russian intelligentsia professed a faith based upon the strange syllogism: man is descended from a monkey, therefore we ought to love one another.[43]

It is understandable that Lev Tolstoy (1828–1910), in the Preamble to his pamphlet *The Decembrists*, should have mocked his own age, an age of

magazines waving the most unlike banners, developing European principles in a European sense, but with a Russian philosophy, and magazines of an exclusively Russian tendency, developing Russian principles, but with a European philosophy. . . . Everybody was trying to dig up new questions and solve them, everybody wrote, read, orated, drew up projects, wanted to reform, to destroy, to change everything—all the Russians were in a state of indescribable exaltation . . .

Who can tell whether Tolstoy feels closer to the Slavophiles than to the Westernizers when he writes: [44]

There is no reason to believe that the Russians are necessarily subject to the law of progress, which governs the European peoples, nor that this progress is a blessing . . .
The Russian people should not become proletarians, in imitation of the peoples of Europe and America, but on the contrary, they should solve the land problem by abolishing land ownership, and show other nations the way to a sensible, free and happy life, outside industrial, factory, or capitalistic coercion and slavery. Such is its high historical mission.

To be sure, to a Slavophile theologian like Vladimir Soloviev, Russia's mission is entirely contained in the spirituality of the Orthodox faith, while according to the pro-Western revolutionary Alexander Herzen (1812–1870), "the Russian people is a social people par excellence, one that strives to realize the social and economical order here below." In either case, we have Mission and Messianism, Russia's mission (divine or historical) face to face with a Europe that has lost the true religion or lacks true social sense.

In the last analysis, cannot the debate between Russia and Europe be reduced to the fundamental debate between the East and the West concerning the role and nature of "civilization"

[43] N. Berdyaev, *op. cit.*
[44] Tolstoy, *A Great Iniquity* (1905).

itself? One of the greatest lyric poets of Russia, Fyodor Ivan Tiutchev (1803–1873), suggests just this:

One great disadavantage of our position is the fact that we are obliged to give the name of Europe to something which should always be called by its right name: Civilization.

DOSTOEVSKY AND RUSSIA'S MISSION

All these contradictions, real or apparent, are to be found, in highly concentrated form, as nervously intense as Van Gogh's cross-hatchings, as piled up as his clouds, in the works of Dostoevsky. To the question whether Russia belongs or does not belong to Europe, no one has given a fuller, more sincere, or more desperately ambivalent answer. In our day many Europeans protest against an alleged "exclusion of Russia," for which, they claim, European statesmanship, not Stalin, is responsible. Is not Dostoevsky part of Europe's cultural treasure? Let us see what he himself had to say.

In 1876 Fyodor Mikhailovich Dostoevsky (1821–1881) began to publish *The Diary of a Writer,* a monthly journal to which he was the sole contributor. A whole book might be put together with the passages he devoted to the relations between Russia and Europe. Here are a few short excerpts.[45]

The author refers repeatedly to the theme of the Orthodox Church's vocation. In this Church "the divine countenance of Christ has been preserved in all its purity. This is perhaps the Russian people's mission, that it had to preserve this image in order to reveal it to a world that has gone astray."

This "world" is in fact Europe.

And in Europe . . . haven't all these cohesive forces, which we had so trusted, been converted into a sad mirage? Isn't their decomposition and segregation even worse than ours? These are questions which cannot be evaded by a Russian. Besides, what true Russian doesn't think first about Europe? . . . [p. 250]

At no time in the past has Europe been loaded with such elements of ill-will as at present. It seems that everything is under-

[45] Dostoevsky, *The Diary of a Writer,* trans. Boris Brasol (New York: Charles Scribner's Sons, 1949).

mined and loaded with powder, and is just waiting for the first spark. . . .

"And what's this to us? All this is there in Europe, and not at home!" Well, it is our concern because Europe will be knocking at our door, crying for help and urging us to save her when the last hour of her "present order of things" strikes. And she will demand our help, as it were, by right; she will demand it with a challenge, commandingly. She is going to tell us that we too are Europe; that, consequently, we have exactly the same "order of things" as she; that not in vain have we imitated her during two hundred years, boasting that we were Europeans, and that by saving her, we are thereby saving ourselves. . . . [p. 258]

And should Europe actually knock at our door, urging us to get up and march to save her *l'Ordre,* then, perhaps, for the first time, all of us would grasp at once to what extent all the while we did not resemble Europe, despite our two-hundred-year craving for, and dreams about, becoming Europe—dreams which used to reach the proportions of passionate fits. But even then, perhaps, we would not grasp it, since it would be too late. And, if so, we should naturally fail to understand what Europe would be expecting and soliciting from us, and how, actually, we could help her. And, on the contrary, should we not, maybe, march to subdue the enemy of Europe and of her order with the same iron and blood as even Prince Bismarck did? Oh, well, in the event of such an exploit, we could boldly congratulate ourselves upon being *thorough Europeans.* [pp. 258–59]

Moreover Dostoevsky thinks that Russia, though not belonging to Europe, will soon be the strongest nation in Europe:

In the March issue of my *Diary* I have recorded some of my meditations concerning the immediate future of Europe. However, no longer meditatingly but almost with certainty, it may be stated that very soon—perhaps, in the immediate future—Russia will prove stronger than any nation in Europe. This will come to pass because all great powers in Europe will be destroyed for the simple reason that they will be worn out and undermined by the unsatisfied democratic tendencies of an enormous portion of their lower-class subjects—their proletarians and paupers. In Russia, this cannot happen: our demos is content and, as time goes on, it will grow even more content because everything tends toward this condition, as a result of the general mood, or —more correctly—by general consensus. And therefore there will remain on the continent but one colossus—Russia. This will come to pass, perhaps, even much sooner than people think. The future of Europe belongs to Russia. [p. 296]

His repeated assertions (in his journal and in his novels) on the Russian's love for Europe, their "second homeland," in fact serve only to stress the existing duality, which some Europeans continue stubbornly to deny. According to Dostoevsky, this duality will be abolished only after all mankind has been united in the true religion—or absorbed by Russia, which no doubt comes down to the same thing in his mind.

We, Russians, have two motherlands—Russia and Europe—even in cases when we call ourselves Slavophiles: let them not be angry at me for this remark. This should not be disputed. The greatest among their great future designations, already apperceived by the Russians, is the designation common to the whole human race—service rendered to mankind as a whole, not only to Russia, not only to Slavs in general, but to humankind *in toto.* . . . [p. 342]

Very much of what we have taken from Europe and transplanted to Russia, we did not copy like slaves from their masters . . . but we have inoculated it into our organism, into our flesh and blood . . . [p. 42]

The French Convention of 1793, when sending the certificate of citizenship *Au poète allemand Schiller, l'ami de l'humanité* ["To the German poet Schiller, the friend of humanity"], did perpetrate a beautiful, stately and prophetic act, nevertheless it did not suspect that at the other end of Europe, in barbarous Russia, that same Schiller was much more national and much more akin to the barbarian Russians than to France—not only in those days but even later, throughout our whole century—where Schiller, the French citizen and *l'ami de l'humanité,* was known, and then but slightly, only by professors of literature, and not even by all of them. Yet, in Russia . . . he soaked into the Russian soul, left an impress upon it, and almost marked an epoch in the history of our development. This measure of Russian attitude toward world literature is an almost unprecedented phenomenon among other nations and all through world history . . . thereby proving the fact that every poet-innovator in Europe, everyone who appeared there with a novel thought and with fresh vigor, cannot help but become forthwith a Russian poet, cannot avoid Russian thought, and almost becomes a Russian force. [pp. 343–44]

No Russia will never belong to Europe . . . unless Europe becomes Russian. He is impassioned on this score:

Russia is something independent and peculiar, not resembling Europe at all, but important by itself. Besides, Europe herself is, perhaps, not in the least unjust when condemning Russians and scoffing at their revolutionary theories: it means that we are revolutionists not merely for the sake of destruction where we did not build—like the Huns and the Tartars—but for the sake of something different, something which, in truth, we do not know ourselves (and those who know, keep silent). In a word, we are revolutionists, so to speak, because of some personal necessity— if you please, by reason of conservatism. [p. 357]

They do not know that nothing in the world can conquer us; that we may, perhaps, be losing battles, but that nevertheless we shall remain invincible precisely because of the unity of our popular spirit, and by reason of the people's consciousness; that we are not France, which is all in Paris; that we are not Europe, which is altogether dependent upon the stock-exchanges of her bourgeoisie and the "tranquillity" of her proletarians which is being purchased—and this only for one hour—with the last resorts of their local governments. [p. 664]

If necessary, we shall draw the sword on behalf of the oppressed and unfortunate, even though to the detriment of our immediate advantage. But let at the same time our faith grow still firmer that precisely herein lies Russia's genuine mission, her strength and truth, and that the self-sacrifice for the oppressed and forsaken by everybody in Europe, in the interest of civilization, is a real service to its actual and true interests.

Nay, it is necessary that in political organisms the same Christ's truth be recognized as by any believer. Somewhere at least this truth must be preserved; some nation at least must radiate. Otherwise what would happen? [p. 609]

In the name of the true religion, and for their own good, the Europeans oppressed by a false civilization are invited to let themselves be enlightened and liberated by Holy Russia. If they do not accept, they will "sink into cynicism," and this will mean their end, an end "toward which they seem indeed to be moving."

In his novels Dostoevsky restates the same "ideas"—or rather prophecies—expounding them somewhat less breathlessly, more fully, and wistfully. What seemed contradictory in his articles becomes a play of poetic symbols. He is haunted by a "dream of Europe" which is dreamed successively by Stavroguin in *The Possessed*, by Versilov in *A Raw Youth*, and by the "ridiculous man" in *The Diary of a Writer*. We quote here the most complete and beautiful version found in *A Raw Youth*. The sunset in a painting by Claude Lorrain, after illuminating the Golden Age of European mankind, becomes suddenly the setting sun of the last day of civilization, when the hero learns that the Tuileries has been on fire.

I shall never forget my first moments in Europe. . . . I will tell you about one of my first impressions, one of the dreams I had in those days, a real dream. . . .

In the gallery at Dresden there is a picture by Claude Lorrain, called in the catalogue "Acis and Galatea," but I used to call it "The Golden Age," I don't know why. I had seen it before, but I had noticed it again in passing three days earlier. I dreamed of this picture, but not as a picture, but, as it were, a reality. I don't know exactly what I did dream though: it was just as in the picture, a corner of the Grecian Archipelago, and time seemed to have gone back three thousand years; blue smiling waves, isles and rocks, a flowery shore, a view like fairyland in the distance, a setting sun that seemed calling to me—there's no putting it into words. It seemed a memory of the cradle of Europe, and that thought seemed to fill my soul, too, with a love as of kinship. Here was the earthly paradise of man: the gods came down from the skies, and were of one kin with men. . . . Oh, here lived a splendid race! they rose up and lay down to sleep happy and innocent; the woods and meadows were filled with their songs and merry voices. Their wealth of untouched strength was spent on simple-hearted joy and love. The sun bathed them in warmth and light, rejoicing in her splendid children . . . Marvelous dream, lofty error of mankind! The Golden Age is the most unlikely of all the dreams that have been, but for it men have given up their life and all their strength, for the sake of it prophets have died and been slain, without it the peoples will not live and cannot die, and the feeling of all this I lived through, as it were, in that dream; rocks and sea, and the slanting rays of the setting sun—all this I still seemed to see when I woke up and opened my eyes, literally wet with tears. I remembered that I was glad, a sensation of happiness I have never known before thrilled my heart till it ached; it was the love of all humanity. It was by then quite evening;

through the green of the flowers that stood in the windows of my little room, broke slanting rays that flooded me with light. And then, my dear—that setting sun of the first day of European civilization which I had seen in my dream was transformed for me at once on waking, into the setting sun of the last day of civilization! One seemed to hear the death-knell ringing over Europe in those days. I am not speaking of the war and the Tuileries; apart from that I knew that all would pass away, the whole face of the old world of Europe—sooner or later, but I, as a Russian European, could not accept it. Yes, they had only just burnt the Tuileries. . . .

Oh, rest assured, I know it was logical; I quite understand the irresistible force of the idea, but as the bearer of the idea of the highest Russian culture, I could not accept it, for the highest Russian thought is the reconciliation of ideas, and who in the whole world could understand such a thought at that time; I was a solitary wanderer. I am not speaking of myself personally—it's the Russian ideal I am speaking of. There all was strife and logic; there the Frenchman was nothing but a Frenchman, the German was nothing but a German, and this more intensely so than at any time in their whole history; consequently never had the Frenchman done so much harm to France, or the German to Germany, as just at that time! In those days in all Europe there was not one European; I alone among all the vitriol-throwers could have told them to their face that their Tuileries was a mistake. And I alone among the avenging reactionaries could have told them that the Tuileries, although a crime, was none the less logical. And that, my boy, was because I, as a Russian, was the only *European* in Europe. . . .[46]

"I emigrated," he went on; "and I regretted nothing I had left behind. I had served Russia to the utmost of my abilities as long as I was there; when I went away I went on serving her, too, but in a wider sense. But serving her in that way I served her far more than if I had remained only a Russian, just as the Frenchman at that time was a Frenchman, and the German only a German. In Europe they don't understand that yet. Europe has created a noble type of Frenchman, of Englishman, and of

[46] Cf. Dimitri Merejkovsky, in *Rule of the Antichrist* (Paris, 1921): "The Europeans, in Europe, are English, Italian, French, German. Only the Russians are universal Europeans. We have two fatherlands, Russia and Europe." Rousseau in *Government of Poland* deplored on the contrary that there were only Europeans in Europe, and no Frenchmen, Italians, Germans . . . (cf. *supra*, pp. 154–55). That was more than a hundred years earlier.

German, but of the man of the future she scarcely knows at present. And, I fancy, so far she does not want to know. And that one can well imagine; they are not free and we are not free. I, with my Russian melancholy, was the only one free in Europe. . . .

"Take note, my dear, of a strange fact: every Frenchman can serve not only his France, but humanity, only on condition that he remains French to the utmost possible degree, and it's the same for the Englishman and the German. Only to the Russian, even in our day, has been vouchsafed the capacity to become most of all Russian only when he is most European. . . . That is the most essential difference between us Russians and all the rest, and in that respect the position in Russia is as nowhere else. . . . Oh, it was not only the bloodshed in those days that appalled me, and it was not the Tuileries, but all that was bound to follow it. They are doomed to strife for a long time yet, because they are still too German and too French, and have not yet finished struggling in those national characters. And I regret the destruction that must come before they have finished. To the Russian, Europe is as precious as Russia: every stone in her is cherished and dear. Europe is as much our fatherland as Russia. Oh, even more so. . . . You must admit, my dear, the remarkable fact that for almost the last hundred years Russia has lived absolutely not for herself, but only for the other States of Europe! And, what of them! Oh, they are doomed to pass through fearful agonies before they attain the Kingdom of God." [47]

Finis Europae . . . In *The Brothers Karamazov*, Ivan speaks of his impending departure for Europe in the following terms: "I know very well that I am going to a graveyard, but it is the dearest of all graveyards."

Very close to the Russians by his spiritual passions, anticipating Nietzsche (who discovered him shortly before his mind gave way), Sören Kierkegaard (1813–1856) belongs to his century just as the eye belongs to the tomb of Cain,[48] though it was not until our own day that this was recognized. How is he to be classified? All existentialism stems from him, yet it is the opposite of a system. Let us place him at the end of one chapter,

---

[47] Dostoevsky, *A Raw Youth*, trans. Constance Garnett (New York: The Macmillan Company), excerpts from Part III, chap. vii, 2–3.
[48] The allusion is to Hugo's well-known poem *Cain.—Translator's note.*

before the beginning of the next, as he might have wished, he who requested that "The Lonely One" be inscribed on his grave.

All Europe, impatiently, with mounting passion, is trying vainly to solve worldly problems that can be solved only by the godhead and that Christianity alone could solve, in fact, solved long ago. Since the Fourth Estate—that is, all men—made its appearance, it has become impossible to move one step ahead toward the solution of the problem of man's equality with man in accordance with the law of this world which is diversity; yes, even if all movement in Europe were stopped, if we were to swim in blood, if all ministers were to lose their sleep through excess of reflection, and if every day a dozen of them lost their minds, while a dozen others were to pick up the problem at the point the others had left it, risking madness in their own turn—this road is barred forever; and this frontier scorns all human efforts, scorns the pettiness of the temporal in the face of the supreme and lordly seignorial right of the eternal, when the temporal pretends to explain in worldly terms what must remain a riddle in time, and what the eternal alone can and will explain. The problem is religious. . . . To conquer the eternal, massacres and bombardments may be necessary, *item*, many ministers may have to lose their minds. . . . But no one can know how much time will be spent in sheer convulsions.[49]

4: From Historicism to Pessimism

WHEN WE TURN abruptly from the passionately ambivalent or apocalyptic pages that the Russians devoted to Europe to the calm, objective and classical works by the great German historian Leopold von Ranke (1795–1886), we are confronted with a dilemma. Either the Russians are raving no end, expressing only what goes on in their own minds, or the sober interpreter of Europe has simply failed to see the realities among which he lived for nearly a century. At all events, the two worlds are not contemporary, despite the dates. When we ask which is true, it would be vain to hope for a serious answer: the method used in each case are not comparable, the aims in view are of different orders.

[49] Kierkegaard, *Posthumous Papers* (Danish edition), IX B, 10.

In more than one sense Ranke is the antithesis of Hegel, by his will to objectivity, spiritual sobriety, controlled description of "what really happened," and by his rejection of any dialectical system that ignores the facts and attributes capacity for evolution to some undefined immanent force. "Each generation is immediate to God," as the famous formula goes.

According to him, a nation conquers the right to play an active part in history only by its "culture." For this reason he grants primacy to Europe as a whole, which he defines as the "Romano-Germanic" domain: Italy-France-Spain on the one hand, Germany-England-Scandinavia on the other. By his conquest of the Gauls, Caesar made possible this configuration which was first unified by Charlemagne, "prince of culture." Under the leadership of the Roman popes and the Germanic emperors, "the interrelationship of all of Europe" has never stopped developing and asserting itself. Ranke does not think at all that the conflict between Papacy and Empire, and later between Catholicism and the Reformation were great misfortunes, for this bipolarity "has deep roots in the very nature of things, and it is even thanks to these conflicts that the spirit of Europe came of age." In other words, these were fruitful tensions, not catastrophic rifts; they must not prevent the historian faithful to facts from seeing "that the complex of the Christian states of Europe must be regarded as a whole, as a kind of State."

To be sure, Ranke saw that the essential unity of Europe was far more seriously threatened by the absolute national sovereignties:

However, those who try to regard this ever greater importance assumed by national sovereignties as a mere tendency of world history are utterly deaf to the danger signaled. The fact is that as a result of all these efforts, so many destructive tendencies have joined together that if they ever gained the upper hand, culture and Christianity themselves would be threatened.[50]

He undoubtedly underestimated the imminence and the scope of the danger. His last works—contemporary with Dostoevsky's

[50] Ranke, *Sämtliche Werke,* Vol. IX, 2, p. 235.

The Diary of a Writer—glorify Europe's civilization and Christian spirit as the *summum bonum* of humanity.

Let us elevate ourselves—and I don't mean in fantasy, but on the basis of a clear vision of the facts—to a general view of world history. . . .

However numerous our inner conflicts may be, however different and often antagonistic our tendencies, we nonetheless face the rest of the world as a single body. The past saw the flowering of other nations and other groups of peoples, animated by other principles. They created their own institutions and developed them to a remarkable extent: today, virtually nothing is left of them. How threatening and powerful Islam once stood in the face of Europe! Not so long ago the Tartars swept across Poland as far as the borders of Germany; the Turk occupied Hungary and besieged Vienna; today, however, we have left these dangers far behind us. . . .

The Ottoman Empire has been overwhelmed by Christianity, and penetrated from all sides. When we speak of "Christianity" we do not refer to religion alone; the term "culture" or "civilization" would be just as inadequate. It is the genius of the West. It is the spirit that transforms peoples into well organized armies, that builds roads, digs canals, takes possession of the seas by covering them with fleets, fills distant continents with colonies, probes the depths of nature by means of exact science, penetrates into all domains of knowledge renewing them through incessant labors, without however losing sight of the eternal truth, the spirit that maintains the rule of law and order among men despite the diversity of their passions. This spirit is making tremendous advances before our very eyes. It wrested America from the raw forces of nature and the indomitable tribes that inhabited it, and transformed it utterly; by various roads it penetrates into the most distant regions of Asia where only China remains closed to it; it encompasses Africa along her entire coastline. Irresistible, multiform, unequaled, invincible thanks to its arms and science, it is conquering the world.[51]

Ernest Renan (1823–1892), too, lived in a spiritual and historical world, in which Europe's pre-eminence could not be doubted. Although Renan believed in progress more than Ranke, not without indulging in some rationalistic illusions (for instance, in *The Future of Science*), he saw more clearly than the German his-

[51] *Ibid.,* XLIII–XLIV, 518.

torian what danger nationalism presented to Europe, to "the interests of reason and civilization." The war of 1870, which illustrated the tragic consequences of state nationalism, compelled him to face the historical and moral problems raised by nationalism.

To the romantic and Herderian idea of a nation founded on race, language, birth, the past, Renan opposes the idea of a nation federated by the "actual consent" of the populations and their "will to live together" in prospect of a common future. This analysis is of basic importance for the whole evolution of the European idea. He formulated his thesis during the war, and he chose to address it personally to one of his equals in the new "science of civilization," the German professor David Strauss. His first letter is dated early in the war, his second toward its end. The idea of federation once again emerges as the obvious solution to the absurd conflicts that were tearing Europe apart:

It seems that peace cannot be concluded directly between France and Germany; it can only be the work of Europe, which has condemned the war and which must desire that none of the members of the European family should become too weak. You are right in speaking of guarantees against the revival of morbid dreams; but what guarantee would be more effective than one given by Europe, which would once again consecrate the existing frontiers and forbid all to consider changing the boundaries established by old treaties? Any other solution would leave the door open to endless wars of revenge. If Europe does this, she will have planted the seed of the most fruitful institution, namely, central authority, a kind of congress of the United States of Europe, which will, by passing judgment on the nations, impose its will on them, and right what was wrong in the principle of nationality by the principle of federation.

The principle of European federation can provide a basis of mediation similar to the one the Church provided in the Middle Ages.[52]

The war will never end, if we do not apply something like a statute of limitations in respect to past outrages. Lorraine was part of the Germanic empire, there is no question about it; but Holland, Switzerland, even Italy as far as Benevento, and all of France including Catalonia, before the treaty of Verdun, were

[52] Renan, "Première Lettre à M. David Strauss," September 16, 1870, in *Réforme intellectuelle* (Paris, 1884).

also part of it. Alsace is now a Germanic country by language and race; but before being invaded by the Germanic race, Alsace was a Celtic country, as was a part of southern Germany. We do not conclude that southern Germany must be French; but let no one maintain either that, by virtue of ancient law, Metz and the Luxembourg must be German. No one can say where this archeological approach would stop. In almost all cases where the impetuous German patriots speak in the name of Germanic rights, we could speak in the name of even older Celtic rights, and prior to the Celtic period, it is said, there were the allophyles, the Finns, the Laplanders; and before the Laplanders, there were the cavemen; and before the cavemen there were the orangutans. According to this philosophy of history, the only legitimate claim in the world would be that of the orangutans, so unjustly dispossessed by the perfidy of civilized men.

Let us be less absolute; next to the claims of the dead, let us recognize, to some extent, the claims of the living.

. . . The European nations, such as history has formed them, are the peers of a great Senate in which every member is inviolable. Europe is a confederacy of States united by the common idea of civilization. Each nation's individuality is undoubtedly constituted by race, language, history, religion, but also by something much more tangible, by the present consent, the will of the different provinces of a State to live together.[53]

Twelve years later, in a lecture given at the Sorbonne on the subject "What is a Nation?" [54] Renan deepens and clarifies his approach. To begin with, in a preface to an edition of his text dated May 8, 1887, he reiterates his fundamental thesis:

Man belongs neither to his language nor to his race; he belongs only to himself, for he is a free being, a moral being. We no longer recognize that it is permissible to persecute people in order to compel them to change their religion; to persecute them in order to compel them to change their language or fatherland seems just as bad. . . .

What constitutes a nation is not speaking the same language or belonging to the same ethnographic group, it is having done together great things in the past and wanting to do great things in the future.

[53] Renan, "Deuxième Lettre à M. David Strauss," September 15, 1871, ibid.
[54] Renan, "Qu'est-ce qu'une nation?" (Conférence faite en Sorbonne, le 11 mars 1887. Réédition. [Paris: R. Helleu, 1934]).

Here are the main ideas of the lecture itself, which was a land-mark, and isolated sentences from which have often been quoted.

Introduction and preliminary considerations:

At the time of the French Revolution it was thought that the institutions of independent city-states such as Sparta and Rome, could be taken over by our great nations of thirty to forty millions of souls. In our day, a more serious error is committed; the Race is confused with the nation, and ethnographic or rather linguistic groups are regarded as entitled to a sovereignty similar to that of actually existing peoples. Let us try to arrive at some exactitude in these difficult questions, where the slightest confusion in the meaning of terms at the beginning of the discussion may produce the most fatal errors in the end. What we are about to do is nearly as delicate a task as vivisection. We are to deal with living man as normally only the dead are treated. In doing so we shall use coolness, and the most absolute impartiality. . . .

Europe has constituted herself by rejecting the hegemony of any one nation or region:

Since the end of the Roman Empire, or, more accurately, since the dismemberment of Charlemagne's Empire, western Europe has been divided into nations, some of which, at certain epochs, have sought to exercise a hegemony over others, always without lasting success. What Charles V, Louis XIV, and Napoleon I were unable to achieve in the past is hardly likely to be achieved by anyone in the future. The establishment of a new Roman Empire or a new Carolingian Empire has become an impossibility. Europe is so deeply divided that any attempt at universal domination must very quickly provoke a coalition which would compel the ambitious nation to withdraw within its natural border.

The nation and its citizenship are specifically modern European concepts:

The nations, in this sense of the word, are relatively new in history. Antiquity did not know them: Egypt, China, ancient Chaldea were not nations to any extent. They were flocks led by a son of Heaven or a descendant of the Sun. There were no Egyptian citizens, as there are no Chinese citizens. Classical antiquity had republics and city-kingdoms, confederations of local republics, and it had empires; it had no nations in our sense of the word. Athens, Sparta, Sidon, Tyre were little centers admi-

rable for their patriotism; but they were city-states with comparatively limited territories. Gaul, Spain, Italy, before their absorp-
tion in the Roman Empire, were groupings of tribes, often allied
with one another, but without central institutions or dynasties.
Nor were the Assyrian Empire, the Persian Empire, and the
empire of Alexander nations. There was never such a thing as an
Assyrian patriot. . . .

Can a nation be properly defined in terms of race, language,
cutlure?

The instinct that presided over the making of the map of
Europe took no account of race, the greatest nations of Europe
are nations of essentially mixed blood.

The reality of race, which was all-important in the beginning,
is thus continually losing its importance. Human history differs
essentially from zoology. Race is everything, as it is in the case
of the rodents and the felines, and no one has the right to go
about the world feeling people's skulls and then taking them by
the throat, and saying, You are of our blood, you belong to us! . . .

. . . What we have just said about race, is also true of
language. Language is an invitation to unity, it is not a compulsion
to unite. The United States and England—and the same is true of
Spain and Spanish America—speak the same language, and yet
do not form a single nation. On the other hand, Switzerland,
which is so perfectly united thanks to having been founded on
agreement between her several parts, speaks three or four languages. In man there is something superior to language: namely,
will. Switzerland's will to be united, despite the variety of her
idioms, is a fact far more important than any similarity of language, often obtained by persecution.

Can a nation be better defined by its "natural borders"?

Geography, or so-called "natural boundaries," certainly plays a
major part in the divisions between nations. Geography is one of
the essential factors in history . . . Can we say, however, as some
believe, that the frontiers of a nation are inscribed on the map,
and that this nation has the right to annex what is needed to round
off given contours, to reach a given mountain or river, to which
a kind of a priori faculty of forming boundaries is attributed? I
know of no doctrine more arbitrary and more disastrous. It justifies all acts of violence. To begin with, do mountains or rivers
constitute these so-called natural boundaries? Incontestably,
mountains separate; but, on the other hand, rivers unite. And

then, not all mountains can serve as boundaries of states. Which are those that separate and which are those that do not separate? From Biarritz to the Tornea there is not a single river mouth that possesses the character of a boundary more than another. But for the grace of history, the Loire, the Seine, the Meuse, the Elbe, the Oder would have, to the same extent as the Rhine, the character of a natural boundary and would have caused no fewer infractions of that fundamental right, which is the will of men.

A nation is a "soul," but is not immortal:

A nation is a soul, a spiritual principle. Two things which, in fact, are only one, constitute this soul, this spiritual principle. One is in the past, the other in the present. . . .
In the past, an inheritance of shared glories and regrets; in the future, a common program to be carried out; to have suffered, enjoyed, hoped together; all these are more valuable than customs unions and "strategic" boundaries; so much is clear despite the diversities of race and language.
. . . By their diverse and often antithetical faculties the nations serve the common work of civilization; each contributes a note to that great chorus of mankind, which, when all is said, is the highest ideal reality we can attain to. Isolated, their parts are weak. I often tell myself that an individual having the faults regarded by nations as good qualities, would be vainglorious, jealous, selfish, and quarrelsome as are the nations. He could not put up with anything without drawing the sword, he would be the most unbearable of men.
. . . The nations are not eternal. They began, they will end. The European federation will probably replace them.

Jakob Burckhardt (1818–1897), citizen of Basel, author of *The Civilization of the Renaissance* and *Considerations on World History*, embodied the tradition of a humanistic city, German by language, Swiss in its civic spirit, and nourished on French and Italian influences. In his writings we find no systematic or metaphysical approach, but a kind of classical impersonality, a subdued passion, and a keen imaginative vision which revives those parts of the past he loves, "assessing" it with a high and serene severity, as befits the historian of "the realities of the present." By the lucidity of his diagnosis, he foresaw the future with more accuracy than any inspired prophet. Nietzsche, so intemperate in all things, was forever seeking the friendship of this temperate thinker. Burckhardt warmly supported the brilliant young philologist at the time he taught in Basel, but politely rejected the pathetic advances made by the prophet of Zarathustra. Shortly before his mind entirely gave way in Turin, Nietzsche sent two last telegrams: one to Cosima Wagner ("Ariadne I love you [signed] Dionysos") and the other to Burckhardt, who did not reply. Burckhardt's closest intimate happened to be a *Polizeidirektor* in Karlsruhe, one Friedrich von Preen.

When Burckhardt speaks of "world history," he very deliberately confines himself to Europe, just as Auguste Comte did:

Only the peoples in the state of civilization, not those which are in the state of nature, belong to history in the highest sense of the term.

And even among the civilized peoples, history does not include in its field those whose culture is not a branch of Europe's, for instance, Japan and China. Similarly, in respect of India, we are concerned with only very remote epochs, first those in which Aryan peoples lived in India (also in Persia), and then those in which contacts were established between Hindus on the one hand and Assyrians, Persians, Macedonians, etc., on the other. The object of our studies is thus confined exclusively to the past which is clearly related to the present and the future.[55]

This Europe which is the center of the world is in turn centered on the tradition of antiquity:

When we learn that the happy epoch called the Golden Age, in the mythical sense of the term, never existed and will never exist, we refrain from rashly overvaluing a certain past or rashly despairing of the present or rashly pinning our hopes on the future; nevertheless we look upon the study of the past as one of the noblest occupations. The past is nothing but the history of the life and sufferings of mankind taken as a whole.

And yet, for certain reasons, Antiquity is very important: it is to it that we owe our conception of the state; it saw the birth of our religions, and even today it remains the most enduring element of our civilization. Its creations in the domains of the plastic arts and literature are models which have never been equaled. Its heritage is important as much by virtue of what we have in common with it as by virtue of our differences from it. . . .

[55] Burckhardt, *Historische Fragmente* (Basel: B. Schwabe, 1925), p. 225.

Even though we are the descendants of peoples which, still in their childhood, slumbered by the side of the great civilized nations of antiquity, we nonetheless feel ourselves to be the descendants of the latter, because their spirit has become our own, and because their labors, their mission, and their fate live again in us.[56]

But what is it that has held Europe together for the last twenty centuries? Burckhardt asks. His answer is: the Papacy, the Holy Roman Empire, the overseas conquests, a few great individuals, and the continued struggle against the hegemony of any one great power:

A single mortal danger seemed constantly to threaten Europe: overwhelming mechanical superiority, whether of a conquering barbarian people, an accumulation of military resources by a single state, or a single movement, even that perhaps of the present-day masses.

It was not the worst enemies of Rome that saved Europe, but the most stubborn enemies of Spain—the Dutch, England (both Protestant and Catholic), and Henri IV in spite of his conversion. More than that, Europe is saved by those who free it from the danger constituted by attempts at unification and political, social, and religious leveling which some try to impose on it by force, and which threaten its most specific quality, the infinitely varied richness of its spirit. It is a commonplace to repeat that the spirit is invincible and that it will always be victorious, while in fact the degree of energy of one man at a given moment sometimes determines whether nations or entire civilizations will or will not disappear. Great individuals are needed, and these need to be successful. But Europe often had great men at the crucial moments of its history.[57]

But what is Europe, in the last analysis? The historical but also public-spirited definition given by Burckhardt is perhaps the most satisfactory and least debatable:

There is one thing we need not wish for, since we have it all around us (whether we rejoice in it or deplore it), namely, Europe, Europe as the home, both old and new, of an infinitely varied life, which has given birth to the richest creations, a home in which all contrasts merge in a common unity; here, everything spiritual attains expression in words or other ways.

[56] *Ibid.*, pp. 226–227.
[57] *Historische Fragmente*, ed. W. Kaegi (Basel, 1942), Fragment 144.

What is European is this: the manifestation of *all* energies, including the individual ones, in the form of monuments, plastic representations, words, institutions, parties; the personal experience of every tendency of spiritual life; the aspiration of the spirit to make known everything it contains, never surrendering without protest to world monarchies or theocracies, as they do in the East. If we occupy a sufficiently high and distant vantage point, as the historian should, we find that all the bells in all the towers are ringing in harmony, even though up close we can hear some dissonances: *Discordia concors. . . .*

It is possible that an obscure need led certain branches of Indo-Europeans to the West simply because here they found a different climate (one of freedom and diversity), a whole world broken up into islands and capes. For here is something else that is European: to love not only power, idols, and money, but also the spirit. It was these peoples that created the Hellenic, Roman, Celtic, and Germanic civilizations—civilizations which are far superior to those of Asia because they are varied in form and appearance, and because in them the individual can develop fully and render the greatest services to the whole of which he is a part. . . .

The historian can only rejoice in this richness and leave the desire for conquest to the champions of this or that tendency. Considering the extreme violence of the past struggles, the constant desire to annihilate the enemy, we, latecomers of mankind, cannot champion one party, even if it is a party which in our hearts we believe to be our own.[58]

"We, latecomers of mankind . . ." This casual phrase (which brings to mind Nietzsche) betrays the pessimism latent in this historian of civilization. Although he noted that in Europe every evolution leads to a transition, to a higher stage rather than a decline, he passes a very harsh judgment on the immediate future (the twentieth century) in one of his letters to Von Preen, a judgment that is confirmed today:

You will never believe how important these drum rolls become as the years go by; the masses in their confusion need a rhythm to march to, without which they would have "no style." In the meantime we are left in peace, and so we can indulge in our thoughts.

Of all classes, the workers are going to have the strangest time;

[58] *Ibid.,* Fragment 142 (lecture of May 14, 1869).

I have a suspicion that, for the time being, sounds completely mad, and yet I cannot rid myself of it: that the military state will have to turn "industrialist." The accumulations of beings, the mounds of men in the yards and factories cannot be left for all eternity in their need and thirst for riches; a planned and controlled degree of poverty, with promotion and uniforms, starting and ending daily to the roll of drums, that is what ought to come logically. (I know enough history, of course, to know that things do not always work out logically.) . . .

It has long been clear to me that the world is moving towards the alternative between complete democracy and absolute, lawless despotism, and the latter would certainly not be run by the dynasties, who are too soft-hearted, but by supposedly republican Military Commands. Only people do not like to imagine a world whose rulers utterly ignore law, prosperity, enriching work, and industry, credit, etc., and who would rule with utter brutality. But those are the people into whose hands the world is being driven by the competition among all parties for the participation of the masses on any and every question. . . .

The picture I have formed of the *terrible simplificateurs* who are going to descend upon poor old Europe is not an agreeable one; and here and there in imagination I can already see the fellows visibly before me, and will describe them to you over a glass of wine when we meet in September. Sometimes I meditate prophetically on how our learning and quisquilian researches will fare when these events are in their very early stages, and culture, in the interval, has only sunk a peg or two. Then, too, I picture to myself something of the lighter side of the great renovation: how the pale fear of death will come over all careerists and climbers, because once again real naked power is on top and the general *consigne* is "shut your mouth." [59]

Friedrich Nietzsche (1844–1900) marks a high point in his century. He died with it, and lives on beyond it. With Kierkegaard and Baudelaire on the one hand, and with Tocqueville and Burckhardt on the other, he saved it from spiritual stupidity and political foolishness, but only the better to condemn it both as a whole and in its social and cultural detail. Everything is contradictory in Nietzsche, including his passion for Europe, though it is constant, but it leads him to sarcasm as well as to praise, according to the epoch he treats. It so happens that his historical likes and

[59] *The Letters of Jacob Burckhardt,* selected, edited and translated by Alexander Dru (New York: Pantheon Books, n.d.).

dislikes are the same as Burckhardt's. First of all, Greece; then, the Renaissance. He prefers the French moralists and non-Romantic music—hard, clear, pure values. As for the modern chaos, Nietzsche believes that it is leading us downward, but in the end, he says, "the spirit may profit by it." Who can tell whether the "plebeian" and "semibarbarian" period that our civilization must go through will not favor, by an instinctive reaction, "the rearing of a new ruling caste for Europe." This, Nietzsche writes, is "my serious topic, the European problem, as I understand it." [60]

In § 242 of *Beyond Good and Evil* this European process is described without the slightest regard for contemporary taboos:

Whether we call it "civilization," or "humanising," or "progress," which now distinguishes the European; whether we call it simply, without praise or blame, by the political formula: the *democratic* movement in Europe—behind all the moral and political foregrounds pointed to by such formulas, an immense *physiological process* goes on, which is ever extending: the process of the assimilation of Europeans; their increasing detachment from the conditions under which, climatically and hereditarily, united races originate; their increasing independence of every definite *milieu*, that for centuries would fain inscribe itself with equal demands on soul and body;—that is to say, the slow emergence of an essentially *super-national* and nomadic species of man, who possesses, physiologically speaking, a maximum of the art and power of adaptation as his typical distinction. This process of the *evolving European*, which can be retarded in its *tempo* by great relapses, but will perhaps just gain and grow thereby in vehemence and depth—the still raging storm and stress of "national sentiment" pertains to it, and also the anarchism which is appearing at present—this process will probably arrive at results on which its naïve propagators and panegyrists, the apostles of "modern ideas," would least care to reckon. The same new conditions under which on an average a levelling and mediocrising of man will take place —a useful, industrious, variously serviceable and clever gregarious man—are in the highest degree suitable to give rise to exceptional men of the most dangerous and attractive qualities.

[60] Nietzsche, *Beyond Good and Evil*, end of § 251, in *The Philosophy of Nietzsche*, trans. Helen Zimmern ("The Modern Library," New York: Random House).

According to Nietzsche Europe suffers from several spiritual diseases. First of all, nationalism, disguised as "jovial and solemn" patriotism:

We "good Europeans," we also have hours when we allow our-selves a warm-hearted patriotism, a plunge and relapse into old loves and narrow views—I have just given an example of it—hours of national excitement, of patriotic anguish, and all other sorts of old-fashioned floods of sentiment. Duller spirits may perhaps only get done with what confines its operations in us to hours and plays itself out in hours—in a considerable time; some in half a year, others in half a lifetime, according to the speed and strength with which they digest and "change their material." Indeed, I could think of sluggish, hesitating races, which even in our rapidly moving Europe, would require half a century ere they could sur-mount such atavistic attacks of patriotism and soil-attachment, and return once more to reason, that is to say, to "good Euro-peanism." [61]

Music, above all, that essentially European creation, makes it possible for us to follow the process of disintegration which leads from cosmopolitan Europeanism to narrow nationalism:

The "good old time" is past, it sang itself out in Mozart—how happy are *we* that his *rococo* still speaks to us, that his "good company," his tender enthusiasm, his childish delight in the Chinese and its flourishes, his courtesy of heart, his longing for the elegant, the amorous, the tripping, the tearful, and his belief in the South, can still appeal to *something left* in us! Ah, some time or other it will be over with it!—but who can doubt that it will be over still sooner with the intelligence and taste for Beethoven! For he was only the last echo of a break and transition in style, and *not*, like Mozart, the last echo of a great European taste which had existed for centuries. Beethoven is the inter-mediate event between an old mellow soul that is constantly breaking down, and a future over-young soul that is always *coming;* there is spread over his music the twilight of eternal loss and eternal extravagant hope,—the same light in which Europe was bathed when it dreamed with Rousseau, when it danced round the Tree of Liberty of the Revolution, and finally almost fell down in adoration before Napoleon. But how rapidly does *this* very sentiment now pale, how difficult nowadays is even the *apprehension* of this sentiment, how strangely does the language

[61] *Ibid.*, § 241.

of Rousseau, Schiller, Shelley, and Byron sound to our ear, in whom collectively the same fate of Europe was able to *speak*, which knew how to *sing* in Beethoven!—Whatever German music came afterwards, belongs to Romanticism, that is to say, to a movement which, historically considered was still shorter, more fleeting, and more superficial than that great interlude, the transition of Europe from Rousseau to Napoleon, and to the rise of democracy. . . . Schumann was already merely a *German* event in music, and no longer a European event, as Beethoven had been, as in a still greater degree Mozart had been; with Schumann German music was threatened with its greatest danger, that of *losing the voice for the soul of Europe* and sinking into a merely national affair.[62]

Romanticism begot nationalism, and as fate would have it, the greatest men of the first half of the nineteenth century all succumbed to it:

Owing to the morbid estrangement which the nationality-craze has induced and still induces among the nations of Europe, owing also to the short-sighted and hasty-handed politicians, who with the help of this craze, are at present in power, and do not suspect to what extent the disintegrating policy they pursue must necessarily be only an interlude policy—owing to all this, and much else that is altogether unmentionable at present, the most unmistakable signs that *Europe wishes to be one*, are now overlooked, or arbitrarily and falsely misinterpreted. With all the more profound and large-minded men of this century, the real general tendency of the mysterious labour of their souls was to prepare the way for that new *synthesis*, and tentatively to anticipate the European of the future; only in their simulations, or in their weaker moments, in old age perhaps, did they belong to the "fatherlands"—they only rested from themselves when they became "patriots." I think of such men as Napoleon, Goethe, Beethoven, Stendahl, Heinrich Heine, Schopenhauer: it must not be taken amiss if I also count Wagner among them.[63]

[62] *Ibid.*, § 245.
[63] *Ibid.*, § 256. In a posthumously published fragment which outlines the same theme, Nietzsche goes further: he foresees the inevitability of a common European market: "I see farther, beyond all these national wars, these 'empires' and other foreground matters. What matters is the One Europe, and I see it being prepared slowly and hesitantly. All the vast and profound minds of this century were engaged in the work of preparing, working out, and anticipating a new synthesis: the European of the future. It was only once they became old, or in moments of weakness, that they relapsed into

With Romanticism was born the historical sense which dominated European thought in the period. Nietzsche's attitude toward historicism is inevitably ambivalent, for his vision of Europe was historical-minded while his value judgments aimed more and more at timelessness:

The *historical sense* . . . which we Europeans claim as our specialty, has come to us in the train of the enchanting and mad *semi-barbarity* into which Europe has been plunged by the democratic mingling of classes and races—it is only the nineteenth century that has recognised this faculty as its sixth sense. Owing to this mingling, the past of every form and mode of life, and of cultures which were formerly closely contiguous and superimposed on one another, flows forth into us "modern souls"; our instincts now run back in all directions, we ourselves are a kind of chaos: in the end, as we have said, the spirit perceives its advantage therein. By means of our semi-barbarity in body and in desire, we have secret access everywhere, such as a noble age never had; we have access above all to the labyrinth of imperfect civilisations, and to every form of semi-barbarity that has at any time existed on earth; and in so far as the most considerable part of human civilisation hitherto has just been semi-barbarity, the "historical sense" implies almost the sense and instinct for everything, the taste and tongue for everything: whereby it immediately proves itself to be an *ignoble* sense. . . .
That as men of the "historical sense" we have our virtues, is not to be disputed:—we are unpretentious, unselfish, modest, grave, habituated to self-control and self-renunciation, very grateful, very patient, very complaisant—but with all this we are perhaps not very "tasteful." Let us finally confess it, that what is most difficult for us men of the "historical sense" to grasp, feel, taste, and love, what finds us fundamentally prejudiced and almost hostile, is precisely the perfection and ultimate maturity in every culture and art, the essentially noble in works and men, their

---

narrow nationalism and became patriots. I am thinking of men like Napoleon, Goethe, Beethoven, Stendahl, Heinrich Heine, Schopenhauer. However, next to what awakened and formed in these minds the need for a new unity, or the new needs for a new unity, we must place a great economic reality which throws light on the situation: the small states of Europe—I mean all our present empires and states—will become economically untenable, within a short time, by reason of the absolute tendency of industry and commerce to become bigger and bigger, crossing natural boundaries and becoming world wide."

moment of smooth sea and halcyon self-sufficiency, the golden-ness and coldness which all things show that have perfected themselves.[64]

If Europe is further removed than ever from conceiving and achieving this highest ideal by her own strength, it is because she suffers from a sickness of the will, an inability to will herself ONE, which Russia will exploit to her advantage:

Our present-day Europe, the scene of a senseless, precipitate attempt at a radical blending of classes, and *consequently* of races, is therefore sceptical in all its heights and depths, some-times exhibiting the mobile scepticism which springs impatiently and wantonly from branch to branch, sometimes with gloomy aspect, like a cloud overcharged with interrogative signs—and often sick unto death of its will! Paralysis of will; where do we not find this cripple sitting nowadays! And yet how bedecked oftentimes! How seductively ornamented! There are the finest gala dresses and disguises for this disease; and that, for instance, most of what places itself nowadays in the showcases as "objec-tiveness," "the scientific spirit," "*l'art pour l'art*," and "pure . . . knowledge," is only decked-out scepticism and paralysis of will— I am ready to answer for this diagnosis of the European disease. —The disease of the will is diffused unequally over Europe; it is worst and most varied where civilisation has longest prevailed; it decreases according as "the barbarian" still—or again—asserts his claims under the loose drapery of Western culture. It is therefore in the France of today, as can be readily disclosed and compre-hended, that the will is most infirm; and France which has always had a masterly aptitude for converting even the portentous crises of its spirit into something charming and seductive, now manifests emphatically its intellectual ascendancy over Europe, by being the school and exhibition of all the charms of scepticism. The power to will and to persist, moreover, in a resolution, is already somewhat stronger in Germany, and again in the North of Ger-many it is stronger than in Central Germany; it is considerably stronger in England, Spain, and Corsica, associated with phlegm in the former and with hard skulls in the latter—not to mention Italy, which is too young yet to know what it wants, and must first show whether it can exercise will; but it is strongest and most surprising of all in that immense middle empire where Europe as it were flows back to Asia—namely, in Russia. There the power to will has been long stored up and accumulated, there the will—

[64] *Ibid.*, § 224.

uncertain whether to be negative or affirmative—waits threateningly to be discharged (to borrow their pet phrase from our physicists). Perhaps not only Indian wars and complications in Asia would be necessary to free Europe from its greatest danger, but also internal subversion, the shattering of the empire into small states, and above all the introduction of parliamentary imbecility, together with the obligation of every one to read his newspaper at breakfast. I do not say this as one who desires it; in my heart I should rather prefer the contrary—I mean such an increase in the threatening attitude of Russia, that Europe would have to make up its mind to become equally threatening—namely to *acquire one will*, by means of a new caste to rule over the Continent, a persistent, dreadful will of its own, that can set its aims thousands of years ahead; so that the long spun-out comedy of its petty-stateism, and its dynastic as well as its democratic many-willedness, might finally be brought to a close. The time for petty politics is past; the next century will bring the struggle for the dominion of the world—the *compulsion* to great politics.[65]

Will Europe be capable of pursuing this "grand policy" on a world scale, that is, will she be capable of meeting the challenge of the twentieth century? In his Preface to *Beyond Good and Evil*, Nietzsche's answer is "perhaps" (referring to the fruitful tensions of which Europe is the historical scene):

But the struggle against Plato, or—to speak plainer, and for the "people"—the struggle against the ecclesiastical oppression of millenniums of Christianity (for Christianity is Platonism for the "people"), produced in Europe a magnificent tension of soul, such as had not existed anywhere previously; with such a tensely-strained bow one can now aim at the furthest goals. As a matter of fact, the European feels this tension as a state of distress, and twice attempts have been made in grand style to unbend the bow; once by means of Jesuitism, and the second time by means of democratic enlightenment—which, with the aid of the liberty of the press and newspaper-reading, might, in fact, bring it about that the spirit would not so easily find itself in "distress"! . . . But we, who are neither Jesuits, nor democrats, nor even sufficiently Germans, we *good Europeans*, and free, *very* free spirits—we have it still, all the distress of spirit and all the tension of its bow! And perhaps also the arrow, the duty, and, who knows? *the goal to aim at.* . . .[66]

[65] *Ibid.*, § 208.
[66] *Ibid.*, end of Preface.

Later on, pessimism, and even catastrophism will dominate Nietzsche's view of the twentieth century. To be sure in his unpublished notebooks he wrote at the time he was writing *Human, All-Too-Human:* "The diversity of languages, above all, prevents us from seeing what is taking place in the depths: the disappearance of national man and the appearance of European man." And in *Will to Power:*

A little more fresh air, for Heaven's sake! This ridiculous condition of Europe must not last any longer. Is there a single idea behind this bovine nationalism? What possible value can there be in encouraging this arrogant self-conceit when everything today points to greater and more common interests?—at a moment when the spiritual dependence and denationalisation, which are obvious to all, are paving the way for the reciprocal *rapprochements* and fertilisations which make up the real value and sense of present-day culture? [67]

However, the conditions of a restoration, as he listed them in his unpublished notes of the 1880's, are clearly impossible of realization. He is well aware of it: pessimism, this "hammer of philosophy," remains the last weapon available to "good Europeans." Rather death than the coming mediocrity:

For the supreme struggle, a new weapon is needed. The hammer. To provoke the terrible decision, to place Europe before her choice: does she want her decadence? Be on guard against mediocrisation. Rather perish.[68]

From the Swedish historian Harald Hjärne (1848–1922) we borrow our conclusions on the nineteenth century, viewed as "The Century of Nationalism." This was the title of an article he published in *Svenska Dagbladet,* the great liberal newspaper of Stockholm, on December 31, 1899:

The century that is ending tonight witnessed many efforts and many illusions in the life of nations. To determine which of its countless tendencies was the most important, is perhaps a question of taste. For my part, in these last hours of the century, I should like to meditate on one of the forces that were at once the

[67] *The Will to Power,* in *Collected Works* (New York: The Macmillan Company, 1910 ff.), Vol. XV.
[68] *Zucht und Züchtung,* III, "Die ewige Wiederkunft."

most creative and the most distinctive in the communities where they operated: nationalism. . . . To be sure, the national tendencies also served culture in the sense that they made it possible to surmount many obstacles which previously had prevented the scattered peoples from sharing in a cultural community. But these advantages weigh less heavily than the drawbacks resulting from them, which made nationalism the dominant political factor. The demand for full equality of rights by all nationalities once they became sovereign states is just as contrary to History and foreign to reality as is the world state to which some aspire. . . . The hatred of everything foreign, kept up in the name of patriotism, is closely akin to the passion for persecuting heretics; it rapidly transforms national sentiment into an instinct which escapes the control of reason. By the same token nationalism stops being a factor of cultural development and becomes superstition. In what measure will the coming century favor the gentling of national passion, no one can foresee as I write. It seems at least as likely that nationalism, by combining with other forces, both old and new, is leading us irresistibly toward new catastrophes, which will not be on a smaller scale than the Thirty Years' War or the French Revolution and its sequel.

However, politically and culturally, the nineteenth century did not end in 1900: it was the First World War that finished it, in every sense of the word. Of this normal, logical, and yet criminal finish, the most cynical and most lucid witness was Georges Sorel (1857–1922). His *Réflexions sur la Violence* is said to have directly influenced Lenin and Mussolini. (The latter is supposed to have said, "I owe what I am to Sorel.") And yet Sorel wanted to be no more than a "disinterested theoretician." No doubt more European-minded than any of his fellow citizens at the beginning of this century, he spoke of Europe only in the tone of somber prophetic resentment. Here are some statements taken down by one of his disciples on the eve of the First World War:[69]

October, 1908. Europe is the land of warlike cataclysms par excellence. The pacifists are either imbeciles ignorant of elementary laws, or clever demagogues who earn their living by lies.

No one has the courage to say or to write that the state of peace in Europe is an abnormal state.

Why is Europe the land of warlike cataclysms par excellence? Because it is inhabited by a number of races which are singu-

[69] Jean Variot, *Propos de Georges Sorel* (Paris, 1935).

larly opposed to one another in immediate interests, ways of life, and ambitions. Europe has no luck. Her inhabitants make bad neighbors.

. . . And then there is Slavism to rub salt on the wound. Pan-Slavic politics. . . . There is something to look forward to!

I say here and now, war is coming and from Russia.

October 12, 1908. In America people wholly like one another, living in entirely similar states, were federated . . . No great feat. But how will you federate Slavs, those religious or revolutionary mystics, sober-minded Scandinavians, ambitious Germans, Englishmen jealous of their authority, stingy Frenchmen, Italians clamoring for room to live, Balkan poachers, warlike Hungarians? What can you do with a basket of crabs that keep pinching each other?

Unhappy Europe! Why hide what lies in store? Ten years from now it will sink into war and anarchy, just as she has always done two or three times a century.

November 8, 1912. There is no hope for Europe's future. Why should there be? What is this old optimism, always waiting for things to work out? Nothing at all. Chemical compounds, which are amorphous separately, catch fire when they are poured into the same retort. Europe is a retort filled to the brim with this sort of chemical mixture. It's catching fire. Hang it all, you've got to face it!

December 18, 1912. Europe is a graveyard, inhabited by peoples who burst into song as they go off to kill each other. The French and the Germans are going to be singing pretty soon.

Sorel, who despaired of "this Europe which is the very type of human wretchedness" and who reinvented Ivan Karamazov's expression "the European graveyard," [70] was doubtless the most pessimistic observer of nationalism's fatal course. The year 1914 proved him right.

For 1914 rang the knell of nationalist Europe's world leadership.

This catastrophe began in a spirit of happy nationalism, with flower-bedecked regiments, and widespread unawareness of the war's true implications. In 1914, as Jules Romains was to write later:

Neither the Kings, the Emperors, nor the Peoples knew really why they set such store on battle, nor for what end they fought. None of them had ever clearly viewed the miracle of this conti-

[70] Cf. p. 314.

nent, nor stopped deeply to consider the more fragile miracle that had determined its position in the world. This Europe, their Europe, which had become the mother and the teacher of all the countries of the earth, the source of all thought, of all invention, the guardian of all the high secrets of mankind, was less precious to them now than was a flag, a frontier line, the name of a battle to be graven on a stone, a deposit of phosphates, the comparative statistics of ocean tonnage, or the pleasure of humiliating a neighbour.[71]

It is a pleasure to give here a page from one of the few French writers who has had the courage and lucidity to fight for a united Europe—"*Europe, mon pays que j'ai voulu chanter!*"—throughout a long career which begins with a poem titled "Europe," published in 1915, and has continued down to newspaper campaigns in favor of the European Defense Community. This is not to mention the long series of novels, *Men of Good Will*. While the war of the nations was at its height, Romains launched his pamphlet *Pour que l'Europe soit*, the message of which was drowned in chauvinist clamor for victory. The same or a worse fate befell Romain Rolland's appeals from September, 1914, on, when he published his pamphlet *Au dessus de la mêlée*. This pamphlet expressed his

intuition that a crime was being committed against Europe and against civilization, to which the people have been led by the policies of their government, and by the failure of the powers responsible for keeping the peace: socialism and Christianity.[72]

The revival of the *projects* for union dates from the period following the First World War.

The birth of a political, economic, and cultural program to realize these projects dates from the period following the Second World War.

It was necessary to touch bottom. A united Europe has come to birth amid the ruins of its latent civil war. And we shall see the prophets of her final decadence contradicted by the facts and refuted by a better-informed generation.

[71] Jules Romains, *Men of Good Will* (New York: Alfred A. Knopf, 1938), VII, 548–49.
[72] Romain Rolland, *Journal des années de guerre*, p. 735.

PART SIX
EUROPE AT ISSUE

From Spengler to Ortega

1: "Everything has sensed that it might perish"

TOUCHED OFF by a short circuit between nationalist tensions which had been building up for a century, the conflagration of 1914 was put down temporarily with the help of the Americans and contingents recruited in Asia, Australia, and Africa. We asked them to rescue us; they did so whether or not of their own free will, and then went back home without further ado, but having learned something about us. From their bitter experience of European reality, some concluded that they could from now on appropriate our material strength and adopt a number of our political principles, ready to turn them against us, taking advantage of our moral weaknesses and our passionate disputes among ourselves. This was how the Soviets were thinking too; others concluded that nationalism, the cause of our disasters, must at last be surmounted, but by means of a system of world arbitration, that is to say, to the same scale as the problems that Europe had just created.

The political leaders of Europe were far from believing in the world's threats and needs, and in the measures required to meet them. Far from realizing the extent of our crisis, they consecrated their "victory" with treaties which were eventually to aggravate the evil. In 1914 Europe had no fewer than twenty sovereign nations. After the Treaties of Versailles, Trianon, and Saint-Germain, she had thirty-one (plus two international zones), redesigned or invented in accordance with the most contradictory principles (which had been eloquently denounced by Renan and by Nietzsche) of a schoolbook nationalism. The colonial problem was not dealt with: the colonies had not yet risen in rebellion. Thus, all that was done was to hand them over to the officially victorious nations of Europe as a bonus! The architects of the treaties kept their eyes fixed on a nineteenth century whose

[339]

nationalist ideals they carried to the point of absurdity. Stubbornly blind to world realities, they paved the way for the eventual failure of the League of Nations and the eventual success of
the totalitarian regimes, and hence for the Second World War.

This is how Paul Valéry judges them:

Europe had it within her to conquer, rule, and organize the rest
of the world to European ends. She had invincible means and the
men who created them. But far inferior to these men were those
who controlled her destiny. They had fed on the past; they could
do nothing but imitate the past. . . . Her . . . village feuds . . .
have caused Europe to lose her tremendous opportunity, the
existence of which she did not even suspect at the right time.
Napoleon seems to be the only one who had any presentiment of
what was bound to happen and what might be done. . . . But
he had come too soon, the time was not ripe, and his means were
far less than ours. After him, people went back to eyeing their
neighbors' acres and thinking in terms of the moment.

The wretched Europeans preferred to play at the game of
Armagnacs and Burgundians rather than assume over the whole
earth the great role that the Romans knew how to assume and
to hold for centuries in the world of their time.[1]

At the same time, however, several thinkers of a new type tried
to study the reality of Europe, which was being neglected by the
realists. Taking into account history, sociology, the arts, the new
sciences, morality, and politics, they attempted to evaluate our
opportunities. They rightly judged them to be seriously compromised. And since they realized that neither the political leaders
nor the masses would listen to them, they indulged in the exqui-
site pleasure of foreseeing the worst, overcompensating for the
cynicism and the naïveté that dominated the actual course of
history by a clear-sighted despair.

The first of these thinkers was Spengler.

It is noteworthy that Oswald Spengler (1880–1936) arrived at
the title of his major work as early as 1912: *The Decline of the
West*. The best minds had sensed our decadence before the devel-

[1] Paul Valéry, "Notes on the Greatness and Decline of Europe," in *History and Politics (Collected Works,* trans. Denise Folliot and Jackson
Matthews [Bollingen Series XLV], X, 226–27).

opments that our political leaders could not even grasp after they had occurred.

Spengler owes most of his celebrity to the title of his work. An immense public that has never read him knows that he is famous and that he prophesied our decline. What does his epoch-making book actually say?

In a sparkling series of planetary and millenary analogies, bearing upon the most varied forms of art and the remotest civilizations, he extends the tradition of Vico and German Romanticism, and anticipates André Malraux's *Imaginary Museum*. Through a comparative study of the cyclical laws governing the formation, growth, apogee, and decline of cultures and civilizations, he extends the tradition of Hegel and anticipates Toynbee. All in all, his great book is a utopia based on an interpretation of the past and the present. His examples are debatable, especially when he draws them from a present that has already become obsolete. (In 1917 he said that plein-air painting—"modern" at the time—"is not made for the people"; but it is this very type of painting that the "people" today looks upon as true painting, as opposed to abstract art.) Of an undertaking as vast as his, which lends itself to such a variety of verifications by means of striking examples—examples either familiar to everyone or pointed out by the author for the first time—we may retain a style of thinking which found many followers, and a pessimistic bias which influenced a whole epoch. His glimpses into a Caesarian future, which will drown the power of money in "blood," i.e. in an eruption of instinctual forces and "the will to power," were confirmed by Hitler much sooner than he had expected, and this "future" is now a thing of the past. Nevertheless Spengler remains one of the sincerest and most important witnesses to twentieth-century Western experience.

His two teachers were Goethe and Nietzsche. From Goethe he borrowed, perhaps unfairly, an "organic" theory of culture: according to him, every culture is comparable to a plant or any other living thing, which is destined to die after it has flowered and matured. From Nietzsche he borrowed a way of looking catastrophes in the face and of loving a fate that cannot be averted. For all that, however, he does not turn his back on the Faustian myth of the active and creative individual. . . . The two excerpts below illustrate the central themes of this enormous work.

Organicism: like nations for Hegel, so cultures for Spengler must realize their formative *idea,* bring their vocation to its flowering, and then disappear:

A Culture is born in the moment when a great soul awakens out of the proto-spirituality *(dem urseelenhaften Zustande)* of ever-childish humanity, and detaches itself, a form from the formless, a bounded and mortal thing from the boundless and enduring. It blooms on the soil of an exactly-definable landscape, to which plant-wise it remains bound. It dies when this soul has actualized the full sum of its possibilities in the shape of peoples, languages, dogmas, arts, states, sciences, and reverts into the proto-soul. But its living existence, that sequence of great epochs which define and display the stages of fulfillment, is an inner passionate struggle to maintain the Idea against the powers of Chaos without and the unconscious muttering deep-down within. It is not only the artist who struggles against the resistance of the material and the stifling of the idea within him. Every Culture stands in a deeply-symbolical, almost in a mystical, relation to the Extended, the space, in which and through which it strives to actualize itself. The aim once attained—the idea, the entire content of inner possibilities, fulfilled and made externally actual—the Culture suddenly hardens, it mortifies, its blood congeals, its force breaks down, and it becomes *Civilization,* the things which we feel and understand in the words Egypticism, Byzantinism, Mandarinism.

This—the inward and outward fulfillment, the finality, that awaits every living Culture—is the purport of all the historic "declines," amongst them that decline of the Classical which we know so well and fully, and another decline, entirely comparable to it in course and duration, which will occupy the first centuries of the coming millennium but is heralded already and sensible in and around us to-day—the decline of the West.[2]

Amor fati: if you want to forestall the disaster, all you can do it to understand its law; better still, last recourse as your freedom of choice narrows down, you can will this law.

[2] Spengler, *The Decline of the West,* authorized translation by Ch. F. Atkinson (New York: Alfred A. Knopf, 1928), I, 106–7.

A power can be overthrown only by another power, not by a principle, and no power that can confront money is left but this one. Money is overthrown and abolished only by blood. . . .

Ever in History it is life and life only—race-quality, the triumph of the will-to-power—and not the victory of truths, discoveries, or money that signifies. *World-history is the world court,* and it has ever decided in favour of the stronger, fuller, and more assured life—decreed to it, namely, the right to exist, regardless of whether its right would hold before a tribunal of waking-consciousness. Always it has sacrificed truth and justice to might and race, and passed doom of death upon men and peoples in whom truth was more than deeds, and justice than power. And so the drama of a high Culture—that wondrous world of deities, arts, thoughts, battles, cities—closes with the return of the pristine facts of the blood eternal that is one and the same as the ever-circling cosmic flow. . . .

For us, however, whom a Destiny has placed in this Culture and at this moment of its development—the moment when money is celebrating its last victories, and the Caesarism that is to succeed approaches with quiet, firm step—our direction, willed and obligatory at once, is set for us within narrow limits, and on any other terms life is not worth the living. We have not the freedom to reach to this or to that, but the freedom to do the necessary or to do nothing. And a task that historic necessity has set *will* be accomplished with the individual or against him.

Ducunt Fata volentem, nolentem trahunt.[3]

Conceived before the First World War and completed in 1917, Spengler's book was actually anticipatory: it revealed the causes of the catastrophes that were to come. As early as 1919, there began to appear that series of dismaying observations on the tragedy we had just lived through—and of which we have today perhaps seen only the first act. . . .

Paul Valéry (1871–1945) in a few noble pages was among the first to take inventory of the disaster:

We later civilizations . . . we too know that we are mortal.

We had long heard tell of whole worlds that had vanished, of empires sunk without a trace, gone down with all their men and all their machines into the unexplorable depths of the centuries, with their gods and their laws, their academies and their sciences pure and applied, their grammars and their dictionaries, their

[3] *Ibid.,* II, 506–7.

Classics and their Romantics, and their Symbolists, their critics and the critics of their critics. . . . We were aware that the visible earth is made of ashes, and that ashes signify something. Through the obscure depths of history we could make out the phantom ships laden with riches and intellect; we could not count them. But the disasters that had sent them down were, after all, none of our affair.

Elam, Nineveh, Babylon were but beautiful vague names, and the total ruin of those worlds had as little significance for us as their very existence. But France, England, Russia . . . these too would be beautiful names. *Lusitania*, too, is a beautiful name. And we see now that the abyss of history is deep enough to hold us all. We are aware that a civilization has the same fragility as a life. The circumstances that could send the works of Keats and Baudelaire to join the works of Menander are no longer inconceivable; they are in the newspapers. . . .

So the Persepolis of the spirit is no less ravaged than the Susa of material fact. Everything has not been lost, but everything has sensed that it might perish.

An extraordinary shudder ran through the marrow of Europe. She felt in every nucleus of her mind that she was no longer the same, that she was no longer herself, that she was about to lose consciousness, a consciousness acquired through centuries of bearable calamities, by thousands of men of the first rank, from innumerable geographical, ethnic, and historical coincidences.

So—as though in desperate defense of her own physiological being and resources—all her memory confusedly returned. Her great men and her great books came back pell-mell. Never has so much been read, nor with such passion, as during the war: ask the booksellers. . . . Never have people prayed so much and so deeply: ask the priest. All the saviors, founders, protectors, martyrs, heroes, all the fathers of their country, the sacred heroines, the national poets were invoked. . . .

And in the same disorder of mind, at the summons of the same anguish, all cultivated Europe underwent the rapid revival of her innumerable ways of thought: dogmas, philosophies, heterogeneous ideals; the three hundred ways of explaining the World, the thousand and one versions of Christianity, the two dozen kinds of positivism; the whole spectrum of intellectual light spread out its incompatible colors, illuminating with a strange and contradictory glow the death agony of the European soul. . . .

Standing, now, on an immense sort of terrace of Elsinore that stretches from Basel to Cologne, bordered by the sands of Nieuport, the marshes of the Somme, the limestone of Champagne, the granites of Alsace . . . our Hamlet of Europe is watching millions of ghosts.

But he is an intellectual Hamlet, meditating on the life and death of truths; for ghosts, he has all the subjects of our controversies; from remorse, all the titles of our fame. He is bowed under the weight of all the discoveries and varieties of knowledge, incapable of resuming this endless activity; he broods on the tedium of rehearsing the past and the folly of always trying to innovate. He staggers between two abysses—for two dangers never cease threatening the world: order and disorder.

Every skull he picks up is an illustrious skull. *Whose was it?* This one was *Leonardo.* He invented the flying man, but the flying man has not exactly served his inventor's purposes. We know that, mounted on his great swan (*il grande uccello sopra del dosso del suo magnio cecero*) he has other tasks in our day than fetching snow during the hot season to scatter it on the streets of towns. And that other skull was *Leibnitz,* who dreamed of universal peace. And this one was *Kant . . . and Kant begat Hegel, and Hegel begat Marx, and Marx begat. . . .*

Hamlet hardly knows what to make of so many skulls. But suppose he forgets them! Will he still be himself? . . . His terribly lucid mind contemplates the passage from war to peace: darker, more dangerous than the passage from peace to war; all peoples are troubled by it. . . . "What about Me," he says, "what is to become of Me, the European intellect? . . . And what is peace? . . . *Peace is perhaps the state of things in which the natural hostility between men is manifested in creation, rather than destruction as in war.* Peace is a time of creative rivalry and the battle of production; but am I not tired of producing? . . . Have I not exhausted my desire for radical experiment, indulged too much in cunning compounds? . . . Should I not perhaps lay aside my hard duties and transcendent ambitions? . . . Perhaps follow the trend and do like Polonius, who is now director of a great newspaper; like Laertes, who is something in aviation; like Rosencrantz, who is doing God knows what under a Russian name?

"Farewell, ghosts! The world no longer needs you—or me. By giving the name of progress to its own tendency to a fatal precision, the world is seeking to add to the benefits of life the advantages of death. A certain confusion still reigns; but in a little while all will be made clear, and we shall witness at last the miracle of an animal society, the perfect and ultimate anthill." [4]

[4] Paul Valéry, "The Crisis of the Mind" (1919), *op. cit.,* pp. 23-30.

At about the same time—between the year Valéry wrote his famous letters and the year they were published—a young Swiss diplomat, Carl J. Burckhardt, who was to have a great career but who had as yet published nothing, addressed to his teacher and friend, the Austrian poet Hugo von Hofmannsthal, a few pages prophetic of Europe's fate: [5]

These weeks in Italy have changed my outlook in many ways. In Bologna, someone said to me, "You are a European." As I was driving up the St. Gothard, I thought about what it meant to be a European. Are you one? Have you the courage to be one still—or once again—today? Is this not a condition which, everywhere and always, relates to the past? Is it not the hope for the Christendom of bygone days? Has humanism, the Greek heritage, ever been more than a moral atmosphere, an atmosphere that is neither compelling nor binding?

Perhaps you are the last true European. Yes, there could have been a Europe, a convergence of the Germanic, Spanish, Italian, and Slav natures, with the Slav nature singing the bass.

A federation can be conceived only on the basis of a common denominator, a strong fundamental idea, a conviction. But they are lacking. Or perhaps a common danger, like the Turk in former times? Nothing today is as it used to be, in our much divided world, so far as our contemporaries are concerned who were brought up in the "yes-but-on-the-other-hand" school. Everything is interpreted, analyzed, explained away, even danger.

Everywhere in the monarchy, your fellow countrymen have been won over to nationalism; it began already under Joseph II. Natural science, Romanticism, the Romantic idea of the French Revolution which were aimed indirectly against Germany, all played their part; and the Austrian intellectuals, those opportunists without instinct, certainly could not have checked this process.

And what about us, here, in Switzerland? There is a persistent feeling of affinity with Germany, but it is not tinged with nationalism. Gotthelf, Keller, Meyer, Jakob Burckhardt applied themselves to demonstrating to the German Swiss that they were Germans by their nature, but not politically. They had already turned their backs on Germany in 1848, and refused to have anything to do with Bismarck's *Reich* which was so largely modeled on the seventeenth-century French prototype. The last global federalist and citizen of a polyphonic world in which

[5] C. J. Burckhardt, to Hugo von Hofmannsthal, in *Briefwechsel* (Frankfort, 1956).

Antiquity and Christianity are fused in a belated alloy, was Goethe, the citizen of the free cities. Precisely because he was so receptive to the world, he was German in a sense which is no longer current. In him, the *sanctum Imperium*, which had been reduced to a shadow, became a reality. As for Herder's message, it is precisely against its spirit that the majority of the German people, born of the defeat, is in revolt.

We can only wait, and try to outlive the period, but we'll have to wait a long time for the nationalist strain to die away. It is a hypnotic state, that wins more and more people to it; anyway, you always get them at the same time, great ideas and great chimeras. . . .

Technological progress may lead to some sort of world organization in our own century. For the moment, however, it seems that the world would crumble before any of the great European nations gave up its claim to primacy. The "great powers," the "concert of powers"—what a fine sound it makes, really a splendid concert. And with this we have long since been in the situation of the Greeks after the first Roman victories, and we too may one day be occupied. One more fratricidal European war, and we'll have reached the point where we can hardly fail to contaminate the rest of the world with our miasmas. Are there really so few of them, people capable of reading what our present-day art and music are writing on the wall? Are there so few capable of meditating on the death of *melody*—something so profoundly European?

There is no turning back, nothing lost can be retrieved; but those who can stay faithful and can stand being alone, will perhaps rise from the dead some day, in a very remote future. That is the secret of all the Renaissances. Possibly, after heavy defeats and devastations, the seed already sown may germinate one day, in the deeply plowed soil. . . .

To stay faithful, the secret of all the Renaissances. . . . But some want to be faithful to liberal humanism, while others see in it the source of all our troubles. If we do not save the values of freedom, tolerance, and free inquiry, says one—if we do not save the emotional values, says another—if we do not restore the rigorous disciplines and the immutability of Catholicism, says a third—Europe will perish.

Thus, Thomas Mann (1875–1955):

In every humanism there is an element of weakness which stems from its repugnance to fanaticism of every kind, from its

348 THE IDEA OF EUROPE

tolerance, and from its leanings toward an indulgent skepticism, in a word, from its natural kindness. And this, under certain circumstances, can be fatal to it. What we may need today is a militant humanism, a humanism that would assert its virility and be convinced that the principle of freedom, tolerance, and free inquiry has no right to let itself be exploited by the shameless fanaticism of its enemies. Has European humanism become incapable of a resurrection that would restore to its principles their combative value? If it is no longer capable of taking stock of itself, of preparing for the struggle by renewing its vital energies, it will perish and Europe with it. Her name will be no more than a purely geographical and historical expression, and we would have no other choice but to seek, even now, a sanctuary outside time and space.[6]

This very humanism, this modern European ideal of Reason, Progress, Science, and Culture was repugnant to the "superessential and Quixotic" Spaniard that Miguel de Unamuno (1864–1936) tried to be. Here is his argument, or rather his refusal to argue the question:

Two words sum up what the rest of the world expects of Spain. These two words are "European" and "modern." "We must be European," "we must be modern," "we must modernize ourselves," "we must keep step with the century," "we must Europeanize ourselves"—one commonplace after another. . . .

I want no other method but that of passion: and when my breast is heaving with disgust, with loathing, with pity or with contempt, I let my mouth speak out of the fullness of my heart, and I let the words fall where they will.

We Spaniards, they say, we are impractical charlatans, filling in the gaps of logic with rhetoric, refining more or less intelligently but perfectly uselessly, lacking a sense of causality and determinism, we are scholastics, casuists, etc. etc. . . . I have heard things of the same kind said about St. Augustine, the great fiery African who poured out floods of rhetoric, who twisted language into antitheses, paradoxes, and other subtleties. St. Augustine was a Gongorist and a conceitist all in one. This suggests to me that conceits and Gongorism are the most natural forms of passion and vehemence.

The great African, the great ancient African! Here is an expression, "ancient African," to set against "modern European"

[6] Thomas Mann, *Avertissement à L'Europe* (Paris: Gallimard, 1937).

and every bit as good, if not better. St. Augustine is African and ancient; so is Tertullian. And why should we not say, "We must Africanize ourselves in the ancient way," or "we must ancientize ourselves in the African way"?

I am coming back to myself after two years of traveling through various domains of modern European culture. Alone with my conscience, I ask: "Am I European? am I modern?" and my conscience answers: "No, you are not European, what is called European; no, you are not modern, what is called modern." And I ask: "And the fact that you feel yourself neither European nor modern, does it not deprive you of your Spanishness?" . . .

Above all, and so far as I am concerned, I must confess that the more I think about it, the more I discover the deep-seated repugnance my mind has for everything that passes as the leading principles of the modern European mind, for today's scientific orthodoxy, for its methods and tendencies.

There are two things that are mentioned very often, science and life. One is as antipathetic to me, I must confess, as the other.

. . . The only way to enter into a living relationship with another is aggression; only those achieve true interpenetration, spiritual fraternity, who try to subjugate each other spiritually, whether they are individuals or nations. Only when I try to put my mind in the mind of my fellow man, do I receive his mind in mine. The blessing of the apostle is that he receives in himself the souls of all those he evangelizes: this gives nobility to proselytism.

. . . I have the profound conviction, however arbitrary it may be (the more profound the more arbitrary, as is the case with all the truths of faith), I have the profound conviction that the true and inner Europeanization of Spain, i.e. our digestion of that part of the European mind which can become our mind, will not begin until we have tried to impose ourselves on the European spiritual order, have made it swallow what is ours, essentially ours, in exchange for what is its, when we shall have tried to "Spanify" Europe.[7]

This is not a nationalist who speaks. It is a man who "desires and needs a soul, and a substantial soul." [8] And it is the Europe of Passion, of the most subversive spirit that through his mouth

---

[7] *Vérités arbitraires,* chapter on Europeanization dating from 1906.
[8] Cf. *The Tragic Sense of Life* (1912).

rejects the lukewarm, humanitarian Europe, concerned with survival. Hitler was to attempt to kill both.

The English essayist Hilaire Belloc, too, condemns the cult of Science and Progress, but he does it in the name of Authority and the Church:

> My thesis . . . is this:
> That the culture and civilization of Christendom—what was called for centuries in general terms "Europe," was made by the Catholic Church gathering up the social traditions of the Graeco-Roman Empire, inspiring them and giving the whole of that great body a new life. It was the Catholic Church which made us, gave us our unity and our whole philosophy of life, and formed the nature of the white world. That world—Christendom —went through the peril of the barbaric assault from without as also from the victorious pressure of great heresy—which soon became a new religion—Mahommedanism.
>
> These perils it survived, though shorn of much of its territory; it re-arose after the pressure was past to the high life of the Middle Ages, which in the 11th, 12th, and especially the 13th centuries reached a climax or summit wherein we were most ourselves and our civilization most assured. But from various causes of which perhaps old age was the chief, that great period showed signs of decline at the beginning of the 14th century; a decline which hastened rapidly throughout the 15th century. The Faith by which we live was increasingly doubted; and the moral authority upon which all depended was more and more contested. The society of Christendom underwent a heavy strain threatening disruption; it equally became more and more unstable, until at last in the early 16th century came the explosion which had been feared and awaited for so long. That disaster is called in general usage "The Reformation."
>
> From that moment onwards throughout the 16th and 17th centuries and the 18th, on through the 19th, the unity of Christendom having disappeared and the vital principle on which its life depended having become weak or distracted, our culture became a house divided against itself, and increasingly imperiled. This evil fortune was accompanied by a rapid increase in external knowledge, that is in science and the command of man over material things, even as he lost his grasp of spiritual truths. It was the converse of what had happened in the beginning of our civilization, when our religion had saved the ancient

world and formed a new culture, though burdened by a decline in science and the arts and material things.

Our increase in knowledge of the externals and in our power over nature did nothing to appease the rapidly growing internal strains of our world. The conflict between rich and poor, the conflict between opposing national idolatries, the lack of common standards and of the fixed doctrines upon which they depend had led up by the beginning of the 20th century to the brink of chaos; and threatened such dissension between men as to destroy Society. In this crisis the only alternatives are recovery through the restoration of Catholicism or the extinction of our culture.[9]

Another Catholic philosopher, Jacques Maritain, denounced the "errors" of liberal humanism in the name of Thomism. However, he puts his faith not in any reactionary utopia, but in a new humanism, an "integral humanism." On the eve of the Second World War, in a lecture on the "Twilight of Civilization," he expressed his faith in the "paths of liberty and the Spirit":

The fatality which worked against the modern democracies was that of the false philosophy of life which for a century altered their vital principle and which, paralyzing this principle from within, caused them to lose trust in themselves. In the meantime, the totalitarian dictatorships, much better versed in Machiavelli, have confidence in their own principle of force and trickery, and they risk everything upon this. The historical trial will continue until the root of the evil has been discovered and, at the same time the principle . . . of a renewed hope and of an invincible faith.

If the Western democracies are not to be swept away, and a night of long centuries is not to come down on civilization, it is on condition that they discover in its primitive purity their vital principle, which is justice and love, and whose source is of divine origin. It is on condition that they reconstruct their political philosophy, and thus rediscover the sense of justice and of heroism in rediscovering God.

In the coming twilight in which we stand there are signs . . . which lead us to think that already the uncertain rays of a dawn are beginning to show themselves. . . . As concerns France, the spiritual renewal which was carried on in the pre-war years

[9] Hilaire Belloc, *The Crisis of Civilization* (New York: Fordham University Press, 1937).

has been of great moment to the whole future of civilization. So is the development of political and social concepts founded on the value of the human person among the best sections of French youth. . . .

And Europe, is it too late for Europe? In the Europe of 1939, who would have dared to hope for the possibility of a new Christendom? But Europe can no longer be considered isolated, it is not Europe alone, it is the world, it is the whole world which must now resolve the problem of civilization. . . .

The totalitarian states are not unaware of the importance of moral unanimity; they strive to attain it, but they can arrive at it by intimidation and coercion. In the last analysis, with regard to the internal adhesion of hearts, these means are of doubtful worth.

The question now is whether the peoples of the countries which are still free are capable of attaining, by the paths of liberty and the spirit, a sufficient moral unanimity, and whether they are capable of resisting the adulterations which threaten their conscience from within.[10]

In the course of his lecture Maritain said among other things: "The important thing for each is not to know what the world will do, but to know what he himself will do." The same idea is to be met with in many essays of the same period: It seems to mark an existential limit to the value of the predictions we have been quoting.

Moreover, whether we are dealing with modern Cassandras (Thomas Hobbes, Swift, Butler, Spengler, Huxley, Orwell), or with the great utopians (Bacon, Thomas More, Campanella, Cyrano de Bergerac, Jules Verne, H. G. Wells, latter-day science fiction), the very concept of prediction needs serious revision. Karl Jaspers, author of one of the most significant works of the period between the two world wars, *Die gestige Situation unserer Zeit* (published in 1931), felt this as he reflected on the prophets of nihilism, who were heralding Hitlerism. Before proclaiming that everything is lost, let us correct our sense of proportion, by recalling the relativity of human history:

As compared with the thousands of millions of years since the beginning of the world, the six thousand years of human tradi-

[10] Jacques Maritain, *The Twilight of Civilization*, trans. Lionel Landry (New York: Sheed and Ward, 1943), pp. 62–65.

tion seem no more than the first second of a new period in the transformation of our planet. As contrasted with the hundreds of thousands of years during which (as disinterred skulls and other bones show) man has lived upon the earth, written and traditional history are but the earliest beginnings of what man can become as soon as he sets himself in movement to escape from slothfully recurrent conditions. No doubt from the outlook of a species for which thirty years are a generation, six thousand years is a long time. Man's memory makes him aware of the age of his race, so that now, just as two thousand years ago, he feels himself to be living in a terminal period, and he is apt to fancy that his best days lie in the past. But perspectives of terrestrial history have made him aware of the brevity of his undertakings and of the situation which has prevailed since he became man. He knows, now, that all lies in front of him. The speed of technical advances from decade to decade seems an infallible proof of this. Still he cannot but ask himself whether the whole of human history may not be a transient episode in the history of the world. Perhaps man is destined to perish from off the face of the planet, whose history may continue in his absence for interminable ages.[11]

All things are possible in the future: our sources of energy may become exhausted; the planet may turn cold, or the opposite may happen, with the progress of technology and the conquest of outer space man may be presented with new conditions; we may be at the end of a culture or on the contrary we may be at the beginning of an era of continuous development. To be sure, there are negative signs all around us, and we imagine that we can infer a law from them:

Questions arise concerning the obscure laws of an inexorable course of human destiny. May not some absolutely essential substance be slowly used up, so that we shall infallibly perish when the supply is exhausted? May not the decay of art, poesy, and philosophy be symptoms of the approaching exhaustion of this substance? Is it not possible that the way in which contemporary human beings become merged in the enterprise, their present modes of intercourse, the fashion in which they allow themselves to be driven like slaves, the futility of their political life, the chaos of their amusements—whether all these things be

[11] Karl Jaspers, *Man in the Modern Age,* trans. Eden and Cedar Paul (London: G. Routledge & Son, 1933).

not indications that the supply of the aforesaid hypothetical substance is running very low? We, perhaps, have still enough of it to note what we are losing; but in the near future our descendants, when its exhaustion has gone a stage further, will, one may suppose, no longer understand what is happening.[12]

To make predictions on the basis of such signs or militant doctrines, can signify spiritual capitulation, but can also and should signify an existential decision:

A contemplative forecast of the whole, a forecast in which the will plays no part, is nothing more than a flight away from that true activity which begins with the individual's inward activity. If I am content with a contemplative forecast, I allow myself to be dazzled in the "theatre of universal history"; I let myself be anaesthetized by prophecies of a necessary progress, whether on Marxian lines as an advance towards a classless society, or culturo-morphologically as a process in accordance with a law of supposed ripening, or dogmatico-philosophically as the expansion and realisation of some definitively attainable absolute truth. . . .

The nearer I am to the future I forecast, the more relevant is it, because it gives me more scope for interference; on the other hand, the more remote I am from the future I forecast, the more indifferent is it to me, because it is more out of touch with my possibilities of action. A forecast, in this sense, is the speculation of a man who wants to do something. He does not keep his eyes fixed on what will inevitably happen, but on what may happen; and he tries to make the future what he wants it to be. The future has become something that can be foreseen because it is modifiable by his own will. . . .

Such a forecast is something more than mere knowledge of actual happenings, for, as such knowledge, it is simultaneously a factor of what happens.[13]

2 : Twilight or a New Dawn?

THE DIAGNOSES QUOTED in the foregoing are scarcely cheering, but the reader may have noted that between Spengler and Maritain there emerged the possibility of new hope, in spite of the

[12] *Ibid.*
[13] *Ibid.*

rising tide of Hitlerism. Fatalism, pride, and nostalgic resignation were followed by more "militant" attitudes. (In the passage quoted above, Maritain alludes to the "personalist" movement which as early as 1933 launched the slogan of "commitment," i.e. the Spirit's refusal to resign in the face of the allegedly "fatal" laws of our decline.)

Between the two wars, a number of intellectuals went back to the old religious faiths, which oppose fatalism. This was a symptom of a new vitality, a renewal of the tensions, which from the beginning had constituted the dynamism of our culture. But these intellectuals refer to Europe only as their natural homeland. What about Europe herself, regarded as an entity, in the face of the twentieth-century world? Has she betrayed her world vocation? Is she still aware of herself? Is not the very fact that Ortega and Benda ask such questions—the former on the eve, the latter on the morrow, of the Second World War—the harbinger of a rebirth?

José Ortega y Gasset (1883–1955), in his best-known book, *The Revolt of the Masses* (1930), deals with a major problem— and at the time he was alone, at all events the first, to see so clearly—the problem of Europe's ability to rule. It was from this political angle, in the highest sense of the term, that he in turn addressed himself to the question that was haunting the period:

There has been so much talk of the decadence of Europe that many have come to take it for a fact. Not that they believe in it seriously and on proof, but that they have grown used to taking it as true, though they cannot honestly recall having convinced themselves decidedly in the matter at any fixed time. . . .

The frivolous spectacle offered by the smaller nations to-day is deplorable. Because it is said that Europe is in decadence and has given over ruling, every tupenny-ha'penny nation starts skipping, gesticulating, standing on its head or else struts around giving itself airs of a grown-up person who is the ruler of his own destinies. Hence the vibrionic panorama of "nationalisms" that meets our view everywhere. . . .

It is really comic to see how this or the other puny republic, from its out-of-the-way corner, stands up on tip-toe, starts rebuking Europe, and declares that she has lost her place in universal history.

What is the result? Europe had created a system of standards whose efficacy and productiveness the centuries have proved. Those standards are not the best possible; far from it. But they are, without a doubt, definite standards as long as no others exist or are visualised. Now the mass-peoples have decided to consider as bankrupt that system of standards which European civilisation implies, but as they are incapable of creating others, they do not know what to do, and to pass their time they kick up their heels and stand on their heads. Such is the first consequence which follows when there ceases to be in the world anyone who rules; the rest, when they break into rebellion, are left without a task to perform, without a programme of life.

The gypsy in the story went to confession, but the cautious priest asked him if he knew the commandments of the law of God. To which the gypsy replied: "Well, Father, it's this way: I *was* going to learn them, but I heard talk that they were going to do away with them."

Is not this the situation in the world at present? The rumour is running round that the commandments of the law of Europe are no longer in force, and in view of this, men and peoples are taking the opportunity of living without imperatives. For the European laws were the only ones that existed. . . .

This for those people who, with the thoughtlessness of children, announce to us that Europe is no longer in command. To command is to give people something to do, to fit them into their destiny, to prevent their wandering aimlessly about in an empty, desolate existence.

It would not matter if Europe ceased to command, provided there were someone able to take her place. But there is not the faintest sign of one. New York and Moscow represent nothing new, relatively to Europe. They are both of them two sections of the European order of things, which, by dissociating from the rest, have lost their meaning. . . .

If the European grows accustomed not to rule, a generation and a half will be sufficient to bring the old continent, and the whole world along with it, into moral inertia, intellectual sterility, universal barbarism. It is only the illusion of rule, and the discipline of responsibility which it entails, that can keep Western minds in tension. Science, art, technique, and all the rest live on the tonic atmosphere created by the consciousness of authority. If this is lacking, the European will gradually become degraded. Minds will no longer have that radical faith in themselves which impel them, energetic, daring, tenacious, towards the capture of great new ideas in every order of life. The European will inevitably become a day-to-day man. Incapable of creative, specialised effort, he will be always falling back on yesterday, on custom, on routine. He will turn into a commonplace, conventional, empty creature, like the Greeks of the decadence and those of the Byzantine epoch.[14]

Such, then, according to Ortega y Gasset, are the causes of our decadence. But here are the formulas for our rebirth:

The European cannot live unless embarked upon some great unifying enterprise. When this is lacking, he becomes degraded, grows slack, his soul is paralysed. We have a commencement of this before our eyes to-day. The groups which up to to-day have been known as nations arrived about a century ago at their highest point of expansion. Nothing more can be done with them except lead them to a higher evolution. They are now mere past, accumulating all around Europe, weighing it down, imprisoning it. With more vital freedom than ever, we feel that we cannot breathe the air within our nations, because it is a confined air. What was before a nation open to all the winds of heaven, has turned into something provincial, an enclosed space.

Everyone sees the need of a new principle of life. But as always happens in similar crises—some people attempt to save the situation by an artificial intensification of the very principle which has led to decay. This is the meaning of the "nationalist" outburst of recent years. And, I repeat, things have always gone that way. The last flare, the longest; the last sigh, the deepest. On the very eve of their disappearance there is an intensification of frontiers—military and economic.

But all these nationalisms are so many blind alleys. Try to project one into the future and see what happens. There is no outlet that way. . . . Nationalism is nothing but a mania, a pretext to escape from the necessity of inventing something new, some great enterprise. Its primitive methods of action and the type of men it exalts reveal abundantly that it is the opposite of a historical creation.

Only the determination to construct a great nation from the group of peoples of the Continent would give new life to the pulses of Europe. She would start to believe in herself again, and automatically to make demands on, to discipline, herself.[15]

[14] Ortega y Gasset, *The Revolt of the Masses,* authorized translation from the Spanish (New York: W. W. Norton & Company [Copyright 1932]).
[15] *Ibid.*

Spengler's romantic dialectic had reached the conclusion of inevitable decadence. Ortega y Gasset, reaching the conclusion that union was necessary, introduces a new factor, and contributes to creating it.

In his polemical manner, which is not so much disillusioned as provocative, Julien Benda is taking the same line when he accuses Europe of unconsciousness; it is to awaken her that he castigates her:

Europe has never been aware of herself as a political entity. From the political point of view Europe's will has been exclusively nationalist. It consisted of a twofold effort to form nations on the one hand, and to make them independent on the other. The movement begins with the Barbarians who were the true originators of the nationalities, in that they opposed the *gentes* to the internationalist elements, namely, the Roman Empire and the Church; they themselves embodied the negation of the *Imperium* and the *Ecclesia.* This movement took shape when the unity created by Charlemagne was broken up and his empire divided among his heirs. There were a few men—clerics nurtured in the religion of the Roman empire—who deplored this partition, but the majority rejoiced in it. It rejoiced, within each of the three divisions, at the thought that it would now be capable of achieving an independent destiny. From that moment on Europe's tendency to form separate groups became more and more pronounced. As is the case with all deep human impulses, everything that was done to check it served only to strengthen it. The universalist claims of the Hohenstaufens, and later of Charles V only crystallized the will to secede on the part of France, Austria, the Italian cities, the Swiss cantons, Flanders. The claims of the papacy produced the same effect on the various parts of Christendom. All adopted the slogan of one of them, "We are Venetians first, Christians afterwards." Finally, in the nineteenth century after the French Revolution and its great imperial heir, who sought to "denationalize" the peoples (particularly Germany!), Europe's will to be disunited and to form nations independent of one another reached its apogee. This was shown in a craze for separate status: Belgium broke away from Holland, and Sweden from Norway. It was strikingly embodied in Bismarck who, the exact opposite of Napoleon, sought to create his own nation by conquests, who resolutely rejected every idea of Europe as stupid idealism. As a logical consequence of his achievement, a regime was set up from the Niemen to the Atlantic, in which each state

was isolated in a devotion to itself and a contempt for the others
—"sacred egoism" of a kind never seen before—while new philosophical doctrines, acclaimed by all nations—Treitschke in Germany, Barrès in France—taught them to adore the instinct that
divided them and to despise the intelligence that might unite
them. The twentieth century, which will perhaps see the formation of Europe, opened with the striking triumph of anti-
Europe. . . .

The fact that Europe has never constituted a political entity is
reflected in this other fact, that a history of Europe has never been
written. The books bearing that title—except perhaps the admirable work that the great Belgian historian Henri Pirenne composed as a prisoner during the war of 1914—treat the history of
different parts of Europe, of their respective development, above
all of their conflicts, not of Europe as a historical entity tran-
scending them. I have occasionally reproached teachers of history
whom I knew to favor European unification for not giving their
pupils a few lessons on Europe treated as an indivisible political
reality. They replied that they were obliged to follow the state-
prescribed curriculum.

Nor has Europe ever had the consciousness of being a spiritual
entity. Here again we must distinguish between facts and
consciousness of facts. Christopher Dawson, an eminent English historian, shows us how in the Middle Ages the nations
were more or less shaped by the Church, thus justifying the saying of Stendahl: "Modern Europe is a child of Christianity." Let
us grant our historian that a community of civilization did exist
in Europe at the beginning. We may go further and recognize
that for a long time there was no tendency to national separatism.
No Parisian student in the twelfth century was surprised that the
German Albertus Magnus or the Italian Thomas Aquinas was
guiding his studies; nor did any bachelor of arts in Vienna find it
undesirable to entrust the formation of his mind to the Frenchman Jean Gerson. As late as the eighteenth century, during the
wars between France and Germany, most of the minor German
courts spoke French, read French books, followed French fashions. A certain spiritual European community thus existed de
facto, but consciousness of it, of its incompatibility with national
particularisms, did not exist. On the contrary, what very soon
appeared as consciousness, as manifest will, was the self-affirma-
tion of nations in their particular genius and very often in their
antagonisms. From now on scholars began to speak their native
languages rather than Latin, the tongue which now united them
above their nations: from now on the peoples began to pray and

preach in their own languages; and men of letters began to free the vernaculars from nonnational elements. . . .

There was, however, one period which really knew the consciousness of a European spirit, namely the close of the eighteenth century, when men not only possessed a cosmopolitan culture inculcated by the Jesuits, but took pride in it and regarded it as superior to the narrowly national cultures. Of these men Voltaire wrote in 1767 that "an immense republic of cultivated minds is being formed in Europe." Typical of them was the Prince de Ligne, whose tradition may be said to have continued with Goethe, Taine, Renan, Liszt, Nietzsche, Romain Rolland, André Gide. Do I need to say that this movement was violently counteracted in the nineteenth century, in the name of the national cultures; in Germany, with the Schlegels, the Lessings, the Görreses, who attacked French literature and its universalizing tendency; in France, with a Barrès who recognized only French truths, with a Maurras who vilified, in the person of Romain Rolland, everything that served the European spirit. This intellectual nationalism seems today to have contaminated the best minds.

. . . In the spiritual as well as in the political order, the twentieth century, which, we repeat, may see the realization of Europe, began with the fiercest and most conscious affirmation ever seen of anti-Europe. . . . Today, the idea of the nation seems to have finished its career, to have become harmful to the European, and the idea of Europe has made its appearance. But we must not indulge in illusions, we must not imagine that this idea will triumph as a matter of course, we must realize that it will encounter, on the part of those it seeks to dethrone, strong opposition, steady resistance, very serious obstacles.[16]

The Austrian poet Hugo von Hofmannsthal (1874–1929) asks us not so much to break down the nationalist obstacles as to go around them, by a new conscious realization of our spiritual assets:

There is no doubt that the concept of "Europe," like many other noble overall conceptions, has become problematic—nor is there any doubt that our spiritual survival depends on restoring it.

We shall never arrive at it by a process of abstraction, by subtracting from—or adding to—the concept of the nation, and still less by sentimental appeal. To rise to this great concept, the mind

[16] Julien Benda, in *L'Esprit Européen* (*Conférence des Rencontres internationales de Genève 1946* [Neuchâtel: Ed. de la Baconnière, 1947]).

must employ its finest powers: lived experience, acquired experience, spiritualization. It is to be found in every nation's highest achievements, wherever are expressed clearly and purely the noblest things a nation possesses as its very own. Without it, great geniuses are unthinkable. They are universal. If the Nation is their fate, Europe is their lived experience.

A great man or a great achievement *becomes* European: this happened to Caesar and to Napoleon, to Petrarch and to Kant, to German music from Bach to Beethoven, to French painting from Ingres to Cézanne. Where a great idea is conceived, there is Europe. If it is conceived within the national sphere, its only desire is to flower in the universal sphere. Today, as in the age of Anaximander, every philosophy is European. Every effective great political idea is European. Every fruitful insight into the past is European. And is there anything we need more urgently than a profound, wholly new and purified vision of what is not Europe?

Our epoch is an epoch of recovery—even though never before has the expression of weakness been so shameless, the will to disintegration so unrestrained. Behind all the noise made by the prophets of decadence and the Maenads of chaos, the chauvinists and the cosmopolitans, the worshipers of the fleeting moment, of appearances, against the great serious background of things European, I see a very few individuals who matter, scattered among the nations, uniting in a great idea: that of creative restoration.[17]

It was Martin Heidegger who summed up the problem of the very *Being* of the "western twilight" in its most compact form, that of the questioning in itself, which seems to be the keyword of his philosophy:

Anaximander, it is said, lived from the end of the seventh to the middle of the sixth century B.C. on the island of Samos, and one of his sayings is regarded as the oldest in Western thought. Here it is, according to the generally accepted text: "From what source things arise, to that they return of necessity when they are destroyed; for they suffer punishment and make reparation to one another for their injustice, according to the order of time." Thus it was translated by the young Nietzsche, in his essay completed in 1873 and entitled, "Philosophy in the Epoch of Greek Tragedy."

Coming from the depths of a chronological and historical distance of two millennia and a half, does Anaximander's maxim still

[17] Hugo von Hofmannsthal, article dated 1925, in *Gesammelte Werke* (S. Fischer Verlag, 1955), *Prosa* IV.

have something to say to us? By what authority would it speak? Would it be enough that it is the oldest? Antiquity of itself has no weight. Moreover, if the maxim is the oldest of those that have come down to us, we nevertheless do not know whether it is the most primitive maxim of Western thought. We can suppose this only in so far as we think that the essence of the West starts at the very point where that primitive maxim speaks.

But by what right would that which comes first speak to us, who are no doubt the latest of the latecomers to philosophy? Are we the latecomers to a History which is today reaching its end, which puts an end to all things, in an order ever more lugubrious and uniform? Or does the chronological and historical remoteness of the maxim conceal a historical proximity of the unformulated, which speaks to that which is to come?

Are we then on the eve of the most unheard-of transformation of the whole Earth and historical time? Are we approaching the twilight of a night which prepares another dawn? Does the land of the Evening come first? Will it be, beyond the West and the East, and through that which is European, the place where the History to come will begin? Are we already, we the men of today, Western in a sense that will be revealed first thanks to our entry into universal night? . . . *Are* we really the latecomers that we are? But are we not at the same time forerunners of the morning of another world era, which will leave behind it our present representations of History?

Nietzsche, from whose philosophy Spengler deduced, by a crude misunderstanding, his historical doctrine of the decadence of the West, wrote in *Traveler and His Shadow* in 1880: "It is a high state of mankind, that in which the Europe of the nations is no more than a dark forgotten past, but in which Europe still lives thanks to thirty very old books, which will never age."[18]

Ortega y Gasset was perhaps the first to see in the crisis of Europe a prerequisite for its rebirth. And so we shall let him conclude this chapter:

Is it as certain as people say that Europe is in decadence; that it is resigning its command; abdicating. May not this apparent decadence be a beneficial crisis which will enable Europe to be really, literally Europe? The evident decadence of the *nations* of Europe, was not this *a priori* necessary if there was to be one day possible a United States of Europe, the plurality of Europe substituted by its formal unity? [19]

[18] Martin Heidegger, *Holzwege.*
[19] Ortega y Gasset, *op. cit.*

PART SEVEN
THE ERA OF
FEDERATIONS

From Cultural Unity to Political Unity

1: The Living Sources

SULLY'S GRAND DESIGN was published posthumously. The Abbé de Saint-Pierre was not listened to. Victor Hugo was merely applauded. By contrast, those who write on Europe in the twentieth century, whether they will or no, are involved in history in the making. Some could imagine that they were no more than commentators, objective analysts. They overlooked the fact that newspapers mold public opinion which serves as guide to political leaders, and that newspapers find their doctrines (even if they do not realize this) in an intellectual atmosphere which the authors we shall quote below have largely helped to shape.

In this final part of our book we shall not follow chronological order—it is of little importance for such a short period, in which everyone reacts to everyone else almost simultaneously. Our choice of texts will be determined by this very simple reasoning: Europe, challenged by the World, and tending to unite for her own salvation seeks first of all to go back to the *sources* of her specific constitutive values; the better to see what she was, what she is, and what she can be, she compares herself with other civilizations, and then rediscovers both the nature of her world function and the nature of her very special unity, which is unity in diversity; it is up to her to draw the consequences from this rediscovery. . . .

We shall not list again the well-known historical sources of Western civilization: Near-Eastern antiquity; Athens, Rome, Jerusalem; the Germans, the Celts, and finally the Arabs. We shall confine ourselves to quoting a few key texts illustrating the rediscovery of our diverse origins, and our awareness of them at the present stage of our evolution. In every epoch of her history Europe redefined herself by what she picked out—discovered or chose to ignore—in her various Ancient Histories. In our day, it seems that the choice proposed by Paul Valéry as early as 1922 [1] exerted a determining influence on most subsequent writing on Europe. Here, then, is his famous definition of the three sources of any culture deserving the name "European" in his views.

I shall consider as European all those peoples who in the course of history have undergone the three influences I shall name.

The first is that of Rome. Wherever the Roman Empire has ruled and its power has asserted itself; and further, wherever the Empire has been the object of fear, admiration, and envy; wherever the weight of the Roman sword has been felt; wherever the majesty of Roman institutions and laws, or the apparatus and dignity of its magistrature have been recognized or copied, and sometimes even incongruously aped—there is something European. Rome is the eternal model of organized and stable power. . . .

Then came Christianity. . . . As St. Peter testifies, although it was one of the very few religions to be looked on with disfavor in Rome . . . Christianity, born of the Jewish people, itself spread to the gentiles of every race; through baptism it conferred on them the new dignity of Christians, as Rome conferred its citizenship on its former enemies. It gradually spread throughout the area of Roman power, adapting itself to the forms of the Empire, even adopting its administrative divisions (in the fifth century, *civitas* meant the episcopal city). It took all it could from Rome, and fixed its capital there rather than in Jerusalem. It borrowed Rome's language. A man born in Bordeaux could be a Roman citizen and even a magistrate and at the same time a bishop of the new religion. The same *Gaul* could be imperial prefect and in pure *Latin* write beautiful hymns to the glory of the Son of God born a *Jew* and a subject of Herod. There, already, we have almost a complete European. A common law, a common God; one and the same temporal judge, and one and the same judge in eternity.

But while the Roman conquest had affected only political man and ruled the mind only in its external habits, the Christian conquest aimed at and gradually reached the depths of consciousness. . . .

Christianity proposed to the mind the most subtle, the greatest,

[1] In a lecture at the University of Zurich, November, 1922: "The European," in *Collected Works*, X, 316-22.

and indeed the most fruitful problems. Whether it were a question of the value of testimony, the criticism of texts, or the sources and guarantees of knowledge; of the distinction between faith and reason, and the opposition that arises between them, or the antagonism between faith, deeds, and works; a question of freedom, servitude, or grace; of spiritual and material power and their mutual conflict, the equality of men, the status of women—and how much else?—Christianity educated and stimulated millions of minds, making them act and react, century after century. . . .

However, this is not yet a finished portrait of us Europeans. Something is still missing from our make-up. . . .

What we owe to Greece is perhaps what has most profoundly distinguished us from the rest of humanity. To her we owe the discipline of the Mind, the extraordinary example of perfection in everything. To her we owe the method of thought that tends to relate all things to man, the complete man. Man became for himself the *system of reference* to which all things must in the end relate. He must therefore develop all the parts of his being and maintain them in a harmony as clear and even as evident as possible. He must develop both body and mind. As for the mind, he must learn to defend himself against its excesses and its reveries, those of its products which are vague and purely imaginary, by means of scrupulous criticism and minute analysis of its judgments, the rational separation of its functions, and the regulation of its forms. . . .

These, it seems to me, are the three essential conditions that define a true European, a man in whom the European mind can come to its full realization. Wherever the names of Caesar, Caius, Trajan, and Virgil, of Moses and St. Paul, and of Aristotle, Plato, and Euclid have had simultaneous meaning and authority, there is Europe. Every race and land that has been successively Romanized, Christianized, and, as regards the mind, disciplined by the Greeks, is absolutely European.

Let us now review the Three Sources.

First of all Jerusalem, the oldest.

It might be thought that the preceding centuries had said all there is to say about the Biblical heritage. The Protestant countries were nurtured on an Old Testament whose heroes, wars, and miracles had become their true antiquity since Luther. As for Catholicism, Chateaubriand, in *Génie du Christianisme,* demonstrated brilliantly that the secret of great European literature lies in the synthesis between Greek tradition and Biblical tradition.

In the twentieth century, however, Europeans are becoming aware of several "new" aspects of their Semitic heritage.

Let us first recall the theories of Victor Bérard, who derives the Homeric epic from the myths and the history of the Phoenicians and the Hebrews, and who discerns a formal affinity between the Chronicles of the Old Testament and Hesiod's *Works and Days*. Thus the Biblical source reappears among us blended with the most ancient and most living Hellenic source.

More specifically, the European of today discovers that some of his most typical attitudes, which have usually been derived from Roman and Greek origins, actually derive from the Hebrew source.

For instance, the Jacobins thought that the prototypes of the revolutionary spirit were to be found in Rome. But, André Siegfried tells us:

Our spiritual, not merely intellectual, conception of man . . . we owe to the Jewish tradition, which flowers magnificently in the Gospels. The prophets of Israel, those thunder-and-lightning holy demagogues, filled our minds with the revolutionary thirst for justice which distinguishes the West, socially speaking.

Similarly, Siegfried adds, today's revolutions do not echo the Graeco-Roman tradition:

Marxist passion goes back rather to the spiritual leaven of ancient Israel, at once destructive and yet filled with indestructible hope for the future.

We find a no less surprising aspect of the Hebrew heritage in an entirely different domain, an aspect which the preceding centuries had been unaware of, or had even repressed, because of their antireligious scientism: we are told that the origin of modern science is far less Greek than Biblical. Karl Jaspers has emphasized this, in connection with Nietzsche: [2]

[2] In a short and compact work on Nietzsche and Christianity. The text quoted above which sums up the argument of chapter III of that work, is an excerpt from a lecture by Karl Jaspers included in *L'Esprit Européen* (Neuchâtel: Ed. de la Baconnière, 1947), pp. 303-4.

Love of science is characteristic of Europe, and the same is true of the immense scientific conquests made by modern research.

European science is limitlessly turned toward everything that is and can be thought. According to it there is nothing that is not worth the trouble of knowing; it seems almost to be losing itself in the infinite. But whatever its object may be, it situates it relationally. It reconciles universal extension with concentration of all knowledge in the universe of sciences.

It allows no blinds to be drawn; it shatters the peace and quiet of opinions formed once and for all. Its pitiless criticism reveals facts and possibilities. But its critical freedom is also constantly turning against itself. It casts light on its own methods, recognizes the modes of its knowledge, the meaning and limitations of its insights. Such a science goes far beyond the rudiments that existed in China, in India, and in ancient Greece; Greek science was merely an introduction, a pedagogic instrument. Whence comes modern science, what impulses engendered it? It would not exist without Biblical religion. This thesis is advanced in the following sense:

The world having been created by God must be essentially good. This is why everything that is deserves to be known, as a part of the creation. But often a new insight contradicts the systematic constructions that were previously taken for granted. Even if these constructions seem to be implied in a logical whole —as was the case with the Greeks' conception of the world and consciousness of Being—science as logical construction bursts the confines of logic. The advantages of a coherent, self-contained system of knowledge are sacrificed to endless research for its own sake; the peace of systematic certainty is sacrificed to never-ceasing doubt. The logic of science opens out onto the irrational, and penetrates into it as it submits to it. The interaction between theoretical conceptions and actual experiment makes it possible to keep advancing in the continuous struggle to attain reality. But even more profoundly than this struggle against appearances for the discovery of Being, another impulse is at work here. God, having created the world, seems responsible for what it is. Knowledge becomes an attack against God. On the other hand, such a knowledge meets God's demand for absolute truthfulness. Thus at the source of science there develops the need to interrogate God in criticism of God. This impulse, stemming from the Book of Job, permeates all European thought. This passionate and restrained indictment of God, linked to love for everything that is God's creation, gave birth to European science—a science which keeps progressing for some time even after these particular impulses have lost their momentum.

As can be seen, the Hebrew source still holds surprises for us, even apart from archeological finds such as the Dead Sea scrolls. Patiently, through the Bible, the Hebrew tradition remains the most present and most active of the three in millions of individuals' lives.

As for the Greek source, which waters only the intellectual strata of our countries, it seems decidedly to be rising, at the expense of the Roman source.

The revival of our interest in things Greek is reflected in the twentieth century by the most varied symptoms: discovery of the pre-Socratic philosophers (which can now be read even in paperbacks); the vogue for mythology (Freud's Oedipus complex, the *Ulysses* of Joyce or Kazantzakis, Spitteler's *Prometheus,* Gide's *Theseus,* Cocteau's *Orpheus,* etc); revival of the themes and titles of Greek tragedy by many playwrights, poets, and composers ("Choephores and Eumenides," by Claudel and Darius Milhaud, to mention only one example, re-created the sacred thrill of the ancient drama, of which a poet like Racine retained only the plot); rediscovery of the secret of the Doric style; passionate researches into the mystery religions. . . .

Dr. Bruno Snell, of Hamburg, one of the leading contemporary Hellenists, formulates the problem of the vitality of the Greek tradition as follows:

Man, at least Western man, attempts to steer his future course with a will and a purpose. But since he cannot very well plan in a vacuum, since he must accept the guidance of given facts, he orientates his search along the bearings of his own past. The question: "What do I want to do?" is in his mind always linked with the further question: "Who am I, and what have I been?" . . . If we hope to be Europeans—and such an intent must be implied in our desire to read and write, and to preserve the arts, technology, philosophy—the question which looms before us is: "What were the Greeks?" And especially if we are dissatisfied with this or that aspect of our modern European culture, we must ask with an added emphasis: "What was the original form of this culture at a time when the modern distortions had not yet marred its face?" [3]

According to him, this is what twentieth-century man, in his specific historical situation, can and should expect of Hellenism:

About the middle of the twenties of the present century, after the first world war, when men began again to consider what values were worth saving in Europe, we entertained doubts whether the traditional forms of humanism were not obsolete. The humanism of Erasmus, it was claimed, had placed too much emphasis on scholarship and learning; the humanism of Goethe was overly aesthetic. What was needed was a new humanism which took account of the whole of man, not only of his thinking and his feeling, but also of his acting. This ethical and political humanism put the concept of *paideia*, of education and culture, in the centre, and thus actually reached back to the sources of the humanism of Isocrates and Cicero. And yet this humanism did not trace its descent from Cicero and Isocrates, but hoped to drink at the common well of all antiquity, particularly Plato, the opposite number of Isocrates, in whose eyes man and his education merited no special status; for he considered God, not man, the measure of all things. . . . The gods are the measure of all things: this dictum signalizes to the Greeks that the world is a cosmos and that everything is controlled by a stable order. It is a concept of nature upon which the Greeks pinned their faith; but more than believing in it, they also attempted to comprehend its principles. The more deeply they probed into the mystery, the clearer it became to them that behind the gods there existed an even more universal plan which controlled the life of man and gave it its meaning. Our European culture may well be said to rest on the discovery of the Greeks that this plan takes different manifestations: to the intellect it appears in the shape of law, to the senses it is beauty, and to the active spirit it is justice. The persuasion that truth, beauty, and justice exist in the world, even though their appearance is largely hidden, is our ever-present heirloom from the Greeks, and even today this conviction is unimpaired. [4]

However, the Greek heritage, when questioned by twentieth-century man, holds more in store for us than the golden mean. Two Greek myths fascinate the modern European, according to

[3] Bruno Snell, *The Discovery of the Mind*, trans. T. G. Rosenmeyer (Oxford: Basil Blackwell, 1953), p. 261.
[4] *Ibid.*, pp. 256–59, *passim.*

whether he thinks he recognizes in them his passion for scientific daring or for sailing the political seas—the proud Prometheus and the cunning Ulysses.

Louis Rougier, a philosopher of sciences, describes a European Prometheus: [5]

Toynbee maintains that a fundamental myth presides over the genesis of every civilization. In the case of the civilization we are dealing with, this myth is easy to discover: the myth of Prometheus. . . .

The myth of Prometheus prefigures the spirit of the West. It is the spirit of revolt against the prohibitions of the jealous gods, who symbolize the fears of primitive man in the face of nature's blind forces which dominate and terrify him. It is the spirit of curiosity and adventure that drives Ulysses to unknown horizons, makes him face the perils of the sea and Poseidon's trickery, and makes him surmount the dangers that assail him by intelligence and courage. It is the cult of labor and effort that induces Hercules to purge the earth of tyrants, brigands and monsters, to tame rivers, to drain marshes, to cut through mountains, to build canals, to tame and civilize nature. It is the critical spirit that rises against superstition, the spirit that Lucretius celebrated in his praise of Epicurus: "When man's life lay for all to see foully groveling upon the ground, crushed beneath the weight of a Religion, which displayed her head in the regions of heaven, threatening mortals from on high with horrible aspects, a man of Greece was the first that dared to uplift mortal eyes against her, the first to make stand against her . . . liberating men from the vain terrors of the Acheron and the Tartarus."

In the eyes of one of the men who contributed most to the union of Europe, the count Richard Coudenhove-Kalergi, it is Ulysses who prefigures the adventurous European spirit:

Ulysses is the true prototype of the European at the same time as he is the hero of the earliest adventure novel in the West. He appears in his full stature, both modern and timeless, when we compare him with the hero of the *Iliad*. Achilles, the idol of antiquity on whom Alexander the Great modeled himself, was the Greek Siegfried, a youthful hero, brave and strong, not too bright, who rushed into the fray, there to die promptly and be-

[5] Louis Rougier, article in *Revue des Deux Mondes,* October 1, 1958.

come immortal. Ulysses is far more complex. His character has several dimensions. He is not only courageous and magnanimous, but also shrewd and cunning. He is European in that his passion is tamed by a sense of measure. He does not seek out dangers, but is equal to them when he meets them. He does not seek out fights, but when he fights he wins. The fate of his companions matters to him as much as his own. Despite his amorous adventures, he remains a faithful loving husband, a good son and an exemplary father. He does not contend with the gods who persecute him, but bears his harsh fate with the patience of Job.

In modern dress, Ulysses would be instantly taken for an authentic twentieth-century European. We can very well imagine him with the thickset features and high forehead of a Churchill. It is likely that Churchill would have acted with the same astuteness and the same daring as Ulysses did when he helped his companions to escape from Polyphemus' cave. Both were sailors, first and foremost. Ulysses is not only a warrior, like his comrades in the *Iliad*, but a hero of the sea.

Throughout the *Odyssey* his main effort is not directed against men but against the elements, the winds and waves. In this too he is a prototype of the European who conquered world hegemony because he learned to dominate the seas, and whose major accomplishment lies in the triumph of his technology over nature.

Lastly, he is a true European because in him, a Greek, came together the most diverse national traits—French, English, German, Italian. . . . Reborn today he could be the son of any of these nations. He could also distinguish himself in any profession —as engineer or foreman, as landowner or officer, as diplomat or parliamentarian. His greatness derives from the fullness with which he realizes body, will, and spirit. This is why he is the forerunner of the human ideal type that came after him—the medieval knight and the gentleman of our own epoch. His royal bearing contradicts the proverb that clothes make the man. When a storm tosses him naked on the shore of Alcinous, the king himself and his daughter Nausicaa receive him as a guest of honor without knowing who he is: they sensed that they were dealing with a great lord, a hero, as well as a man of elevated and free mind. We cannot imagine the old Menelaus composing hymns to Helen, but we can very well imagine the aged Ulysses in his eagle's nest at Ithaca, writing his memoirs, his "Poetry and Truth," This primitive *Odyssey*, revised and rewritten later by a poet, may very well be the one which has survived the centuries, and which, in our own day, still entrances European youth by its direct freshness, vitality and humanity.[6]

Now we come to a most unusual voice which resembles no other, yet which has aroused deep echoes in many of our best minds. This is the voice of Simone Weil (1909–1943), who for a short time was the most naturally Greek and Christian soul in our time. Speaking with the utmost intransigence from the sole point of view of spirituality and divine love, she discarded from the European tradition everything that is not Greek or evangelical. More particularly, she rejected the Roman and the Hebrew traditions:

The Gospels are the last and most marvellous expression of Greek genius, as the *Iliad* is its first expression. The spirit of Greece makes itself felt here not only by the fact of commanding us to seek to the exclusion of every other good "the kingdom of God and his righteousness" but also by its revelation of human misery, and by revealing that misery in the person of a divine being who is at the same time human. The accounts of the Passion show that a divine spirit united to the flesh is altered by affliction, trembles before suffering and death, feels itself, at the moment of deepest agony, separated from men and from God. This sense of human misery gives these accounts of the Passion that accent of simplicity which is the stamp of Greek genius. And it is the same sense which constitutes the great worth of Attic tragedy and of the *Iliad*. . . .

Particularly rare is a true expression of misfortune: in painting it one almost always affects to believe, first, that degradation is the innate vocation of the unfortunate; second, that a soul may suffer affliction without being marked by it, without changing all consciousness in a particular manner which belongs to itself alone. For the most part the Greeks had such strength of soul as preserved them from self-deception. For this they were recompensed by knowing in all things how to attain the highest degree of lucidity, of purity and of simplicity. . . .

The Romans and the Hebrews both believed themselves exempt from the common misery of man, the Romans by being chosen by destiny to be the rulers of the world, the Hebrews by the favour of their God, and to the exact extent in which they obeyed him. The Romans despised foreigners, enemies, the vanquished, their subjects, their slaves; neither have they any epics or tragedies. The Hebrews saw a trace of sin in all afflic-

[6] *Odysseus der Europäer*, article published in various journals in 1954.

tion and therefore a legitimate motive for despising it. They saw their vanquished as an abomination in God's sight and therefore condemned to expiate their crimes. Thus cruelty was sanctioned and even inevitable. . . .

Despite the brief intoxication caused, during the Renaissance, by the discovery of Greek letters, the Greek genius has not been revived in the course of twenty centuries. Something of it appears in Villon, Shakespeare, Cervantes, Molière, and once in Racine. . . . But nothing of all that the peoples of Europe have produced is worth the first known poem to have appeared among them. Perhaps they will rediscover that epic genius when they learn how to accept the fact that nothing is sheltered from fate, how never to admire might, or hate the enemy, or to despise sufferers.[7]

"Never to admire strength . . ." The exact opposite was the motto of fascism, obsessed as it was by imperial Rome; though we may doubt whether the Fascists understood imperial Rome better than the Jacobins understood republican Rome.

Thus Rome has a bad press among present-day intellectuals. According to Simone Weil, Rome is the "Great Beast." The Romans were gangsters, and worse than that:

The Romans . . . that handful of adventurers brought together by necessity. . . . The Romans could not tolerate anything rich in spiritual content. Love of God is a dangerous fire whose contact could prove fatal to their wretched deification of slavery. So they ruthlessly destroyed spiritual life under all its forms. They very cruelly persecuted the Pythagoreans and all philosophers associated with any authentic traditions. . . .
They wiped out all the Druids in Gaul; destroyed the Egyptian religious cults; drowned in blood and brought into disrepute by ingenious calumnies the worship of Dionysus. We know what they did to the Christians at the beginning. . . .
The truly Christian inspiration has fortunately been preserved by mysticism. But apart from pure mysticism, Roman idolatry has defiled everything. . . . If a Christian worships God with a heart disposed like that of a pagan of Rome in the homage rendered to the Emperor, that Christian is an idolator also.[8]

[7] Simone Weil, *Intimations of Christianity Among the Ancient Greeks,* trans. E. C. Geissbuhler (London: Routledge and Kegan Paul, 1957), pp. 52–55.
[8] Simone Weil, *The Need for Roots,* trans. Arthur Wills (New York: G. P. Putnam's Sons, 1952), pp. 274–77, *passim.*

Spengler's judgment was just as severe. According to him, Roman civilization was merely external and artificial, and it "finished" (by killing it off) Hellenic "culture":

Unspiritual, unphilosophical, devoid of art, clannish to the point of brutality, aiming relentlessly at tangible successes, they stand between the Hellenic Culture and nothingness. An imagination directed purely to practical objects—they had religious laws governing godward relations as they had other laws governing human relations, but there was no specifically Roman sage of gods—was something which is not found at all in Athens. In a word, Greek *soul*—Roman *intellect;* and this antithesis is the differentia between Culture and Civilization. . . .

Not till the Romans came with their practical energy was slave-holding given that big collective character which many students regard as the die-stamp of Classical economics, legislation and way of life, and which in any event vastly lowered both the value and the inner worthiness of such free labour as continued to exist side by side with gang-labour. . . . Not till the Roman Caesarism—foreshadowed by C. Flaminius, shaped first by Marius, handled by strong-minded, large-scale men of fact—did the Classical World learn the *pre-eminence of money.* Without this fact neither Caesar, nor "Rome" generally, is understandable. In every Greek is a Don Quixote, in every Roman a Sancho Panza factor, and these factors are dominants.[9]

However, T. S. Eliot reminds us that the Roman Empire was not only the military and bureaucratic slave state of the later period, but also the lofty ideal of Virgil, one of Europe's spiritual fathers:

. . . even those who have as little Latin as I must remember and thrill at the lines:

His ego nec metas rerum, nec tempora pono:
Imperium sine fine dedi . . .
Tu regere imperio populos, Romane, memento
[hae tibi erunt artes] pacique imponere morem,
parcere subiectis et debellare superbos . . .

I say that it was all the end of history that Virgil could be asked to find, and that it was a worthy end. And do you really think

[9] Spengler, *The Decline of the West,* authorized translation by Ch. F. Atkinson (New York: Alfred A. Knopf, 1928), I, 32, 36.

that Virgil was mistaken? You must remember that the Roman Empire was transformed into the Holy Roman Empire. What Virgil proposed to his contemporaries was the highest ideal even for an unholy Roman Empire, for any merely temporal empire. We are all, so far as we inherit the civilization of Europe, still citizens of the Roman Empire, and time has not yet proved Virgil wrong when he wrote *nec tempora pono: imperium sine fine dedi*. But, of course, the Roman Empire which Virgil imagined and for which Aeneas worked out his destiny was not exactly the same as the Roman Empire of the legionaries, the pro-consuls and governors, the business men and speculators, the demagogues and generals. It was something greater, but something which exists because Virgil imagined it. It remains an ideal, but one which Virgil passed on to Christianity to develop and to cherish.

In the end, it seems to me that the place which Dante assigned to Virgil in the future life, and the role of guide and teacher as far as the barrier which Virgil was not allowed to pass, was not capable of passing, is an exact statement of Virgil's relation to the Christian world. We find the world of Virgil, compared to the world of Homer, to approximate to a Christian world, in the choice, order, and relationship of its values. I have said that this implies no comparison between Homer the poet and Virgil the poet. Neither do I think that it is exactly a comparison between the worlds in which they lived, considered apart from the interpretation of these worlds which the poets have given us. It may be merely that we know more about the world of Virgil, and understand it better; and therefore see more clearly how much, in the Roman ideal according to Virgil, is due to the shaping hand and the philosophical mind of Virgil himself. For, in the sense in which a poet is a philosopher (as distinct from the sense in which a great poet may embody a great philosophy in great poetry) Virgil is the greatest philosopher of ancient Rome. It is not, therefore, simply that the civilization in which Virgil lived is nearer to the civilization of Christianity than is that of Homer; we can say that Virgil, among classical Latin poets or prose writers, is uniquely near to Christianity. There is a phrase which I have been trying to avoid, but which I now find myself obliged to use: *anima naturaliter Christiana*. Whether we apply it to Virgil is a matter of personal choice; but I am inclined to think that he just falls short: and that is why I said just now that I think Dante has put Virgil in the right place.[10]

[10] T. S. Eliot, *On Poetry and Poets* (New York: Farrar, Straus and Cudahy, 1957), pp. 145–47.

A German Catholic essayist, Reinhold Schneider (1887–1959), in a valuable little book, *Europa als Lebensform,* stresses the emotional value that the Pax Romana still holds for us:

The Piazza of the capitol, conceived by Michelangelo, and given by him to the City, is a wellspring of present European history. It is best approached at nightfall; when Marcus Aurelius sits astride his horse, a lonely figure in the fading light, reflected by the fountains onto the columns that line the square. Very little of the gold of antiquity, of the age of imperial peace, remains on the Emperor's armor; but, according to a Roman popular tradition, this gold increases, and when the whole statue is covered with it, the Emperor, who died in the course of a military campaign, will inaugurate a new reign of peace. Thus Europe finds her image in the Emperor who protects and blesses the City and the World. But let us not escape from reality by sharing the dreams of the suffering masses: nothing could be farther from the spirit of Marcus Aurelius! "He who saw what exists today contemplated with a single glance what was from all time and will be for all eternity." The present contains the whole history of the world. And if Europe exists within us, in the plentitude of her contradictory diversities and her infinite mission, Europe is here and now, as a destiny; however, if this image does not come to dwell in the inwardness of our being, if she is not our "heart's core," our "heart of hearts," as Hamlet says to Horatio, then Europe has ceased to exist and the land has become a battlefield of the technological powers of the inhuman.[11]

Paul Valéry in his speech of 1922 does not as much as mention the Germanic source. This Frenchman of Genoese origin was conscious only of his Mediterranean heritage. In the 1930's the very concept of *Germanentum* was to be obscured and repressed under the impact of the fantastic neo-barbarian doctrines of National Socialism. There was a reaction of universal horror with the discovery of the crimes which those doctrines allegedly justified.

Moreover, the Nordic democracies are as instinctively hostile to the "Holy Roman Empire of Germanic nation" as the Latin democracies are. Would perhaps the first be hostile because it was "Roman," the second because it was "of Germanic nation"?

[11] Reinhold Schneider, *Europa als Lebensform* (Hegner, 1957).

The truth is that the very concept of the Holy Empire is no longer understood. (And it never was in France or in Scandinavia.)

How then are we to do justice to the Germanic contribution? Gonzague de Reynold, the Swiss historian, of an old Fribourg family, writing in France, but living on the border of the German-speaking world, devoted one of the eight volumes of his major work, *La Formation de l'Europe*, to the Germans, from their origin down to the Carolingian period. Reynold describes "the fusion of the Barbaricum with Romania, under the auspices of the Church," a fusion which can be said (as can also be said of Charlemagne) to have truly created Europe. According to Reynold the two principal "discoveries" of twentieth-century historiography concerning the Germanic heritage can be summed up as follows:

1. It is not true that the Empire was ruined by the "great invasions":

. . . Without divisions and weaknesses in the Empire, there would have been no Germanic peril. The Germans were not sufficiently numerous to conquer it. It is foolish to speak of Germanic invasions, let alone of "great invasions."

There were the Germans outside the Empire, and those within: the latter defended the Empire against the former, took over leading commands, and became the Empire:

. . . In the end the question was: which German people was capable of taking over from the Roman people and restoring the imperium? [12]

The Franks turned out to be capable of that. Charlemagne, "the father of Europe," [13] was a Frank. The first concrete attempt at a European federation in the twentieth century, that of the Six, was, not without reason, baptized "the Europe of Charlemagne."

[12] *La Formation de l'Europe* (Paris: Plon, 1937), VII, 340.
[13] This epithet, quoted above *(rex pater Europae)*, is not merely symbolic. According to O. Forst de Battaglia, in *Traité de Généalogie* (Lausanne, 1945), the number of Charlemagne's descendants alive today can be estimated at twenty million!

2. Germanism, which recognizes the rights of "folk" communities, is one of the two sources of European federalism, the other being, according to Reynold, the trinitarian doctrine formulated by the earliest Councils of the Church:

The political and social organization [of the Germans] made them opponents of Roman bureaucratic centralization. Their organization was federative in the full sense of the term, being founded upon the oath: clans combined into tribes, and tribes into a people; there were assemblies of free men and warriors; the *Volksthing* survives in the mountain cantons of Switzerland today as the *Landgemeinden*. Hence a law which—between two extremes of the *jus romanum:* the individual and the State—provided for checks and balances to prevent the individual, the weaker element, from being absorbed by the State, the stronger element. The principle of Germanic law, indeed, is the idea of association, *Genossenschaftsrecht,* as the great jurist Gierke said.
. . . When the *imperium romanum* by miracle became Christian, the emperor ceased to be a god himself and became God's representative on earth. Constantine humbled himself before the Church, but his successors who were Arians found in their heresy justification for absolutism and Caesaropapism. The god of the Arians, one and monolithic, was hypostatized in the all-powerful emperor. With the triumph of the trinitarian doctrine, this conception was no longer possible. "The emperor is not above the Church but inside the Church," St. Ambrose harshly reminded the penitent Theodorus.
St. Augustine was St. Ambrose's disciple. . . . To match a Christian emperor with a Christian regime was one of the goals that the author of *The City of God* set himself. It was Charlemagne's breviary. In the centuries to come it was to have as much influence as Rousseau's *Social Contract* or Marx's *Capital.* There is a passage in it, which describes the Church as traveling for the term of its earthly pilgrimage, alongside human diversity, which it accepts, protects, and follows. St. Augustine's political ideal, the *societas civitatum,* is an association of free cities united in the same faith and the same love. Thus diversity becomes the first condition of unity. This is federalism of which we are justified in saying that it is the Christian conception of political and social life, the order that secures peace and quiet for all.

This last quotation invokes the Christian heritage.
Two great schools of cultural historians differed violently with each other on this score during the so-called interwar period

(1919–1939). One, programmatically optimistic, continued the tradition of the Enlightenment, of Promethean science and technology, and regarded Europe as a creation of the Renaissance. The other, pessimistic more by allegiance than by nature, regarded the great centuries of the Catholic Middle Ages (from the eleventh to the thirteenth) as the only Europe worthy of the name. The Europe of Man and the future *vs.* the Europe of Christendom and the past? What we have here is rather a polemic between two parties both genuinely concerned with saving the present-day Europe—a Europe threatened from without by the rise of "quantitative empires," and from within by age-old divisions. But to which of the saints should we appeal? Or to which of the scientists?

We will allow one of the deans of European historiography, Christopher Dawson, to define the symmetrically similar errors committed by both schools:

Modern historians, particularly in England, have frequently tended to use the present as an absolute standard by which to judge the past, and to view all history as an inevitable movement of progress that culminates in the present state of things. There is some justification for this in the case of a writer like Mr. H. G. Wells, whose object is to provide the modern man with a historical background and a basis for his view of the world; but even at the best this way of writing history is fundamentally unhistorical, since it involves the subordination of the past to the present, and instead of liberating the mind from provincialism by widening the intellectual horizon, it is apt to generate the Pharisaic self-righteousness of the Whig historians or, still worse, the self-satisfaction of the modern Philistine.

There is, of course, the opposite danger of using history as a weapon *against* the modern age, either on account of a romantic idealisation of the past, or in the interests of religious or national propaganda. Of these the latter is the most serious, since the romanticist at least treats history as an end in itself, and it is in fact to the romantic historians that we owe the first attempts to study mediaeval civilisation for its own sake rather than a means to something else. The propagandist historian, on the other hand, is inspired by motives of a nonhistorical order, and tends unconsciously to falsify history in the interests of apologetics. This is a danger to which Catholic historians of the Middle Ages are peculiarly exposed, since the romantic revival first brought in the conception of the Middle Ages as "The Ages of Faith," and of mediaeval culture as the social expression of Catholic ideals. . . . But for the last century and more there has certainly been a tendency among Catholic writers to make history a department of apologetics and to idealise mediaeval culture in order to exalt their religious ideals. Actually this way of writing history defeats its own ends, since as soon as the reader becomes suspicious of the impartiality of the historian he discounts the truth of everything he reads.[14]

To be sure, Christopher Dawson is not content to turn his back on both schools. Better than anyone he has described the crucial influence of the Church on the formation of the earliest European synthesis during the dark age between the decline of the Roman empire and the dawn of "medieval unity" (fifth to eleventh centuries). He does not think that humanism and technology alone will save us. Nor does he decree, however, that unless we go back to the philosophy of St. Thomas Aquinas or the Christendom of Gregory the Great, no viable Europe, no European unity, is possible.

With the ending of the Middle Ages, Europe turned its back on the East and began to look westward to the Atlantic.

Thus the mediaeval unity was not permanent, since it was based on the union of the Church and the Northern peoples, with a leaven of oriental influences. Nevertheless its passing did not mean the end of European unity. On the contrary, Western culture became more autonomous, more self-sufficient and more *occidental* than ever before. The loss of spiritual unity did not involve the separation of the West into two exclusive and alien cultural units, as would almost certainly have been the case if it had occurred four or five centuries earlier. In spite of religious disunion, Europe retained its cultural unity, but this was now based on a common intellectual tradition and a common allegiance to the classical tradition rather than on a common faith. The Latin grammar took the place of the Latin liturgy as the bond of intellectual unity, and the scholar and the gentleman took the place of the monk and the knight as the representative figures of Western culture. The four centuries of Nordic Cathol-

[14] Christopher Dawson, *The Making of Europe* (1932), ("Meridian Books"; Cleveland and New York: World Pub. Co.), pp. 16–17.

icism and oriental influence were followed by four centuries of Humanism and occidental autonomy.

To-day Europe is faced with the breakdown of the secular and aristocratic culture on which the second phase of its unity was based. We feel once more the need for spiritual or at least moral unity. We are conscious of the inadequacy of a purely humanist and occidental culture. We can no longer be satisfied with an aristocratic civilisation that finds its unity in external and superficial things and ignores the deeper needs of man's spiritual nature. And at the same time we no longer have the same confidence in the inborn superiority of Western civilisation and its right to dominate the world. We are conscious of the claims of the subject races and cultures, and we feel the need both for protection from the insurgent forces of the oriental world and for a closer contact with its spiritual traditions. How these needs are to be met, or whether it is possible to meet them, we can at present only guess. But it is well to remember that the unity of our civilisation does not rest entirely on the secular culture and the material progress of the last four centuries. There are deeper traditions in Europe than these, and we must go back behind Humanism and behind the superficial triumphs of modern civilisation, if we wish to discover the fundamental social and spiritual forces that have gone to the making of Europe.[15]

Dawson warns us against a certain Romantic idealization of the Middle Ages, too often described as an epoch of universal faith and profound spiritual harmony down to the moment when the Reformation treacherously shattered this unity. Such a reverse utopia, which Novalis promulgated in *Christendom or Europe*, became a commonplace among Catholic historians in the first half of this century. No one has more effectively refuted it than the Viennese historian Friedrich Heer, who was himself a convinced Catholic:

There is continual talk about Europe's Christianization and de-Christianization. These erroneous terms reflect a false formulation of the problem: as though Europe had one day been Christian, and then ceased to be Christian! This is nothing but a legend. The facts revealed in the archives of History prove only too fully that things happened very differently. They demonstrate the unity, the inner and even intimate coherence of

[15] *Ibid.*, pp. 243–44.

European history, to which belong St. Augustine, Luther, Voltaire, Thomas Aquinas, Descartes, Kant, the medieval emperors, and the French and the Spanish kings "by the grace of God." All of them are part of the evolution of a historical phenomenon by their allegiance to Europe.

. . . Early in the thirteenth century, Cesar de Heisterbach quoted this proverb which was to be repeated with variations down to the nineteenth century: "Lots and lots of things are possible, but not a German bishop gaining Paradise." In the *Vita Heriberti*—a biography of an Othonian bishop of Cologne, dating from the middle of the twelfth century—we read the story of a poor man who roamed the streets of "Holy Cologne," the cathedral city, and visited its famous religious establishments without finding a single priest willing to baptize his newborn son except for a fee the poor man could not pay. Fifty years later, the burghers of Cologne petitioned Pope Innocent II to divide into two parishes their community of 60,000 souls which had only one priest. They had hitherto been unable to afford more than the one.

The common people of Europe, down to the age of Joan of Arc and even later, knew no individual cure of souls, instruction in the faith, or parish institutions in the present-day sense. Thus, until long after the Reformation, the Lord's Prayer, the Ave Maria, and the Credo constituted the sole transmitted doctrine, plus the silent predication of Romanesque architecture and frescoes.

Friedrich Heer goes on to point out that Bible reading was forbidden the faithful by the Synod of Toulouse in 1229. The Bible in the vernacular was put on the index by Pope Paul IV in 1559. "Charles V on his deathbed had to beg the Inquisition for permission to read the Gospels in French (there was no Spanish translation)." In the meantime, monachism went into decline; the Roman curia had become bureaucratic; "national" Churches were formed as early as the thirteenth century (and not just from the sixteenth on) in France, England, Spain, and Germany; it was not the Pope, but laymen who tried to reform the Church at the Council of Basel, but in vain. . . . Friedrich Heer concludes:

Time and again, in numerous publications devoted to Europe and Christianity, we find repeated the dangerous commonplace according to which the secularization and de-Christianization of the West began in the sixteenth century with the Renaissance, Humanism, and the Reformation. The truth is very different: in the sixteenth century secularization had already run its course.

On the other hand—and this is the point Friedrich Heer was trying to make—if the Novalis-type myth of the Middle Ages has been exploded, if this past was far from being as Christian as claimed, what followed and will continue to follow it is far more Christian than what either the Catholic pessimists or the free-thinking optimists recognize:

Incontestably, as a result of individual, national, and historical diversities, the single faith provided at an early date a fertile soil for the harshest divergencies and conflicts. This fact must not obscure for us awareness of close bonds, whether positive or negative, which have never stopped existing between the opposing denominations and religious conceptions of the world. The twelfth- and thirteenth-century heretics "belong" to the Christianity of their time, just as Post-Tridentine Catholicism from the sixteenth to the nineteenth century remained closely connected with the Protestantism of those centuries, both by its achievements and by its failures.

What we must keep in mind is this: From the ninth to the nineteenth century Europe possessed a certain number of fundamental unifying elements. The internalized secular liturgy which we find in German classical poems is just as inconceivable without the Church liturgy as German idealism is inconceivable without Christian theology—Goethe without Raban Maur, Kant without Thomas Aquinas, Hegel without Eusebius of Caesarea. From 800 to 1815 all the European peace treaties concluded *in nomine sanctae et individuae Trinitatis.* Until 1850 Latin remained the language of European clerics and scholars (and in Hungary, even the language of the chancelleries). Our task now is to show how this millennial unity was broken up, giving rise to positions and counter-positions, affirmations and negations, the tensions between them growing ever stronger, the dangers of conflict ever more numerous. The true living heritage of Europe is this extraordinary wealth of dangerously conflicting possibilities and aspirations, which Europe presents to the world's gaze today.[16]

The Greek heritage and the Christian heritage are today the most alive. Simone Weil tried to fuse them. A great liberal hu-

[16] Friedrich Heer, *Das Experiment Europa* (Einsiedeln: Johannes Verlag).

manist, Salvador de Madariaga, preferred to present them as complementary. He takes up again a classical theme, "The dialogue between Socrates and Christ":

The primacy of will and intellect, and the close kinship between these two faculties in the European psyche, account for the fact that the strongest European traditions are the Socratic tradition and the Christian tradition. Socrates dominates the intellect of Europe; Christ, its will. It is pointless to ask whether these two traditions are the cause or the effect of the European character; the two are both cause and effect; and, more important, given the intimacy between intellect and will, the two traditions have influenced each other, so that in the course of centuries of European life, Socrates has become Christian, and Christ has become Socratic. . . .

It is only when the European deliberately repudiates them, that he betrays Europe and his own essential nature.

What we call the Socratic spirit is a spirit open to facts, in the service of logic and loyal to truth, but free and resistant to any preconceived doctrine or conclusion. The Socratic spirit is proud in relation to other spirits, but humble in the face of facts. These two virtues of the Socratic spirit are at the bottom of European freedom of thought. . . . In depth, the internal history of Europe must be understood as an effort to achieve the Socratic style in the development of its spirit, despite all obstacles inherent in the preceding stages.

In this struggle the European spirit has been both helped and hindered by the other tradition, that of Christ. The characteristic feature of Christendom is this, that in dying on the Cross for all men and every man, Christ founded humanism on an indestructible spiritual basis and invested the individual with a value that no one can challenge. In choosing voluntarily to drink the hemlock rather than to disown his teaching, Socrates freed the human mind from falsehood; in consenting to die on the Cross, to expiate the sins of all men, Christ definitively freed the will of Europe from all inhumanity. To be sure, falsehoods and inhumanity have gone on dishonoring Europe since the deaths of these two great men who gave it life, but only as negations of its essential being. European individualism was not born on Golgotha, but it is from Golgotha that it draws its strength and inspiration; and as for those individualists who remain blind to the Christian origin of their faith, let us refer them to the Spaniard who, to the question, What is your religion? replied, I am an atheist, thank God!

Next to this powerful tradition whose spirit strengthened our active individualism, Christianity brought to Europe a supernatural system which brooked no rival. To the extent that Christianity destroyed or eliminated the "natural" pagan or barbarian beliefs which haunted the shadowy forests and the misty riverbanks, it furthered the Socratic tendency to freedom and intellectual clarity. However, the contribution of the Old Testament, which came from Asia Minor, and even a certain local and pagan "folklore," which was added in the course of time, soon made the Christian tradition a danger to the Socratic tradition. This was the period of struggle between science and Church, the era of the Inquisition, of Giordano Bruno and Galileo, when Descartes had to be careful about what he said and even hold back some of his manuscripts. The errors, however, were not all on one side. In the nineteenth century, when a number of spectacular inventions (the steam engine, gas, electricity, the telephone) popularized science, certain scientists and philosophers lost their heads: they imagined that science could provide an answer to everything, and made it a faith; "science" then threatened to invade the domain of religion, having as little regard for the essential reality of things, as religion had previously had when it invaded the field of science. This episode was closed thanks to a clearer understanding of the limits of knowledge.

Gradually the two domains were better defined and more clearly delimited. The Socratic tradition no longer trespassed on the domain of revelation; the Christian tradition accepted the methods and principles of the Socratic tradition in respect of the natural world.

The Socratic tradition strongly influenced the intellectual side of the Church and helped to endow the Christian religion with a clear and firm system of thought, under the influence of St. Thomas Aquinas. This amounted to Europeanizing a religion that originated in Asia Minor. From then on, religion has not only dominated the hearts of Europeans, by subjecting them to the discipline of the Sermon on the Mount, but has also appealed to their minds by founding its intellectual system on the principles of Socrates.

Christianity in turn sets limits to the inhuman neutrality of the Socratic quest. To be sure, we must increase our knowledge by every possible means and method; but Christianity insists that all investigations must in the last analysis be useful to the human mind, and that we must never forget that we have no right to transform a human being into a mere instrument without his consent. The researches made by Goering's physicians on concentration camp inmates in order to determine the limits of human resistance were Socratic, not Christian. Therefore they were contrary to the European spirit.[17]

2 : European Values and Virtues

THIS BEING THE European heritage, what are we resolved to make of it or extract from it, we, twentieth-century Europeans? For a third of a century, intellectual Europe—in this respect in advance of political Europe, and of organized public opinion— has not stopped questioning herself concerning her true goals, those which are within her capacities and express her aspirations.

What are our specific values, those the world at large would miss if Europe were suddenly to vanish, swallowed up in one or another of the catastrophes we can imagine only too well?

The answers that will be quoted below may not be the best but they are certainly the most typical and the "truest," in the sense that they faithfully convey Europe's aspirations as translated by her best minds. As for the inevitable repetition of certain themes —freedom and its denial, for example—it is noteworthy how often they turn up, and how often the shades of meaning given them vary.

Edmund Husserl (1859–1938), founder of phenomenology and teacher of Heidegger and most of the philosophers who matter today, asks the fundamental question, What is Europe in respect of the spirit? and he answers: Europe is the spirit of philosophy born in Greece:

The typical form of Europe—what is it? It is the philosophical idea immanent in the history of Europe, or, what amounts to the same, her immanent teleology, as expressed by the irruption of a new epoch of humanity, that in which it can and will find its life and meaning as it freely shapes its existence, its history, and its infinite aspirations with the help of rational ideas. . . .
The Europe of the spirit has a birthplace. And by that I mean not so much a geographical place situated in a certain country

[17] Salvador de Madariaga, *L'Esprit de l'Europe* (Brussels: Mouvement Européen, 1952).

(even though this can be maintained), as a spiritual place situated in a certain nation amid certain individuals and groups of that nation. It was the ancient Greek nation in the seventh and sixth centuries B.C. Within it the individual began to display a new attitude to the world around him. Thanks to this attitude there was a breakthrough to a new spiritual formation, which developed rapidly into a form of coherent and systematic culture: the Greeks called it "philosophy." . . . In this irruption of philosophy bringing all the sciences in its train, I see, however paradoxical this may seem, the primordial phenomenon of the Europe of the spirit.

It will be objected at once that philosophy, the science of the Greeks, is not something that characterizes them specifically, and that it did not appear in the world for the first time with them. Did they not themselves speak of the sages of Egypt, of Babylonia, etc., and did they not accept their teaching? We have today a mass of works on the Indian and Chinese philosophies, which put these philosophies on the same plane with the Greek, and look upon all of them merely as varied historical configurations reflecting one and the same conception of culture. Naturally, they do not lack common elements. However, the merely morphological generality must not prevent us from seeing the profound intentionality, nor blind us concerning the very essential differences of principle.

And it is quite true that we have to go to the Greeks to find this new attitude to "theory," which led them to search together for universal truths rather than for solutions for practical problems.

They were men whose effort bore on *theoria* and nothing but the *theoria*, who did not investigate individually but together, helping each other, in an interpersonal community of labor whose growth and constant improvement, as the circle of collaborators broadened and the results acquired by generations of investigators followed one upon the other, led in the end to taking upon their shoulders an endless universal task. The theoretical attitude has historical origin in the Greeks.

The "crisis of European existence," which is so much discussed and is expressed in numerous symptoms of devitalization, is not a dark fate, nor an impenetrable fatality; it becomes comprehensible if we see it against the background of the teleology of European history, which is philosophically interpretable. However, the condition for such comprehension is first of all to grasp the phenomenon "Europe" in the central core of its existence. To conceive everything that is nonessential in the present "crisis," we would have to elaborate the concept of Europe as the historical teleology of infinite rational goals. The purpose would be to show how the European "world" was born from rational ideas, that is, from the spirit of philosophy. Then the "crisis" could clearly be interpreted as the apparent failure of rationalism . . . in its commitment to naturalism and objectivism.

. . . The crisis of European existence can have only one of two outcomes: either the decadence of Europe estranged from her own rational sense of life, her fall into anti-spiritualism and barbarism, or the rebirth of Europe in the spirit of philosophy, which will definitively surmount naturalism by the heroism of reason. The greatest danger to Europe resides in weariness. If we combat this greatest of all dangers, as "good Europeans," with a courage that does not shrink from endless tasks, then, out of the flaming faggots of disbelief and despair in the human mission of the West, the phoenix of a new inwardness and spirituality will be reborn from the ashes of weariness, the promise of a great future for humanity. Only the spirit is immortal.[18]

Another "good European" long revered as the authoritarian father of Liberal thought, Benedetto Croce (1866–1952), holds that the history of Europe is the history of the ideas of liberty and humanity:

Because this is the sole ideal that has the solidity once owned by Catholicism and the flexibility that this was never able to have, the only one that can always face the future and does not claim to determine it in any particular and contingent form, the only one that can resist criticism and represent for human society the point around which, in its frequent upheavals, in its continual oscillations, equilibrium is perpetually restored. So that when the question is heard whether liberty will enjoy what is known as the future, the answer must be that it has something better still: it has eternity. . . . It lives in many noble intellects in all parts of the world, which, no matter how they are dispersed and isolated and reduced almost to an aristocratic but tiny *respublica literaria,* yet remain faithful to it and surround it with greater reverence and pursue it with more ardent love than in the times when there was no one to offend it or to ques-

[18] Edmund Husserl, *Die Krisis der europäischen Wissenschaften und die transzendentale Phänomenologie,* ed. W. Biemel, in *Complete Works,* ed. H. L. Van Breda (The Hague: Martinus Nijhoff, 1954), Vol. VI.

tion its absolute lordship, and the crowd surged around it hailing it by name, and in the very act contaminated its name with vulgarity, of which it has now been cleansed.

Nor does liberty live only in these men, nor does it exist and resist only in the government of many of the major states and in institutions and customs, but its virtue operates even in things themselves, it opens a path for itself with more or less slowness through the rudest difficulties. This can be seen principally in the sentiment and the idea that is arousing general solicitude, of a truce and a diminution of "preparedness" and armaments, of a peace and alliance between the states of Europe, of an agreement of intentions and efforts between her nations that shall save in the world and for the good of the world, if not their economic and political supremacy, at least their supremacy as creators and promoters of civilization, their acquired aptitude for this unceasing task. This is the only political project that, among all those formed since the war, has not been lost and dissipated but on the contrary gains ground from year to year and converts to itself minds that were hostile to it or displayed incredulity or would have liked to but did not dare to believe in it. . . . The World War—which perhaps future historians will consider as the *reductio ad absurdum* of all nationalism—may have embittered certain relations between states because of the iniquitous and stupid treaty of peace that ended it, but it has brought into intimate communion the nations who have felt themselves, and will always more and more feel themselves, equal in their virtues and their errors, in their strength and their weakness, subject to the same fate, troubled by the same loves, saddened by the same sorrows, proud of the same ideal heritage. Meanwhile, in all parts of Europe we are watching the growth of a new consciousness, of a new nationality (because, as we have already remarked, nations are not natural data, but historical states of consciousness and historical formations). And just as, seventy years ago, a Neapolitan of the old kingdom or a Piedmontese of the subalpine kingdom became an Italian without becoming false to his earlier quality but raising it and resolving it into this new quality, so the French and the Germans and the Italians and all the others will raise themselves into Europeans and their thoughts will be directed towards Europe and their hearts will beat for her as they once did for their smaller countries, not forgotten now but loved all the better.[19]

[19] Benedetto Croce, *History of Europe in the Nineteenth Century,* trans. Henry Furst (New York: Harcourt, Brace & Co., 1933), pp. 358–60.

However, freedom is not merely a political and social demand. Salvador de Madariaga, who was also a great liberal, considered it the very "essence of life." It would not be a crucial form of existence, if it were not linked to another value which spiritual Spain has always proclaimed, from Don Quixote to Unamuno: disinterestedness.

Europe clings to freedom; she clings to the qualitative; she understands the supreme value of the useless. . . .

To us Europeans, life is a creative process that goes on in the heartbeat of every individual, thanks to his freedom to decide which possible combination of events he chooses. . . . By his free decision, the individual contributes to giving form to his own life, to choosing his own soul, as Plato would say.

This belief in freedom is implicit in two axioms or affirmations. The first is that when he is free to choose, each man will choose what is best, so that in the overall combination of individual choices, the level of the world will be raised. This affirmation is self-evident provided it is tempered with the second: that his "good" choice is made according to the lights that the man in question possesses at a given moment, and that it is good that it should be so; for, if he had to choose (even freely) according to standards borrowed from others, this would be of little profit to his personal experience, which is what matters.

All this, however, presupposes a general principle: the existence of a criterion of perfection acceptable to all. What is the source of this presupposition? It is an intuition of the human mind, in which are integrated the best and most powerful elements of all human faculties. We may imagine this "human mind" as a symbolic sphere each radius of which represents a human energy: in poetry, the yardstick would be Shakespeare; in music, Bach or Beethoven; in mathematics, Newton and Leibniz, and so on. We admit instinctively that every individual, within this sphere, is represented by a number, which is for the most part pitifully small, but capable of increasing.

The degrees that we observe in this increase and in the particular direction it takes, is what we call "quality." We Europeans insist on freedom because we believe in quality. Quality is as inseparable from individualism as freedom. Through the creative process of freedom, the individual produces quality, as he accumulates his differences. Diversity, quality, distinction are thus the essential features of European life. They account for the abundance, the variety, the human richness of the numerous European types, from the Irish to the Greeks, and from the Portuguese to the Finns. It is true that some of these features have sometimes become petty and superficial; at the end of the eighteenth century, a man of quality was often enough a booby, and in the twentieth century a man of distinction is often merely a graceless parasite. But for all these frivolous distortions of their original meanings, distinction and quality remain the essential characteristics of European life.

This is especially true of quality, for quality is for us Europeans the very essence of life. All life is qualitative, and that is why we must be on guard in Europe against the two dangers that threaten us, the two antipodes of quality: quantity and equality. Our repugnance for these two concepts is expressed in the wise French saying: "I don't have a big glass, but I can drink out of it." . . .

Quality and variety, as expressed in one's own bit of land, in the type of grape and the particular vintage, the particular year, are concepts that spring up like choice mushrooms in the shadow of taste. They are forms of European life which will forever escape the straitjacket of statistics. Where they are concerned, no five-year plan, no electronic machine applies. They exclude every form of socialization, mass production, standardization. They remain themselves and cannot be improved upon save in their own terms. They are at once the flower and the forcing bed of form.

Form is another specific expression of the European spirit. Nothing could be more erroneous than to qualify form as superficial. Although external in appearance, it actually arises out of the depths of the objects that it fashions and is part of their very substance. The potter knows this instinctively. Civilization, in particular, is a question of form. . . . Often, a decision that would be opportune, and the morality would not reject explicitly, is not taken by a European because it would lack form.

The refusal to grant first place to the opportune proves the nonutilitarian character of the European spirit. Utilitarianism is a sign of insufficient maturity. It is the key symptom of an arrested culture. For, when we carry out a useful action, it is by definition to serve a useful end, which is in turn useful because it serves a third useful end, and so on. But what would be the usefulness of this whole chain of usefulnesses did not the glorious star of the useless preside over the process? Men remain slaves as long as they let themselves be chained to the utilitarian by fetters of their own making. They liberate themselves only when their everyday useful actions are inspired by a spirit of lofty inutility which gives life its true meaning, its poetry, its drama and its eternal value.[20]

[20] S. de Madariaga, *op. cit.*, chap. v.

So much for quality, as the goal of culture. What about power? In Europe, power depends on a happy balance between intellect and will:

When we come from the west, we are inclined to look upon Europe as the land of general ideas. When we come from the east, it seems the land of harsh reality. Situated between America, where will is stronger than intellect, and India, where intellect is stronger than will, the essential characteristic of Europe is a balance between the two.

This happy mixture of the two most differentiated human faculties, intellect and will, is probably at the bottom of our intuitive feeling that we Europeans are one. All this is obviously very relative and very broad, and must not be understood in the sense that this mixture of intellect and will is denied to persons born on other continents. We claim only that the essential quality characterizing the actions and achievements of European men is precisely this harmonious development of intellect and will.

Intellect and will are the most individualized human faculties. . . . Our continent is incontestably the most individualistic of all. The individual is only just beginning to matter in Asia; in America he is beginning not to matter at all. America's conformism, slogans, and standardized men are farther from the European spirit than from that of any other continent. In Europe the individual is king. . . .

This accounts for the active quality of the European spirit. It does not confine itself to observing the object, but goes right to it and takes possession of it, seizes it. The spirit of the European is "acquisitive." Knowledge is a means for taking possession of nature: an attitude which is halfway between that of the American (for whom knowledge is a tool for action) and that of the Hindu (for whom it is a means for liberating himself from himself).

Therefore it is perhaps in Europe that intellect and will are most closely linked, to such a point that they are inseparable. This determines the special rhythm of all European life. Here will, stronger than intellect, first proceeds directly to the goal, deliberately, individualistically, unreflectively. Then comes a second phase: intellect, stronger now than will, tries to order the initial chaos. Finally there is a third phase governed by a balance between intellect and will, which achieves a synthesis. This three-phase rhythm is characteristic of the European type of life, in the scientific as well as in the political domain, in the history of law as well as in that of geographical expansion.[21]

[21] *Ibid.*, chap. ii.

"To construct the schema of that which is specifically European," Karl Jaspers has chosen three terms—freedom, history, science.

We have quoted him on science. On freedom and history, he tells us something new, namely, that the one would be inconceivable without the other:

The content of freedom is revealed by two fundamental European phenomena. These are:
Life in tension between two opposite poles.
Life at extreme limits.
First: life in tension between two poles. For every position taken, Europe herself has asserted the inverse position. She alone perhaps possesses this capacity for being all things. This is what makes her capable not only of conceiving what comes from outside as opposition to herself, but also of assimilating it and making it an element of her own essence. Europe knows the majesty of vast ordered structures, and she knows the restlessness of revolution. She is conservative, and she effects the most radical breaks with the past. She knows the peace of religious meditation, and she knows the leap into nihilistic negation.
She favors the idea of authority in its universal, Christian purport, as well as the idea of free investigation. She builds great philosophical systems, and she lets them be torn down by prophets of the truth. She lives with awareness of the political whole, and at the same time with what is most private and inward in the personal sphere.
Europe's essentially dialectical reality is rooted in her oldest traditions: the Bible, the foundation of European life, already conceals within it, in unique fashion, the tension between the poles. It is the holy book which in the course of millennia allowed all contradictory possibilities to flower with its blessing. Then we find at the basis of Europe the great antithesis between Antiquity and Christianity; the two have been at odds with each other and have been joining forces with each other down to our own day. European too are the fruitful oppositions between Church and State, the nations and the Empire, the Latin and the German nations, Catholicism and Protestantism, theology and philosophy—and today, Russia and America. Europe links what she at the same time sets in extreme opposition—world and transcendence, science and faith, material technology and religion.
Europe becomes unfaithful to her freedom when she drops

these antagonisms for peace and quiet, whether by setting up an order heedless of its limitations, or by going to extremes of partiality which exclude all order, or by clinging to one of the poles and taking it for the whole. Europe finds herself again when she is open, free in tension between the opposites, when she preserves her possibilities, and when, as the situations change, she draws upon her own sources and unceasingly, unpredictably, freshly unfolds her creative genius.

Second: life at extreme limits. If to be free means necessarily to know the Truth, then our freedom remains always fragmentary because we are never sure of the Truth in its totality or once and for all. Our freedom remains relative to something else, it is not *causa sui*. If it were, man would be God. Here the European reaches his extreme limit. Subjectively, as individual, he has the experience of the origin of his being; I am not free by myself; when I know myself to be truly free, I know by the same token that I am given to myself as a gift from transcendence. I can be absent from myself. That is the enigmatic limit which corresponds to the possible experience of being a gift to oneself. The Existence we can be is real only if it is united with the transcendence that gives us being. When Existence becomes aware of itself, it becomes aware by the same token of transcendence.

Objectively, we can say of freedom what follows: freedom needs the freedom of all others; this is why political freedom cannot be realized under the form of unchanging institutions. Freedom requires that the Truth be attained; however, the truth is multiple and whatever its form, always in movement; scientific knowledge founders on insurmountable antinomies and remains limited to the finite, to appearances. Every achievement in the world immediately engenders dissatisfaction. What manifests itself in time is doomed to failure.

But failure itself, taken in one of those tensions between opposite poles characteristic of Europe, has become a symbol there: the tragic consciousness, such as it existed in Greece, knows the significance of failure itself and the desire for authentic failure; and the Christian cross, which makes it possible to vanquish the tragic consciousness or to avoid it in the first place, gives life its meaning in transcendent reconciliation.

The freedom of the European tends to extreme limits, it seeks out the deepest abysses. The European goes through despair toward resurrected trust, through nihilism toward well-founded self-awareness; he lives in the anguish, which is the goad to his good faith.

In freedom are rooted two other European phenomena: the consciousness of history and will to science.

Only in the West is freedom, even in the individual consciousness, linked with freedom from external circumstances. Social freedom, religious freedom, personal freedom depend upon one another. But since freedom is never for all, and since for this reason it is, in the Western sense, for no one, history is indispensable for the conquest of freedom. Thus the need for freedom produces history.

Our history is not made up of mere change, of the fall and restoration of an eternal idea; it does not tell us how an over all situation conceived of as definitive realizes itself; rather it tells us of a significant succession of facts deriving from one another, a succession which becomes aware of itself as a struggle for freedom. In this sense history exists at all events in Europe, even if the mass of happenings appears, as everywhere else in the world, in the form of an effort forcibly to transform one kind of misfortune into another. Suffering becomes the cradle of the man who wills history. Only the man who exposes himself inwardly to unhappiness can know by experience what is, and acquire the necessary impulse to change. If he does not close himself to reality, if he does not let himself be destroyed blindly, if he is not content to wait "until it has passed" in order to live afterward as though nothing had happened, then the conditions are met for the birth of his concrete freedom. . . .

Only in the West has the demand for freedom been ahead of history, in the sense of a search for political freedom.[22]

As for science, we have seen that according to Jaspers it originates in respect for the truth and a "pitiless" critical sense, both of which are Christian values.

And yet the rest of the world has been most struck by Europe's cultivation of Promethean values. In the more traditional Asian view, our technology was produced by defying the sacred orders rather than by any respect for the divine creation or any desire to serve mankind by liberating it from nature.

Of course we may think that this view is mistaken, but it can be explained; indeed, the mistake was inevitable. At the very heart of European civilization there is a refusal to bow to

[22] Karl Jaspers, in *L'Esprit Européen* (Neuchâtel: Ed. de la Baconnière, 1947), pp. 298–302.

Fate, a refusal which those who identify Fate with God must find unsettling. On this score, Louis Rougier writes: [23]

There are societies which submit passively to the impact of the events, not even attempting to do something about them: such was in general the case of the underdeveloped peoples. There are societies which, through the ups and downs of their history, sought to perpetuate a status quo, without attempting original responses to new challenges: the Celestial Empire, with its millennial morality and social order modeled on the cosmic order, presented for centuries the image of just such an immobility. There are civilizations characterized by a flight from reality, a mystical escape based on detachment from the things of this world, from individuality (considered an illusion), on an escape into nirvana from the cycle of rebirths so as to be re-absorbed in the great whole: such were the civilizations of India. What characterizes Western civilization, is that it has never run away from a challenge or a threat. It has taken them up and tried to surmount them.

And yet European technology was not born of a Promethean impulse. After all, Prometheus was a Greek, and it is not from the Greeks that technology comes to us. Plato: Between the exercise of a mechanical trade and the duty of citizenship, there is radical incompatibility. And Aristotle: Slavery will disappear when the shuttle moves of itself. (Which is the case today.) Now, Rougier goes on to say, Christian humanism rehabilitated manual work: Jesus the carpenter, Paul the tentmaker, the "confraternities of freedom," the medieval guilds and corporations, the cathedrals. . . . And then came the Renaissance and the Reformation. Henceforth:

Science is no longer regarded as pure intellectual speculation, in the manner of the ancients, nor as a mere leisure-time diversion for the worldly. We expect it to be useful, practical, to promote the mechanical arts, to lighten toil, and to improve the human condition. The great Renaissance scientists, Leonardo da Vinci, Tartaglia, Agricola, Galileo, were as much engineers as pure thinkers. Bernard Palissy in his *Discours admirables* gave "Practice" a speaking role in the dialogue. Leone Alberti praised technology for having transformed the face of the earth for our convenience. Jérôme Cardan shocked humanists such as Scaliger

[23] *Op. cit.,* p. 424.

by assigning Archimedes a higher rank than Aristotle because of his mechanical inventions. The Chancellor Bacon was willing to have all of Aristotle's books burned, "because he was incapable of producing works serving the well-being of man." "Truly, it is to be worth nothing, to be useful to no one," Descartes said. To "the speculative philosophy usually taught in the schools," the *Discours de la Méthode* opposes "a practical philosophy by means of which, knowing the force and action of fire, water, air, the stars, the heavens, and all the other bodies around us, as distinctly as we know the various crafts of our artisans, we might apply them in the same fashion to all the uses to which they are suited, and thus make ourselves as though nature's lord and master." Bacon had already said it: We master nature by obeying her laws. It is not enough to know the world; it is time to change it.[24]

The reader has surely recognized the last sentence as the second of Karl Marx's *Theses on Feuerbach.* Now Marxism came after the great upsurge of European technology, and contributed nothing to it. On the other hand, we know today the part played in that domain, at the end of the eighteenth century, by the Pietists and the mystical heirs of the old dream of alchemy: to complete God's creation and to co-operate in its redemption.

How did it come about that these preoccupations became fused with the demand for freedom, technological advance, defiance of custom and tradition? Are they incompatible, or really interrelated? In a speech at the European Congress for Culture (1949), in Lausanne, Carlo Schmid reduced all these values to Europe's refusal to bow to fate:

What is it, then, that characterizes Europe? What a question, and how many different answers could be given to it! And yet there are some data that give us a clue as to where we should look for an answer, even though this answer may be as uncertain as the flickering shadows on the wall of Plato's cave.

One of these shadows might be Prometheus who, having formed man out of clay, stole fire from heaven to give life to his creature, and thereby initiated the struggle against everything that is mere fate. Indeed, to struggle against everything whose only claim to dignity is its materiality, to refuse to be merely a passive and determined element in the order of the Creation—

[24] *Ibid.,* p. 433.

this seems to me the primordial virtue which transformed an Asian peninsula into Europe. Dante, the European, puts the following words in the mouth of Ulysses who wanted to

divenir del mondo esperto

although he had been strictly forbidden to go beyond the straits of Gibraltar:

> *O frati . . .*
> *Considerate la vostra semenza:*
> *fatti non foste a viver come bruti*
> *ma per seguir virtute conoscenza.*

What is this but the refusal to be merely a particle of nature, a creature accepting the Paradise of Fate? Is not Dante's Ulysses brother to Prometheus who, though himself a creature of the gods, wished in his turn to become a creator, and not by any delegation of powers, but by his own right?

From this, as well as from the need to suffer knowingly the weight of history in order to shake off the yoke of the past which it has created, from this need to base his actions on a perpetual present which he forever sees as spontaneous (despite his knowledge of cause and effect), European man has drawn his happiness no less than most of his misfortunes. In the fortunate moments of his history he succeeded in being moderate. We call these fortunate moments "the classical period."

Prometheus is also, in some mysterious way, Antaeus, son of Earth and Neptune, who to regenerate himself and double his strength seeks out the Earth, Nature; but European man does not abandon himself to Nature; he accepts her with all her powers only after having "recognized" her, that is, measured and counted her, and on this score there is no substantial difference between Thales and Anaxagoras, between Descartes' *decompositio* and *recompositio* on the one hand and that nature which is literally "reproduced" by Claude Lorrain (it is his term) and by the great nineteenth-century painters—and even by our contemporary painters who, though they often seem exotic, nevertheless merely recompose the life of the human soul which the human mind has decomposed. (And did the Romantics do any differently?)

Similarly, the European, by isolating human consciousness from its relations with all that is outside the Self, made it possible for man, drowned in the collectivity and the interplay of its contingencies, to become an individual. The dignity of the individual consists precisely in this, that it is no longer permitted to man to justify his acts merely in terms of nature, history, society. He must justify himself before the court of his own conscience and reason (which, wherever it refers to evidence, is nothing but the secularized individual conscience).

If we want society to respect the decisions of our own conscience, we must respect the dignity of the conscience of every human being. This is one of the reasons which forced us to look beyond the truths of the individuals (absolute to them) for a truth higher than subjective truths, a truth that is true in and for itself, not because it is approved by traditional doctrines or by the collective soul. It is here that the miraculous advance of European thought and science—both born of Plato's *Logos geometretos*—puts down its deepest roots. And we would have passed over in silence one of the purest glories of Europe if, in this order of ideas, we had forgotten to mention music.

Nor must we forget that it is indeed European man who refused to let his material and political existence become a mere function of circumstances. More than his fellow men he has always fought against everything that obstructs man's march toward a future ever richer in spiritual, political, and social freedom. Ours is the continent that has sown everywhere in the world the seeds of resistance to the tyranny of circumstances and history. From our continent, too, comes the will to modify the crucial factors of temporal existence, its very substance, so as to permit man to overcome the alienation to which a brutal economic and social mechanism had reduced him, preventing him from determining himself. European man has always refused to regard the stability of the social order as a law of fate, and this is why, in every age, the third estate has fought in the streets for liberty, equality, and justice.

Nonetheless, this liberty, this equality, this justice have always been invoked as the originary virtues. In short, what the peoples and classes sought in the European revolutions was neither utopia nor abstraction. They have always sought, as Machiavelli said, initial virtues, those we recognize in Socrates, in Cicero's Republic, in the *agi et pati fortia* of Titus Livius, in the *pax et justicia* of St. Augustine, and in the American State of Virginia's Declaration of Rights—a precious gift by which the New World paid back Europe for what it had borrowed.

Three years before the Congress of Lausanne, the first Geneva "International Meeting" (September, 1946) had formulated in memorable fashion the problem of "the European spirit" in the

unsettled postwar world. We have previously given excerpts
from speeches made on that occasion by Julien Benda and Karl
Jaspers: they tried to define Europe's idea of herself and the
values of her culture. Denis de Rougemont, for his part, attempted to evaluate the prospects for Europe's specific genius
by comparing it with the ideals of the great world empires to
the east and to the west. Of these empires he said:

It is they who won the war, not we. It is they who have taken
over responsibility for progress and the faith in progress. . . .
Before the war Europe's name evoked a focus of activities
which extended to every other continent. Europe seemed bigger
to us than she really was. Hence the shock to our minds after
the other war, when Valéry referred to Europe as "a little cape
of Asia." Today Europe, as seen from America, and I imagine
also as seen from Russia, seems smaller than it actually is: physi-
cally hemmed in between two great empires which throw their
long shadows across her, damaged and nibbled at around her
borders, morally closed in on herself. And that's not all. To the
profit of these two empires Europe has been as though drained
of certain ambitions, certain dreams, and certain beliefs which
had first appeared here, and which seemed sometimes to define
her genius. For instance, our dream of progress seems to have
emigrated from Europe to America and Russia. . . .
From the Middle Ages on, Europe dominated the world for
centuries primarily through her culture: by her curiosity and
her trade in the era of the great discoveries; by her arms and
her art of war in the service of rapacious princes and nations,
now and again by ideals that caught on elsewhere, and lastly,
by her machines and capital.
Now America and Russia have taken away from her, one after
the other, her machines, her capital, her ideals, her arms, her
trade, even her curiosity about the planet! All this happened
over a period of thirty years, and there is no going back as far
as can humanly be foreseen. What, then, is left to us that is
specifically our own? A unique monopoly: that of culture in the
broadest sense of the term, that is to say, a certain conception
of man, a principle of continuous criticism, a certain human
balance resulting from countless tensions. This much is still left
to us, and to tell the truth it would be rather hard to take away
from us! At the same time it is not easy to keep our culture vital
and effective.
At the origin of European religion, culture, and morality is

the idea of contradiction, of fruitful antagonism, of creative conflict. The cross is the emblem of contradiction par excellence.
On the other hand, at the origin of the two new empires is the
idea of mankind's unification by its own efforts, of the elimina-
tion of antitheses, and of the triumph of efficient organization,
trouble-free and frictionless. The European hero, then, is the
man who attains the highest point of consciousness and signification through conflict: the saint, the mystic, the martyr. Whereas
the American or Russian hero is the man who best conforms
to the norm of happiness, the man who succeeds, the man so
perfectly adjusted that he does not suffer. The model for Europeans is the exceptional man, the great man; the model for the
others is the average man, the common man, the object or the
result of statistics. To us, the exemplary man is the loftiest example; to them, the exemplary man is the standard sample. . . .
To us, life arises out of permanent conflict, and the goal of life
is not happiness, but keener awareness, discovery of a meaning,
a signification, if only in the unhappiness of passion, in failure.
They aim at happy unconsciousness, we at consciousness—whatever it may cost. They want life, we want reasons for living—
even though they prove deadly.

This is why the typical European is sometimes a revolutionary,
sometimes an apostle; sometimes a passionate lover, sometimes
a mystic; sometimes a polemicist, sometimes a warrior; sometimes a maniac, sometimes an inventor. His good and his evil are
inextricably linked in the marrow of his bones. The European
knows the essential value of antagonisms, of creative opposition,
while the American and the Soviet Russian look upon these as
symptoms of something gone wrong, something to be eliminated
gently or brutally so as to achieve unanimity, homogeneity. The
Americans will achieve it through advertising, the movies, and
mass production; the Russians, as we know, by less flexible
means, but the results are similar, and are becoming ever more
so.

Thus the comparison between Europe and these two sometimes ungrateful children of the West suggests a definition of
the typically European man: he is the man of contradiction, the
dialectical man par excellence. In the purest type, we see him
crucified between the opposites he has himself named: im-
manence and transcendence, the collective and the individual,
group discipline and liberating anarchy, security and risk, the
rules of the game which are for all and the vocation which is
for one. I say "crucified," for European man as such will not let
himself be reduced to either of these terms. He will take them

both upon himself, and define himself in terms of the tension between them, his balance forever threatened, in unending agony. This agony—literally, this struggle—consumes immense energies. And this is why the gigantic plans and enterprises that proliferate elsewhere are rare among us. On the other hand, the effect of this agony is to turn man in upon himself, to see himself as victim or creator of these tensions, and the latter as his main spiritual achievement. Typically European, then, is the will to refer all institutions to man, to measure them on the human scale. This man of contradictions (when he dominates them creatively) is what I call "a *person*." The institutions to his own measure, to his own scale, which translate the same fundamental tension into the life of culture as well as into political structures, I call "federalist." [25]

At about the same time, André Malraux gave a lecture in Paris, which was widely discussed. In it, he concentrates and carries to the highest point of dramatic tension several of the themes illustrated in this chapter. We can do no better than to conclude it with his words:

At this moment, what are the Western values? We have seen enough to know that they are neither rationalism nor progress. Optimism, faith in progress, are American and Russian rather than European values. The first European value is will to consciousness; the second, will to discovery. . . .

The strength of the West resides in accepting the unknown. This implies a kind of humanism, but we must recognize, and say clearly, that it is a tragic humanism. We are confronted by an unknown world; we face it with consciousness. This is something we alone try to do. Let there be no mistake about it: will to consciousness and will to discovery belong to Europe and to Europe alone as fundamental values. You have seen them at work in an everyday fashion in the scientific sphere. At the present time, the forms of the spirit are defining this humanism both by the fundamental assumptions of the sciences and by the nature of their investigations. Columbus had a better idea of what he was leaving than of what he would find. We can found a human attitude only on humanism because man knows what he is leaving and what he wants to do, and this humanism must be tragic because man does not know where he is going. . . .

We are at a crucial point where the European will should be

[25] Denis de Rougemont, in *L'Esprit Européen* (Neuchâtel: Ed. de la Baconnière, 1947), pp. 148–56.

reminded that heirs do not respect and sometimes squander what has been bequeathed them; all they truly inherit is their intelligence and their strength. Pascal was the heir to Christianity at its most contented. Europe's heritage is tragic humanism. . . .

We have made a certain number of images worth talking about, not just in the arts, but in that wider area of all that man finds in himself with which to accuse himself, to deny himself, to make himself greater, or to try to make himself eternal. We have made notable harvests within the noblest solitudes, even in God's own: for who on this earth, if not we, invented the idea of the saint and the hero as productive? The Assyrian hero was alone with his corpses; Buddha was alone with his charity. Are Michelangelo and Rembrandt merely relations of volumes and colors, or are they also prey to their divine faculties, for the benefit of all who are worthy? The justice of the Bible, the old freedom of the cities—who imposed them on the world? But justice and freedom by themselves, as we have recently seen, are all too soon threatened. It is Europe that has tried to find something beyond them.

I maintain that she is still trying, and that, as far as I know, she alone is trying, face to face with the unknown, fully aware of the torments she has just lived through. To be sure, over the centuries man has always been bowed down by the same fate which is death, but at the same time, here in this place called Europe—and in this place alone—men bowed down under this fate have risen up and tirelessly hurled themselves into the dark, to make intelligible the world's immense confusion and to pass on their discoveries rather than to keep them secret, endowing this ephemeral world with death's victory, in the realization that man is not born of his own affirmations, but by putting the universe in doubt. As was said of England, of the Battle of Britain, let us say: "If this must die, may all dying cultures have an equally noble death."

Despite the most sinister appearances, it cannot be proclaimed too loudly that those who are to come will perhaps look back on our fears with amazement. The Europe of Nicopolis, the taking of Rome, the fall of Byzantium, such events will perhaps seem to them no more than a miserable backwash in comparison with the indomitable spirit which says, as the threatening shadows begin to fall: "We shall use you, as we used the others, to make something of the common clay." [26]

[26] Lecture at the Sorbonne (November 4, 1946), published in *Unesco Lectures* (Paris: Editions de la revue Fontaine, 1947).

3:   Europe and the World

To KNOW OURSELVES, we must compare ourselves with others. We Europeans least of all dare evade such a comparison, though we need not underestimate the risk it involves. When we review the judgments that the world passes on us, the first thing we discover is that we inspire hatred, and secondly we discover reasons for doubting ourselves.

The great comparative historian Arnold Toynbee tried to carry out such an investigation in space and time. His conclusions are alarming:

A Westerner who wants to grapple with this subject, must try, for a few minutes, to slip out of his native Western skin and look at the encounter between the world and the West through the eyes of the great non-Western majority of mankind. Different though the non-Western peoples of the world may be from one another in race, language, civilization, and religion, if any Western inquirer asks them their opinion of the West, he will hear them all giving him the same answer: Russians, Muslims, Hindus, Chinese, Japanese, and all the rest. The West, they will tell him, has been the arch-aggressor of modern times, and each will have their own experience of Western aggression to bring up against him. The Russians will remind him that their country has been invaded by Western armies overland in 1941, 1915, 1812, 1709, and 1610; the peoples of Africa and Asia will remind him that Western missionaries, traders, and soldiers from across the sea have been pushing into their countries from the coasts since the fifteenth century. The Asians will also remind him that, within the same period, the Westerners have occupied the lion's share of the world's last vacant lands in the Americas, Australia, New Zealand, and South and East Africa. The Africans will remind him that they were enslaved and deported across the Atlantic in order to serve the European colonizers of the Americas as living tools to minister to their Western masters' greed for wealth. The descendants of the aboriginal population of North

America will remind him that their ancestors were swept aside to make room for the West European intruders and for their African slaves.

This indictment will surprise, shock, grieve, and perhaps even outrage most Westerners today.

Thus Europe is summoned to confess to the world a guilt unprecedented in the history of mankind. Does Tonybee deny the charge? Far from it:

"When the world passes judgment, it can be sure of having the last word," according to a well-known Latin proverb. And certainly the world's judgment on the West does seem to be justified over a period of about four and a half centuries ending in 1945. In the world's experience of the West during all that time, the West has been the aggressor on the whole; and if the tables are being turned on the West by Russia and China today, this is a new chapter of the story which did not begin until after the end of the Second World War. The West's alarm and anger at recent acts of Russian and Chinese aggression at the West's expense are evidence that, for us Westerners, it is today still a strange experience to be suffering at the hands of the world what the world has been suffering at Western hands for a number of centuries past.

But did the Europe which discovered the world and brought what the whole world calls civilization to every continent contribute only aggression, tyranny, and suffering? According to Toynbee, we are guilty of overweening pride when we ask such a question:

We Westerners, being human, are inclined to feel that what we have done to the world within the last few centuries is something unprecedented. An effective cure for this Western illusion of ours is to glance back at what, not so very long ago, was done to the world by the Greeks and Romans. We shall find that they too overran the world in their day, and that they too believed for a time that they were not as other men are. . . .

In the second century B.C. the Greeks conquered India right across to Bengal, and in the same century the Romans won for the Graeco-Roman world a frontage on the Atlantic Ocean in what are now Southern Spain and Portugal. The Basic Greek in which the New Testament was written in the first century of the Christian Era was spoken and understood from Travancore to the hinterland of Marseilles. At the same date Britain was being annexed to the Graeco-Roman world by force of Roman arms, while Greek art in the service of an Indian religion—Buddhism— was travelling peacefully northeastwards from Afghanistan along a road that was eventually to carry it across China and down Korea to Japan. Thus, in sheer physical range, the Graeco-Roman culture, in its day, spread as widely in the Old World as our Western culture has spread in its day; and, in an age which had not yet seen the emergence of the indigenous civilizations of the Americas, the Greeks could boast, as we can today, that every contemporary civilization on the face of the planet (whose shape and size the Greeks had accurately calculated) had been reached and penetrated by the radiation of their world-conquering culture.

This impact of Greek culture on the world in and after the fourth century B.C. gave the world as sharp a shock as the impact of our modern Western culture has been giving it since the fifteenth century of our era; and, as human nature has not undergone any perceptible change within the last few thousand years, it is not surprising to find the standard alternative psychological reactions to a cultural assault, which we have observed in the history of the world's encounter with ourselves, making their appearance likewise in the history of the world's earlier encounter with the Greeks and Romans. . . .

Of course I am not meaning to suggest that we can cast a horoscope of our own future by observing what happened in Graeco-Roman history beyond this point, where our own record breaks off, and then mechanically translating this Graeco-Roman record into modern Western terms. History does not automatically repeat itself; and the most that any Graeco-Roman oracle can do for us is to reveal one among a number of alternative possible future denouements of our own drama. In our case the chances may well be against the plot's working out to its Graeco-Roman conclusion. It is conceivable that we Westerners and our non-Western contemporaries may give the course of our encounter with each other some quite different turn which has no counterpart in Graeco-Roman history. In peering into the future we are fumbling in the dark, and we must be on our guard against imagining that we can map out the hidden road ahead. All the same, it would be foolish not to make the most of any glimmer of light that hovers before our eyes; and the light reflected upon our future by the mirror of past Graeco-Roman history is at any rate the most illuminating gleam that is visible to us.[27]

These texts call for several replies.

Leaving moral questions aside, a few incontestable major facts remain, which ought to be kept in mind:

1. The Europeans discovered the entire earth; it never occurred to any other people to discover Europeans. Thanks to them mankind became aware of its unity. The idea of universality, the very idea of "the human race" are creations of Christian and technological Europe.

2. The prophets of European decline—Spengler, Valéry, and Toynbee—all based themselves on the precedent of the fall of the Roman Empire, of the Graeco-Roman world. Is this a valid precedent? Is European civilization a civilization like the others? Can its fate be predicted by extrapolation from ancient examples? Has it not gone beyond a certain world threshold, such that its destiny is not, strictly speaking, comparable to any other?

3. European civilization is the only one which has actually become universal. The Chinese emperors and Alexander the Great imagined that they ruled the entire world: they were simply mistaken; any good travel agency could set them straight on this today. *Der Erdenkreis ist mir genug bekannt,* says Faust, that great modern European.

4. All the European creations (Church, philosophy, science, technology, history, geography, sociology, psychology, museums, laboratories, etc.) are spreading throughout the world. They attract the world and feed on it, paving the way for world unity. And only they have done so.

5. There are no serious candidates to take the place of our civilization which has become universal. Who but it can teach the use of its creations, or find remedies for the diseases of which it spread the germs?

On all this in general and on Toynbee in particular, the Spanish historian Luis Diez del Corral has a great deal to tell us in

[27] Arnold Toynbee, *The World and the West* (New York and London: Oxford University Press, 1953), pp. 2-4, 85-87, 90 f.

a work entitled *The Rape of Europe*, a meditation on the fate of a culture "dispossessed" of its conquests by the very world which it brought into being.

This is how he states the problem:

The disbalance between the old European (in the geographical sense) political structure and that of the whole world (also European by origin) had developed to such a degree that new political powers and mentalities had grown up beside those of the old European nations and had finally turned against them and shattered the historical landscape of Europe. In a kind of immense reversion the universal history of the West, the expression of its fecundity, of its rational objectivity and of the expansiveness of many of its creations now adopted by non-European peoples, had been turned against the concrete history of geographical Europe. The very ideas, habits and styles discovered or produced by Europe had suffered transformations and above all simplifications, and had been levelled against their mother's breast. . . .

Sophocles says of his Oedipus, the greatest exponent of patience in the face of fate: . . . "Of all ills the most painful are those that are of our own choosing."

Europe, with her supreme genius for creating, has likewise created directly or indirectly most of her own misfortunes. Her great weakness lay in her spirit of enterprise, her youthful eagerness and her incapacity for renunciation.

However, we should speak of her crisis rather than her decline. For the worst, as predicted by Toynbee, is not certain:

Universal history in Toynbee's *Study of History* is like a vast hospital ward containing twenty-two beds. Most of the patients are already dead. Some are dragging out their existence in a state of lethargy. The most prominent of these, Europe, has been struck down by a sudden but grave affliction against which her stout constitution is putting up a gallant resistance. But nothing can be done. The doctor . . . knows that her days are numbered. She is but a mortal body doomed to dissolution as her organic forces fail, and no political medicine can avail her.

In the circumstances all that is left is to count the days that remain and profit by them, doing nothing that might hasten the end and adopting an attitude of resignation. . . . Spengler thought that by the year 2200 Western civilization would reach a stage comparable with that of the ancient world between 100 and 300 of our era, the age of Trajan and Marcus Aurelius to Septimius Severus, a not unattractive prospect, despite some of its basic deficiencies such as "the petrification without history" which Spengler provided for, and which could not fail to offer the prospect of rest to the feverish brains of contemporary Europeans.

But the fact is that Europe's situation is at once more optimistic and more pessimistic than such historians usually imagine, more optimistic in the long view and in terms of the positive significance of European culture, and more pessimistic and perplexing as regards the present. Unfortunately perhaps the Western world was far less decadent in its science, technology, vital temper and will to organize than Spengler supposed. Unfortunately too, Western culture is much less of a closed compartment than Spengler thought, and precisely because of its enormous fertility, the spontaneous multiplication of consequences and its frenzied expansibility, it may yet inflict severe trials on the historical entity that has produced it.

Diez del Corral discusses the precedent of the Hellenistic decline, which is invoked by Toynbee, and he finds in it new grounds for believing in the European future:

Hellas too ceased to be Hellenic and became Hellenistic, with its typical political, economic and spiritual problems. Hellenism, derived from the expansion of the Hellenes, flowed back to the motherland and transformed it into a new historical subject, now only a part of the extended constellation that inflated and multiplied the problems of the Greek polis. But from our own perspective, the engaging of the Hellenic and Hellenistic epochs, that jarring of the wheels of the times that the ear of Demosthenes detected, is scarcely perceptible to a historiography that searches for the great historical connections and discerns the guiding-lines of Greek philosophy, art, science, and technology with their prolongation into the Hellenistic period, beneath the turn of the events.

The comparable guiding-lines of European culture seem even more vigorous as it attains universality, and there is no cause to expect a reaction like that of the peoples of the Near East to Hellenization. If Europeans have anything to reproach those of Asia for, it is their ductility, the rapidity of their accommodation to European ideologies, their lack of genuine powers of resistance. The impress of Europe on them is much deeper than that of the Greek world on the East, and has sunk in one fashion or

another (sometimes by substitutes) even down to the level of
religion, which was the line of defence and counter-attack for
Asia against Greece.

So, as we trace the universal projection of the problems of
European culture, it would seem that the study of the modes
they acquire in the course of projection, and the inflections they
may suffer in their new setting would prove more interesting
than the mere circumstances of the dispossession which may
seem . . . already outdated by the march of events. Europe's
only course is to adapt herself to the new situation, to forget
her past greatness, to draw new vitality from her own bowels,
unifying her energies which have hitherto been dispersed among
the multiplicity of her nations, and so matching herself with the
gigantic young heroes of the present day.

Moreover, the problem of the Europeans' future and their
"dispossessed civilization" is no longer separable from that of
all mankind's future:

The plight of the dispossessed concerns not only the victim,
but her despoiler as well, who, however much he takes, is still
unsatisfied. He is shaping his own existence by forms that come
from without, that he has not produced, that may not survive
the transfer, that may suddenly contract and impair his own
vitality. . . .

Until a few decades ago it was believed that European civilization was the monopoly of its owner, or at most, that a few
purely technical externals might be copied by others. Ranke
wrote, "how is it possible to imitate that from which not only
the foundations of history spring but also the spirit that links
past and present, and must give life to the future?" Yet as we
have seen, it has been imitated and appropriated and made
their own by other societies. . . .

The truth is that not only have the products of this civilization
been copied, but exotic elements have been introduced into its
very motor where the facile distinction between civilization and
culture disappears or is greatly diminished. As we have seen,
technology does not belong to the epidermis of European culture, but is nurtured on its very life blood and its most spiritual
aspirations, and has so developed that it pervades and conditions
all, and being in its mature form an easily appropriable instrument, it takes with it, even if only obliquely and implicitly, the
most varied impulses, values and ideals of European life.

It certainly cannot convey them all, or even perhaps the most essential of them. . . . Europe's mission is not over, far from it, though in some aspects of life it is surpassed and reduced. Europe has not only established the premises which have later been developed by non-Europeans, but it has largely been intellects bred in its medieval cities and trained in its ancient, but advanced universities who have supplied the decisive impetus for the great and tragic discoveries that technology has made outside Europe itself. The achievements of nuclear physics have been made possible by theoretical discoveries that form an almost strictly European intellectual feat. Hence the phenomenon of dispossession is clearly discernible.

But in general the phenomenon is so new and so sudden that we cannot say what consequences it may produce over the years in its new setting. If it has involved surprising losses from the storehouse of Europe, the ancient spiritual matrix is not finally expropriable. Intellectual activity is something so delicate, so much conditioned by multiple circumstances that it may be doubted if, beneath the apparent continuity of development of the premises established by European learning, the latter can continue to progress in different circumstances with the driving genius of which the old world has given ample proofs in the last half-century.

Does not Europe's mission henceforth consist in rethinking the problem of how mankind is to make best use of her conquests?

After such decisive advances as those made in the order of technology, science, material ease, social organization, may not a pause and a reassessment of the gains be necessary, bringing a new and fuller burgeoning of humanism? And who better than Europe can face so real a problem? She alone has the breadth of vision, the experience, the degree of integration of the various sectors of life, so variously developed in the expansion of the contemporary world: she alone can actualize the old and imperishable storehouse of ancient and Christian humanism. Her obligations to the future may have been reduced in some respects, but they have increased in others, for she is responsible not only for her own historical destiny but for that of a subject but independent planet, now fully of age, and if truculent, made so by energies drawn from the European patrimony, for whose investment parental consent is necessary.[28]

[28] Luiz Diez del Corral, *The Rape of Europe*, trans. H. V. Livermore (London: Allen & Unwin, Ltd., 1959), pp. 47–49, 58–59, 296–301.

Concerning Europe's world mission, let us now question two great elders who earned the right to speak from a world point of view. Few men have devoted themselves so wholly to all traditional aspects of the problem—both physical and spiritual—as Keyserling and André Siegfried.

The Count Hermann von Keyserling (1880–1946), famous for his *Travel Diary of a Philosopher* (which is especially full of striking intuitions on the score of India), arrived at a "spectral analysis" of Europe after going around the world. Even more striking is the fact that it is to Europe, in the end, that he assigns the mission of saving the Spirit—that Europe so often looked down upon by the spiritual elite of the East, where the masses nonetheless envy Europe's material achievements:

The proper thing will be to make of every nation the best, the very best which its possibilities permit. And that, no longer for the sake of exclusive self-glorification, but for the sake of a higher unity—not at the expense of the others, but for the best interests of all. . . .

I will only seek to show to what extent *Europe as a whole* must effect an inner transposition, in what things it must look for its true task in order that it may remain a positive factor in the development of mankind.

The material supremacy of Europe is of course at an end. As contrasted with the new world, it has become very weak, very small. Its power in the east will also end before long. It may be that the industrial centre of this planet will shift over to Asia. Invention is difficult, but even the ape can imitate. Before long all our technical ability will be common human property. Before long, if we continue to plume ourselves on our achievements, we Europeans will be stared at just as Cornelius Nepos would be if he suddenly appeared in our midst with a general claim to the world's worship; we have become our own classics. Thus our prestige, the mightiest of all factors for power, has disappeared. But above all it was the social achievements of the last few decades that undermined our material power. . . . Under these circumstances, the mere self-preservation of Europe compels it to adjust itself to what it can do best, to what no one can take away from it. And that is its intellectuality. . . .

We should not be called upon to be the bearers of spirituality, the logos principle, on earth, we should be God's hands . . . if, for us, the exclusive emphasis did not lie on mind. Greek form still lies at the base of Far-Eastern art; the Jewish Ethos still lies at the base of whatever ethos is at work throughout the world. All science is of European origin. And as regards Christianity, its power to expand and transform derives from the fact that it embodies understanding directed toward practical use. There are, in Asia, religions which are equally deep, if not deeper; but the principle of the earth-conquering spirit does not live in them. In and for itself spirit is indeed . . . without earthly power; the most tremendous spirituality can achieve nothing if he toward whom it turns will not come forward to meet it—we have but to think of the second thief on the cross. Now in Europe the spirit is essentially earth-conquering. Because of this it can be an effective historic force. . . . The European presents a specific synthesis of spirit, soul, and body; because of this synthesis, and by virtue of the law of correspondence between meaning and expression, the ultimate essence of the spirit becomes effective on earth. . . .

If Europe has from time to time also acquired external power, it was not a primary expression of the European spirit, but the consequence of its practical application—just as great fortunes are built up on the basis of inventions produced by some unworldly scientist in pursuit of purely intellectual interest. And today the significance of Europe is based on its spirituality to a degree unknown before. *For that is the one thing in which it is still unique.* It is at the same time the one thing which is, precisely at this moment, susceptible of the most tremendous intensification. . . .

The chief reason why Europe's greatest prospects lie in this direction derives from the fact that the spirit can rule only where the entire emphasis is laid on the unique and its value. All values are personal. Just as Christ proclaimed and taught the infinite worth of the human soul, just as all ethics have their unique meaning in the free will of man, just as all creative originality derives from the unique, and just as there is no other form of understanding than personal understanding, so the rule of the spirit on earth stands or falls by whether or not the emphasis is laid on the individual, and on him only. Today this condition obtains only in the case of the European. . . .

Europe's ability to fulfil this task resides in the fact that its entry into the new world in the making—and its entry alone among all the regions—is taking place without a *solution de continuité.* Science and technical development are authentic children of Europe's spirit: their acceptance therefore implies no revolution in the psychic structure. Thus, for us, socialism merely signifies one consequence, among others, of Christianity; it goes back directly to the deepest spiritual roots. Accordingly, not only the European elite, but the European masses, too, are fundamentally immune to both Americanism and Bolshevism. In Europe no movement of consequence can ever again repudiate the spirit for the sake of matter. It is psychologically in advance of the rest of the world.[29]

In one of his last writings—a preface to the French translation of Diez del Corral's *Rape of Europe*—André Siegfried sums up, with his admirable grasp of the larger issues, the crucial problem of our time, namely, the problem of the worldwide spread of technology divorced from the spirit which created it.

Siegfried first of all notes the "sensational, almost unbelievable" spread of Europe's civilizing influence:

The world is in process of adopting Europe's armaments, technical methods, and—so it imagines—her very spirit. Europe has let herself be robbed of these instruments of power; more than that, she has generously offered them to the very nations which were to use them against her. But the genius of creative civilizations perhaps consists in working for others.

From the point of view of her civilizing influence, Europe's victory is extraordinary, sensational, almost unbelievable. The whole planet is borrowing not only her technology but her ways of life, including even her clothing. But this is at the price of her former hegemony, which is slipping from her hands, at the price perhaps of her spiritual integrity, which is compromised by subtle and dangerous counter-influences. An era of omnipotence since the sixteenth century, of high and unique culture since the sixth century B.C., is, I fear, on the point of ending. What is coming in its place is a new age whose true mainspring is technology. Such is the more than Shakespearean, indeed apocalyptic drama which we are witnessing today. Tomorrow the very existence of our continent will be at stake.

We can measure the difference between European civilization and Western civilization. The latter was a product of the former, a transformation of it which perhaps was false to it by its very expansion. "Rome is no longer to be found in Rome," says Corneille's hero. It may very well be that even today the West's center of gravity is no longer to be found in Europe, and this

[29] Count Hermann Keyserling, *Europe*, trans. Maurice Samuel (New York: Harcourt, Brace & Co., 1928), pp. 371, 377, 379–81, 391.

induces us to analyze the essential features of European civilization proper. We gave little thought to such analysis until the First World War compromised the solidity and what we had supposed to be the intangibleness of our power. We thought it was enough that Europe existed, as irresistible and brilliant as the sun, but we did not ask what she was, where lay the secret spring of her incomparable hegemony.

The secret of this hegemony, in the modern era, seems to have resided in our continent's industrial and technological power. But where is the secret of this industrial power to be found?

Its initial source may be sought in Greek antiquity, for the latter had already discerned the essence of our modern scientific methods; Greek antiquity, however, used them in a contemplative, disinterested quest for knowledge. (Recall Plato's reservations on technique and Archimedes' apologies for having applied his science to practical purposes!) Modern industrial achievements, which had paradoxically to wait two thousand years to be realized, became possible only when the ancient methods of thought were brought up to date in a new geographic environment. Civilization's center of gravity shifted to the cold northern countries where the physical necessities of food, clothing, and shelter were more urgent. In the late Middle Ages, the use of coal put England on the road she was to follow, down to the industrial revolution. However, after the symbolic birth of the latter in 1764, with Watt's invention of the steam engine, it could not have produced all its immense consequences had not those "masters of thought"—Descartes, the true ancestor of "rationalization," and Bacon, the father of induction—improved the intellectual tools, without which mechanical technology would not have known its astonishing achievements.

It was all this that gave rise, in the nineteenth century, to Europe's irresistible hegemony. Until then Asia could have matched the West with techniques and armies comparable to those of the West. But now, for one hundred and fifty years, Europe was to benefit from an industrial advance which outdistanced all rivals and overcame all resistance.

The two dates—1764 and 1914—marked the beginning and end of the period when Europe dominated the world. This was her optimum. Already benefiting from all the advantages of the machine, she continued to feed her strength on the dynamism she derived from her conception of knowledge and of the individual. This extraordinary hegemony, however, could not last forever.

Her technology could be borrowed from her, and the more readily because she did not try to keep it to herself.

The "third world" of the underdeveloped nations, however, far from crediting Europe with what it had received from her (remembering only the conquests) will now turn her own weapons against her.

The revolt was at first purely technical, a matter of engineers and equipment, and Europe casually, imprudently furthered it. But with the socialist revolution, and then with the Chinese revolution, this protest took on, under the aegis of Marxism, the passionate accents of a dynamism turned against the West. An amazing doctrine with built-in power, Marxism was transformed into an instrument of revenge against us. As practiced in Russia, and later in Asia, it appears as a nationalist anti-Western movement as much as a program for social and industrial advance. In this new atmosphere, the acquisition of mechanical equipment, acclaimed as liberating, is charged with passion. Tractors or power houses are hailed with mystical enthusiasm. Marx himself thought that his system would be first accepted by the most developed industrial societies, but it is among the technologically most backward peoples that it is today received with the greatest conviction. What a subject of reflection for a twentieth-century Bossuet—the technological lesson of Europe, transmitted to Asia not by its initiators, but through the intermediary of a barely Europeanized Russia—no doubt a disciple of Europe, but a rebellious one!

But what will the "third world" make of our techniques, if it is unaware how they came into being and what their true purpose was, namely, the freedom of the person?

Here arises a fundamental question, namely, to what extent can European civilization, transmitted as technology, be transmitted equally as culture. We have to go into this matter. We have to determine what is primordial and cannot be transmitted in our European thinking.

The industrial revolution would not have borne all its fruits if its technology, however marvelous, had not been nourished at the deep source of a creative thought equipped with the resources of logical reasoning. What the logical mind and its practical applications hinge on, let there be no mistake about it, has so far been an exclusively European thing, only by extension

Western. True Western superiority lies here: European skill is efficient because it is nourished on spirit. The spirit listeth where it wills, this is its nature, but it needs a special branch circuit to be transposed into practical results. In these conditions, technology alone cannot suffice, at least in the long run. For in the long run the practitioner does not find means for renewal in himself, and industry wilts if it imagines it owes everything to the workshop and nothing to pure thought. When the world borrows European machines and related notions as to their use, does it by the same token borrow Europe's creative spirit? Asia's intellectual gifts are incontestable; but there is Europe's essentially creative climate, and we may ask whether it can in fact be transplanted.

The demand that there should be a sphere in which freedom of the spirit rules supreme is typically European. Were we to renounce it, we would no longer be ourselves. But this is by no means true in countries which, under the aegis of Marx, have recently committed themselves to a technological, social, and political revolution. Their totalitarian conceptions do not just misunderstand, they integrally condemn all dualism which may leave room for some secret garden in which thought can blossom in accordance with its own laws. They do not respect the individual as such, only the workingman, an all but anonymous agent of the collectivity. Yet the individual alone is creative, and more through the spirit than through the technical means at his disposal. Such is the lesson of two thousand years of history which have led to this new miracle, this extraordinary technological tide that is sweeping across the world.

By outlining the principle of a "program for Europe," which assumes ineluctable contradictions in her nature, contradictions that she has projected into the world around her, Siegfried reaches the same conclusions as Keyserling:

In truth Europe's fate has been contradictory because of the contradictory nature of her genius. Europe could renew the world only because her spirit was a spirit of critical freedom. Europe's creations were continually renewed because they were forever under discussion. The very makeup of the old continent, its division into nations forever at odds with one another, reflects this climate of creative freedom. But in the end Europe suffered from this age-old division, from her exhausting fratricidal wars. And yet, would a Europe unified by Hitler or leveled down by the Soviet steamroller still be herself? Above all, would she preserve the capacity for renewal that has left so striking a mark in history's pages?

Consequently, we are at the beginning of a new period of human evolution. It succeeds the Graeco-Roman period, but in coming after it does not continue what was winged spirituality and divinely free radiance in the former. The coming age, primarily technological in inspiration, judging human greatness less in terms of thought than by standards of living, rests upon a collective anonymous society, in which the masses, not the individual, are the source of all effectiveness. What we have supposed to be essential seems to be lacking in it.

In this contrast one might find the basis for a program for the Europe of today and tomorrow. Still, she would have to preserve a body capable of serving as support for what remains of her soul.

4: Unity in Diversity:
Foundation of Federal Union

IF IT IS TRUE that such is Europe's special vocation in a world that has been awakened by her efforts, two general conclusions follow:

1. The political union of our peoples is henceforth the condition not only of their survival but also of the just exercise of their world function.

2. This union must take a form dictated by structures, both historical and living, of the complex organism of our culture: that is, a federal form.

Political union presupposes "a common European awareness," as Christopher Dawson said in 1932:

No doubt it was easy to lose sight of this unity during the eighteenth and nineteenth centuries, when European civilisation had attained such prestige that it seemed to have no rivals and to be identical with civilisation in general. But the case is very different to-day, when the hegemony of Europe is challenged on every side; when Russia and America can no longer be regarded as colonial extensions of European culture, but are beginning to rival Europe in population and wealth and to develop independ-

ent cultures of their own; when the peoples of the East are re-
asserting the claims of oriental culture, and when we ourselves
are losing confidence in the superiority of our own traditions.

Unfortunately it is nobody's business to defend the cause of
Europe. Every national state creates a thousand vested interests
that are concerned in its defence, and the cause of internationalism also has its champions in the forces of Liberalism and Socialism and international finance. Even the oriental cultures
have attained self-consciousness by borrowing the forms of
western nationalism and developing a nationalist propaganda
after the western model. But nobody has ever thought of calling
Europe a nation, and so the cause of Europe goes by default.

Yet if our civilisation is to survive it is essential that it should
develop a common European consciousness and a sense of its
historic and organic unity. We need not fear that this will prejudice the cause of international peace or cause an increase of
hostility between Europe and the non-European cultures. What
the oriental resents is the arrogant claim that our civilisation is
the only kind of civilization that matters, and he is far more
likely to view it with sympathy if he sees it as a spiritual whole
than if, as at present, he regards it as an incomprehensible material power that is seeking to control his life. If a true world-
civilisation is ever to be created, it will not be by ignoring the
existence of the great historic traditions of culture, but rather
by an increase of mutual comprehension.[30]

As for the basic cultural unity on which our Federation will
have to be built, we must recapture a sense of it and strengthen
it anew. We must aim at a unity that goes partly beyond and
is partly in terms narrower that the "nations" which have been
formed over the last few centuries:

But before it is possible to give European culture its due place
in the international society of the future, it is first necessary to
undo the false view of the past that has gained currency and to
recover an historic sense of the European tradition. We must
rewrite our history from the European point of view and take
as much trouble to understand the unity of our common civilisation as we have given hitherto to the study of our national individuality. . . .

The fact that this truth is not generally realised is due, above
all, to the fact that modern history has usually been written
from the nationalist point of view. Some of the greatest of the

[30] C. Dawson, *op. cit.*, p. 21.

nineteenth-century historians were also apostles of the cult of nationalism, and their histories are often manuals of nationalist propaganda. This influence shows itself in the philosophic historians, who were affected by the Hegelian idealisation of the State as the supreme expression of the universal idea, as well as in writers like Treitschke and Froude, who were the representatives of a purely political nationalism. In the course of the nineteenth century this movement permeated the popular consciousness and determined the ordinary man's conception of history. It has filtered down from the university to the elementary school, and from the scholar to the journalist and the novelist. And the result is that each nation claims for itself a cultural unity and self-sufficiency that it does not possess. Each regards its share in the European tradition as an original achievement that owes nothing to the rest, and takes no heed of the common foundation in which its own individual tradition is rooted. And this is no mere academic error. It has undermined and vitiated the whole international life of modern Europe. It found its nemesis in the European war, which represented a far deeper schism in European life than all the many wars of the past, and its consequences are to be seen to-day in the frenzied national rivalries which are bringing economic ruin on the whole of Europe. . . .

The evil of nationalism does not consist in its loyalty to the traditions of the past or in its vindication of national unity and right of self determination. What is wrong is the identification of this unity with the ultimate and inclusive unity of culture which is a supernational thing.

The ultimate foundation of our culture is not the national state, but the European unity.[31]

Historians who have approached Europe as a cultural unity have elaborated this thesis. Most of them—Dawson, Halphen, Marc Bloch, Reynold, Denys Hay, Jürgen Fischer, Friedrich Heer—have centered their works on the problem of the "formation of Europe," i.e. on the pre-national periods of our history. The most recent of these, Henri Brugmans, sums up in a few felicitous formulas the principles common to them all:

Eternal nationhood seems to us a concept that needs careful handling. . . . European history cannot be explained in terms of national histories regarded as "windowless monads," immutable entities: it is not the sum total of the juxtaposed national histories. On the contrary, Europe is prior to the nations

[31] *Ibid.*, pp. 21–22, 20.

and accounts for them. Now Europe and the nations are subject to change. . . .

Even nationalism was an international phenomenon, and the conflicts of modern imperialism revealed a common acquisitive tendency. The collectivity of European nations as it has developed has never ceased being the backdrop of our history. . . .

An incomparably dynamic civilization, Europe continually reinterprets her great traditional authorities. The variations in her history can only be accounted for by what is common to them all.[32]

It is noteworthy that all the authors who have contributed to our becoming aware of the unity of our culture conceive it as unity in diversity. Just what do they mean by the ever recurring term "diversity"? Does it merely denote the multiplicity of nations today? No, European diversity is something deeper, something organic, as Ortega y Gasset reminded us:

When Guizot, among others, opposes European civilization to all others, pointing out that never has any principle, any idea, any group, any class in Europe triumphed absolutely, and that this fact accounts for its continuous development and progressive character, we cannot help pricking up our ears. The man knows what he is talking about. . . . Freedom and pluralism are reciprocal and together constitute the permanent essence of Europe.

The division of modern Europe into nations does not reflect this "permanent essence," does not translate our true regional, religious, ideological, linguistic diversities, does not make them fruitful. On the contrary, it accounts for the feeling of paralysis and decadence that prevailed in the first half of this century.[33]

The only thing that appears, and that not in great detail, when an attempt is made to define the actual decadence in Europe, is the complex of economic difficulties, which every one of the European nations has to face to-day. But when one proceeds to penetrate a little into the nature of these difficulties, one realises that none of them seriously affect the power to create wealth, and that the Old Continent has passed through much graver crises of this order.

[32] *Les origines de la civilisation européenne* (1958), Vol. I.
[33] We may recall that Ortega y Gasset wrote this in 1930.

Is it, perhaps, the case that the Germans or the English do not feel themselves to-day capable of producing more things and better things, than ever? Nothing of the kind; and it is most important that we investigate the cause of the real state of mind of Germany or England in the sphere of economics. And it is curious to discover that their undoubted depressed state arises not from the fact that they feel themselves without the capacity; but, on the contrary, that feeling themselves more capable than ever, they run up against certain fatal barriers which prevent them carrying into effect what is quite within their power. Those fatal frontiers of the actual economics of Germany, England, France, are the political frontiers of the respective states. The real difficulty, then, has its roots, not in this or that economic problem which may present itself, but in the fact that the form of public life in which the economic capabilities should develop themselves is altogether inadequate to the magnitude of these latter. . . .

The pessimism, the depression, which to-day weighs down the continental mind is similar to that of the bird of widely-spreading wings which, on stretching them out for flight, beats against the bars of its cage.

The proof of this is that the situation is repeated in all the other orders, whose factors are apparently so different from those of economics. Take, for example, intellectual life. Every "intellectual" to-day in Germany, England, or France feels suffocated within the boundaries of his country; feels his nationality as an absolute limitation. . . .

If we were to make in imagination the experiment of limiting ourselves to living by what is "national" in us, and if in fancy we could deprive the average Frenchman of all that he uses, thinks, feels, by reason of the influence of other sections of the Continent, he would be terror-stricken as the result. He would see that it was not possible to live merely on his own; that four-fifths of his spiritual wealth is the common property of Europe.

It is impossible to perceive what else worth while there is *to be done* by those of us who live on this portion of the planet but to fulfil the promise implied by the word Europe during the last four centuries. The only thing opposed to it is the prejudice of the old "nations," the idea of the nation as based on the past. We are shortly to see if Europeans are children of Lot's wife who persist in making history with their heads turned backwards.[34]

Ortega personally believed that the need for political union could be read in the lineaments of the present:

[34] Ortega y Gasset, *Revolt of the Masses*, pp. 145, 146, 180.

The unity of Europe is not an idle fancy. It is reality itself; what is fantastic is the contrary thesis: the belief that France, Germany, Italy, and Spain are substantive, independent realities.

And from this he drew these curiously prophetic conclusions:

It is extremely unlikely that a society, a collectivity as mature as that already formed by the European nations should not be on the verge of creating the political machinery of a state, in order to give form to the exercise of the already existing European public authority. . . .

It is historical realism that has taught me to recognize that the unity of Europe as a society is not an *ideal* but a very old everyday fact. And once this has been seen, the probability of a general European state can no longer be discounted. As for the occasion that will suddenly bring the process to its completion, it may be God only knows what! the pigtail of a Chinese emerging from behind the Urals or a tremor in the great Islamic magma.

Hermann von Keyserling, too, at about the same time, sensed that union is implicit in the logic of Europe's development:

Europe is emerging as a unity because, faced at closer range by an overwhelming non-European humanity, the things which the Europeans have in common are becoming more significant than those which divide them, and thus new factors are beginning to predominate over the old ones in the common consciousness. . . .

A living "Europe" is therefore arising today as a branch of the all-human ecumene. It already exists as a psychological reality in all leading minds. The specific subconscious which is conditioned by its own peculiar history and which has the last word today on a man's attitude toward the external world, is beginning to work itself out in the conscious. . . . Hitherto the difference between the French and the German being could be regarded as a primary significance. Today it is outweighed by the consciousness of that difference from the Russian being, and above all from the Asiatic. . . . Thus the inhabitants of Europe are steadily becoming more conscious of the fact that above the individual nations and cultures of Europe broods a new, living reality, that of the *European*. Accordingly, the French, the German, etc., is becoming different from what he has been hitherto: the basis of his relationship to the whole has shifted.[35]

The founding of a European "supernationality" (we believe the term appeared here for the first time) must not, however, be

[35] H. Keyserling, *op. cit.*, pp. 355, 357.

allowed to standardize our peoples. On the one hand, our internal oppositions will be relativized in the face of the other cultures; on the other hand, within European unity, they will yield to a stronger feeling that the different styles of life complement one another:

The European, and with him Europe, is emerging inevitably. He is emerging as a specific product of differentiation out of an already existent all-human unity, itself the product of spiritual experience. He is emerging from a consciousness of difference vis-à-vis that which lies to the East and that which lies to the West of Europe, and the consciousness of difference causes the common consciousness of all Europeans to outweight the consciousness of those things which divide them. Now, if our spiritual journey through Europe has taught us anything at all, it has taught us this: we are dealing, in the case of Europe, with an astoundingly manifold, astoundingly riven structure. That is why there can be no question of the unification of Europe in the sense of an effacement of all differences, as a desirable goal. To seek its unification on the Russian or American plan is, on the theoretical side, to misunderstand it completely; on the practical side it is to desire its destruction. Should things go well, there will ensue a new unity on a higher plane, a unity which the nations, continuing in all their old force, will themselves build up. . . .

The glorification of one's own country at the expense of the others, once accepted as the eleventh commandment, has suddenly become an absurdity. We suddenly understand again what Dr. Johnson meant by his harsh dictum, Patriotism is the last refuge of a desperate scoundrel; and what Grillparzer meant by his statement that the way of humanity lies through nationalism to bestiality. It is becoming a primary spiritual experience that the various nations *supplement* each other.[36]

To be sure, Keyserling does not underestimate the dangers of virulent "supernationalism," nevertheless he sees it as a step forward to European unity:

But is the "European" after all the highest type of man? There will surely arise, before long, a corresponding type of supernationalism which will for the time be as virulent as any nationalism ever was; this would then be the European equivalent of American Messianism. But of course the European, too, is not the ideal man. . . . But he is more than any previous inhabitant of Europe because he is of wider scope. All superiority depends

[36] *Ibid.*, pp. 363, 369.

on the integration of those values, which, on their own plane, are exclusive, into a higher unity.[37]

We have noted above that the fruitful diversity of Europe exists on a deeper, organic level than the national level. Paul Valéry, in attempting to define Europe, does not even mention the nation as one of the diverse elements which, according to him, constitute the "system" called Europe:

> Europe has been built up gradually like a gigantic city. It has its museums, parks, workshops, its laboratories and salons. It has Venice, Oxford, Seville, Rome, Paris. There are cities of Art, other cities of Science, and still others that join ornament and instrument in one. It is small enough to be traveled over in a very short time—which may soon be too short to count. It is large enough to contain all climates, diverse enough to afford the most varied crops and terrain. From the physical point of view, it is a masterpiece of temperament, combining all conditions favorable to man. And here man has become the European. You will forgive my using the words "Europe" and "European" in a somewhat more than geographical and historical . . . rather in a *functional* sense. I would almost say (allowing my thought to abuse my language) that a *Europe* is a kind of system composed of human variety and a particularly favorable locality, and, lastly, fashioned by a singularly vivid and eventful history. The product of this conjunction of circumstances is a European.[38]

Valéry, writing in 1922, in a victorious France, could rise above the political facts of national life. At the height of the Second World War, on the contrary, it took a certain courage for a writer in Germany to predict the day when the nations will have disappeared and be supplanted by a democratic federation of states. Ernst Jünger did just this in a little book entitled *The Peace* which circulated clandestinely in 1943, and was published in 1946.

Developing the theme of unity in diversity, Jünger imagines that a future European Constitution will have to take careful account of two necessarily opposing principles: in the realms of economics, technology, trade, etc., *unity* of organization must rule; in the realm of nature, and in the cultural sphere, freedom must assure *diversity:*

[37] *Ibid.*, p. 370.
[38] *Collected Works*, X, 314–15.

What the steam engine, coal, railways, and telegraphy were for the development and unification of the national state, electrical science, the combustion engine, flight, radio, and the forces streaming out of the atom are, in their turn and at new levels, in other spheres. It follows that complaints are being renewed that the old world has become too small. Frontiers, variations in political and economic forms which hinder the exchange of men and goods, deny free passage to the many means of communication.

That is particularly true of Europe, which is rich in old heritage, and in its manifold divisions, bears the mark of history's sufferings and experience. Thus it becomes understandable that from its center the great wars have flared out to lay waste the world; it is at the weakest part of the body, which is, however, also its heart and vital point, that its suffering becomes apparent. For this reason this is also where healing must begin.

Europe must become a partner in the great empires which are forming on this planet, and are striving towards their final form. It must share in the higher freedom won in the face of an inheritance of restricted space. . . .

To set up a European state means, therefore, to give geographical and political unity to a territory which historical development was already shaping. . . . Land hunger will be relieved by the unification of the nations; nor is there any more just solution. How they are to live together in their new home will be laid down in the constitution.

In this connection there is no point in going into details. Yet there are two supreme principles which must find expression in the constitution, irrespective of how they may be incorporated in it. These two principles are those of unity and diversity. The new dominion must be a union of all its members, but must respect their individuality.

In this combination the two main trends which democracy has assumed in our time must be reconciled—that of the authoritarian and that of the liberal state. There is good reason for both; but life cannot be either entirely disciplined nor completely dominated by free will. It is rather a question of distinguishing the levels appropriate to each.

The forms of the authoritarian state apply where men and things can be organized technically. On the other hand, freedom must have control where more organic processes are the rule. . . . There should be uniformity of organization in whatever concerns technical matters, industry, commerce, communications, trade, weights and measures, and defense. . . . Liberty, on the other hand, dominates in diversity—wherever nations and men differ.

That applies to their history, their speech and race, to their customs and habits, their art and their religion. Here there cannot be too many colors on the palette.

Thus the European constitution must skilfully distinguish the cultural plane from that of material civilization, forming them into picture and frame so as to unite their benefits for the human race. It must create territorial and political unity while preserving historical diversity. That implies at the same time distinguishing between the technical and the organic world. The state as supreme symbol of technical achievement takes the nations in its toils, yet they live in freedom under its protection. Then history will take a hand and give contents to old forms. . . .

Within this framework the nations large and small will flourish more strongly than before. As the rivalry of the national states dies away, the Alsatian, for instance, will be able to live as German or as Frenchman without compulsion from one or the other. But above all he will be able to live as an Alsatian, as he wishes. This regained freedom will dawn even for racial minorities, for septs and towns. In the new home it will be possible to be Breton, Wend, Basque, Cretan or Sicilian—and that with greater freedom than in the old.[39]

A fairly similar distinction between Europe as a political organization (as a union to be created) and Europe as cultural organism (an existing unity) was proposed and defined more closely by T. S. Eliot in his short essays on "The Unity of European Culture" (destined for the German radio). He clearly defines the relations between culture and politics: [40]

A nation's political structure affects its culture, and in turn is affected by that culture. But nowadays we take too much interest in each other's domestic politics, and at the same time have very little contact with each other's culture. The confusion of culture and politics may lead in two different directions. It may make a nation intolerant of every culture but its own, so that it feels impelled to stamp out, or to remould, every culture surrounding it. An error of the Germany of Hitler was to assume that every other culture than that of Germany was either decadent or barbaric. Let us have an end of such assumptions. The other direction in which the confusion of culture and politics may lead, is

[39] Ernst Jünger, *The Peace*, trans. Stuart O. Hood (Chicago: Henry Regnery Co., 1948), pp. 45–46, 59–62.

[40] *Notes Towards the Definition of Culture* (London: Faber and Faber, 1948), Appendix: "The Unity of European Culture."

towards the ideal of a world state in which there will, in the end, be only one uniform world culture. I am not here criticising any schemes for world organisation. Such schemes belong to the plane of engineering, or devising machinery. Machinery is necessary, and the more perfect the machine the better. But culture is something that must grow; you cannot build a tree, you can only plant it, and care for it, and wait for it to mature in its due time; and when it is grown you must not complain if you find that from an acorn has come an oak, and not an elm-tree. And a political structure is partly construction, and partly growth; partly machinery, and the same machinery, if good, is equally good for all peoples; and partly growing with and from the nation's culture, and in that respect different from that of other nations. . . .

It is necessary to be clear about what we mean by "culture," so that we may be clear about the distinction between the material organisation of Europe, and the spiritual organism of Europe. If the latter dies, then what you organise will not be Europe, but merely a mass of human beings speaking several different languages. And there will be no longer any justification for their continuing to speak different languages, for they will no longer have anything to say which cannot be said equally well in any language; they will, in short, have no longer anything to say in poetry. I have already affirmed that there can be no "European" culture if the several countries are isolated from each other: I add now that there can be no European culture if these countries are reduced to identity. We need variety in unity; not the unity of organisation, but the unity of nature.

Eliot warns against any sort of European planning that does not respect the special nature of our cultural unity:

The Western World has its unity in this heritage, in Christianity and in the ancient civilisation of Greece, Rome and Israel, from which, owing to two thousand years of Christianity, we trace our descent. I shall not elaborate this point. What I wish to say is, that this unity in the common elements of culture, throughout many centuries, is the true bond between us. No political and economic organisation, however much goodwill it commands, can supply what this culture unity gives. If we dissipate or throw away our common patrimony of culture, then all the organisation and planning of the most ingenious minds will not help us, or bring us close together.

This unity of culture, in contrast to the unity of political organisation, does not require us all to have only one loyalty: it means that there will be a variety of loyalties. It is wrong that the only duty of the individual should be held to be towards the State; it is fantastic to hold that the supreme duty of every individual should be towards a Super-State.

Eliot gives an example of cultural unity nourished on diversity, which is the more striking for being drawn from poetry—Romanticism had taught us to think of poetry as the most "typically national," the least exportable of cultural activities:

The unity of European culture is a very large subject indeed, and no one should try to speak about it, unless he has some particular knowledge or experience. . . . I am a poet and a critic of poetry. . . . I shall try to show what the first of these two professions has to do with my subject, and what conclusions my experience has led me to draw.

It has often been claimed that English, of all the languages of modern Europe, is the richest for the purpose of writing poetry. I think that this claim is justified. . . . The real reason . . . in my opinion, is the variety of the elements of which English is made up. First, of course, there is the Germanic foundation. . . . After this we find a considerable Scandinavian element, due in the first place to the Danish conquest. Then there is the Norman French element, after the Norman conquest. After this there followed a succession of French influences, traceable through words adopted at different periods. The sixteenth century saw a great increase of new words coined from the Latin. . . . And there is another element in English, not so easy to trace, but I think of considerable importance, the Celtic. But I am not thinking, in all this history, only of the Words, I am thinking, for poetry, primarily of the Rhythms. Each of these languages brought its own music; and the richness of the English language for poetry is first of all in its variety of metrical elements. There is the rhythm of early Saxon verse, the rhythm of the Norman French, the rhythm of the Welsh, and also the influence of generations of study of Latin and Greek poetry. And even today, the English language enjoys constant possibilities of refreshment from its several centres: apart from the vocabulary, poems by Englishmen, Welshmen, Scots and Irishmen, all written in English, continue to show differences in their Music. . . . I think the reason why English is such a good language for poetry is that it is a composite from so many different European sources. . . .

The possibility of each literature renewing itself, proceeding to new creative activity, making new discoveries in the use of words, depends on two things. First, its ability to receive and assimilate influences from abroad. Second, its ability to go back and learn from its own sources. As for the first, when the several countries of Europe are cut off from each other, when poets no longer read any literature but that in their own language, poetry in every country must deteriorate. As for the second, I wish to make this point especially: that every literature must have some sources which are peculiarly its own, deep in its own history; but, also, and at least equally important, are the souces which we share in common: that is, the literature of Rome, of Greece and of Israel. . . .

What I have said of poetry is I think true of the other arts as well. . . . In the practice of every art I think you find the same three elements: the local tradition, the common European tradition, and the influence of the art of one European country upon another.

No one has better illustrated how cultural influences interpenetrate within the fundamental unity of European literature than Ernst Robert Curtius, the greatest student of comparative literature in our time. In the Introduction to his last work, he insists on the impossibility of interpreting any of our "national literatures" in artificial isolation from the others, as our textbooks all do:

Europe is merely a name, a "geographical term" (as Metternich said of Italy), if it is not a historical entity in our perception. But the old-fashioned history of our textbooks cannot be that. General European history does not exist for it; it sees merely a coexistence of unconnected histories of peoples and states. . . .

The "Europeanization of the historical picture" which is to be promoted today must also be applied to literature. . . .

European literature is coextensive in time with European culture therefore embraces a period of some twenty-six centuries (reckoning from Homer to Goethe). . . .

European literature is an "intelligible unit," which disappears from view when it is cut into pieces. . . . The "timeless present" which is an essential characteristic of literature means that the literature of the past can always be active in that of the present. So Homer in Virgil, Virgil in Dante, Plutarch and Seneca in Shakespeare, Shakespeare in Goethe's *Götz von Berlichingen*, Euripides in Racine's *Iphigenia* and Goethe's. Or in our day: The *Thousand and One Nights* and Calderón in Hofmannsthal; the *Odyssey* in Joyce; Aeschylus, Petronius, Dante, Tristan Corbière,

Spanish mysticism in T. S. Eliot. There is here an inexhaustible wealth of possible interrelations. Furthermore, there is the garden of literary forms—be they genres . . . or metrical or stanzaic forms; be they set formulas or narrative motifs or linguistic devices. . . . Finally, there is the wealth of figures which literature has formed and which can forever pass into new bodies: Achilles, Oedipus, Semiramis, Faust, Don Juan. André Gide's last and ripest work is a *Theseus*.[41]

Jean-Paul Sartre, too, drew upon his own experience as a writer when, in 1949,[42] he listed the conditions for defending our cultural diversity. He, too, saw the need for integrating our diverse cultures within the unity of European culture:

Can French culture be defended as such? To this, I answer simply: No. . . . Is there some other way of saving the essential elements of that culture? Yes. But on condition that we attack the problem in an entirely different manner, and that we understand that today there can no longer be question of a French culture, no more than of a Dutch, a Swiss, or a German culture. If we want French culture to survive, it must be integrated within the framework of one great European culture.

And he added, coming to political conclusions as though against his will:

Naturally, this cultural unity cannot be constituted of itself. To be sure, we can even now ask governments, associations, private individuals to inaugurate a cultural policy; to be sure, we can have cultural interchange, more translations, personal contacts, we can draw up a program for books, for international newspapers. All this was tried before the 1939 war. Such attempts, though very interesting, would be fruitless today, because they would create a superstructure of cultural unity, which would not be matched by any unity in the infrastructures. Therefore we must conceive—and I shall stop here because I wish to avoid the political question—European cultural unity as the only one capable of saving what is valid in each country's culture.

By striving for a unified European culture, we will save French culture. However, a unified culture would have no meaning, would be a purely verbal achievement unless set within the

[41] E. R. Curtius, *European Literature and the Latin Middle Ages,* trans. Willard R. Trask (Bollingen Series XXXVI), pp. 6–15, *passim.*

[42] In an article in the magazine *Politique Etrangère,* excerpts from which were submitted to the European Congress for Culture (Lausanne, 1949).

framework of far more profound efforts to bring about Europe's political and economic unity.

Summing up and clarifying the contributions of his elders, anticipating those of his juniors, Robert de Traz (1884–1951), the guiding spirit of the *Revue de Genève*, as early as 1929 called upon Europe to respond to the challenge of History by uniting:

The men of the West to whom has been bequeathed a priceless heritage have no reason for deserting their own cause. They should come together and discuss it thoroughly. Calmly, coolly, they should take inventory of their common patrimony. European civilization is the product of age-old collaboration, and no people's contribution to it can be subtracted without disfiguring and weakening it. Our inventive genius is intact. Thanks to their very principles our critical methods can always adapt themselves to unforeseen circumstances. We are still about equal in capacity for labor—useful, conquering, transfiguring labor. Our greatest potentiality resides perhaps in our capacity for self-renewal. I should say, our capacity for rising from the dead. By dint of courage and imagination, our aspirations are not dissipated in slumbering ecstasy: they are active.

Is it dreaming, to advise Europe that in order to recover, to silence her detractors, she must recognize that she has a new mission? In asserting her unity over and above all differences without destroying them, she would set the world an example. Against the dangers from within, her children might conclude a pact of alliance: in time she might ask the rest of the world to join. She might forestall the great conflicts of the century to come by bringing harmony, not just to tiny states separated by a line of hills, but to continents separated by vast oceans. She might take the lead among the nations of the earth because she alone could give them rational principles of order, a program for joint action, in short, she would supply the guiding ideas.[43]

These last words echo Ortega y Gasset's prophetic pages quoted above. They are addressed to Europeans to remind them of a vocation more difficult than self-denigration: the vocation to create Europe because the World has to be created, and because Europe alone, in creating the World, will fulfill her own vocation.

[43] *L'Esprit de Genève* (Paris: Grasset, 1929), pp. 259–60.